Investments in a Sustainable Workforce in Europe

AF763470

A sustainable European workforce has become increasingly relevant in the present day. Flexibility and job insecurity are omnipresent; organizational workforces are displaying growing diversity with respect to age, gender, ethnicity and family status; and Europe's welfare states are delegating more and more responsibility for the well-being of workers to employers. Now, more than ever, organizations need to consider investing in workers to improve their performance and their level of satisfaction. These investments can take many forms, including flexible work arrangements, training plans, child-related policies and health programs. The crucial question is how to make this happen. Why do some organizations invest more and others less in their employees? Why do some employees make use of these investments while others do not? Why do such investments sometimes improve employee performance and satisfaction whereas in other instances they do not? *Investments in a Sustainable Workforce in Europe* addresses these questions. It contributes a new, large-scale survey of 259 organizations, 869 work units and 11,011 employees in 6 diverse economic sectors in Bulgaria, Finland, Germany, Hungary, the Netherlands, Portugal, Spain, Sweden and the UK to study the causes and consequences of organizational investments in employees.

This book will be of interest to undergraduate and postgraduate students, researchers and lecturers in the fields of sociology, business and management and organizational studies. It will also be useful for practitioners of human resource management and others interested in workforce sustainability.

Tanja van der Lippe is Professor of Sociology at Utrecht University, the Netherlands.

Zoltán Lippényi is Assistant Professor of Organizational and Economic Sociology at the University of Groningen, the Netherlands.

Routledge Advances in Sociology

Populism and the Crisis of Democracy
Volume 3: Migration, Gender and Religion
Edited by Gregor Fitzi, Jürgen Mackert and Bryan S. Turner

The Challenge of Modernity
Simmel's Sociological Theory
Gregor Fitzi

The World Multiple
The Quotidian Politics of Knowing and Generating Entangled Worlds
Edited by Keiichi Omura, Grant Jun Otsuki, Shiho Satsuka, Atsuro Morita

DIY Cultures and Underground Music Scenes
Edited by Andy Bennett and Paula Guerra

ISIS
Ideology, Symbolics, and Counter Narratives
Masood Ashraf Raja

Ethnographic Inquiry and Lived Experience
An Epistemological Critique
Wing-Chung Ho

European Solidarity in Times of Crisis
Insights from a Thirteen-Country Survey
Jürgen Gerhards, Holger Lengfeld, Zsófia S. Ignácz, Florian K. Kley and Maximilian Priem

Investments in a Sustainable Workforce in Europe
Edited by Tanja van der Lippe and Zoltán Lippényi

For more information about this series, please visit www.routledge.com/Routledge-Advances-in-Sociology/book-series/SE0511

Investments in a Sustainable Workforce in Europe

Edited by
Tanja van der Lippe and Zoltán Lippényi

Routledge
Taylor & Francis Group
LONDON AND NEW YORK

First published 2019
by Routledge
2 Park Square, Milton Park, Abingdon, Oxon OX14 4RN

and by Routledge
605 Third Avenue, New York, NY 10017

First issued in paperback 2020

Routledge is an imprint of the Taylor & Francis Group, an informa business

© 2019 selection and editorial matter, Tanja van der Lippe and Zoltán Lippényi; individual chapters, the contributors

The right of Tanja van der Lippe and Zoltán Lippényi to be identified as the authors of the editorial matter, and of the authors for their individual chapters, has been asserted in accordance with sections 77 and 78 of the Copyright, Designs and Patents Act 1988.

All rights reserved. No part of this book may be reprinted or reproduced or utilized in any form or by any electronic, mechanical, or other means, now known or hereafter invented, including photocopying and recording, or in any information storage or retrieval system, without permission in writing from the publishers.

Trademark notice: Product or corporate names may be trademarks or registered trademarks, and are used only for identification and explanation without intent to infringe.

British Library Cataloguing-in-Publication Data
A catalogue record for this book is available from the British Library

Library of Congress Cataloging-in-Publication Data
A catalog record has been requested for this book

ISBN 13: 978-0-367-72794-9 (pbk)
ISBN 13: 978-1-138-47726-1 (hbk)

Typeset in Goudy
by Wearset Ltd, Boldon, Tyne and Wear

Contents

Figures

Tables

Contributors

Anja-Kristin Abendroth is a junior professor in Technical and Social Change in the Department of Sociology at Bielefeld University, Germany. Her research interests include social inequalities, the interplay of work and family life, digitalization of work, and organizational and cross-national comparative research. Currently, she is one of the principal investigators in the project "Organizational Inequalities and Interdependencies between Capabilities in Work and Personal Life: A Study of Employees in Different Work Organizations" funded by the German Science Foundation. She is also the German Collaboration Partner in the Sustainable Workforce project. Recently, she published her research on women's access to power and the gender earning gap in *ILR Review* and her research on telework and work–family conflict across workplaces in *Contemporary Perspectives in Family Research*.

Paul de Beer is Henri Polak Professor of Industrial Relations at the University of Amsterdam, affiliated with the Amsterdam Institute for Advanced Labour Studies/Hugo Sinzheimer Institute (AIAS-HSI), and Director of the Scientific Bureau for the Dutch Trade Union Movement, de Burcht. His research focuses on labor market issues, social policy, income distribution, industrial relations, and solidarity. He is also Chair of the Knowledge Platform Work and Income (KWI) of the Dutch Ministry of Social Affairs and Employment. He co-edited *The labour market triangle* (Edward Elgar, 2009) and *Ethic diversity and solidarity* (Cambridge Scholars, 2017).

Katia Begall is Assistant Professor of Sociology at Utrecht University. Her main research interests are in the division of paid and unpaid work within households, gender norms, family formation, and the interplay between organization context and the career outcomes of parents. Her publications have appeared in, among others, *Population Studies*, *Demographic Research*, *European Sociological Review*, *Social Forces*, and *Journal of Marriage and the Family*.

Jannes ten Berge is a PhD candidate in the Department of Sociology and Research School (ICS) at Utrecht University. His research interests include technological change within enterprises and its effects on workers and enterprises, and the relation between interethnic contact and interethnic attitudes. His work has been published in *European Sociological Review*.

Paul Boselie is Professor of Public Administration and Organization Science at the Utrecht University School of Governance (USG) at Utrecht University, Head of Department of USG, and Dutch Human Resource Management Network Board Member. His research interests are in the area of HRM and performance, high performance work systems, talent management, employer engagement, performance management, private equity, and public service performance. He was co-editor of *Managing social issues – A public values perspective* (Edward Elgar, 2013) and author of the SHRM textbook *Strategic human resource management – A balanced approach* (McGraw-Hill, first edition 2010, second edition 2014). He is guest editor of special issues of *Personnel Review* (HRM and balanced approaches, 2009), *Human Resource Management Journal* (employer engagement, 2018) and the *International Journal of HRM* (SHRM and public sector performance, 2018). His research is in health care organizations, schools, national governments, international governmental organizations, and financial services organizations.

Leonie van Breeschoten obtained her PhD in Sociology in April 2019 in the Department of Sociology and Research School (ICS) at Utrecht University. Her research interests are in the area of work–family linkages, specifically parental leave and part-time work, and the role organizations play in this. She conducts her research as part of the "Investments in a sustainable workforce in Europe" project, and collected data for the European Sustainable Workforce Survey. Previously, she obtained an MSc in International Crimes and Criminology (the social science of human rights violations) from VU University Amsterdam (cum laude) and a BA in Sociology and Human Rights from University College Roosevelt in Middelburg (cum laude).

Vincent Buskens is Professor of Theoretical Sociology in the Department of Sociology and Research School (ICS) at Utrecht University and Director of Teaching in the Department of Sociology. His research interests are in the areas of cooperation and trust, experimental sociology, and social networks for which he has received prestigious national grants. He was elected member and secretary of the European Academy of Sociology in 2010. His work is published in prominent journals including *American Journal of Sociology*, *Social Networks*, and *Scientific Reports*. His edited books include *Micro–macro links and microfoundations* (Routledge, 2012), *eTrust: Forming relationships in the online world* (Russell Sage, 2009), and *The governance of relations in markets and organizations* (JAI Press, 2003).

Wieteke Conen is a postdoctoral researcher at the Amsterdam Institute for Advanced Labour Studies, University of Amsterdam. Her research interests are in the area of changing labor markets, the value of work, self-employment, and employers' personnel policies. She has contributed to a number of national and international books and journal articles on these topics and is editor of *Self-employment as precarious work: A European perspective* (Edward Elgar, 2019).

Anneke van Doorne-Huiskes is Emeritus Professor of Sociology in the Department of Sociology and Research School (ICS) at Utrecht University. Her major research interests lie in the areas of the welfare state, labor market and gender, gender and organization, organizational culture, and work–life balance. She has been engaged in the international research project "Transitions: Gender, Parenthood and the Changing European Workplace," co-ordinated by Professor Suzan Lewis, Manchester Metropolitan University, UK (2003–2006) and in "Quality," an international comparative project on quality of life and work of European citizens, financed by the European Commission (2006–2009). She represented the Netherlands in the EU-Network Family & Work (1995–2001). Her co-edited books include *Women and the European labour markets* (Paul Chapman, 1995), *Flexible working and organisational change* (Edward Elgar, 2005), and *Quality of life and work in Europe: Theory, practice and policy* (Palgrave, 2011).

Maria das Dores Guerreiro, is a professor in the Department of Sociology and the research coordinator at the Center for Research in Sociology (CIES-IUL), ISCTE-University Institute of Lisbon (ISCTE-IUL), Portugal. She is a member of the Department of Sociology Scientific Council and of the Portuguese Sociological Association Advisory Board. She represented Portugal in the EU-Network Family & Work (1995–2001). Her research interests are in the fields of work–life balance, gender and work, equal opportunities, generations, family, organizations and professions, social policies, new forms of work, and employment. She has published many books, book chapters, and articles in scientific journals and social policy publications, both at national and international levels. One of her edited books is *Welfare and everyday life, Portugal in the European context* (Oeiras, 2009). She was editor of the journal *Sociologia, Problemas e Práticas* (2000–2017).

Laura den Dulk is Professor of Employment, Organization, and Work–Life issues in the Department of Public Administration and Sociology at Erasmus University Rotterdam. Her main area of expertise is cross-national research on work–life policies in organizations. Her current research interests include the integration of work and personal life at the individual level (how women and men manage their work and personal/family life), the organizational level (the role of managers, workplace flexibility), and country level (cross-national comparisons). She is co-editor of *Quality of life and work in Europe: Theory, practice and policy* (Palgrave, 2011), *Flexible working, organizational change and the integration of work and personal life* (Edward Elgar, 2005), *Work–family arrangements in Europe* (Thela-Thesis, 1999), and leading author of the paper "National context in work–life research: A multi-level cross-national analysis of the adoption of workplace work–life arrangements in Europe" which won the 2014 Rosabeth Moss Kanter Award for Excellence in Work–Family Research. She is editor of *Community, Work & Family*.

Éva Fodor is a sociologist researching gender inequalities in post-socialist labor markets. Currently, she is Associate Professor of Gender Studies and Pro-rector of Social Sciences and Humanities at the Central European University (CEU) in Budapest. She has written books and papers on gender inequality in positions of authority in Hungary and Austria (*Working difference: Women's working lives in Hungary and Austria 1945–95*, Duke University Press, 2003), on the gendered construction of the ideal worker in the organizational practices of financial sector companies, parental leave regulations and their effects on labor market gender inequalities, as well as on the societal level determinants of gender inequality in relation to poverty from a cross-national perspective. She has participated in four EU funded research projects (EUREQUAL, QUALITY, FLOWS, and EQUALITY) and has worked as program manager for the International Labour Organization (ILO) in Budapest. She has MA degrees from Eötvös Loránd (ELTE) University in Budapest and a PhD in Sociology from the University of California, Los Angeles.

Alessandra Gasparotto works as researcher and analyst for Glocalities in Amsterdam, focusing on company operations in international market environments. She completed her MSc in Sociology and Social Research at Utrecht University in 2017.

Nikki van Gerwen obtained her PhD in January 2019 in the Department of Sociology/ICS at Utrecht University. Her research interests are in the area of employee cooperative behavior, employee training and development, social dilemmas, and experimental research. Her work has been published in several international journals, including *International Journal of Training and Development* and *Social Networks*. Before her PhD research as part of the "Investments in a sustainable workforce in Europe" project, she obtained her bachelor's and research master's degree in Sociology from Utrecht University.

Maarten Goos is Professor of Economics and Institutions in the Faculty of Law, Economics and Governance at Utrecht University. His research focuses on labor markets including technological progress, labor market intermediation, inequality, and institutions. His award-winning research is published in international peer-reviewed journals, books, and magazines. He is a regular speaker at international conferences in the areas of innovation, productivity, economic growth, labor markets, and the ethical, legal, socio-economic, and political consequences of ongoing technological progress. Maarten received his PhD from the London School of Economics (LSE) and has held positions at Erasmus University Rotterdam, University College London, and KU Leuven. He has also held visiting positions at Princeton University, the Centre for Economic Performance at LSE, Fudan University Shanghai, Massachusetts Institute of Technology, and Boston University. He is currently coordinating the Future of Work initiative at Utrecht University and is involved in various initiatives by the European Commission, national policy institutes, and multinational corporations.

Jasmijn van Harten is Assistant Professor at the Utrecht School of Governance (USG) at Utrecht University. She is Chairperson of the Faculty Council of the Faculty of Law, Economics and Governance at Utrecht University. Her research focuses on individuals' employability, the ways in which organizations and supervisors can stimulate their workers' employability through human resource management and people management, and how and whether this is successful. She has presented her research at international conferences such as the Academy of Management, the Work, Employment and Society conference, and the European Group for Public Administration. She has published in international scientific journals including the *International Journal of Human Resource Management*, *Journal of Health Organization and Management*, and *Personnel Review*.

Margriet van Hek is a postdoctoral researcher in the Sociology department at Utrecht University. She is also a member of the Interuniversity Center for Social Science Theory and Methodology (ICS) and a fellow of the German College for Interdisciplinary Educational Research (CIDER). Her research interests include gender issues and educational and labor market inequalities. In her current postdoctoral project, "Do women at the top matter?," she studies the impact of female leadership on social inequalities in public and private organizations, and in public administration. Her work has been published in a number of international scientific journals.

Bram Lancee is Associate Professor of Sociology at the University of Amsterdam. His current research interests include social capital, ethnic minorities and the labor market, inequality and social participation, attitudes towards immigration, and ethnic diversity in neighborhoods. His work has been published in journals such as *Social Forces*, *European Sociological Review*, *International Migration Review*, *Journal of Ethnic and Migration Studies*, and *Social Science Research*. He is also co-editor of *Social cohesion and immigration in Europe and North America: Mechanisms, conditions, and causality* (Routledge, 2015).

Tanja van der Lippe is Professor of Sociology in the Department of Sociology at Utrecht University, She is also member of the board of Utrecht University's Strategic Theme "Institutions for Open Societies." Head of the Department of Sociology, and Chair of the Research School ICS. Her research interests are in the area of work–family linkages in Dutch and other societies, for which she has received a number of large-scale grants from Dutch and European Science Foundations. She received a European Research Council (ERC) Advanced Grant for her research into "Investments in a sustainable workforce in Europe." She is an elected member of the Royal Netherlands Academy of Arts and Sciences (2014), the Royal Holland Society of Sciences and Humanities (2013), and the European Academy of Sociology (2010). Her edited books include *Quality of life and work in Europe: Theory,* *practice and policy* (Palgrave, 2011), *Competing claims in work and family life* (Edward Elgar, 2007), and *Women's employment in a comparative perspective* (Aldine de Gruyter, 2001).

Zoltán Lippényi is Assistant Professor of Organizational and Economic Sociology at the University of Groningen, the Netherlands. He is a member of the Interuniversity Center for Social Science Theory and Methodology (ICS) and the ISA RC28 Social stratification and Mobility. He obtained his PhD in Sociology at Utrecht University in 2014. Between 2014 and 2018, he worked as a post-doctoral researcher with the ERC-financed Sustainable Workforce project, focusing on the consequences of organizational employment practices, in particular, the adoption of flexible work and employment arrangements for workplace inequality and employee outcomes. Since 2015, he has represented the Netherlands in the Comparative Organizations and Inequality Network (COIN), a research collaboration studying workplace wage inequality from an international perspective. In this collaboration, he studies the effects of organizational context and change on inequality in wages, using register-based linked employer–employee datasets. His work is published in the *European Sociological Review*, *Research in Social Stratification and Mobility*, *History of the Family*, and *Social Science Research*.

Jelle Lössbroek is a postdoctoral researcher in the Department of Sociology at Utrecht University, a member of the Research School ICS and a management committee member of COST Action IS1409: Gender, health and extending working lives. He has master's degrees in Political Science and in Social & Cultural Science (both cum laude), and completed his PhD, "Turning grey into gold: Employer–employee interplay in an ageing workforce," in January 2019. He has collected data as part of the Sustainable Workforce research team; his labor market research focuses on older workers and on technological change.

Jornt Mandemakers is Assistant Professor of Sociology in the Department of Sociology and Research School (ICS) at Utrecht University. His research interests are in the areas of the social determinants of health/social inequality in health, human reproductive behavior, and in combining social science with quantitative genetics. His recent publications have appeared in *Nature Genetics*, *Demography*, and the *European Journal of Population*.

Thomas Martens works as external collaboration liaison for and teaches in the Department of Sociology at Utrecht University. With a background in Organizational Psychology, consulting, and project management, he has strong interests in human resources (HR) policy development and bridging the gap between academia and the professional world. As project coordinator for the Sustainable Workforce project, he was tasked with reaching out to organizations to participate in the study. Based on conversations with management from the participating organizations, he designed a benchmark report, using data from the study, to help HR management reflect on their policies.

Silvia Maja Melzer is currently working as an interim professor in Sociology at Bielefeld University, Germany and co-directs a German Research Foundation project that seeks to examine how firms create, mute, and exaggerate social inequality. She has published in the *Journal of Marriage and Family*, *Social Forces*, and *Industrial and Labor Relations Review*.

Jouko Nätti is Professor of Social Policy in the Faculty of Social Sciences, University of Tampere, Finland. His research interests include working life research, the relations between work and time and place, forms of employment, labor market policy, segmentation, unemployment, work and household, job insecurity, knowledge work, gender, and aging at work. He has completed over 20 research projects funded by the Academy of Finland, the Finnish Work Environment Fund, EU-TSER, EU FP6, and Nordforsk. He has published over 200 journal articles, book chapters, research reports, and discussion papers.

Anne-Rigt Poortman is Associate Professor in the Department of Sociology and Research School (ICS) at Utrecht University. She has specialized in family sociology and social demography. She is particularly interested in divorce and separation, new relationship types, and the organization and legal aspects of partner relationships, and has published widely in the area of family studies and social demography (e.g., *Journal of Marriage and Family*, *Journal of Family Issues*, *Population Studies*, *Demographic Research*). Currently, she is program leader of a large data collection and related research program about contemporary parenthood among divorced and intact families.

Anne van der Put is a PhD student in the Department of Sociology and Research School (ICS) at Utrecht University. Having completed her research master's in Sociology and Social Research (cum laude), she is now working on her dissertation focusing on the role of organizations in the influence of workplace health promotion on the lifestyle, health, and performance of employees.

Joop Schippers is Professor of Labour Economics at Utrecht University (since 1999). He graduated from Erasmus University Rotterdam in 1981 (cum laude) in (political) economics and completed his PhD thesis on gender inequality in the labor market in 1987. He is a leading Dutch expert on gender and age-related labor market issues and has published a series of books and articles on gender differences, human capital investments, labor market relations, and labor market flexibility and organizational/employers' behavior with respect to women and older workers. Since 2014 he has been a member of the Board of Supervisors of the University of Humanistic Studies in Utrecht. In 2017 he was invited to become an affiliated researcher of the Netherlands Interdisciplinary Demographic Institute in The Hague.

Stefan Szücs is Associate Professor of Political Science in the Department of Social Work at the University of Gothenburg. His research interests concern democracy and local governance, working-life policies, and innovative sustainable development, for which he has received a number of large-scale grants from Swedish and international science foundations. He has published in high ranking scientific journals such as *European Planning Studies* (2014), *Local Government Studies* (2009), *Governance* (1996), and *The Annals of The American Academy of Political and Social Science* (1995). His edited books include *Local elites, political capital and democratic development: Governing leaders in seven European countries* (Springer, 2006).

Preface

A sustainable European workforce has become increasingly important in the present day. Flexibility and job insecurity are omnipresent; organizational workforces are displaying growing diversity with respect to age, gender, ethnicity, and family status; and Europe's welfare states are delegating more and more responsibility for the well-being of workers to employers. Now more than ever, organizations need to consider investing in workers to improve their performance and levels of satisfaction. These investments can take many forms, including flexible work arrangements, training plans, child-related policies, and health programs. The crucial question is how to make this happen. Why do some organizations invest more and others less in their employees? Why do some employees make use of these investments while others do not? Why do such investments sometimes improve employee performance and satisfaction yet in other instances they do not? This book addresses precisely these questions.

We have organized the chapters of this book into three sections. In Part I, we set the stage with an introduction to the theme of the sustainable workforce and explain how the chapters contribute to this theme. This is followed by a description of the data we gathered and the institutional backgrounds of the selected countries. In Part II, we analyze the organizational availability of various policies and how employees use them, highlighting barriers to investing in workforce sustainability at different levels. Finally, in Part III, we discuss the consequences of organizational policies for employees.

This book is the outcome of the European Research Council Advanced Grant "Investments in a Sustainable Workforce in Europe: Causes and Consequences in a Comparative Perspective" (ERC Grant Agreement no. 340045) awarded to Tanja van der Lippe, for which we are grateful. The team at Utrecht University put enormous effort into unpacking the processes and conditions of creating a sustainable workforce. To do so, we collected information from employees in many organizations in various sectors across nine European countries: Bulgaria, Finland, Germany, Hungary, the Netherlands, Portugal, Spain, Sweden, and the United Kingdom. In our survey, we worked with international collaborators at different universities and research institutes across Europe. Many of them have co-authored chapters in this book. We would like to thank Anja-Kristin Abendroth, Margareta Bäck-Wiklund, Teresa Castro-Martín,

Maria das Dores Guerreiro, Éva Fodor, Siyka Kovacheva, Suzan Lewis, Jouko Nätti, and Stefan Szücs for their indispensable help. Moreover, we are grateful to the members of our advisory board, Arne Kalleberg, Ellen Ernst Kossek, Anneke van Doorne-Huiskes and Laura den Dulk, for the role they played in our large-scale project. We would also like to thank the research assistants in the Netherlands and across Europe who helped us make the data-collection process a success.

We also wish to take this opportunity to express our deepest gratitude to the organizations, human resource managers, supervisors, and employees who shared their insights about their jobs, the quality of work, and policies and arrangements in their organizations. We would like to thank them all for their time and effort.

We are deeply indebted to our authors not only for their invaluable contributions, but also for their ideas on how to draw the contours of a sustainable workforce. We discussed the detail of every chapter during frequent and lively meetings with our team and feel privileged to have such wonderful colleagues who share our devotion to this topic, and to research.

We would like to thank Piet Buitendijk, Wieteke Conen, Esther Havekes, Karoline Gros, Thomas Martens, Sanne Roelfsema, Nina Vergeldt and Wim Zinger for all their practical support during this large-scale project, and Ellen Janssen and Miranda Jansen for their advice on sometimes challenging issues. Jos Slabbekoorn helped us harmonize all the chapters in the book. A special word of thanks goes to Routledge for the trust they have shown in our endeavor and for the painstaking way in which they have guided the publishing process.

Tanja van der Lippe and Zoltán Lippényi

Part I

Organizations and their employees in a sustainable workforce

1 A sustainable workforce in Europe

Bringing the organization back in

Tanja van der Lippe

In need of a sustainable workforce

Globalization, economic fluctuations, the aging population, technological advances, and rapidly changing social structures pose new challenges to creating a sustainable workforce in Europe. The term 'sustainability' comes from the environmental domain and refers to using resources in a way that retains them for future generations. As a concept, sustainability can also be applied to employment relations. The European Commission's Europe 2020 strategy identifies efforts to ensure quality of work and employment conditions as a core tool for promoting a sustainable workforce (European Commission, 2010a, 2016b). Achieving this aim is critical, especially at a time when people are less secure in their jobs, governments are reining in social welfare spending, and the social, economic, and ecological environments are challenging. Generally speaking, a workforce is sustainable when: (1) employees are productive and satisfied (micro level); (2) organizations are profitable and workplaces are cohesive (meso level); and (3) countries have a high labor participation rate and a flourishing economy (macro level) (Appelbaum, Bailey, Berg, & Kalleberg, 2000; Bäck-Wiklund, Van der Lippe, Den Dulk, & Van Doorne-Huiskes, 2011; DiFabio, 2017).

Work organizations play a key role in building a sustainable workforce. It is organizations that invest money, time, and effort in developing human capital, that put work–life policies in place, that establish flexible work and health arrangements for employees, and that address the long-term employability of older workers. These investments may not always have direct payoffs for the organization itself, although managements most definitely count on such benefits. At the societal level, organizational engagement in a sustainable workforce is crucial for retaining talent and tapping into the unused potential of women, migrants, and older workers (Gallie, 2009; Taylor, Loretto, Marshall, Earl, & Phillipson, 2016; Van der Lippe, 2007).

While few would question the centrality of organizations in nurturing a productive and flourishing workforce, sociologists of work have long refrained from engaging with their role. The research agenda typically centers around labor markets and how they value workers' attributes. Analyses focus on formal education and labor market experience, or prioritize the role of occupations and how labor markets 'select' workers for more or less advantaged jobs. Work organizations are often missing from such analyses. Others study organizations' human resources as a system, and its implications for organizational performance. The question of how human resource investments impact individual workers has been left unanswered. At the opposite end of the micro–macro spectrum, we find studies of psychological mechanisms contributing to individual productivity and well-being. By focusing on individual-level mechanisms, however, this body of scholarly work does not problematize the contribution of the organization.

This book proposes to respond to a growing chorus in research that we must 'bring the organization back in' (Barley & Kunda, 2001; Baron & Bielby, 1980; Kalleberg, 2009; Scott & Davis, 2015). Major transformations in the organization of work and employment relations, occurring primarily within organizations, necessitate an organization-focused analysis of a sustainable workforce. The increasing diversity of the workforce and its varied preferences regarding fulfilling work require more knowledge of organizational investments in employees' human capital and their payoffs (Rousseau, Ho, & Greenberg, 2006). New work forms call for in-depth knowledge of the effect of organizations' flexibility policies (Ramsdal & Skorstad, 2016). The growing female employment participation rate makes the study of work–life policies all the more relevant (Acker, 2006). An aging population requires an examination of the employability of older employees in organizations (Kooij, Jansen, Dikkers, & de Lange, 2014). The increase in migrant employees in European countries makes it important to understand to what extent programs for training and development can help to improve their careers (D'Netto & Sohal, 1999). Finally, insecure and dynamic labor markets demand more knowledge of which kinds of employment contracts will help promote a sustainable workforce (Kalleberg, 2012; Rodriquez, Johnstone, & Procter, 2017).

The idea of investing in the workforce has been voiced in many EU directives and national policy initiatives, as well as in the research community (Cappelli, 2008; Den Dulk, Peper, Kanjuo Mrčela, & Ignjatović, 2016; European Commission, 2010a; European Commission's European Political Strategy Centre (EPCS) 2016; Kossek & Michel, 2010; Schalk & Van Veldhoven, 2010). Nonetheless, a comprehensive account of the contribution of work organizations to a sustainable workforce and the impact of this contribution for workers and organizations is missing from the research agenda. This book proposes to fill this void and has the following aims:

1 To provide insight from an international comparative perspective into the availability of organizational policies for a sustainable workforce and their use by employees in different sectors across Europe.
2 To analyze the consequences of the availability and use of investments in productive and satisfied employees and cohesive and profitable workplaces in different sectors across Europe.
3 To introduce and integrate the meso (organizational) level into research on the micro and macro levels of employment.

Organizational policies

This book will address organizational investments that are thought to make important contributions to a sustainable workforce (see Grossmeier et al., 2016; Kelly et al., 2008; Kossek & Michel, 2010; Tsui, Pearce, Porter, & Tripoli, 1997). These investments are training, work–life policies, employability of older workers, flexibility and security, and health arrangements. Often, but not always, these investments are contingent on national laws and regulations regarding labor and employment. Sweden and Finland, for example, have generous family leave policies that organizations are required by law to implement. It remains to be seen, however, whether mandatory policies are also efficient for organizations. The provision of training may also hinge on labor policies that require regular training, for example about health and safety, in certain sectors and jobs (e.g., nurses). In some cases, for instance in Germany, sector or industry-level collective bargaining agreements stipulate the amount of job-related training that must be provided. Although the country or sector does not provide the training, it mandates organizations to do so. Another example is part-time work. Some countries, including Germany and the Netherlands, have statutory regulations that make it easier for individual employees to change their work hours. Finally, with pension rules and retirement ages varying between countries (Organisation for Economic Co-operation and Development, 2017a), national differences have emerged in how organizations deal with the employability of older employees.

Beyond institutional control as a homogenizing force, there are multiple reasons why organizations invest differently in employees. On the organization's part, it can be intentional (e.g., provisions for employees with children), but it may also be the unintended consequence of discrimination (e.g., underinvestment in female employees and minorities). Investments therefore can be, and are, directed toward different groups of employees, and in this book we will focus on groups such as men and women, migrant and non-migrant employees, younger and older workers, and lower- and higher-educated employees. The consequences of investments for employees and for the organization as a whole depend on how much is invested and in whom. In this book, we will address both the availability and use of policies and their consequences for the workplace.

Training. Long-term relationships used to provide a favorable setting for deriving mutual benefits from investments in human capital, such as employee training. These days, however, employment relationships are less secure and the workforce more diverse: employees are more open to job change, and employers readily lay off workers when the market deteriorates. This can discourage the organization from making relationship-specific investments and employees from utilizing them. But who still receives training and why? This is a relevant question, since investments in training programs are found to be related to organizational performance (Hansson, 2007).

Work–life policies. Organizations differ significantly in terms of work–family responsiveness and the extent to which they supplement public work–life policies. That organizations are highly committed to work–life policies might be due to certain economic drivers, but also to institutional pressure. To what extent are statutory arrangements relevant for the way organizations invest in employees with children?

Employability of older employees. Many countries are facing an unprecedented aging of their populations, with consequences for the composition of the workforce. Companies are relying increasingly on the knowledge and skills of older workers; meanwhile, the pool of available workers is shrinking. Some organizations invest more than others in older employees by offering job expansion and other employability plans (Van der Heijde & Van der Heijden, 2006), but under what conditions do older employees make use of these arrangements?

Flexible employment contracts. Despite the new flexible worker paradigm, the implications of flexible contracts for productivity are unclear (Kossek & Thompson, 2016). Increasingly, organizations rely on flexible contracts to safeguard their profits, but they might still need to invest in temporary workers. Employees are expected to make use of flexible contracts, depending on the type of work, their work–life requirements, and the community infrastructure and country culture. Individual employees respond differently to these policies, but in what ways?

Health arrangements A combination of business norms of responsibility toward the workforce and the expected positive impact of health on employees and their performance (Carmichael, Fenton, Pinilla Roncancio, Sadhra, & Sing, 2016; Goetzel & Ozminkowski, 2008) has led many organizations to offer worksite health promotion (e.g., sports facilities, health checks, healthy nutrition programs), designed to improve employees' lifestyle and health (Anderson et al., 2009). Worksite health promotion has the potential to do this because people spend a large part of their lives at work. It is therefore important to understand under what conditions organizations offer these programs.

Approach

To meet the aims of the book, our approach consists of three central elements, namely, (1) a multi-disciplinary theoretical approach, (2) a cross-country and cross-industry comparative perspective, and (3) a multi-level data design.

Multi-disciplinary theoretical approach

To understand *why* organizations invest in certain work arrangements, *if and why* employees actually use these arrangements, and *what* the consequences are, we make use of an analytical framework that allows us to study how the organization (meso level) interacts with both the employee (micro level) and the country (macro level). Because most research concentrates on either the employee or the country (or a combination of the two), their importance may be overstated (Beham, Drobnič, Präg, Baierl, & Eckner, 2018; Blossfeld & Hofmeister, 2006; Lewis, 2009; McGinnity & Whelan, 2009; Van der Lippe, De

Ruijter, De Ruijter, & Raub, 2010). We therefore combine general theoretical insights from economic sociology with field-specific theories from sociology, economics, psychology, and management. In line with economic sociology (Smelser & Swedberg, 2010), we assume that investments by organizations and their use by employees depend on costs and benefits for both parties. Whether an investment benefits a company's performance depends on its employees' behavior, and vice versa; in other words, organizations and employees are *interdependent* (Buskens, Raub, & Snijders, 2003; Williamson, 1989).

Besides the interdependencies that arise during everyday 'transactions' in the workplace, relations between workers are also influenced by stereotypes in society about specific groups – women and minorities in particular. That can have consequences for power relations and inequality in workplaces, as expressed in relational inequality theory (Avent-Holt & Tomaskovic-Devey, 2012a). Culture and norms are therefore influential because tacit norms imposed by the social environment – whether that is the family, the organization, the industry, or the country to which one belongs – shape behavior and actions (England & Folbre, 2005; Ryan & Kossek, 2008; Tomlinson, Baird, Berg, & Cooper, 2018). If a certain group accounts for a large percentage of an organization's employees (be it a group of women, younger employees, or older workers), not investing in relevant policies could lead to costs in terms of hasty resignations, with the organization then losing out on human capital and other skills (Kalleberg, Marsden, Reynolds, & Knoke, 2006; Lazear & Shaw, 2007). For example, if there are no work–family policies available, the costs of staying in the organization are expected to be higher for women (in terms of work–life conflict) than moving to a family-friendly organization. The specific macro-level context also plays a role: extensive government social policies, such as in the Nordic countries, make it less beneficial for organizations to introduce their own policies (Abendroth, Van der Lippe, & Maas, 2012; Esping-Andersen, 2009). Another example involves investing in the long-term employability of older employees: if the organization trains or retrains older employees, it runs the risk of their retiring before the investment can be recouped. Moreover, employer failure to invest in older employees may be tied to status evaluations of this group of employees (Avent-Holt & Tomaskovic-Devey, 2012b).

We deliberately focus on both the availability of investments and their utilization by employees. Research has thus far paid much more attention to the availability of investments in organizations, making it difficult to assess their real impact on workers and organizations (Boxall & Macky, 2009; Thunnissen, Boselie, & Fruytier, 2013). Consider an employee decision to use work–family arrangements. If many of the employee's colleagues and supervisors also have families, that constitutes a meso-level condition that may engender norms that encourage the utilization of work–life arrangements and reduce the risks of doing so (Huffmann, Cohen, & Pearlman, 2010). In addition, the costs of using work–life arrangements will be lower and the benefits in terms of work–life balance and individual performance higher. Interdependence between the parent employee and the supervisor entails more benefits than risks.

We explain the *consequences* for the employee and for the organization. When it comes to the intended consequences at each level, we assume that actors evaluate costs and benefits (including norms) that lead to the intended outcomes. We also study unintended consequences, where the relationship is less straightforward because actors do not evaluate it in terms of costs and benefits. Moreover, consequences at the organizational level might not be a simple aggregation of employees' actions (Hedström & Ylikoski, 2011).

Each of the investments studied in this book is an example of where costs and benefits, interdependencies, and norms are important, and therefore also interesting from a theoretical viewpoint. Our authors come from various scientific disciplines (sociology, economics, human resource management/management studies, public administration), contributing different disciplinary insights to the study of sustainable employment.

Cross-country and cross-industry comparative perspective

Organizations are embedded in diverse institutional, industrial, and professional environments, and resources and constraints from the environment have a profound impact on organizational strategies, practices, and their outcomes (Scott & Davis, 2015). The national welfare regime and economies will influence the feasibility or attractiveness of certain investments (Rubery, Bosch, & Lehndorff, 2008). The nine countries studied in this book, namely, Bulgaria, Finland, Germany, Hungary, the Netherlands, Portugal, Spain, Sweden and the UK, constitute different types of welfare regimes (Bäck-Wiklund et al., 2011; Esping-Andersen, 2009). Although differences between these types are somewhat fluid, Finland and Sweden are typically categorized as socio-democratic regimes, Germany and the Netherlands as conservative regimes, Spain and Portugal as Mediterranean regimes, the UK as a liberal regime, and Hungary and Bulgaria as post-communist regimes. This diverse set of countries provides ample variation in policies, (gender) culture and labor market characteristics (for further elaboration, see Chapter 2).

Within countries, firms are embedded in economic sectors differing in levels of national and international competition and growth, factors that further influence firms' decisions to invest in workers. Existing studies, however, pay little attention to the influence of the institutional and industrial context on organizational investments. Taking environmental dependencies into account is important for understanding differences in organizational investments in a sustainable workforce. The authors address these rich differences by making explicit comparisons between organizational investments and their consequences across different institutional and industrial settings. This book studies six sectors: manufacturing, health care, higher education, transportation, financial services, and telecommunications. These sectors vary widely in the percentage of male and female, younger and older, and lower- and higher-educated employees. This variation has implications for the investments (or lack thereof) in a sustainable workforce at the organizational level. We aimed to include sectors in our study in which investments in a sustainable workforce will become increasingly important due to current demographic and technological pressures as well as globalization in Europe.

Multi-level data design

A unique aspect of this book is that it analyzes multi-level data on organizations and workers. Existing studies on firms' investments in employees typically utilize one-level surveys, interviewing individual employees from a single company, representatives of firms, or the labor force in general, without identifying the employer (Hansson, 2007). A significant drawback of this approach is that none of these designs can simultaneously address variation between firms in investments (Lazear & Shaw, 2007), as well as the consequences of this variation for individual workers. De Menezes and Kelliher (2011) and others have therefore asserted the need for a multi-level design to study the influence of organizations on employee outcomes.

This book contributes a new, large-scale survey of 259 organizations, 869 work units, and 11,011 employees in six diverse economic sectors in the UK, Germany, Hungary, Bulgaria, Spain, Sweden, Finland, the Netherlands, and Portugal (Van der Lippe et al., 2016; see further in Chapter 3) to study the causes and consequences of organizational investments. The organizations studied are in both the private and the public sectors. Once the organization (often the human resources director) had agreed to participate, we contacted employees and their departmental managers at work and asked them to complete an online or paper-and-pencil questionnaire. Topics addressed in the questionnaire included organizational investments and use by employees, performance and satisfaction of employees, and productivity and cohesion of the workplace, as well as many background characteristics of the employee and the organization.

Sustainable workforce: productive and satisfied employees and workplaces

This book is about a sustainable workforce in Europe. Before discussing the structure of the book and the individual chapters, we will look at the general picture of sustainability derived from the European Sustainable Workforce Survey (ESWS) (Van der Lippe et al., 2016). We calculated job satisfaction and self-reported performance at the individual employee level. For job satisfaction, we used the question "All things considered, how satisfied are you with your current job," with answers ranging from 1 (extremely dissatisfied) to 10 (extremely satisfied). For performance, we used the scale by Koopmans, Bernaards, Hildebrandt, De Vet, & Van der Beek, (2014) that distinguishes between task performance and contextual performance, with a 5-point Likert scale of items whereby low values indicated low performance and high values high performance. An example of a task performance item is "I was able to do my work efficiently" and an example of a contextual performance item is "I took on extra responsibilities." Figures 1.1a and 1.1b show individual performance and job satisfaction for all employees by country. Figure 1.1a shows that scores for job satisfaction are relatively high in Finland, the Netherlands, and Sweden,

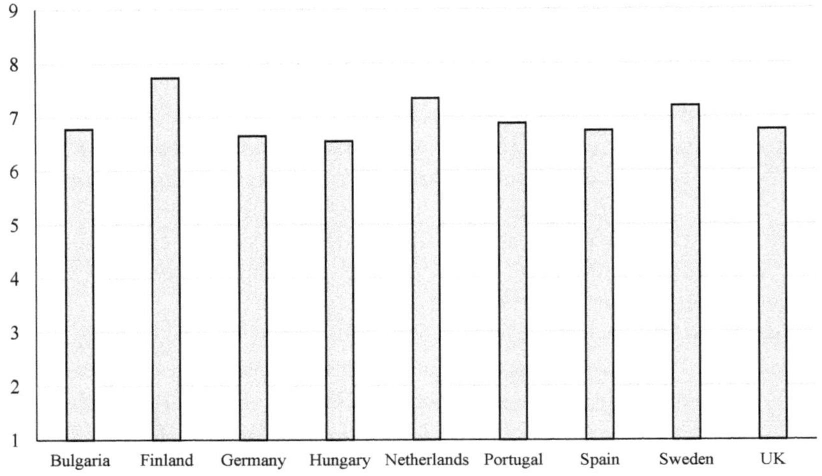

Figure 1.1a Job satisfaction for the nine European countries.

Source: Van der Lippe et al. (2016).

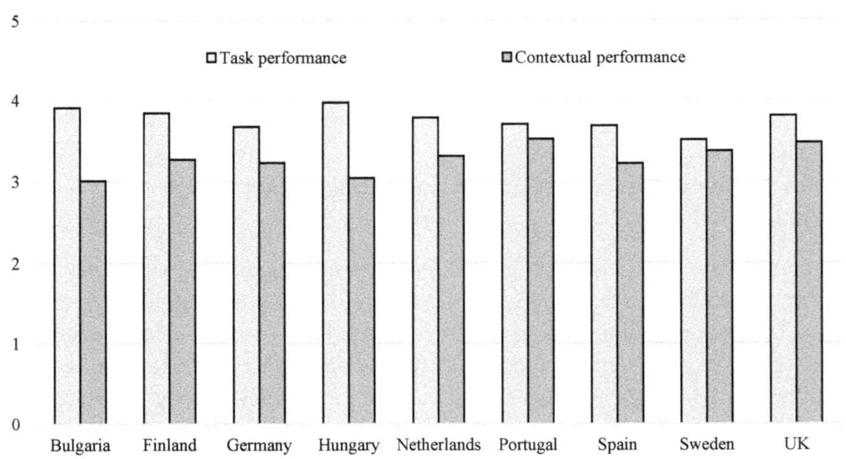

Figure 1.1b Individual performance for the nine European countries.

Source: Van der Lippe et al. (2016).

Note

These figures (1.1 and 1.2) are not necessarily representative of the countries; they are an outcome of the ESWS data.

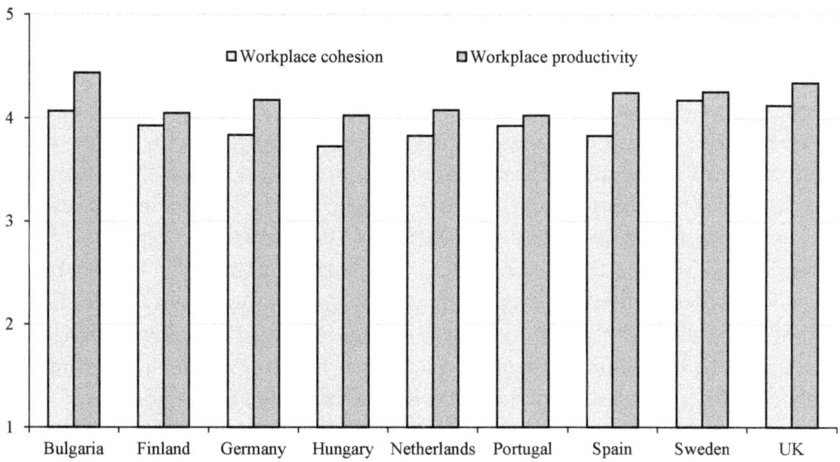

Figure 1.2 Workplace cohesion and productivity for the nine European countries.
Source: Van der Lippe et al. (2016).

and relatively low in Hungary and Germany. Furthermore, self-reported task performance is always rated higher than contextual performance, with the differences being most notable in Bulgaria and Hungary. Scores for contextual performance are also somewhat lower in these two countries than in the others. We performed the same analyses for sectors, and it became clear that there is more variation in job satisfaction and self-reported performance between countries than between sectors. The figures reported by employees who participated in the ESWS were similar to European statistics, but there are no comparable figures for perceived performance (Eurostat, 2015).

We performed a similar analysis for workplace cohesion and productivity using ratings provided by departmental managers. Labor productivity is measured by a single item, while department cohesion is measured by four items. Example items are "Everyone feels like part of the team" and "Employees regularly give one another feedback," using 5-point Likert scale items. Figure 1.2 shows that workplace cohesion is relatively high in Sweden and lower in Hungary, and workplace productivity as reported by the manager is higher in Bulgaria.

Overall, managers' scores for workplace cohesion and productivity are somewhat higher than the ratings provided by employees themselves for job satisfaction and performance. Once again, the differences between sectors are smaller than between countries.

Structure of the book

The book is divided into three parts. Part I, consisting of three chapters and entitled *Organizations and their employees in a sustainable workforce*, sets the stage, describes the problem and background, outlines the institutional context and current trends in the nine countries, and provides details about the ESWS. Part II consists of five chapters and is entitled *A comparative approach to which organizations invest in employees: differences between sectors and countries*. Each chapter focuses on a different investment by the organization in specific groups of employees and explains the reasons for these investments, which vary from training to health programs. The chapters look in detail at variations in investments within the industries and countries studied. Part III, *Returns on investments in a sustainable workforce for employers and employees*, consists of six chapters and focuses on the consequences of investments made by the organizations, not only for individual employees but for organizations as a whole. Since the ESWS does not contain information on self-employed workers, additional data are used to understand the consequences of investments for this group on the labor market. The book – which also makes extensive use of additional data on technological change in firms – concludes by discussing challenges for future research.

Although the book has many authors, it in fact resembles a monograph. It begins by discussing the research problem, data, and institutional context, obviating the need to reintroduce the data in each chapter and leaving more room to discuss theoretical mechanisms, findings, and policy recommendations.

Part I begins with this introductory chapter. In Chapter 2, Katia Begall and Anneke van Doorne-Huiskes analyze the institutional context in the nine countries, i.e., the context in which companies and their employees develop strategies to achieve high productivity and satisfaction. The authors examine economic, labor market, and demographic trends in these countries in recent years and focus on commonality and variance in employment, work–family, and health policies in each participating country. This chapter provides a background against which the results of the empirical chapters can be interpreted and facilitates a comparative perspective on the institutional structures. Despite a shared body of European legislation which has led to harmonization in some areas, national contexts still vary widely with regard to the position of older workers, the provisions surrounding work–family compatibility, and the importance of lifelong learning, implying variation in the institutional preconditions for creating a sustainable workforce.

In Chapter 3, Zoltán Lippényi, Thomas Martens, and Tanja van der Lippe outline the data strategy and data collection for the Sustainable Workforce project. Before the start of this project, multi-actor data of this type were nonexistent. The authors compare the ESWS to other survey designs, and describe the procedures used for sampling organizations, approaching them about the study, and surveying respondents.

In Part II, Nikki van Gerwen, Vincent Buskens, and Maria das Dores Guerreiro (Chapter 4) focus on the question of which employees are more likely to receive training. Trained employees often have better opportunities for promotion and higher wages than untrained employees, which makes unequal access to training a possible mechanism that can foster inequality between men and women. This chapter contributes to the literature on gender differences in training participation. Whereas previous research has focused on either employee or organizational characteristics related to employees' training opportunities, this chapter moves beyond the existing literature by examining whether these characteristics have a differential influence on the training participation of men and women. It does so while focusing on three different types of training: training given by a co-worker, training given by a professional, and enrollment in an educational program. The authors look specifically at which organizations are more likely to invest in training their employees by considering the type of organization (public or private), its size, and the presence of collective bargaining agreements.

In Chapter 5, Leonie van Breeschoten, Katia Begall, Anne-Rigt Poortman, and Laura den Dulk examine the correlation between the organization and the utilization of one specific work–family policy: parental leave. Organizations and national governments are increasingly making work–family policies available to help working parents combine a career and childcare. Nonetheless, many people who might benefit from these policies do not use them, and we know little about why they do or do not. Some studies have suggested that organizations restrain or encourage people's use of these policies, yet no large-scale quantitative studies have been carried out. This chapter specifically combines two ways of looking at organizations: it considers how family-supportive their organizational culture is, and it treats them as rational actors that make strategic choices to invest in policies – choices that are influenced by organizational characteristics such as size, public ownership, or the proportion of women employed. Based on a business-case argument, the authors expect organizations that operate in a competitive climate to be particularly keen to invest in work–family policies, as such policies can attract and retain employees and improve employee satisfaction and performance. At the same time, it is public sector organizations in particular – which tend to be less profit-oriented – that are known for offering work–family policies, as they are more sensitive to institutional pressures.

In Chapter 6, Jelle Lössbroek, Joop Schippers, Bram Lancee, and Stefan Szücs study the older workforce. As the average age of workers increases across Europe, organizations face the challenge of adapting their personnel policies to this situation. Three types of policies have been found to potentially help prolong working lives and are frequently implemented: activating/training policies, flexibility policies, and phasing-out policies. Training participation has been widely studied and is known to decline as workers age. The literature on flexibility policies focuses on younger workers, and little is known about which workers use phasing-out polices. To understand the extent to which human resource arrangements contribute to working longer, it is important to know who uses the options formally available to workers. This chapter studies which older workers are most likely to participate in flexibility and phasing-out policies (in the organizations that offer them). The authors investigate two cost–benefit arguments from both the employee's and the employer's perspective: older workers' age and their job compatibility with certain personnel policies. They also test the importance of two attitudinal considerations: gender roles and managerial agism.

In Chapter 7, Anne van der Put and Jornt Mandemakers focus on the healthy workforce, which is in the interests of employers and employees alike. They investigate what organizations do to promote and facilitate employee health. Their analyses are motivated in part by the large socio-economic disparities in health across Europe. Differential access to health interventions at work constitutes an important pathway for socio-economic health differences among employees, but little is known about the determinants of access to health interventions at the organizational and/or employee level. The authors first map the European organizational landscape in terms of four healthy interventions: (1) healthy nutrition, (2) sports participation, (3) ergonomic facilities, and (4) health checks; they then focus on country and sector differences. Employees generally less often perceive health interventions to be available than is reported by organizations themselves. The authors then move to the employee level to see what explains employee perceptions of health interventions, drawing on information and motivation theory and incorporating employee and organizational characteristics.

In Chapter 8, Silvia Maja Melzer looks at the specific situation of immigrants in achieving a sustainable workforce. Although the wage disadvantages of immigrants are well documented, there has been little interest shown in their access to employer-provided training, although this is likely to create many opportunities for them. As access to employer-provided training is related to various aspects of employment in which immigrants are disadvantaged and they have less chance of integrating successfully into the host country's labor market, it is important to identify the factors that restrict their access. This study examines access to employer-provided formal training and how firms' resources, training costs, and training intensity influence immigrants' opportunities to participate in training. Although training enhances employees' human capital, decisions regarding training are not individual decisions but depend as much on the employer as on the employee.

In Part III, Jasmijn van Harten, Zoltán Lippényi and Paul Boselie provide a general assessment, in Chapter 9, of how different sets of human resource investments in employability impact employee performance and well-being. They address a key debate in human resource management: do human resource investments enhance both employee well-being and performance and generate mutual gains for workers and organizations, or do human resource investments have trade-off effects, meaning that either performance or well-being is negatively affected? This chapter assesses these conflicting hypotheses for investments in organizational flexibility and training.

In Chapter 10, Zoltán Lippényi, Alessandra Gasparotto and Youko Nätti study the consequences of temporary employment for employees' perceived work–life balance. The risks that temporary employment poses to work productivity, due to job insecurity, work intensification, and competition, are well documented in the literature. Much less research has been devoted to the implications of temporary employment for the interface between work and private life. This chapter fills the gap by studying how temporary jobs influence the perceived balance between work and private life. It also addresses the role of the meso level by looking at whether temporary workers perceive their work–life balance as poor when the organization views them as incidental labor as opposed to prospective employees in secure jobs.

In Chapter 11, Wieteke Conen and Paul de Beer look at investments in employability and the value of work, comparing employees and solo self-employed workers. Organizations may invest in their employees to enhance individual (and organizational) performance, for instance by offering various human resource policies (training, health policies, work–family policies). But what if there is no 'organization' to make that investment? In this chapter, the focus is on investments in the employability of employees as compared to solo self-employed workers. The authors first address whether employees differ from solo self-employed workers in their self-assessed skills: do they think their skills correspond well to their own work duties, or would they require further training? Next, they examine to what extent and how solo self-employed workers – as compared to employees – ensure that they remain employable. And finally: do investments in employability have an effect on employees' and solo self-employed workers' current 'value of work' and their (perceived) chances in the labor market – in other words, on their (expected) utility? The authors use data from the sixth European Working Conditions Survey (2015) to address these questions.

In Chapter 12, Margriet van Hek and Anja-Kristin Abendroth focus on male and female leadership and promotional opportunities of men and women. Managers decide on the hiring, promotion and wages of their employees. Male and female managers may differ in the extent to which they promote female and male employees. Female managers might act as agents of change that improve women's chances of obtaining better positions in the organization. Conversely, female managers may act as cogs in the machine; "queen bee" theory asserts that female managers do not benefit women's promotional opportunities because they aim to distance themselves from feminine matters to underscore their (masculine) professionalism. This chapter tests these competing hypotheses and asks: to what extent are women's and men's perceived promotional opportunities affected by the proportion of female managers in their organization, and by being supervised by a female manager?

In Chapter 13, Jannes ten Berge and Maarten Goos study technology implementation and changes in the educational and age composition of enterprise workforces. Their study examines how technology implementation within enterprises impacts the educational and age composition of workforces, those entering and those leaving companies. They advance the literature on the labor market consequences of technological change by focusing on the impact of technology within the workplaces where it is implemented, rather than inferring from aggregate data on structural changes in labor. They use large-scale matched employer–employee panel data from the Netherlands that directly measure technology implementation in over 3,500 enterprises between 2000 and 2014 to test their ideas about the impact of entrants and leavers on the composition of the workforce.

Finally, in Chapter 14, Tanja van der Lippe and Éva Fodor synthesize and discuss the results of all the previous chapters, identify future challenges, and make suggestions for future research.

Investments in a sustainable workforce in Europe offers an agenda for future research regarding the obstacles and opportunities for a sustainable workforce in Europe from a global perspective. The multi-layered analysis presented in this comprehensive book helps us rethink Europe's workforce by providing new empirical as well as theoretical underpinnings.

2 The institutional context of a sustainable workforce

Katia Begall and Anneke van Doorne-Huiskes

Introduction

The aim of this chapter is to describe the opportunity to create a sustainable workforce at the national level within which organizations and individuals operate. It provides a background against which the results of the empirical chapters can be interpreted and facilitates a comparative perspective of the institutional structures. To this end, we present an overview of the institutional context and aggregate population characteristics of the nine countries involved in the Sustainable Workforce Survey to show similarities and differences between them. The focus will be on features and outcomes related to the key organizational policies identified as relevant to the creation of a sustainable workforce (see Chapter 1) and addressed in the empirical chapters. These are *flexibility and security* (Chapter 10), *training* (Chapters 4, 6, 8, 11), *work–life policies* (Chapters 5, 7, 10), *health arrangements* (Chapter 7) and the *employability of older employees* (Chapter 6).

The nine countries from which organizations in the Sustainable Workforce Survey were sampled can be thought of as representing ideal typical settings of institutional structures which correspond to differences in the preconditions for creating sustainable employment relationships. To illustrate this, we place the nine countries within the welfare-regime typology developed by Esping-Andersen (1990), which draws on two theoretical dimensions, namely, the extent to which individuals can maintain an acceptable standard of living independent of the market ("de-commodification") and the degree of social inequality ("stratification"). This is supplemented by discussing country variation across three institutional factors which we take from theories about employment regimes to be central to the creation of sustainable employment relations: the degree to which unions can influence policies and employment conditions, the process of skill formation and the level of state regulation in the labor market (Gallie, 2007, 2009; Holman, 2013). These perspectives are useful in establishing the connection between the country level and sustainable employment practices at the level of organizations and employees. We discuss (clusters of) countries ordered according to the likelihood of sustainable employment relations.

Sweden and Finland represent the social-democratic regime in the Sustainable Workforce Survey, characterized by a high degree of de-commodification and a low degree of stratification. In addition, the strongly institutionalized role of the unions in Sweden and Finland fosters good working conditions and low wage differentials as well as high employment (particularly in the large public sector). Table 2.1 presents information on wage bargaining systems and union density and shows the highest union density and collective bargaining coverage in Sweden and Finland. The active role of the unions is coupled with generous unemployment and work–family policies and high investment in education and training of the general population through access to lifelong learning and extensive vocational programs (Holman, 2013).

The Netherlands and Germany approximate to the corporatist or conservative regime type where social inequality is more pronounced and, besides the state, other institutional actors in civil society provide support to citizens. Union influence is generally less strong, even though industry-level bargaining ensures good working conditions and high wages, but especially so for core workers in large firms which fall under collective labor agreements (see Table 2.1). Strong employment protection makes investments in vocational training and job specific skills worthwhile for the employer, but levels of employment are lower than in social-democratic countries and there exists a peripheral labor market with lower-skilled workers in non-standard jobs. Also, there is less policy support for work–family reconciliation compared to the Scandinavian countries.

The UK represents the liberal welfare regime which is characterized by the predominance of the market as the organizing actor in society, implying a low degree of de-commodification and higher levels of inequality. Here the influence of

Table 2.1 Collective bargaining in the ESWS countries sorted by bargaining coverage

	Level of centralization (2014)[a]	*Degree of coordination (2014)*[a]	*Union density (%) (2012/13)*[b]	*Collective bargaining coverage (%) (2013)*[b]
HU	–	–	11	23
BG	o	–	18	29
UK	–	–	26	30
DE	o	o	18	58
PT	o	o	19	73
ES	+	+	17	78
NL	o	o	18	85
SE	o	+	67	89
FI	+	+	69	93

Sources: a European Observatory of Working Life, 2018. b Source: Visser, 2016.

Notes

+ = centralized/highly coordinated; o = intermediate; – = decentralized/low level of coordination.
HU – Hungary; BG – Bulgaria: UK – United Kingdom; DE – Germany; PT – Portugal; ES – Spain; NL – Netherlands; SE – Sweden: FI – Finland.

unions on policies is weaker and bargaining is more decentralized. The level of state regulation is generally low, particularly with regard to employment protection. Levels of employment are lower and not subject to government intervention; the educational system is comprehensive and less focused on providing vocational skills. There is a high degree of stratification based on skills and class, but relatively small differences between permanent and temporary workers compared to the corporatist countries (Holman, 2013).

Spain and Portugal do not fall into the original welfare regime typology but have been proposed as a separate type, the sub-protective or Mediterranean cluster, which refers to a regime in which there is little state support and a particularly strong role for informal social connections in the family and personal networks (Ferrera, 1996). Unions influence on working conditions is less strong than in the social democratic and corporatist countries and state regulation is relatively weak. This shows in low unemployment- and work–family-support, as well as low investments in education and a relatively weak vocational education system. There is a strongly segmented labor market structure with strong protection for 'insiders' in standard jobs and a weak position for 'outsiders', i.e., workers in non-standard employment forms (Holman, 2013).

Hungary and Bulgaria, like other post-socialist states, are not easily classified into one common or existing regime because they developed different policy directions after 1990. Bulgaria experienced a severe economic crisis during the 1990s and continues to combine austerity and low social spending with low taxation for companies and citizens (Nenovsky & MIlev, 2014). Hungary experienced increasing poverty rates and unemployment after the transformation and the government responded by decreasing social spending accompanied by welfare reforms. The main trend has been increases in self-insurance and a shift from universal to means-tested provisions; however, more recent governments have partly reinstated universal benefits, implying that Hungary has not followed a single ideal typical welfare reform path (Matos, 2013). Hungary and Bulgaria, comparable to Portugal and Spain, are characterized by unions which are relatively weak, autocratic management structures and relatively little state intervention with regard to the regulation of working conditions. Notable exceptions are the generous leave policies for working mothers in both post-socialist states. In addition, efforts toward economic liberalization have decreased job security, even though the extent of non-standard employment is low compared to the other regimes (Holman, 2013).

To complement the discussion of institutional features, the general pattern of wealth and inequality in the nine countries is illustrated in Figure 2.1 which shows GDP per capita, the extent of income inequality and the proportion of the working population at risk of poverty. Finland, Sweden and the Netherlands combine low income inequality (measured by the Gini coefficient) with a low risk of poverty and social exclusion among the working population and high GDP per capita. In terms of inequality, Hungary, Germany and the UK are in the middle of the group of countries studied, while Portugal, Spain and Bulgaria show the highest income inequality. Bulgaria, especially, but also Hungary and

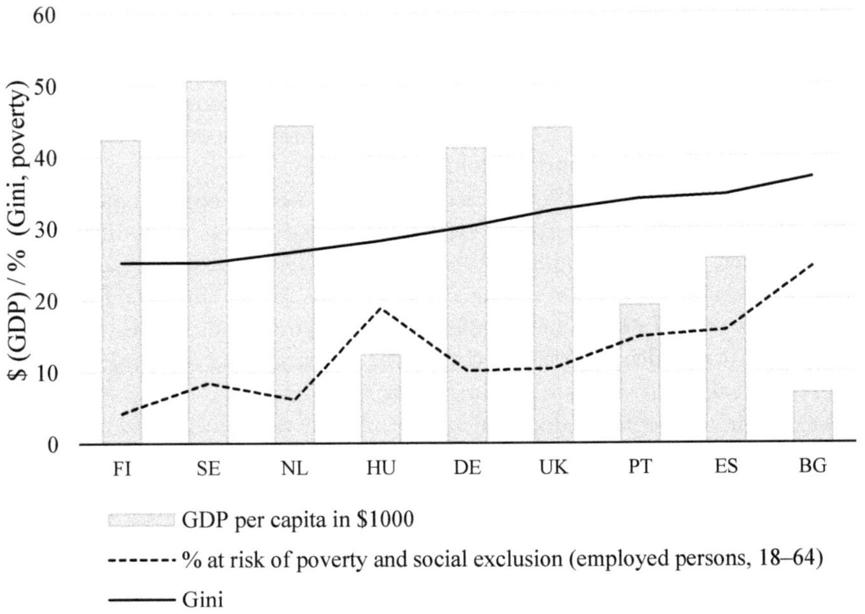

Figure 2.1 GDP per capita, Gini coefficient and percentage of population at risk of poverty and social exclusion (2015); sorted by Gini coefficient.

Sources: Eurostat (2017) Gini coefficient of equivalised disposable income – EU-SILC survey [ilc_di12] (extracted on September 9, 2017); Eurostat (2017) At-risk-of-poverty rate by poverty threshold, age and sex – EU-SILC survey [ilc_li02] (extracted on September 9, 2017); World Bank Data (2018) GDP per capita (current US$): http://data.worldbank.org/indicator/NY.GDP.PCAP.CD?view=chart (extracted on September 9, 2017).

Note
FI – Finland; SE – Sweden; NL – Netherlands; HU – Hungary; DE – Germany; UK – United Kingdom; PT – Portugal; ES – Spain; BG – Bulgaria.

Spain, show relatively high risks of poverty and social exclusion. Considering the national income, Figure 2.1 shows that while Portugal and Spain perform better than the former socialist countries of Bulgaria and Hungary, they fall far below the other five countries. Low per capita income combined with high income inequality (Bulgaria, Spain, Portugal) or high risk of poverty and social exclusion (Hungary, Bulgaria) pose potential threats to the creation of a sustainable workforce because they imply low investments in the productivity and welfare of a part of the workforce.

Flexibility and security

Recent decades have seen a rapid flexibilization of the labor market in many industrialized countries; many people are now employed in jobs that are different from what used to be the standard – full-time, with a permanent contract, worked during office hours (Kalleberg, 2000). During the recent 'great recession' (2008) many countries relaxed their regulations on dismissal of permanent workers, thereby reducing the gap in protection between permanent and temporary workers which had been created in the 1990s when regulations for temporary work were loosened while the protection of permanent workers was maintained (Organisation for Economic Co-operation and Development [OECD], 2013).

Table 2.2 presents the strictness of employment protection legislation for permanent and temporary workers. The employment protection indicators are compiled by the OECD (2013) and range from zero to five, where five implies the strictest regulation. The protection of permanent workers is strongest in the Netherlands, but Germany, Portugal and Sweden exhibit a similar level of strictness. Bulgaria and the UK are the countries with the lowest level of protection from dismissal for permanent workers. Temporary work is most regulated in Spain and Portugal and least regulated in the Netherlands, Sweden and the UK. The combination of the two indicators shows that permanent workers are more protected than temporary workers in all countries except Spain, but that the differences are particularly great in the UK, the Netherlands and Sweden. This can be problematic because it may lead to labor market segmentation, with low levels of mobility between permanent and temporary groups of workers (OECD, 2013).

One indication of such segmentation is the extent to which workers are employed involuntarily in non-standard jobs. Figure 2.2 shows the proportion of

Table 2.2 Indicators of employment protection legislation (2013) and self-employment (2015) in the ESWS countries sorted by protection of permanent workers

	Protection of permanent workers[a]	*Regulation on temporary employment*[a]	*Self-employed workers (% of employed, 2015)*[b]	
			With employees	*Without employees*
BG	1.5[b]		3.4	7.4
UK	1.6	0.5	4.4	5.3
HU	2.1	2.0	4.5	11.0
FI	2.2	1.9	4.4	8.6
ES	2.4	3.2	4.7	4.9
SE	2.5	1.2	4.2	12.0
PT	2.7	2.3	4.5	8.3
DE	2.8	1.7	3.6	5.2
NL	2.9	1.2	2.4	11.6

Sources: a OECD, 2013; b Eurostat Labour Force Surveys (2017), Self-employment by sex, age and educational attainment level (1000) [lfsq_esgaed] (extracted on October 10, 2017); Avdagic, 2015.

Notes

Protection of permanent workers refers to protection from collective and individual dismissal.
Employment protection for BG refers to average employment protection legislation 1980–2009.
BG – Bulgaria: UK – United Kingdom; HU – Hungary: FI – Finland; ES – Spain; SE – Sweden: PT – Portugal; DE – Germany: NL – Netherlands.

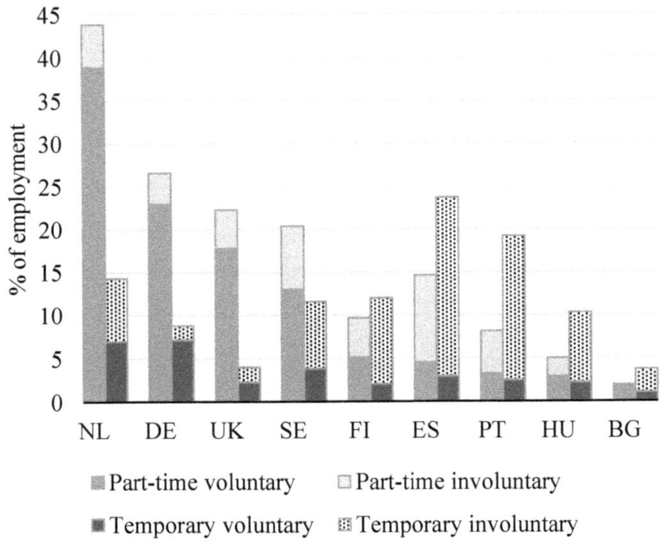

Figure 2.2 Prevalence of non-standard employment (2015, men and women aged 25–59); sorted by voluntary part-time.

Sources: Eurostat European Labour Force Surveys (2018) Temporary employees by sex, age and main reason [lfsa_etgar] (extracted on March 12, 2018); Eurostat European Labour Force Surveys (2018). Part-time employment as percentage of the total employment, by sex and age (percent) [lfsa_eppga] (extracted on March 15, 2018); Eurostat/European Labour Force Surveys (2018). Involuntary part-time employment as percentage of the total part-time employment, by sex and age (percent) [lfsa_eppgai] (extracted on March 15, 2018).

Note
NL – Netherlands; DE – Germany; UK – United Kingdom; SE – Sweden; FI – Finland; ES – Spain; PT – Portugal; HU – Hungary; BG – Bulgaria.

workers employed voluntarily and involuntarily in part-time and temporary jobs in the countries included in the European Sustainable Workforce Survey (ESWS). The only country in which the majority of affected workers claim to be voluntarily employed in a non-permanent contract is Germany. In all other countries temporary contracts appear to be a form of non-standard employment which serves employers' preferences more than those of employees. When comparing the prevalence of temporary contracts between countries, Spain clearly stands out with almost one-quarter of all workers on such contracts. Other countries with a high proportion of workers on temporary contracts are Portugal (about one-fifth) and the Netherlands (15 percent).

Another form of non-standard employment which is increasing is the self-employed without employees or 'freelancers,' a diverse group which is studied in more detail in Chapter 12. This group of self-employed without employees is largest in the Netherlands, Sweden and Hungary (see Table 2.2). Not only does the prevalence of non-standard employment differ between countries, but also the extent to which working conditions such as benefits or wages are different from those in a standard job. Some countries protect certain categories of non-standard workers in order to mitigate differences between groups, a prominent example being part-time workers in the Netherlands who enjoy the same employment benefits and working conditions as full-time workers (Visser, 2002). When the difference in quality between standard and non-standard employment is slight, certain forms of non-standard work can also be a preferred form of employment; for instance, in the case of part-time work and freelancing, which can serve as a strategy for combining work and care responsibilities. With regard to part-time work, a notable figure is of course the high degree of such work in the Netherlands – about 45 percent of all employees – leaving the runner up, Germany, with about one-quarter of its workforce employed part-time lagging far behind. For the majority of workers in the Netherlands, Germany, the UK, Sweden and Finland, part-time work is a choice (albeit possibly one forced by care responsibilities) rather than a constraint. This is not the case in Spain, where more than half of the 16 percent of the workforce who work part-time claim to do so involuntarily (meaning they could not find a full-time job); the same is true in Portugal and Hungary, even though the group of part-timers in the labor market is small in Hungary (5 percent) and even smaller in Bulgaria (2 percent).

Taken together the picture confirms the strong segmentation of the labor market in southern Europe with a high prevalence of involuntary non-standard work and the growing de-standardization of employment in social-democratic and corporatist countries. Notably, the two post-socialist countries show a diverging picture with a low degree of all forms of flexibilization in Bulgaria, but relatively large shares of contractual flexibility in Hungary.

Training

In today's knowledge intensive economies governments and employers stimulate participation in training and the continuous development of skills over the life course in order to achieve higher productivity. The need for employers to offer additional training to employees depends in part on the national educational system, in particular on the extent and nature of vocational training. One can roughly divide the upper secondary educational systems into those that emphasize general skills (United Kingdom, Portugal, Spain, Bulgaria) as opposed to vocational training (Germany, Netherlands, Sweden, Finland, Hungary), and within the latter a distinction can be made between school-based (Sweden, Finland, Hungary) and enterprise-based (Netherlands, Germany) systems. In school- based systems, students are trained in a specific occupation, but training occurs mostly in schools, while enterprise-based or apprenticeship systems combine on-the-job learning with theoretical lectures. Apprenticeship-based systems generally perform well with regard to the school-to-work transition of young people and provide skills well matched to employers' needs (Shavit & Muller, 1998). At the same time, this system requires a high degree of coordination between schools, employers, chambers of commerce and unions which means that adaption of curricula to new technical developments is less flexible than in a school-based system. In systems that emphasize general skills, graduates possess less occupation-specific skills and a larger part of initial training will be carried out on the job and is thus generally less formalized. How the specific skills of employees in the labor market are matched to occupational profiles affects the likelihood of receiving initial training on the job as well as additional training later on, and in this way it impacts the skill level of the population (Gallie, 2007).

Besides the extent of vocational training in upper secondary education, productivity is believed to be enhanced by a higher proportion of the workforce attaining higher education (Wolff, 2001). When comparing the educational attainment of recent cohorts in the labor market in the countries included in the ESWS (Figure 2.3), one can clearly differentiate between countries with an emphasis on vocational education where a large number of recent graduates hold an upper secondary vocational degree – Germany, Hungary and Finland – and countries with a larger proportion of graduates from tertiary education – Sweden, Spain and the UK. In the Netherlands both forms of qualification are quite common, whereas Bulgaria and Portugal are characterized by low attainment in these categories and thus relatively more people hold lower or general upper secondary degrees.

The extent to which training is provided by employers is summarized in Figure 2.4, which differentiates between training for current employees intended to develop and improve their competences ('continued vocational training', CVT, at least partly financed by the enterprises) and training offered as part of a formal education program where working time alternates between periods of education and training at the workplace and in educational institutions or training centers ('initial vocational training', IVT). As can be seen in Figure 2.4, in Spain, Sweden and Portugal the proportion of employees participating in CVT is highest, while the proportion of enterprises employing IVT participants is relatively small. In Finland, the Netherlands and Germany CVT participation is around the European average. The strong prevalence of IVT in Germany and the Netherlands mirrors the enterprise-based nature of vocational training. In the UK, CVT participation is lower than in most other countries included in the ESWS and lower than the European average. The relatively high amount of IVT – given the comprehensive secondary school system – may be explained by the range of vocational degrees with apprenticeship elements which are offered in short-cycle tertiary programs (Universities and Colleges Admissions Service, 2017). Finally, in Hungary and Bulgaria the amount of CVT and IVT provided are comparatively low.

Work–life policies

Among the key policy features which impact on gender inequalities in work and care are work–family policies such as the availability of affordable childcare,

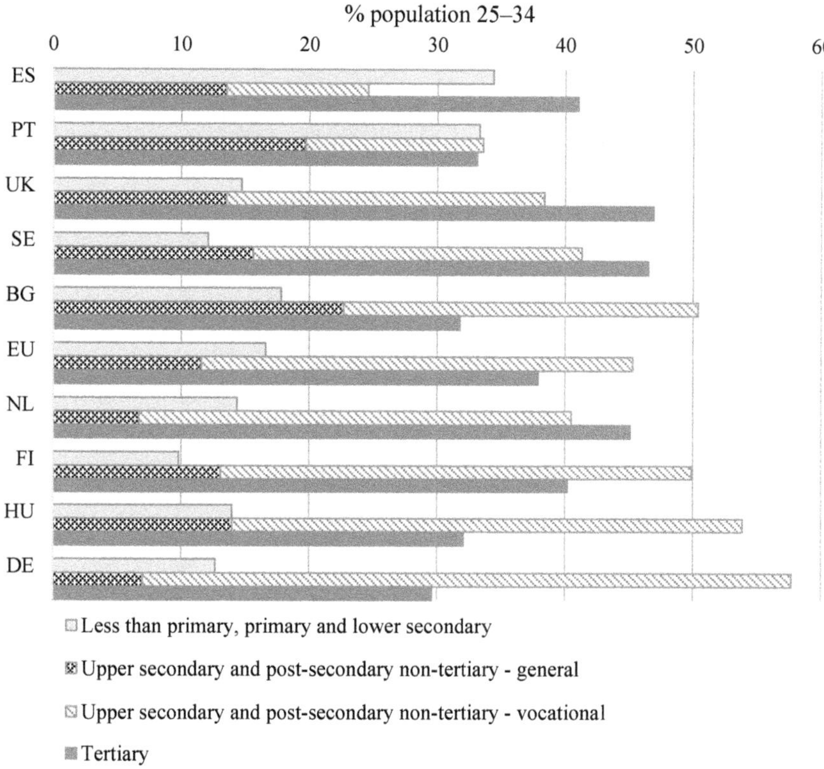

Figure 2.3 Educational attainment of population aged 25–34 in percent (2015); sorted by graduates in upper secondary vocational programs.

Source: Eurostat (2018) Population aged 15-34 by educational attainment level, sex, age and programme orientation (percent) [edat_lfs_9914] (extracted on March 14, 2018).

Note
ES – Spain; PT – Portugal; UK – United Kingdom; SE – Sweden; BG – Bulgaria; EU – European Union; NL – Netherlands; FI – Finland; HU – Hungary; DE – Germany.

parental leave provisions which are well paid and accessible to fathers and mothers and labor market regulations which allow for flexibility in the timing and location of work. These are policies which directly affect organizations' human resource strategies and their investments in employees. Because the combination of childrearing and work is most challenging when children are young, this section discusses work–family policies which target young parents. One of the key policies to consider concerns leave. Important features with regard to the division of work and care are the extent to which leave is paid and whether a part of the leave is reserved for fathers (Grunow, Begall, & Buchler, 2018). Figure 2.5 shows the leave available to mothers and fathers in the countries included in the ESWS. The bars indicate the total amount of paid leave

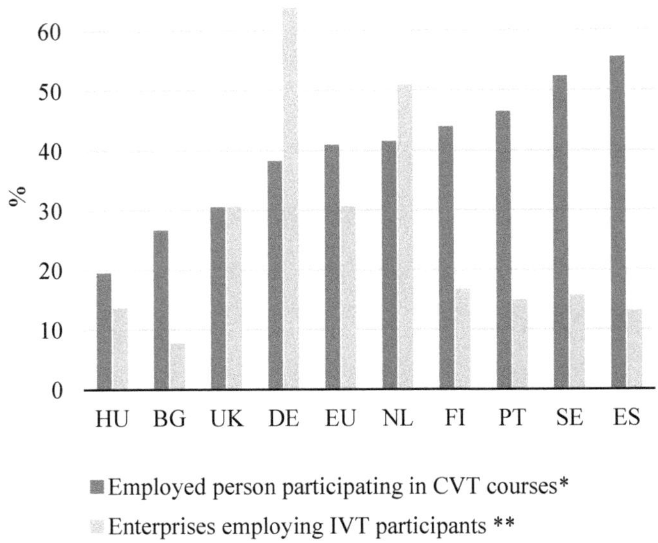

Figure 2.4 Extent of initial vocational training (IVT) and continued vocational training (CVT) in enterprises (2015); sorted by participation in CVT.

Sources: Eurostat (2018) Participants in CVT courses by sex and size class – % percentage of persons employed in all enterprises [trng_cvt_12s] (extracted on March 14, 2018); Eurostat (2018) Enterprises employing IVT participants by size class – percentage of all enterprises [trng_cvt_34s] (extracted March 14, 2018).

Notes
* Percentage of persons employed in all enterprises;
** Percentage of all enterprises.
HU – Hungary; BG – Bulgaria; UK – United Kingdom; DE – Germany; EU – European Union; NL – Netherlands; FI – Finland; PT – Portugal; SE – Sweden; ES – Spain.

and the full-rate equivalent, i.e., the length of leave if calculated at the full income replacement rate. Bulgaria and Hungary offer the longest paid leave with the highest replacement rate for mothers, but reserve almost no leave for fathers. These generous leave policies are a legacy from the socialist past, where the full-employment principle required high female labor force participation, but no efforts were made to involve men in care tasks.

After Bulgaria and Hungary, Germany, Finland and Sweden offer comparable amounts of leave, all with a part reserved for fathers. While Finland and Sweden have pursued gender equality in earning and caring for decades, Germany has only recently reformed its leave policy to mirror the Scandinavian model. This model entails well-paid leave of moderate duration accessible to both parents and conditional on labor market participation, thereby maximizing incentives for mothers to return to work (Dearing, 2016). Portugal also offers relatively generous leave (six months well paid), of which about one-third is reserved for fathers. The Netherlands, Spain and the UK offer

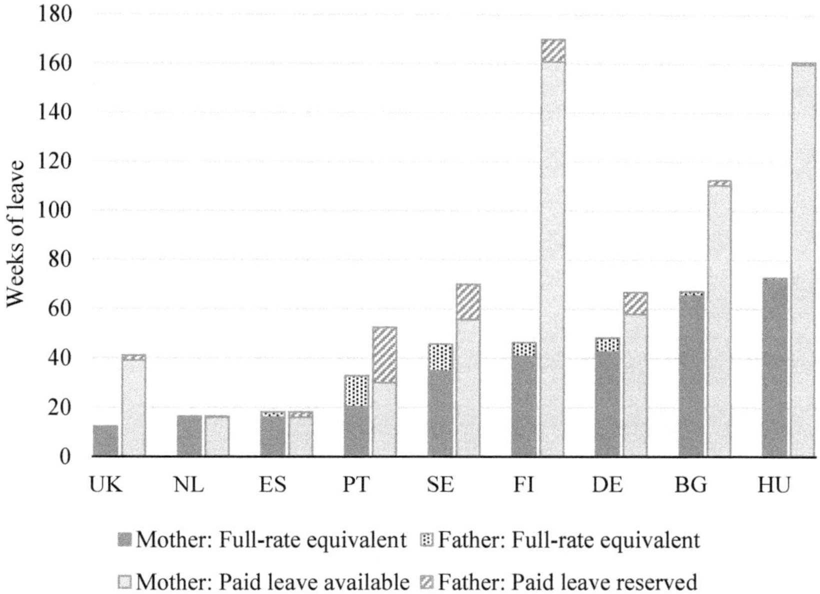

Figure 2.5 Statutory paid leave for mothers and fathers (2016), total paid leave[a] and full-rate equivalent[b] in weeks; sorted by full-rate equivalent.

Source: OECD (2017) OECD family database: www.oecd.org/els/soc/PF2_1_Parental_leave_systems.xlsx (extracted on July 11, 2018).

Notes

a Total paid leave refers to the total (partially) paid maternity/paternity, parental and home care leave available to parents. Mothers: all leave available plus any leave that can be taken by either of the parents. Fathers: non-transferable leave reserved for father plus weeks of shareable leave that must be taken by the father in order for the family to qualify for "bonus" weeks.

b The full-rate equivalent was calculated by multiplying the duration of leave by the extent to which it is paid. (e.g., 10 weeks of leave at replacement rate of 50 percent relate to full-rate equivalent of 5 weeks).

UK – United Kingdom; NL – Netherlands; ES – Spain; PT – Portugal; SE – Sweden; FI – Finland; DE – Germany; BG – Bulgaria; HU – Hungary.

only paid maternity leave of around three months and about one week of paid paternity leave.

Besides leave policies, childcare facilities are of major importance to working parents and, in particular, to the labor market positions of mothers. Figure 2.6 shows men's and women's full-time and part-time employment rates and the enrollment in childcare for children under three years of age, also differentiated by part-time (less than 30 hours per week) and full-time enrollment. Women's employment ranges from 68 percent in Spain to 85 percent in Sweden. Men's employment rates are higher than women's in all countries, the largest gender gaps of about 6 percentage points are found in Hungary, Spain, the Netherlands and the UK. This corresponds roughly to the European average gender employment

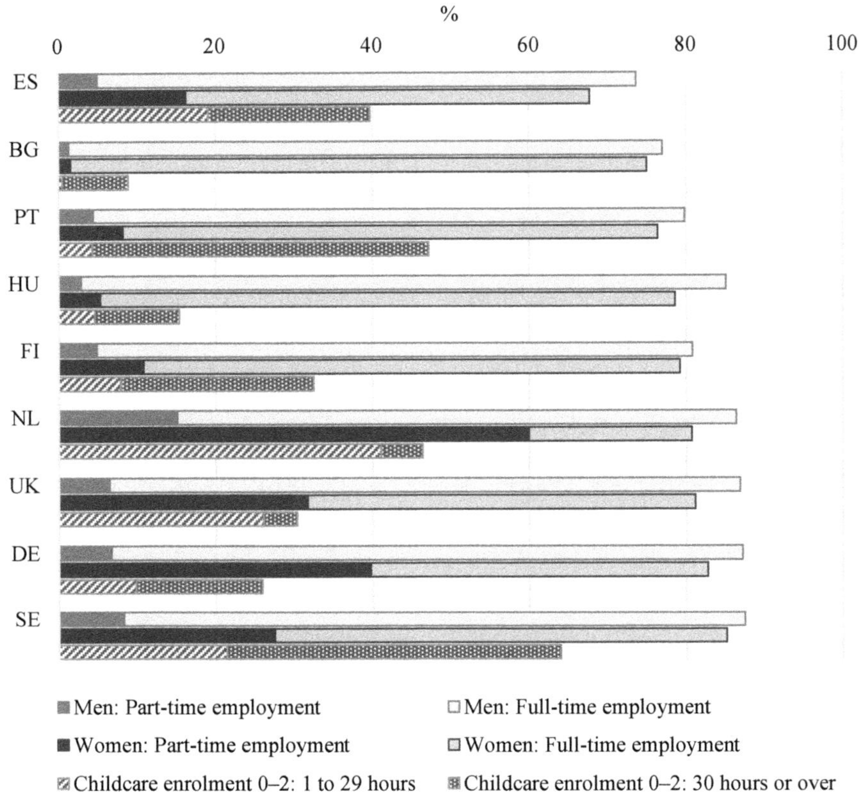

Figure 2.6 Full-time and part-time employment of men and women aged 25–59 in percentage of employed persons and enrolment in formal childcare age 0–2 by duration per week in percent (2015); sorted by women's employment rate.

Sources: Eurostat European Labor Force Surveys (2018) Part-time employment as percentage of the total employment, by sex and age (percent) [lfsa_eppga] (extracted on March 15, 2018); Eurostat European Labor Force Surveys (2018) Employment rates by sex, age and educational attainment level (percent) [lfsa_ergaed] (extracted on March 15, 2018); Eurostat EU-SILC (2018) Children in formal childcare or education by age group and duration – percentage over the population of each age group – EU-SILC survey [ilc_caindformal] (extracted on March 15, 2018).

Note
ES – Spain; BG – Bulgaria; PT – Portugal; HU – Hungary; FI – Finland; NL – Netherlands; UK – United Kingdom; DE – Germany; SE – Sweden.

gap of 5.8 percentage points, implying that in the other countries in the ESWS the gender gap in employment is actually relatively small. The proportion of men working part-time is below 10 percent in all countries except the Netherlands, indicating that the majority of childrearing tasks fall to women. Indeed, variation in women's labor force participation corresponds to work–family policies at the national level. In Sweden, where female employment rates are highest, childcare enrollment is high and mostly full-time. Women's part-time work is moderate at about one-third of all employed women and there are policies in place which allow employees to reduce their working hours temporarily when children are young, indicating that they return to full-time work afterwards (Hegewisch & Gornick, 2011). Contrary to this, the Netherlands, the UK and Germany offer part-time work as the main solution for women who wish to combine work and care, with policies allowing employees to reduce their work hours and low full-time child-care enrollment.

Health arrangements

The question of the extent to which and for how long employers are financially responsible for their employees in case of sickness is of importance for our understanding of employers' investments in health-promoting workplace facilities (see Chapter 6). Furthermore, the extent to which sickness carries a financial risk for individual employees and the degree to which this risk varies by social-economic position, age or gender are potential threats to the creation of a sustainable workforce.

In the nine countries included in our study (as in most EU countries) the employer has to pay for the first 3–12 days of sickness (sometimes after a waiting period of 2–4 days) and for this period the income replacement rate is quite high, around 60–80 percent of gross earnings. Three countries stand out, with longer sickness periods covered by the employer: in Germany it is 6 weeks (at 70 percent of salary), in the UK it is 28 weeks (flat rate, average 20 percent of wages) and in the Netherlands it is 2 years (at 70 percent of wages). After the initial period paid by the employer, the social protection system generally takes over for extended periods of time (at least one year with income replacement of 60–80 percent) (Mutual Information System on Social Protection, 2018). So, in terms of the division of the risk of illness between the employee, the employer and the state we can discern clear differences between the countries in the ESWS: in the Netherlands the employer carries the largest risk, while in the UK the risk of falling ill rests mainly with the individual employee. When the financial responsibility of long-term sickness rests with employers, it may be more difficult for employees who are perceived as having a high risk of falling ill to access permanent positions. When the risk of illness is predominantly borne by the employee this might result in people coming to work while ill, implying lower productivity and the possible aggravation of health problems in the long run (Spasova, Bouget, & Vanhercke, 2016). Both are undesirable outcomes in terms of developing a sustainable workforce.

Related to this is the issue of differences in access to and use of sick leave benefits with regard to gender, age and social class. In terms of use, women, older workers and blue-collar occupations generally show higher absence due to illness in all countries. In terms of formal access, differences might stem from the fact that in some countries collective agreements govern the level and length of sick pay and these may differ between white- and blue-collar workers, the latter generally receiving lower and shorter payments (e.g., Finland).

The differences with regard to sick leave benefits are also visible in variations in work-related health outcomes. The indicators of health and employment in Figure 2.7 relate to the institutional rules regarding sick leave benefits as well as to the composition of the workforce in terms of health. As such they can give us an idea about how dangerous work in the countries in the ESWS is, in terms of accidents and exposure to stress in the workplace, as well as about the generosity and accessibility of sick leave benefits. With regard to the dangers relating

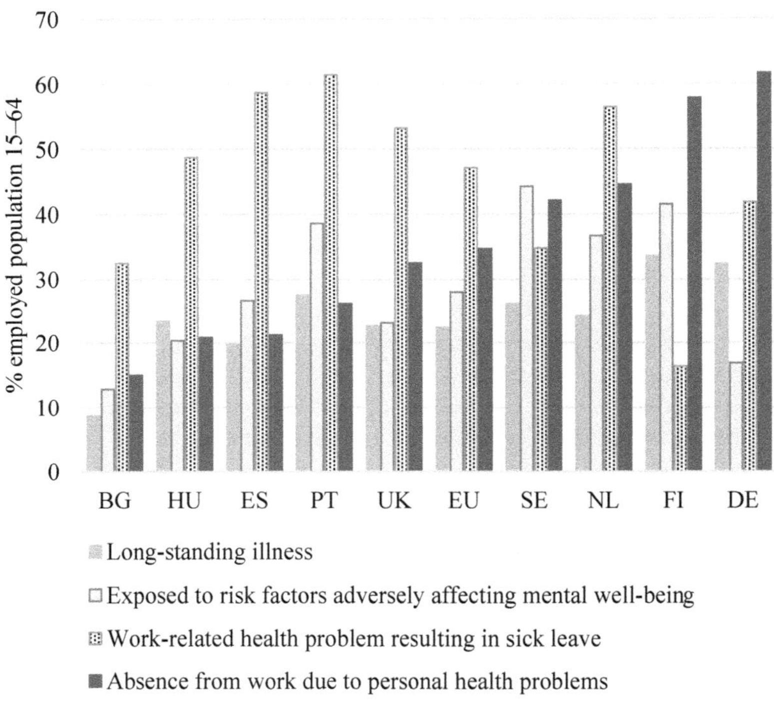

Figure 2.7 Work related health outcomes (2015); sorted by absence from work due to personal health problems.

Sources: *Long-standing illness*: Eurostat (2018) People having a long-standing illness or health problem, by sex, age and labour status [hlth_silc_04] (extracted on January 26, 2018 – data refer to employed persons 16–64 in 2015); *Other*: Eurostat (2018) Persons reporting exposure to risk factors that can adversely affect mental well-being by sex, age and educational attainment level [hsw_exp1] (extracted on January 24, 2018); Eurostat (2018) Persons reporting a work-related health problem resulting in sick leave by sex, age and educational attainment level [hsw_pb2] (extracted on January 26, 2018); Eurostat (2018) Absence from work due to personal health problems by sex, age and educational attainment level [hlth_ehis_aw1e] (extracted on January 26, 2018 – data refer to working population 15–64 in 2013, except NL, 2007).

Note
BG – Bulgaria; HU – Hungary; ES – Spain; PT – Portugal; UK – United Kingdom; EU – European Union; SE – Sweden; NL – Netherlands; FI – Finland; DE – Germany.

to work, Portugal, Spain, the Netherlands and the UK report more work-related health problems than the EU average, while Sweden, Bulgaria and, in particular, Finland score remarkably low. When looking at exposure to risk factors to mental health on the other hand, which relate to time pressures and work overload as well as bullying and harassment experienced at work, Finland and Sweden score highest, followed by the Netherlands and Portugal with above EU average scores. On this indicator, the post-socialist and southern European countries score lowest, which might be related to lower productivity but also to less policy awareness around stress in the workplace. The last two indicators, absence from work due to illness and the presence of long-standing illnesses among employed persons, largely correspond; these show that Germany, Finland, the Netherlands and Sweden have comparatively high scores on both. As noted above, these figures to some extent reflect accessibility and generosity of policies with regard to benefits for disability and sickness.

Employability of older employees

Dealing with population aging and the accompanying challenges of financing welfare systems is a task faced, to some extent, by all industrialized countries. The countries in the ESWS are among those with the largest aging populations in the world. In fact, five out the nine countries (Germany, Portugal, Finland, Bulgaria, Sweden) rank among the top ten of countries with the highest share of the population aged 65+ (World Bank Data, 2018). A major policy response to this development has been to keep older workers in the workforce longer by increasing the statutory retirement age, abolishing early retirement schemes and offering supportive workplace policies to older employees. This has been a successful strategy as throughout the EU the activity rates of older workers have increased over the past ten years, in spite of the economic recession (European Commission, 2016a). While efforts to increase the participation of older workers have been successful, large differences between countries in the employment rates of older workers remain. Figure 2.8 shows the employment rate of older workers (aged 50–64) and prime-age workers (aged 25–49) in combination with the percentage of the population aged 50–64. In all nine countries in our sample the employment rate of older workers is lower than that of prime-age workers, but the size of the gap varies from 25 percentage points in Hungary to only 7 percentage points in Sweden. Sweden also shows the highest participation of older workers in absolute terms; almost 80 percent are in paid employment while the figure is only about 55 percent in Spain. In Hungary, Portugal and Bulgaria older workers also have low employment rates, while at the same time the proportion of people aged 50–64 is comparatively high in these countries indicating that there exists unfulfilled potential in terms of integrating older workers into the labor market.

A major policy development in recent decades concerning older workers has been to raise the retirement age and abolish early retirement schemes in order to adjust the period spent in retirement to growing life expectancy.

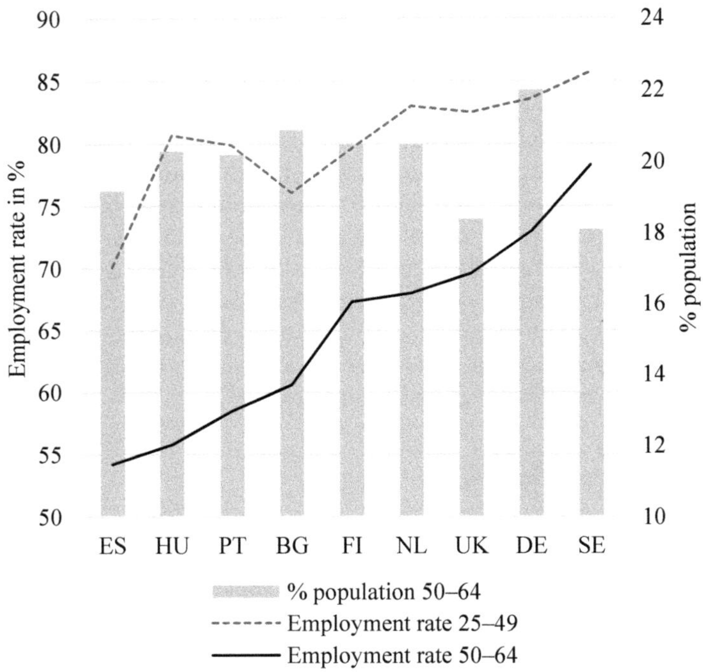

Figure 2.8 Population aged 50–64 and employment rates of population aged 25–49 and 50–64 in the ESWS countries (2015); sorted by employment rate 50–64.

Source: Eurostat European Labour Force Surveys (2018) Employment rates by sex, age and citizenship (percent) [lfsa_ergan] (extracted on March 7, 2018); Eurostat (2018) Structure indicators [demo_pjanind] (extracted on March 7, 2018).

Note
ES – Spain; HU – Hungary; PT – Portugal; BG – Bulgaria; FI – Finland; NL – Netherlands; UK – United Kingdom; DE – Germany; SE – Sweden.

Furthermore, the gender gap in pensionable age that gave women earlier access to retirement has been abolished in many countries. Figure 2.9 shows the current and predicted future retirement age for a person who entered the workforce at age 20 in the nine ESWS countries. Four of the nine countries have adapted some form of adjustment of the pension age to growing life expectancy and are predicted to have a pensionable age of 68+ in 2060: the Netherlands, Portugal, the UK and Finland. The other five countries will increase the pensionable age to 65 or beyond in the years to come. As only Portugal and Sweden currently have an effective pension age higher than 65, most of the countries in our sample will have to make a serious effort to keep older workers in the labor force. For instance, the gap between effective and current retirement age is about two years or more in Finland, Spain, Germany and the Netherlands.

Figure 2.9 Current, effective and future retirement age in the ESWS countries (2016); sorted by current retirement age.

Source: OECD (2017) Pensions at a glance: http://stats.oecd.org/index.aspx?DatasetCode=PAG (extracted on March 8, 2018).

Notes

HU – Hungary; BG – Bulgaria; FI – Finland; DE – Germany; ES – Spain; SE – Sweden; UK – United Kingdom; NL – Netherlands; PT – Portugal.

Effective labor market exit missing for BG.

For each country the black dot indicates the effective age at which people, on average, leave the labor market.

Conclusion

A summary of opportunities and threats to the creation and maintenance of a sustainable workforce, which we distilled from the various policy areas, is presented in Table 2.3.

While the social-democratic countries, Sweden and Finland, score well in terms of training and work–life balance, the flexibilization of the labor market and the aging population pose challenges, as does the relatively high prevalence of work-related health problems. The latter may in part be a result of generous sickness leave policies, but the high proportion of employees reporting exposure to risk factors that can adversely affect mental well-being should be noted (see Figure 2.7). The corporatist countries, Germany and the Netherlands, have labor markets which offer a high degree of flexibility in terms of part-time work, but this is mostly used by women and, combined with inadequate policy support for working parents, this results in large gender inequalities in the labor market.

Table 2.3 Threats of and potential for the creation of a sustainable workforce by policy area

	Flexibility and security		*Training*		*Work–life policies*		*Health arrangements*		*Older employees*	
	Threats	*Potential*	*Threats*	*Potential*	*Threats*	*Potential*	*Threats*	*Potential*	*Threats*	*Potential*
BG	Low flexibility; low employment protection		Low participation in training; low qualified workforce		Low availability of formal childcare and part-time work	Paid leave for mothers		Low prevalence of (work-related) health problems	Low employment rate of older workers; large part of population 65+	
FI	High proportion of labor force on involuntary flexible contracts						High prevalence of (work-related) health problems		Large part of population 65+; low effective retirement age	
DE		Opportunities for part-time work		High participation. in enterprise based IVT	Low availability of formal childcare; high gender employment gap (hours)	Paid leave for both parents	High prevalence of (work-related) health problems		Large part of population 65+	
HU	High proportion of labor force in freelance positions		Low participation in training		Low availability of formal childcare and part-time work; high gender employment gap	Paid leave for mothers		Low prevalence of (work-related) health problems	Low employment rate of older workers; low retirement age	
NL	High proportion of labor force in freelance positions; low protection for temporary workers	Opportunities for part-time work		High participation in enterprise based IVT	Leave low paid; high gender employment gap (hours)		High prevalence of (work-related) health problems		Large gap between effective and formal retirement age	

PT	High proportion of labor force on involuntary flexible contracts		Workforce low qualified			Paid leave for fathers			Low employment rate of older workers; large part of population 65+	High effective labor market exit; high retirement age
ES	High proportion of labor force on involuntary flexible contracts				Leave low paid; high gender employment gap				Low employment rate of older workers	
SE	High proportion of labor force in freelance positions; low protection for temporary workers			High participation in training and tertiary education		Paid leave for both parents; high availability of formal childcare	High prevalence of (work-related) health problems		Large part of population 65+	High employment rate of older workers; high effective labor market exit
UK	Low employment protection	Opportunities for part-time work	Low participation in training		Leave low paid; high gender employment gap (working hours)					

Note
BG – Bulgaria: FI – Finland; DE – Germany; HU – Hungary; NL – Netherlands; PT – Portugal; ES – Spain; SE – Sweden; UK – United Kindgom; IVT - initial vocational training

A notable strong feature is the strongly developed systems of vocational training in both countries.

In the UK, too, we observe that low policy support for working parents and good opportunities for part-time work result in gender disparities in working hours. The low participation in training among employees may be related to low employment protection, which can inhibit mutual investments of employers and employees; however, it should be noted that the actual prevalence of flexible employment is below average in the UK.

Spain and Portugal both have labor markets with a high degree of involuntary flexibility coupled with low employment (particularly of older workers) in Spain and a low-qualified workforce in Portugal, both of which pose risks of segregation and exclusion. Similar structural threats to creating sustainable employment relations are present in Bulgaria and Hungary. Notable for both post-socialist countries is the low prevalence of (work-related) health problems, although these outcomes combined with weak policy support may spark concerns about under-reporting. We conclude that the overall picture which emerges from our description of population characteristics and institutional structures by policy topic broadly confirms the expectations derived from welfare and employment regimes cited at the beginning of the chapter.

3 Collecting cross-country comparative multilevel data in organizations

The research design of the European Sustainable Workforce Survey

Zoltán Lippényi, Thomas Martens, and Tanja van der Lippe

Much research in the past has focused on the factors contributing to a sustainable workforce. Comparative studies research, however, has predominantly focused on the individual employee and the country–labor market context. We know relatively little about the role of organizations and their investments in a sustainable workforce. The Sustainable Workforce project set out to explore the causes and consequences of organizational investments in a sustainable workforce, while also taking into account factors at both the individual and country–sectoral context level. To achieve this goal, we needed to gather data at multiple levels: employees, organizations, and different industrial contexts and labor markets. To study the impact of organizational investments on employees, we also needed a multilevel survey design linking employees to organizations. Multilevel organizational surveys are, however, very rare in current organizational research practice.

We broke new ground with the collection of data in the European Sustainable Workforce Survey (ESWS), a multilevel organizational survey among employees, team managers and human resource (HR) managers in organizations in nine European countries. This chapter focusses on the description of this dataset. Our primarily goal is to provide the reader with a detailed guide to the design of the survey, fieldwork, and the characteristics of the collected dataset. The chapter primarily serves as a companion to subsequent chapters that use this dataset, but it also aims to inform and guide future organizational data-collection projects.

The first part of this chapter reviews the main publicly available surveys in organizational research that study topics related to the sustainable workforce and the characteristics of the organizations' datasets used by researchers in publications in leading sociology and management studies journals. The second part outlines the design and methodology of the ESWS. Here, we aim to provide a detailed justification of our decisions regarding various aspects of the survey – e.g., the sampling design of both organizations and employees, survey methods, instruments, and fieldwork. The third part provides a basic description of the collected dataset, including the response rates at various levels, comparing it with known response rates from earlier studies. Finally, a short conclusion discusses the challenges involved in collecting multilevel organizational data, providing practical suggestions for future research.

Taking stock of data used to study the sustainable workforce

Prior to the research fieldwork and designing our survey, we carried out an overview of the prolific publicly available datasets used to study questions related to the sustainable workforce. Table 3.1 provides an overview of publicly available comparative datasets. The main criterion of inclusion was that the dataset should contain information on organizations and/or on employees. Notably, we focus in this section on survey data rather than other data sources on organizations such as business lists (e.g., Fortune500) and reports by the US Equal Employment Opportunity Commission (EEO-1 reports).[1]

The search revealed the absence of data that include information on employee-, organization-, and country-level. In most comparative studies with data on organizations, no employee-level information is available and large-scale cross-national datasets on employees (such as the European Working Conditions Survey) typically lack information about organizational characteristics and investments. A well-known comparative study that focusses on organizations (but not their employees) is the Cranet Survey (e.g., Den Dulk, Peters, Poutsma, & Ligthart, 2010; Nikandrou, Aspospori, Panayotopoulou, Stavrou, & Papalexancris, 2008) which is a repeated international comparative survey of organizational practices. Another popular dataset is the European Community Innovation Survey, a large-scale comparative study with ample information on investments in innovation and organizational performance (e.g., Hashi & Stojcic, 2014). Lastly, the European Company Survey and the European Survey on Working Time and Work–Life Balance focus on the availability of various policies and on organizational outcomes (Anxo, Fagan, Letablier, Perraudin & Smith, 2007). The common feature of all four datasets is that they only provide organization-level information. Employee-level data are lacking and, from these sources, the consequences of investments at the employee level are little understood.

The Dutch Time Competition Survey and the UK Workplace Employment Relations Study focus on employee outcomes, but these studies only include one country, and are therefore not suitable for cross-country comparisons. To our knowledge, the 2007 Quality of Life in Changing Europe Survey is the only cross-national dataset on organizations and employees. A limitation of this study is that only four organizations (each from a different sector) are surveyed per country. As a result, the possibility of making inter-organizational comparisons between sectors is limited.

We performed a systematic review to provide a benchmark of the design and quality of data represented in high-ranking sociology and management journals.

We confined our search to research articles published in the *American Journal of Sociology*, *American Sociological Review*, *British Journal of Sociology*, *Academy of Management Journal*, and the *Journal of Management* in the period 2010–2014.[2] We did not solely rely on the existing datasets described above as we were interested in authors' own data collections as well.

The results give a clear indication of the scarcity of cross-country comparative multilevel design organizational surveys. We did not come across any articles based on internationally comparative data among employees nested within organizations. In management journals all kinds of self-collected data are reported, and most of them rely on convenience or snowball samples that focus on one sector or even one firm (but seldom on employees). The work of McClean, Burris, and Detert (2013) published in the *Academy of Management Journal* is a rare example of a paper using a multilevel organizational survey. They collected survey data among employees and managers in 136 restaurants in 4 divisions of a corporation-owned chain located in 21 states throughout the US. Nationally representative samples of enterprises, and especially employees nested within these organizations, are rare in the management journals and studies seldom compare economic sectors nationally or internationally. An exception is the Cranet Survey (see Table 3.1) which contains random samples stratified on economic sectors in 32 countries. This dataset contains no employee-level information, however, and the sampling procedure differs by country, making international comparisons problematic.

In the top sociology journals, only a few empirical papers study organizations, and these focus mainly on the level of the organization and/or HR manager. Employee issues are mainly studied from a labor market perspective, and organizational work mostly uses qualitative methods. Compared to the management literature, studies in sociology journals more often employ existing surveys (e.g., the National Organizations Survey) or other organizational data sources (such as EEO-1 reports and Fortune500), rather than collecting their own data. A rare example of a self-collected survey is in Kelly's (2003) paper; here, the managers of 389 US work establishments in the manufacturing, service, public, and nonprofit sectors were interviewed, sampled from the Dun & Bradstreet Market Identifier database.

As this short review reveals, the cross-country multilevel design of the ESWS is unique among organizational surveys. It includes multiple organizations, sectors, and countries, and surveys employees, teams, and the organization.

The design of the Sustainable Workforce Survey

Research population

In designing the ESWS, our aim was twofold: (1) to maximize variation across organizations in HR policies and (2) to minimize individual-level variation within organizations. Taking all sectors of the economy and all employees as the research population was not feasible given the multilevel design; we made a

Table 3.1 Overview of (comparative) datasets and surveys on organizations and employees

Dataset/survey	*Period*	*Countries*
Organizations in countries:		
The Cranet Survey	1989–1993; 1995/1996; 2004/2005; 2008/2009	EU, Australia, Asia,US/Canada
Business Environment and Enterprise Performance Survey	1999/2000; 2002; 2004/2005; 2008/2009; 2011/2013	East EU, Russia, Asia
Community Innovation Survey	2000/2001; 2004; 2006; 2008; 2010	EU
European Company Survey	2004/2005; 2009; 2013	EU
European Survey on Working Time and Work–life Balance	2004/2005	EU
National Study of Employers[a]	2005; 2008; 2012	US
National Organizations Survey	2002	US
Multi-city Telephone Employer Survey	1995	US[b]
Work–Life Balance Employer Survey	2000; 2002; 2007	UK
Human Resource Practices in Multinational Companies in Ireland	2007	Ireland
Netherlands Employer Work Survey	2008; 2010; 2012	Netherlands
Employees in countries:		
European Working Conditions Survey	1990/1991; 1995/1996; 2000; 2005; 2010	EU
European Union Labour Force Survey	1983–2012	EU
National Study of the Changing Workforce	1992; 1997; 2002; 2008	US
Employees in organizations:		
Time Competition Survey	2002	Netherlands
Workplace Employment Relations Study	1980; 1984; 1990; 1998; 2004; 2011	UK
Greek Dataset of Flexible Work	2010/2011	Greece
Employees in organizations in countries:		
Quality of Life in Changing Europe	2007	UK, Finland, Germany, Netherlands, Portugal, Hungary, Bulgaria

Notes

a Follow-up of Business Work–Life Study finished in 1998.

b Four US cities: Atlanta, Boston, Detroit, and Los Angeles.

number of theoretically guided restrictions regarding the organizational level, size, and sector, as well as the employees to survey within organizational units. The nine countries participating in the survey, the UK, Finland, Sweden, Germany, the Netherlands, Portugal, Spain, Hungary, and Bulgaria, were decided at the initial phase of fund application.

Specifying organizational level, size, and sector

Previous organizational surveys either used firms (e.g., the Community Innovation Survey and the Time Competition Survey) or establishments – that is, the local unit in the case of multi-site firms (e.g., the European Company Survey and the Cranet Survey) – as organizational units. We chose the establishment level as the primary sampling unit as a number of determinants and outcomes that we were interested in, such as managerial support and work cohesion, manifest within physical workplaces. In addition, selecting firms would have limited the number of organizations in the dataset.

Most existing surveys focus on larger organizations. The Cranet Survey, for example, focuses on establishments with at least 200 employees, while the European Company Survey and Workplace Employment Relations Study are restricted to establishments with at least 10 and 5 employees, respectively. All studies exclude single person organizations (i.e., self-employed persons). As the Sustainable Workforce project explicitly focuses on HR policies, such as work flexibility and training, we excluded very small organizations as they do not usually have formal HR functions or policies. We chose to limit our study to establishments that have more than 40 employees in cases where the organization only had one establishment, or more than 20 employees where the organization had more than one establishment.

Finally, organizational surveys vary in the scope of economic sectors covered. Large-scale organizational studies that only survey a representative of the organization usually cover all economic sectors, such as the European Company Survey. Multilevel organizational surveys typically select the few sectors that are theoretically most relevant or informative for the topic under study, such as knowledge intensive organizations in the Time Competition Survey. We also aimed to include a limited number of theoretically relevant economic sectors in the ESWS. These sectors are: manufacturing, health care, telecommunications, financial services, transport, and higher education. We selected them to reflect variation in the causes and types of investments in a sustainable workforce at the organizational level.

- An increasing number of women participate in the labor force, changing the ways in which individuals and families arrange their work and family life. As female employees in particular experience pressures due to dual commitments, we selected both high (health care and higher education) and low (manufacturing and transport) female employment sectors for the ESWS.

- The aging of the European workforce poses several challenges to employees and to employers. Organizations with older employees face the challenge of replacement demand and have to develop strategies to maintain older employees' productivity. To reflect these challenges, sectors that have relatively young (telecommunications) and old (higher education) workforces are both included in the ESWS.
- Technological development (e.g., improving production technologies and IT possibilities) is triggering a higher demand for highly-educated workers in Europe. The ESWS incorporates sectors that represent the higher-skilled (higher education and financial services) and lower-skilled (transport and manufacturing) segments of the workforce.
- Globalization and innovation have fundamental impacts on the structure of the European economy. Due to the increasing competitiveness of developing countries manufacturing is declining, whereas innovation-intensive sectors of the economy, such as telecommunications, are growing. We aimed to include both shrinking and growing sectors as their capabilities and priorities to invest in employees may differ substantially.
- Organizations in Europe demand greater flexibility in contracting, hiring, and firing, which has profound implications for investments in the workforce. For the ESWS, we selected sectors that employ a high percentage of temporary workers (manufacturing, transport, and also higher education, which employs high-skilled workers) and those that usually offer long-term employment contracts (financial services).

Table 3.2 shows the sectors in the ESWS and their relevant demographic and economic characteristics, averaged for the countries under study.

Specifying respondents within organizations

In order to minimize individual variation within establishments, we sampled a limited number of employee groups. In larger establishments we usually selected departments, while in establishments without a departmental structure we chose to include teams. A further reason for focussing on groups of employees is that it allowed us to survey managers of teams/departments and match them with employees. Managers are an important employee group to study in their own right, and their reports provide an additional source of information about organizational and workplace characteristics, such as investments and outcomes. A similar strategy, using occupational groups, has also been successfully employed in the Dutch Time Competition Survey (Van der Lippe & Glebbeek, 2003).

The groups selected included at least two departments/teams that represent the organization's core activity: for example, if the organization is a hospital, we interviewed nurses; or if the organization is a university, we included a research unit. Furthermore, we chose at least one department or team whose tasks do not particularly refer to the core activity of the organization, such as a finance, communication, or maintenance departments. The rationale was that support teams

Table 3.2 Characteristics of the economic sectors in the ESWS

Sector characteristics[a]	*Nace Rev. 2:*[b]					
	Higher education	*Transport*	*Telecommunications*	*Financial services*	*Health care*	*Manufacturing*
% female employees (2013)	70.66	22.20	31.41	48.15	78.91	28.04
% workers older than 50 (2013)	34.37	33.15	20.18	26.41	33.04	29.90
% workers high educated (2010)	66.37	23.75	64.34	45.55	50.41	28.27
% change N of enterprises (2008–2011)	10.15	–6.10	5.06	5.30	9.68	–7.35
% temporary employment (2010)	14.81	6.28	5.91	2.45	11.03	6.43
% collective pay agreement (2010)	82.40	64.67	35.62	63.40	65.94	57.89
	Nace Rev. 1.1:					
	Education	*Transport and communications*		*Financial services*	*Health and social work*	
% public sector[c] (2009 % public)	71.73	13.50		11.79	48.86	

Sources: [a]European Commission Eurostat Labor Force Surveys series, detailed annual survey results – https://ec.europa.eu/eurostat/cache/metadata/en/lfsa_esms.htm.

Notes

Figures are averaged for the countries under study: UK, Finland, Sweden, Germany, the Netherlands, Portugal, Spain, Hungary, and Bulgaria.

a Information based on data from all nine countries, except: "% workers high educated," where Germany is not included; "% temporary employment" where Sweden is not included; and "% collective pay agreement" where the Netherlands and Sweden are missing; Finland is partially incomplete (Transport, Financial services, and Higher education).

b NACE 2.2 codes: Manufacturing (section C), Health Care (Q8610, Q8710, Q8720, Q8730, Q8790), Higher education (P8541 and P8542), Transport (section H, excluding H5310), Financial services (section K and M6920), Telecommunications (J6110–J6312).

c Source: Eurofund European Company Surveys, 2009 – HYPERLINK "http://www.eurofound.europa.eu/surveys/european-company-surveys/european-company-survey-2009/ecs-2009-methodology" www.eurofound.europa.eu/surveys/european-company-surveys/european-company-survey-2009/ecs-2009-methodology.

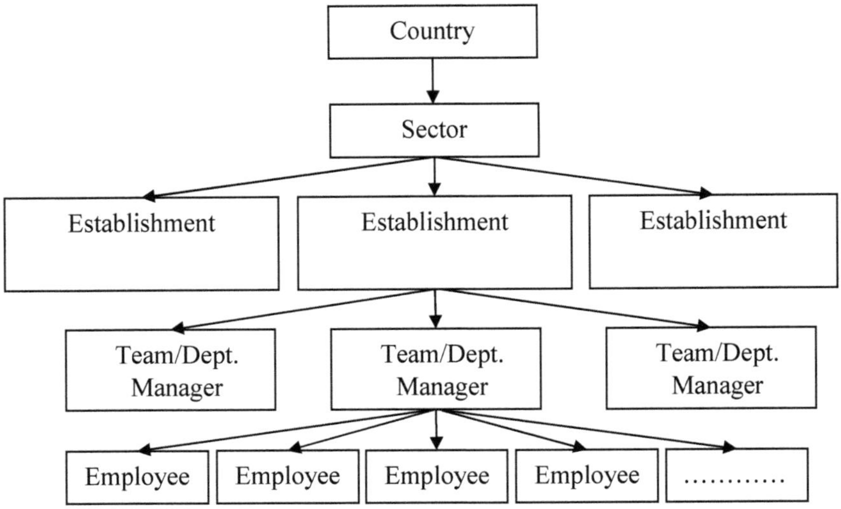

Figure 3.1 ESWS – multilevel design of the data collection.

perform similar activities regardless of sector, and this provides an opportunity to compare organizations while limiting the variability in job characteristics.

The resulting survey design has four layers: employees nested within teams; establishments; sectors; and countries. Figure 3.1 represents the multilevel design of the ESWS.

Sampling establishments and workers

Large-scale organizational surveys use stratified random sampling to select organizations or establishments (e.g., European Company Survey, Community Innovation Survey, and the National Survey of Employers). Based on sampling frames (e.g., commercial or public company/business lists) they sample organizational units stratified by sector and size, resulting in representative samples of organizations. The National Organizations Study and National Study of Employers use a probability proportionate-to-size sample such that larger organizations have a higher likelihood of being selected. These studies do not, however, include the level of employees. Most organizational studies involving employee surveys include a much smaller number of organizations, and rely on a non-probability sampling procedures to select them, such as snowball sampling or convenience sampling (e.g., Chand, 2010; Chang & Smithikrai, 2010; Giannikis & Mihail, 2011). In cases where a random sampling procedure is employed at the enterprise level using a sampling frame, studies are usually limited to one or two economic sectors (e.g., Funk, 2013; Navarro, Dewhurst & Eldridge, 2010).

The unique depth of the ESWS limited the possibilities of drawing a random representative sample from the whole population of organizations. Instead, we used stratified purposeful sampling, which combines qualitative and quantitative sampling (Sandelowski, 2000). We opted to select two or three suggestive cases from multiple sectors and size categories within each country – selecting organizations in highly urbanized areas – building on the plausible assumption that job characteristics, human resource investments, and organizational challenges will meaningfully vary across sector and organization size. We took three size groups: 20–99 employees, 100–249 employees, and 250+ employees. At the start of the project, projections were made to include two establishments per sector-size stratum in our sample.

First, we used quantitative sampling to randomly select cases within sector and size categories from lists of business organizations. We used national business lists as our sampling frame which came the closest to meeting the methodological requirements from organizational sampling frames such as timeliness, representativeness, availability for research (e.g., digitally accessible), and the costs of gaining access (Kalleberg, Marsden, Aldrich, & Cassell, 1990). Important selection criteria were that lists should contain information on sector and size, and that they should list establishments. This latter criterion was the most problematic, as not all countries had lists of establishments. In these cases, we selected organizations at the first step, and gathered information on establishments via online sources or by contacting the organization to select the establishments for the sample. We initially restricted the sample to establishments that are geographically close to the economic center of the country, but relaxed this requirement in most countries due to the difficulty of finding eligible and willing participations in this region. Table 3.3 lists the organizational sampling frames used to sample organizations.

Second, we complemented the random selection with the convenience sampling of suggestive cases from alternative sources, mainly web searches and referrals. We used this method when the random sample from the business lists did not yield enough participants. This occurred either because the 'population' of establishments that satisfied the criteria in the business lists was too small or because none of the approached establishments were receptive to our call. Convenience sampling is often relied upon by studies in management journals, and its main advantage is that it improves organizational cooperation and establishing contact with the right gatekeeper.

The main drawback of convenience sampling is that it potentially leads to sample selectivity, decreasing the out-of-sample generalizability of findings. In addition, the calculation of a response rate requires that the sample is random, which is not truly the case with these methods. However, as the main goal of the ESWS was explanatory, to study the causes and consequences of investments in employees, representativeness was not a major concern. In addition, the low participation rate of organizations makes fully random samples unfeasible.

Among existing studies, only a few sample of employees within organizations. Large-scale datasets, such as the Workplace Employment Relations Study and

Table 3.3 Sampling frames used for selecting organizations in the ESWS

Country	*Sample region*	*Sample source*	*Level*
Netherlands	"Randstad"	LISA	Establishment
Hungary	Budapest and Pest-county	Hungarian Central Bureau of Statistics	Establishment
UK	The Greater London area	Experian Business Database; Blueberry Solutions	Establishment
Germany	Mostly Ruhr-area	Bisnode Deutschland GMBH	Organization
Finland	Tampere-Helsinki	Statistics Finland Register of Enterprises and Establishments and a Register of Public Corporations	Establishment
Sweden	West Sweden and Stockholm	Statistics Sweden's Business Register	Establishment
Spain	Barcelona	Chamber of Commerce of Spain	Organization
Bulgaria	Sofia	Bulgarian National Statistical Institute	Organization
Portugal	Lisbon	Ignios	Organization

the Quality of Life in Changing Europe, randomly select employees from each firm. Similarly, the Time Competition Survey randomly selected employees within principle occupational groups within the organization in order to minimize individual-level variation. In the ESWS, we selected employee groups, in close consultation with the HR manager of each organization, to ensure that they adequately represented the core production and support functions of the establishment. Within these groups, we aimed to include all workers, although in a few cases the organization only supported the participation of a sample of workers.

Survey instruments

The ESWS consisted of three instruments: the organization questionnaire (OQ), the manager questionnaire (MQ), and the employee questionnaire (EQ).[3] The three main topics covered by the questionnaires were: (1) measurement of the forms of investments by organizations (human capital, work–life arrangements, work flexibility, employability) and their utilization by employees; (2) measurement of the returns on the availability and use of organizational investments at the employee, team, and organizational level; and (3) general characteristics of employees, teams, and organizations. Tables A1.1–A1.3 in Appendix 1 provide a comprehensive list of the questionnaire modules.

In addition, the EQ and MQ included one survey vignette experiment, administered after the main questionnaire was completed. Participation in this part of the questionnaire was optional. Three EQ vignette experiments, varying across countries, and one MQ vignette experiment, the same in all countries, was conducted. The topics of the vignette experiments in the EQs were: choice of part-time work (administered in the UK, the Netherlands, and Sweden); readiness to cooperate within teams (administered in Bulgaria, part of the German sample, and part of the Hungarian sample, and Portugal); and job preferences (administered in Finland, part of the Hungarian sample, part of the German sample, and Spain). The vignette experiment in the MQ concerned age-based discrimination and it was administered in all countries.

The source language of the questionnaires was English. The questionnaires were translated into the national languages of the various countries by native translators and compared with the original English questionnaire by proofreading carried by a different native speaker. The translation of the questionnaire was performed by professional translation bureaus.

We tested the surveys to assess their technical properties (i.e., routing, length) and content (apprehension of respondent, scale reliabilities) in a representative Dutch organization (i.e., large organization, presence of a HR manager, existence of various departments and departmental managers, and a diverse workforce) within our own network and made only minor adjustments to the design and content of the questionnaires.

Survey mode

With the spread of computer literacy, web-based surveys and surveys distributed by email have become an increasingly popular method in organizational research (Saunders, 2012). Meta-analyses of management and organizational behavior studies find that web-based research, on average, results in lower response rates than traditional mail-based surveys (Anseel, Lievens, Schollaert, & Choragwicka, 2010; Baruch & Holtom, 2008; Shih & Fan, 2008). Saunders (2012) argues that non-response to electronic surveys might diminish in time with increasing computer literacy. Analyzing a population of IT literate individuals, he found that web-based surveys resulted in a higher response rate than mail-based surveys. Anseel et al. (2010) argue, furthermore, that the effectiveness of web-based administration depends on the type of respondents that is surveyed: web-based surveys are more effective in samples of non-managerial employees than in samples of top executives and managers. They explain this finding by the fact that non-managerial employees receive fewer emails and have more time to complete the questionnaire during work hours than (top) managers.

Taking into account that we had sectors with both high and low IT penetration, high- and low-skilled workers, managerial and non-managerial respondents, as well as country differences in IT literacy, we took a flexible approach to choosing the survey mode for the ESWS. We let participating establishments choose between online and paper-and-pencil modes of administering the survey. We supported mixed mode within a single organization; for instance, managers could receive online and non-managerial workers paper-and-pencil questionnaires. We did not switch modes between first contact and reminders in the case of online surveys to avoid annoyance and non-compliance through complicating the design and overstretching the organization's capacities.

When the organization provided names and/or email addresses we addressed the questionnaire to the respondent personally, as personal addressing produces the highest response rate (Baruch & Holtom, 2008). However, to remove concerns about anonymity, we also offered the option of distributing the questionnaire anonymously. In some cases, we only received the number of workers or managers within the team, and not their names and email addresses. For the online survey mode, we distributed unique log-in tokens in sealed envelopes with which respondents could log in and complete the survey.

Eliciting participation

Eliciting participation of organizations

Eliciting the participation of organizations is becoming a difficult task, as organizations often conduct their own surveys of employees, feel disinclined to grant research access, and see surveys as an extra burden on employees (Van der Lippe et al., 2009). The primary objective of survey fieldwork is therefore to elicit the participation of establishments in the survey.

We followed common organizational research practice of targeting the relevant gatekeepers instead of the top of the organizational hierarchy during initial contact (Buchanan, Boddy, & McCalman, 1988). We identified HR managers as the actors who are potentially most interested in this research. A team of native research assistants in each country performed a web search or made calls to the establishment to get the contact details of the HR manager. In Bulgaria, we contracted a survey organization to perform these tasks. In the UK and Portugal, research assistants proved to be unsuccessful in entering and contacting organizations, so we sought the help of a UK-based professional marketing company to generate leads for our research assistants. Once contact was established, a personalized invitation letter based on online and telephone information was sent to the HR manager of the establishment by post and/or email, followed-up by a phone call to schedule a research consultation. During the research consultation, which took place in person or by phone, we held a five-minute presentation to the HR manager to explain the research and elicit participation. Once organizations consented to participate, we discussed (during the research consultation) which departments or teams could participate, start dates, and survey mode.

To elicit participation, it is important to provide credentials and offer a tangible product in return for cooperation (Buchanan et al., 1988). Credentials are important because organizational decision makers might be reluctant to cooperate if the contact person is considered to be 'low in status' (e.g., a student) (Saunders, Lewis, & Thornhill, 2006). A product offered in return for cooperation could be a research report in a form that is useful for the recipients. To enhance the credibility of the survey, invitation material for the ESWS listed both Utrecht University and our research partner's university located in the given country, because organizations may not be familiar with research institutions and universities outside their own country. We offered a benchmark report as a product based on the survey results; this compares the establishment with establishments from the same sector and country with regard to workforce investments and key productivity outcomes. Organizations value information about what their competitors are doing and how they perform as this is hard to come by, and our experience was that this benchmark report generated much interest among managers.

The three most common concerns of organizations that deter participation are time, anonymity, and confidentiality (Buchanan et al., 1988). In our fieldwork, organizations mentioned seasonal high workload as the most important temporal constraint. We ensured organizations of our efforts to minimize the time investment in the survey, and they could decide on the timing of their participation within the fieldwork period, which particularly helped to overcome these concerns. We emphasized during the initial contact and the research consultation that we would take great care to ensure anonymity and confidentiality. We did not encounter any cases where concerns about anonymity or confidentiality were the reason for declining participation, although some organizations requested a contract prior to participating which specified our data safety procedures.

Eliciting participation of employees and managers

Incentives are key to ensuring high response rates in surveys. Rose, Sidle, and Griffith (2007) and Jobber and O'Reilly (1998) found that monetary incentives significantly increase response rate, regardless of race, age, sex, or company tenure. Monetary incentives have been shown to be especially effective if given as a gift unconditional upon opening or completing the questionnaire (Dillman, 2011). Organizational surveys of employees use monetary incentives to a lesser extent than public opinion surveys (Rose et al., 2007), but there is evidence that monetary incentives work similarly in organizational and consumer populations (Saunders et al., 2006). A cash incentive yields higher response rates than other forms of monetary incentives, such as vouchers or lotteries (Birnholtz, Horn, Finholt, & Bae, 2004), but transferring cash in web-based surveys is complicated and it has also been found to be less cost-effective than other forms of monetary incentive (Gajic, Cameron, & Hurley, 2012). Initially, we planned to give a cash incentive of 5 euro to all non-managerial employees invited to participate in the ESWS, but we encountered ethical objections to handing out cash incentives in several organizations as well as logistical problems. We therefore decided to offer the choice between a lottery among employees who completed the survey and a monetary gift to the organization (based on the number of employees who completed the survey) to spend on organizing activities for staff.

We chose the unconditional cash incentive only in Hungary and Bulgaria, because it was indicated that organizations in these countries highly value compensating workers for their efforts in completing surveys. Seven organizations opted not to give their employees an incentive at all.

In addition to monetary incentives, we implemented a number of response enhancing strategies that had proved to be effective in general survey research and advocated by Anseel et al. (2010) and Baruch and Holtom (2008) for use in organizational surveys. The following methods were used:

- We notified employees about the survey in advance through the HR manager.
- We sent a personalized cover letter and invitation email where we had access to names, and included the name of the organization in all surveys.
- We stressed in the cover letter that sustainable workforce studies benefit employees, to increase topic salience.
- We emphasized confidentially in both the cover letter and at the start of the survey. In paper-and-pencil based surveys we attached a response envelope and shipped a sealed box in which employees could put their envelopes.
- We ensured respondents that the organization supported our research and used university logos in correspondence materials to raise the status and gain trustworthiness.
- We sent reminders, depending on the survey mode: in the case of personalized online surveys we sent four reminders directly to the respondent; in respect of other survey modes, we asked the HR manager or contact person at the organization to remind workers about the survey.

These strategies follow Dillman's (2011) Total Design Method rooted in social exchange and trust mechanisms. Dillman (2011) argues that questionnaire recipients are most likely to respond if they expect that the perceived benefits of participating in the research outweigh the perceived costs (including risks) of filling out the questionnaire.

Survey administration

The administration of the online survey and the printing and distribution of paper-and-pencil surveys took place at Utrecht University in the Netherlands between March and December 2015. Local research assistants consulted with the contact person at the organization about the timing of the survey and, in the case of the paper-based survey, about dispatching and collecting the surveys. Figure 3.2 illustrates the survey procedure for different modes of contacting and administering the questionnaire, specifying the details of the research material used, stages of the survey, and reminder intervals.

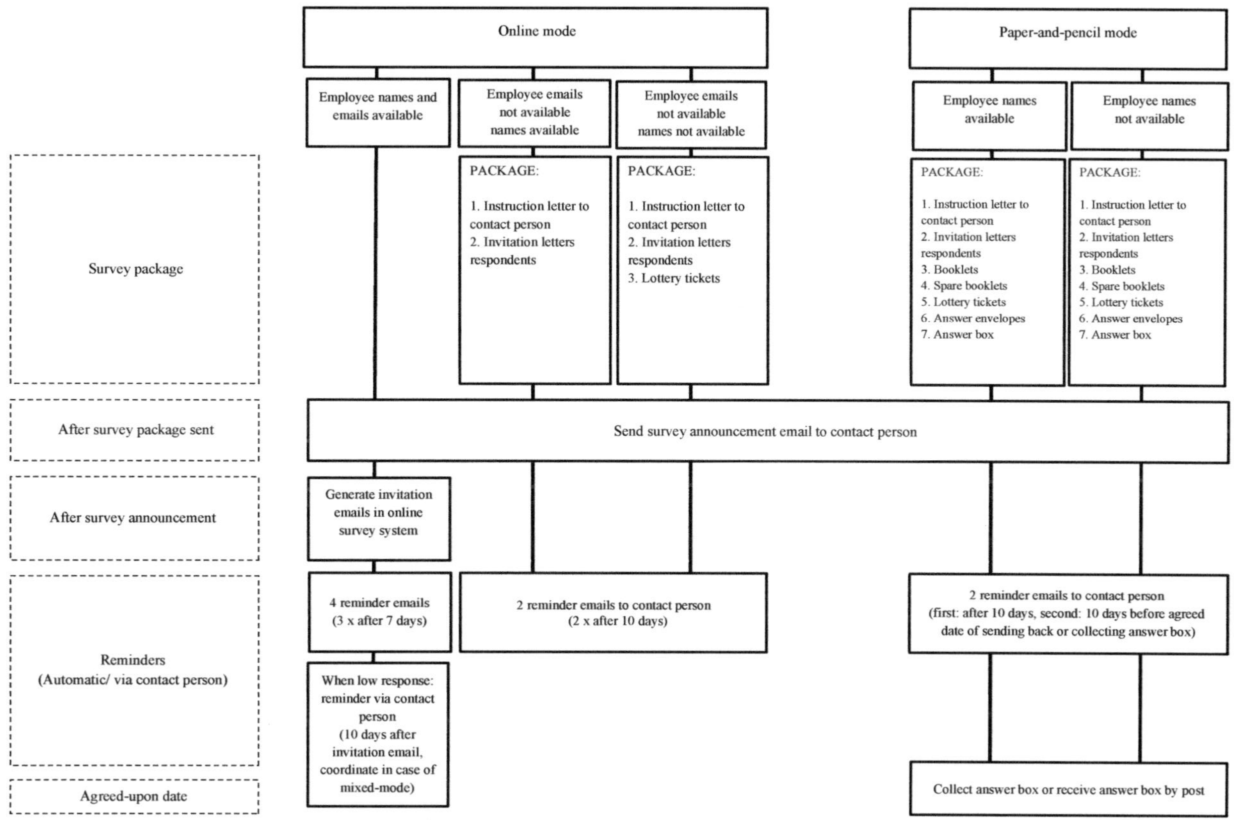

Figure 3.2 ESWS – survey structure and procedures.

Main characteristics of the European Sustainable Workforce Survey

Number of establishments, teams, and workers

The ESWS includes a total of 259 work establishments, 869 teams/departments, and 11,011 employees. The number of employees within the establishment surveyed varies between 2 and 326, with an average of 42.5 employees. The number of teams/departments varies between 1 and 12, with an average of 3.3 teams. Originally, we opted for the selection of three teams/departments, and a maximum of six, but some establishments requested that we include more than six working units. Table 3.4 provides a breakdown of the number of establishments per country and per sector.

At the start of the project, we planned to include 2 establishments per sector-size stratum in our sample to acquire data from 6 establishments per sector-country, 36 establishments per country, and 324 establishments in total. It soon became apparent that not all sectors were receptive to our request for participation.

The manufacturing sector was the least problematic, as many of the issues covered in our study directly apply to manufacturing companies and their employees. Here, we successfully obtained an even distribution of establishment sizes and countries. The Netherlands is over-represented in this sector, where a single manufacturer holding requested that all its subsidiaries should participate. Similarly, managers in health care recognized the value of our survey. Negative decisions about participation were mostly due to the establishment already participating in other studies. The credibility of our study among higher education establishments was high, due to the fact that we had partner universities in all participating countries. Higher education establishments were generally willing to participate in our study. Organizations in the transport sector were also highly receptive and interested in participating, despite our initial concerns that transport organizations would be hard to motivate with a survey about investments and employability due to the growing employment flexibility in this sector.

In many countries it was challenging to elicit the participation of organizations in financial services. Managers expressed concerns about the consequences of bringing investments that their organization does not offer to their employees' attention. Finding organizations in telecommunications proved to be difficult as well, because there was only a small number of organizations in the population – especially large ones – to select from.

While the survey was well received in most countries, we encountered differences across countries in establishments' reactions. HR managers in the UK expressed the most concern about time investment and the sensitivity of the data collected (e.g., wages). In general, they were very upfront about wanting or not wanting to participate. In Germany, HR managers were very eager to discuss the subject of sustainable employment with our research team. However, the time between first contact and participation decision was the longest in

Table 3.4 Number of establishments by country, sector, and size in the ESWS

	Manufacturing			*Health care*			*Higher education*			*Transportation*			*Financial services*			*Telecommunications*			
	20/40–	*100 –*	*>249*	*20/40–*	*100 –*	*>249*	*20/40–*	*100 –*	*>249*	*20/40–*	*100 –*	*>249*	*20/40–*	*100 –*	*>249*	*20/40–*	*100 –*	*>249*	
	99	249		99	249		99	249		99	249		99	249		99	249		
UK	1	1	2	0	1	1	0	0	4	1	0	1	3	0	1	2	0	1	19
DE	1	1	1	3	2	1	1	4	2	1	1	2	1	1	0	1	0	1	24
FI	1	1	1	3	2	1	2	3	0	1	0	1	1	0	2	2	0	1	22
SE	0	2	5	3	2	0	2	0	3	3	3	1	1	2	2	1	3	2	35
NL	8	5	4	2	3	3	2	2	2	4	2	1	3	1	2	1	2	1	48
PT	2	1	1	3	2	1	0	1	3	1	1	2	1	2	3	1	0	3	28
ES	1	3	1	1	0	3	1	2	1	1	1	2	2	0	2	1	0	1	23
HU	2	1	3	2	2	2	2	1	1	0	1	2	0	1	0	2	0	1	23
BG	4	2	2	2	1	3	2	2	2	3	1	2	2	2	2	2	2	1	37
	20	17	20	19	15	15	12	15	18	15	10	14	14	9	14	13	7	12	
		57			49			45			39			37			32		259

Note
UK – United Kingdom; DE – Germany; FI – Finland; SE – Sweden; NL – Netherlands; PT – Portugal; ES – Spain; HU – Hungary; BG – Bulgaria.

Germany, as several organizational stakeholders (including higher management and employee councils) needed to approve the survey. Finding our way through different levels of management and other stakeholders was a time-consuming effort, and in some cases organizations dropped out because we could not reach a key stakeholder. The fieldwork in Sweden and Finland did not pose many problems, as most HR managers were very receptive to our survey and eager to participate. In the Netherlands, likely owing to recent public attention given to employability and work–life issues, most organizations were highly interested in the ESWS project. Spanish HR managers were also enthusiastic about the survey, but we still experienced a high drop-out rate. We found that, subsequently, it was difficult to reach the HR manager, perhaps owing to the high workload that some spoke about during the research consultation. The data collection in Hungary was well received in most sectors, but many organizations declined to participate in the telecommunications and financial services sectors, as managers stated that sustainable employment is not a salient problem.

Despite these challenges during fieldwork, the resulting ESWS presents a sample with a balanced number of organizations in all countries, sectors, and sizes. Importantly, the sample size makes it possible to perform quantitative analyses per country and per sector.

Participation and response

Participation rates are a major concern in employee surveys, especially as the participation of employees is conditional upon the participation of the organization. Low participation at both organization and employee level can produce misleading conclusions which are not generalizable to the population of interest. At the organizational level we cannot provide an estimate of the response (or participation rate) because purposeful sampling is partially non-random. We established contact with decision makers (or their gatekeepers) in approximately 6,000 organizations, were invited for a research consultation in 600 organizations, and in 320 organizations the decision maker decided to participate. For various reasons, such as a board of directors disallowing participation or an unexpected strike, 61 organizations dropped out before data collection started.

Like general population surveys, non-response in organizational studies can be passive (e.g., because of staff turnover, sickness, maternity leave, incorrect mailing address, etc.) or active (i.e., a deliberate decision not to participate). Meta-analyses show that response rates in studies that focus on the organization (or top managers) as the primary unit of analysis are typically lower than in those that focus on individual employees. Cycyota and Harrison's (2006) estimate of the response rate among executive populations is 32 percent, while Baruch and Holtom (2008) provide a similar estimate (35 percent) among organizational representatives. Studies that survey the employee have a considerably higher response rate at 52 percent (Baruch & Holtom, 2008). Anseel et al. (2010) conclude in their meta-analytic review that the higher respondents are situated in the organizational hierarchy, the lower their response rates.

Table 3.5 presents the response rates for our main sample of employees and managers, for both online and paper-and-pencil survey modes, and for each country. It is informative to compare the response rate of the ESWS to the few studies with a similar framework, such as the 2011 Work Employment Relations Study (WERS) and the 2002 Dutch Time Competition Survey (TCS). With a 49.5 percent response rate among non-managerial employees, the WERS produced a figure comparable to the one reported by Baruch and Holtom (2008). The response rate among employees in the TCS was much lower at 29 percent (Van der Lippe & Glebbeek, 2003). However, the TCS also required employees' partners to participate in the study, which may explain the lower participation rates. The response rate in the ESWS was 61 percent among non-managerial employees – around 10 percentage points higher than the figure reported by Baruch and Holtom (2008). The response rate was 81 percent among department or team managers, which is exceptionally high compared to the experience of earlier studies. In the case of the optional vignette survey following the main survey, the participation rate was 61 percent among employees. Managers had a comparable response rate for the vignette survey.

There are two of factors that may have contributed to the high response rate in our survey. First, we had a low number of organizations compared with studies such as the WERS, and this made it possible to focus our efforts on eliciting the participation of employees and managers. We had intensive personal contact with all participating organizations, taking a flexible approach to survey mode, incentives, and administering the survey. Second, we surveyed managerial employees who are in lower-level, non-executive positions and may have had more time to participate than top managers.

Table 3.5 Response rates in the ESWS

	Employee questionnaire			*Manager questionnaire*		
	All	*Online*	*Paper*	*All*	*Online*	*Paper*
All countries	61	59	68	81	79	92
UK	57	58	47	79	83	60
DE	45	46	43	85	83	95
FI	65	65	73	71	74	–
SE	65	64	78	84	83	100
NL	54	56	34	75	76	86
ES	51	51	57	74	77	43
PT	71	77	62	86	84	100
HU	78	71	84	87	83	100
BG	94	93	95	96	88	100

Notes
Figures are percentages.
UK – United Kingdom; DE – Germany; FI – Finland; SE – Sweden; NL – Netherlands; ES – Spain; PT – Portugal; HU – Hungary; BG – Bulgaria.

Conclusions

The ESWS is unique among organizational surveys. It has a multilevel design, including a large-scale sample of employees and managers within teams and organizations, and it is also cross-country comparative. The ESWS fills an important gap within organizational research and we hope that it generates new knowledge and insights that would not be possible without such data.

We encountered numerous country–organization specific challenges during the fieldwork. Getting in contact with establishments and eliciting participation remains a major difficulty in organizational research. Based on our positive experience with professional lead-generation services in the UK and Portugal, we would certainly advice practitioners to consider this as an option. Accommodating organizational requests regarding timing, survey mode, and incentives proved to be highly successful: it contributed to organizations' participation, and generated high response rates and satisfaction with our survey team among participating establishments.

Our advice to future projects is to take a structured, but flexible, approach to survey design. Survey methodologists would undoubtedly concur that differentiating the design across organizations risks comparability, and we can certainly see the validity of these concerns. However, our experience is that without such flexibility it would be an arduous task to elicit acceptable rates of participation. The differences across national and organizational cultures, as well as between the needs and schedules of different employee groups, are too large to make a one-size-fits-all strategy successful. We very much encourage methodological research on flexible design in complex surveys, and hope that our study will be an interesting case for developments in this area.

Notes

1 The US Equal Employment Opportunity Commission collects data on the gender and racial composition of the workforce from organizations with more than 100 employees. Employers that meet the reporting thresholds have a legal obligation to provide this data. For more information, see www.eeoc.gov/.

2 It appeared that not many articles in the top sociology journals focus on the level of the firm; therefore, we expanded our search for these journals to the period 2000–2014.

3 For the complete questionnaires we refer to the following: Van der Lippe et al., 2015a, 2015b, 2015c.

Part II

A comparative approach to which organizations invest in employees

Differences between sectors and countries

4 The differential influence of employee and organization characteristics on men and women's training participation

Nikki van Gerwen, Vincent Buskens, and Maria das Dores Guerreiro

Introduction

The ability of men and women to continue learning by participating in on-the-job training has become a crucial determinant of continuing career success (Hansson, 2007; Hillmert, Hartung, & Weßling, 2017; Vogtenhuber, 2015). Participating in training allows employees to update their skills and knowledge, leading to lower risks of unemployment, improved job opportunities both within and outside the organization, and often to higher wages (Dearden, Reed, & Van Reenen, 2006; Haelermans & Borghans, 2012; Konings & Vanormelingen, 2010). Previous research has been inconclusive as to whether training opportunities are equally available to men and women. Given that women are already at risk of receiving lower wages and fewer promotion opportunities (Booth, Francesconi, & Frank, 2003; Evertsson, 2004), unequal access to training might lead to further social inequality between men and women (Hillmert et al., 2017). In this chapter we assess the determinants of men and women's participation in training and look at how employee and organization characteristics might differentially affect their participation.

Although the majority of studies put forward arguments that women are less likely to receive training than men, the empirical evidence is mixed (Arulampalam, Booth, & Bryan, 2004; Dieckhoff & Steiber, 2011; Evertsson, 2004; Grund & Martin, 2012; Kristal, 2017; O'Halloran, 2008; Simpson & Stroh, 2002). While some studies indeed indicate that women are less likely to be trained than men (Evertsson, 2004; Grund & Martin, 2012), others illustrate that women are more likely to participate in training than men (Dieckhoff & Steiber, 2011; O'Halloran, 2008; Simpson & Stroh, 2002) or find no differences between men and women's participation in training (Arulampalam et al., 2004). Most of these studies rely on employee data and although they have identified several employee characteristics that affect training participation in general, such as educational attainment (Grund & Martin, 2012), age (Carmichael & Ercolani, 2014), and contract type (Arulampalam et al., 2004), they largely neglect to examine whether these characteristics promote men and women's training opportunities in differential ways. Moreover, previous research largely neglects the importance of organizational characteristics in determining training opportunities.

Training participation has been found to vary according to whether the organization operates in the public or private sectors (Grund & Martin, 2012), the size of the organization (Carmichael & Ercolani, 2014), and whether collective labor agreements are in place (O'Halloran, 2008). The literature on wage inequality has underlined that such organizational characteristics play an important role in explaining wage differences between men and women (Anderson & Tomaskovic-Devey, 1995; Arulampalam, Booth, & Bryan, 2007). Similar processes might also foster unequal access to training opportunities. Without taking these characteristics into account, our understanding of the factors contributing to men and women's training participation remains limited. This chapter accordingly examines whether men and women differ in training participation and pays specific attention to the differential influence of individual and organizational characteristics on men and women's participation in training. We formulated the following research questions: (1) *What are the determinants of men and women's participation in training?* (2) *Do employee and organizational characteristics have a differential influence on men and women's participation in training?*

To aid understanding of the determinants of participation in training, we provide demand- and supply-side arguments. We focus on how employers are more likely to select specific groups of employees for training and how these groups are more likely to opt for training themselves. This means that we pay attention to how the opportunity structure set by the employer relates to employees' individual preferences to be trained. We subsequently add to the literature by being among the first to study the differential influence of organizational characteristics in men and women's participation in training. We suggest that such an endeavor may prove worthwhile insofar as it sheds light on the relation between individual determinants of men and women's participation in training and the contextual factors that promote these opportunities.

The lack of research on how individual and organizational characteristics affect men and women's participation in training might be partially due to difficulties in gathering appropriate data. The European Sustainable Workforce Survey (ESWS) was specifically designed to examine the interplay between individual and organizational characteristics and has a number of unique advantages. First, the large number of organizations and teams included in the ESWS dataset allows for comparison between and within organizations, which helps us to understand how individual and organizational characteristics relate to men and women's training opportunities. Second, the multi-level, multi-actor structure of the data allows for a strong test of cross-level hypotheses by reducing the common-method bias that plays a role in research that relies on reports from the same actor for individual and organizational characteristics (Podsakoff, MacKenzie, Lee, & Podsakoff, 2003). Third, the ESWS contains information on three types of training: training given by a co-worker, training given by a professional, and participating in an educational program. As questions regarding training opportunities were asked in a standardized manner across multiple industries and countries, the ESWS allows for the study of a broad range of training types across different industries and countries.

Theory and hypotheses

Men and women's training participation

The literature on gender differences in organizations provides a range of explanations as to why women are less likely to be trained than men. These explanations can broadly be divided into explanations that focus on demand-side factors (i.e., employer decisions) and those that focus of supply-side factors (i.e., employee decisions).

Becker's (1975) human capital theory is one of the most prominent theories to focus on demand-side factors in explaining gender differences in training participation. Becker situates the decision to train employees in a cost–benefit analysis: employers are only willing to train an employee if the expected benefits from this investment exceed the expected costs. Expected costs include, among others, hiring an instructor and continuing salary payments during the training (Zwick, 2006). Benefits include increased employee productivity (Zwick, 2006) and higher levels of cooperative behavior (Lambooij, Flache, Sanders, & Siegers, 2007; Van Gerwen, Buskens, & Van der Lippe, 2018). Whereas the costs of training only occur once, the benefits can be obtained for as long as the employee stays with the organization. Human capital theory therefore strongly relies on differences in expected labor force participation to explain gender differences in training participation. Men are often expected to have longer periods of realized tenure than women. This is partly due to women and, in particular, younger women, being more likely to scale-back or even take time off after giving birth to children or to care for young children (Dieckhoff & Steiber, 2011; Simpson & Stroh, 2002; Van Breeschoten, Roeters, & Van der Lippe, 2018). As a result, employers profit longer from investing in the training of male employees compared to investing in the training of female employees.

Statistical discrimination processes are another demand-side argument often put forward to explain gender differences in training participation (Biebly & Baron, 1986; Grund & Martin, 2012). Employers cannot observe everything they would like to know about employees and therefore rely on group membership (i.e., being a woman) as a signal for determining the potential benefits from investing in a specific employee (Biebly & Baron, 1986; Dieckhoff & Steiber, 2011; Spence, 1973). These benefits are partly determined by the perceived job attachment and productivity of employees. If employers perceive all women to have weaker attachments and lower productivity levels than men – without knowing if this is indeed the case – the expected benefits from investing in training are lower for women than for men. Consequently, when employers base training decisions on this expectation, even strongly attached, highly productive women do not receive training. Previous research has shown that gender-based statistical discrimination plays a role in employers' hiring and promotion decisions and in the allocation of training (England, 2005; Grund & Martin, 2012).

In contrast to demand-side explanations, supply-side explanations argue that for various reasons men and women self-select or are sorted into different types of jobs. Several explanations have been proposed that provide insight into how this selection might occur. The first pertains to the concept of gender ideology: the idea that society prescribes different personality characteristics, attitudes, and behaviors to men and women (Corrigall & Konrad, 2006; West & Zimmerman, 1987). Through socialization, men learn that they must provide for their family, while women learn to be homemakers. Behaving contrary to these roles might result in negative reactions, reinforcing people to conform to their gender role (Corrigall & Konrad, 2007). Although the increase in women's labor participation has led to significant changes in the way couples arrange their task division, the male breadwinner model still "profoundly impacts how gender organizes societies" (Kanji & Samuel, 2017, p. 349). Previous research has found that internalized gender roles affect what individuals aspire to in their jobs (Corrigall & Konrad, 2006; Van der Horst, Van der Lippe & Kluwer, 2014). On average, women's aspirations are less ambitious, which might result in women being less likely to opt for training than men. Other research regards gender differences in training participation as resulting from segregation processes (Reskin & Bielby, 2005). More specifically, market segmentation theories argue that women often take on jobs where the need to be continuously trained is less. Or they find themselves in jobs that do not allow for advancing one's career and consequently alter their aspirations accordingly (England, 2005; Polachek, 1981; Renaud, Lakhdari, & Morin, 2004; Simpson & Stroh, 2002). Both demand-side and supply-side theories lead to the following hypothesis:

Hypothesis 1: Women are less likely to be trained than men.

The role of employee characteristics in men and women's training participation

We consider three employee characteristics that are likely to influence participation in training: educational attainment, age, and contract type. Demand-side factors and supply-side factors are expected to play a role here too. We first briefly elaborate on how each of these characteristics affects employees' likelihood to be trained, before we turn to how they relate to differences in men and women's training participation.

Participating in training is often aimed at acquiring new skills and knowledge or complementing skills and knowledge acquired in formal schooling. The ability to learn and the efficiency of learning increase as individuals become more educated. Lower-educated employees are presumed to need longer, costlier training to achieve the same outcomes as higher-educated employees. From the perspective of the employer, investing in higher-educated employees is therefore not only less costly, but also more beneficial in terms of productivity gains than investing in the training of lower-educated employees. This means that the costs of training are more quickly amortized by the benefits when training higher- compared to lower-educated employees. Ample research has corroborated this positive association between level of education and workplace training (Bassanini, Booth, Brunello, Paola, & Leuven, 2005; Connell & Byrne, 2010; Grund & Martin, 2012). At the same time, because higher-educated employees are more efficient at learning they are more eager to participate in training than lower-educated employees (Oosterbeek, 1998).

There is a large strand of literature illustrating that training participation rates decrease with age. Human capital theory is often put forward to explain the relationship between employee age and training participation. Older employees are less likely to receive training than younger employees because the benefits from participating in training are experienced for a shorter period of time due to the proximity of retirement age (Carmichael & Ercolani, 2014; Van Dalen, Henkens, & Schippers, 2009). Previous research has illustrated that employers tend to view older employees as less productive, less flexible and as having reduced ability to adapt to new technology. This means that processes of statistical discrimination are likely to occur and explains why participation in training decreases with age (Carmichael & Ercolani, 2014; Fleischmann, Koster, & Schippers, 2015; Remery, Henkens, Schippers, & Ekamper, 2003). Moreover, research shows that differences in training participation between older and younger employees are partly driven by older employees being less interested in learning activities, compared to their younger co-workers (Carmichael & Ercolani, 2014; Felstead, 2010; Setti, Dordoni, Piccoli, Bellotto, & Argentero, 2015).

A similar argument can be made as to why employers are more likely to invest in the training of employees with permanent contracts than in that of employees with fixed-term contracts. Since fixed-term contracts are short, human capital theory predicts that having this type of contract results in fewer training opportunities due to the shorter period over which the returns in training can be realized (Arulampalam et al., 2004; Leuven & Oosterbeek, 1999). This also explains why employees with fixed-term contracts are less willing to actively seek to be trained in firm-specific skills than employees with permanent contracts. However, this does not mean that employees with fixed-term contracts are less willing to participate in general training that may increase their labor market position.

> *Hypothesis 2*: Employees are more likely to be trained when their level of education increases or when they have a permanent rather than a fixed-term contract, and are less likely to be trained when they are older.

The differential influence of employee characteristics on men and women's training participation

Now that we have an idea as to how level of education, contract type, and age relate to employees' chances of participating in training, we turn to how these characteristics might differentially influence men and women's training participation. As outlined above, employers base their training decisions largely on the (expected) pay-off period of the investment. How the employer perceives an employee's job attachment and the potential increase in productivity after participation in training is therefore crucial. Employers often lack complete information on these aspects and are therefore likely to statistically discriminate against women. Here, we argue that, rather than just relying on employees' gender, employers can complement their information regarding the perceived job attachment and productivity of female employees with other employee characteristics: their level of education, contract type, and age.

For employers, it is more attractive to invest in higher-educated than in lower-educated employees as employee productivity increases with level of education (Bassanini et al., 2005; Connell & Byrne, 2010; Grund & Martin, 2012). Being higher educated might especially promote women's training opportunities. One of the reasons why employers are less willing to train female employees is because women are expected to have shorter periods of realized tenure than men. However, research has shown that higher-educated women more often work full-time, making their periods of realized tenure similar to those of higher-educated men (Portegijs & Den Brakel, 2016). If employers statistically discriminate against women due to lack of information regarding the productivity or job attachment of female employees, being higher educated might serve as a signal to the employer that investing in such employees is worthwhile. For men, having a higher level of education does not add much to the perception of the employer: male employees are already perceived to be more productive and to be more attached than female employees. Therefore, the positive relationship between level of education and training participation can be expected to be stronger for women than for men. Research has also shown that higher-educated women are equally ambitious in their careers as higher-educated men, which implies that the differences in willingness to participate in training are also reduced when employees become more educated (Portegijs & Den Brakel, 2016).

Having a permanent rather than a fixed-term contract might similarly work to the advantage of women. Since job attachment is often higher among employees with a permanent rather than a fixed-term contract (Arulampalam et al., 2004; Leuven & Oosterbeek, 1999), having a permanent contract can signal to the employer that an employee is highly attached to the organization. This makes investing in female employees with a permanent contract less risky as returns on the investment can be expected to be reaped over a longer period. On the other hand, having a fixed-term contract might harm women's chances of being trained more than it does for men, as it reinforces the employer's belief that the employee will soon leave the organization.

Lastly, research has shown that employers become more willing to invest in female employees when they grow older as career interruptions occur less frequently (Bassanini et al., 2005). This means that, although investing in older employees in general seems less profitable than investing in younger employees, being older might be less disadvantageous for women than for men. Combining these points, we propose the following hypothesis:

> *Hypothesis 3*: The positive relationship between level of education or having a permanent contract and likelihood of being trained is stronger for women than for men, while the negative relationship between age and likelihood of being trained is less strong for women than for men.

The differential influence of organizational characteristics on men and women's training participation

Which organizations are more likely to invest in employee training and how do their characteristics relate to women's training opportunities? In this section, we elaborate on how three organizational characteristics influence men and women's participation in training: whether the organization resides in the public or in the private sector, organization size, and unionization of the organization. For each of these characteristics, we furthermore hypothesize how they might differentially influence men and women's participation in training.

Organizations in the public sector spend a larger part of their budget on employee training than organizations in the private sector (Arulampalam et al., 2004; Boyne, 2002; Grund & Martin, 2012). The reason for this difference is simple: organizations in the private sector are more profit-oriented. The fear of losing trained employees, and thus the investment, means that organizations in the private sector generally invest less in employee training (Arulampalam et al., 2004). Whereas private sector organizations are mainly concerned with profit-maximization and market performance, public sector organizations have numerous goals that are imposed by different stakeholders. Public sector organizations are often guided by concerns about equity and accountability, goals that are less prominent in private sector organizations (Boyne, 2002). Providing equal opportunities for men and women is considered more important in public sector organizations than in those in the private sector. This can be seen in differences in the availability of work–life policies (Den Dulk & Groeneveld, 2013). Even though women might still be less likely to be trained than men, these differences might be decreased for women who work in public sector organizations compared to those employed in private sector organizations.

It is also widely reported that larger organizations invest more in employee training than smaller organizations (Black, Noel, & Wang, 1999; Carmichael & Ercolani, 2014; Hoque & Bacon, 2006; O'Halloran, 2008; Tam & Chiu, 2010). There are several explanations for this difference. First, training costs decrease with firm size due to economies of scale making investments in training less costly for larger organizations. Second, when more employees participate in training the returns from this investment can be reaped over a larger group of employees making investments in training more cost effective for larger organizations than for smaller organizations. Finally, internal labor markets in large organizations often require employees to train for new positions and facilitate employee retention, which consequently benefits the returns from investments in training (Frazis, Gittleman, & Joyce, 2000). Taken together, training opportunities are therefore often expected to increase with size of the organization. The more formalized structure of larger organizations benefits women, as there is less room for individual managers to select employees to participate in training based on an ad-hoc basis and to accidentally discriminate against women (Abendroth, Melzer, Kalev, & Tomaskovic-Devey, 2017; Arulampalam et al., 2004).

Lastly, training participation is more frequent in organizations where collective labor agreements are in place (O'Halloran, 2008; Tam & Chiu, 2010). Employee benefits, such as wages and career opportunities, are often high on the agenda in collective bargaining procedures. Collective labor agreements increase employees' training opportunities either directly, through the inclusion of training opportunities in labor agreements, or indirectly through the negotiation of employee wages (Connell & Byrne, 2010). When collective labor agreements are in place, employee wages are higher, which helps to reduce staff turnover. Low turnover rates reduce the uncertainty of investing in employee training and, hence, makes such investments more attractive to employers. Subsequently, organizations have fewer costs involved in recruiting and selecting new employees, leaving a higher budget for training opportunities (Hoque & Bacon, 2006). Collective labor agreements might especially promote women's training opportunities as they leave less room for individual employees to negotiate the conditions of their employment contract, such as wages, holidays, and training. Hence, collective labor agreements may be a way of increasing gender equality at work (Dickens, 2000). Women's training participation rates can be expected to be higher when women are employed in organizations where collective labor agreements are in place.

Taking these points together, we propose the following hypothesis:

> *Hypothesis 4*: Employees are more likely to be trained when they work in organizations in the public rather than the private sector; in larger compared to smaller organizations; or in organizations where collective labor agreements are in place compared to organizations where such agreements do not exist.

Regarding the differential influence of these organizational characteristics on men and women's participation in training, we formulate the following hypothesis:

Hypothesis 5: The positive relationship between working in organizations in the public sector, larger organizations, or organizations where collective labor agreements are in place and employees' likelihood of being trained is stronger for women than for men.

Data and methodology

Data selection

This chapters relies on data from ESWS (Van der Lippe et al., 2016). For the analyses conducted in this chapter, we exclude employees with a trainee contract, subcontract, or on-call contract and all employees younger than 18 ($N = 357$). There are 464 employees with a missing value regarding training participation or gender. Cases with incomplete data on the other variables were excluded list-wise from the analyses, leaving 9,489 employees in 811 teams and 240 organizations.

Measurements

Training participation

We distinguish three types of training: training given by a co-worker, training given by a professional from outside the organization, and participating in an educational program. Employees were asked the following questions regarding their participation in training: "In the past 12 months, have you been trained by a co-worker?" [training by co-worker], "In the past 12 months, have you been trained by a professional instructor from outside your organization?" [training by professional], and "In the past five years, have you been enrolled in an educational program?" [educational program]. Employees were assigned the value 1 on the respective training variable when they answered "Yes" to the question and the value 0 when they answered "No."

Employee characteristics

The variable *female* indicates 1 for females and 0 for males. The variable *years of education* was measured by asking employees for their highest level of completed education and was recoded to years. The variable *age* measured the respondent's age in years. The variable *permanent contract* is a dummy variable indicating whether employees have a permanent or a fixed-term contract.

Organization characteristics

The dummy variable *public* was constructed to indicate 1 for organizations in the public sector and 0 for organizations in the private sector. There were nine organizations that indicated that they are semi-private; these were coded as being private organizations. The variable *organization size* represents the number of employees working for an organization as indicated by the human resource (HR) manager. We recoded this variable into three categories: small (<101 employees), medium (100–250 employees), and large (>250 employees). The dummy variable *collective labor agreement* indicates 1 for organizations that stated that pay is determined by collective bargaining and 0 for organizations that stated that pay is set by senior management, through negotiations with individual employees, or in other ways.

Control variables

Previous research has shown that, especially for women, having a young child living at home influences participation in training. We follow previous research and control for whether respondents have any children younger than eight years old living at home (Evertsson, 2004). For similar reasons, we also control for whether employees work part-time or full-time. To take more contextual differences into account, we control for the overall gender distribution in the organization. The variable *percentage of females* was constructed by asking the HR manager of each organization to indicate on a 9-point Likert scale. Dummy variables are added to the model to control for industry and country differences. Table 4.1 presents the descriptive statistics of the variables in the sample.

Analytical strategy

Given the nested structure of the ESWS dataset and the binary nature of the dependent variable, logistic multi-level models are used to analyze the data. The analytical strategy is as follows: for each type of training, we first present a model including the independent variables while controlling for several employee and organization characteristics. In this model, we determine whether men and women differ in their participation in training and examine which other employee and organization characteristics relate to training participation. Next, we add the interaction terms to the model to test whether the employee and organization characteristics have a differential influence on men and women's training participation. Industry and country differences are controlled for and included as fixed effects in each model (the results are not shown in Table 4.2). Since we expect women's training participation to differ depending on organizational characteristics, a random term for the variable *female* is included in the model. Results are presented in terms of average marginal effects, as estimated coefficients from logistic regression models can be difficult to interpret. The average marginal effects express how the probability of the dependent variable being 1 (i.e., participating in training) changes for each 1-unit increase in the independent variable while holding the other variables constant.

Table 4.1 Descriptive statistics

	Mean/Prop.	*Std.*	*Min*	*Max*
Employee level variables				
Training by co-worker	0.38		0	1
Training by professional	0.42		0	1
Educational program	0.27		0	1
Female	0.56		0	1
Years of education	13.49	2.93	2	20
Permanent contract	0.91		0	1
Age	42.18	1.87	18	77
Organization level variables				
Public	0.39		0	1
Organization size				
Small	0.28		0	1
Medium	0.26		0	1
Large	0.46		0	1
Collective labor agreements	0.48		0	1
Control variables				
Young children living at home	0.21		0	1
Part-time	0.17		0	1
Proportion of female workers	0.50	0.24	0	1
Sector				
Manufacturing	0.24		0	1
Health care	0.23		0	1
Higher education	0.17		0	1
Transport	0.12		0	1
Financial services	0.13		0	1
Telecommunications	0.10		0	1
Country				
Bulgaria	0.13		0	1
Finland	0.08		0	1
Germany	0.08		0	1
Hungary	0.13		0	1
The Netherlands	0.24		0	1
Portugal	0.11		0	1
Spain	0.07		0	1
Sweden	0.10		0	1
UK	0.07		0	1

Note
N = 9,489.

Results

Training given by a co-worker

Model 1 in Table 4.2 presents the tests of the hypotheses regarding participation in training given by a co-worker. In this model, we test how employee and

Table 4.2 Average marginal effects from logistic multi-level analyses of training participation in organizations

	Hyp.	*Training by co-worker*		*Training by professional*		*Educational program*	
		(Model 1)		*(Model 2)*		*(Model 3)*	
		B	s.e.	B	s.e.	B	s.e.
Independent variables							
Female	–	–0.04**	0.01	–0.02	0.02	–0.03**	0.01
Years of education	+	0.03*	0.01	0.07***	0.01	0.04***	0.01
Permanent contract	+	–0.10***	0.02	0.07***	0.02	–0.00	0.02
Age	–	–0.05***	0.01	–0.03***	0.01	–0.04***	0.01
Public	+	–0.01	0.04	–0.07	0.04	0.02	0.02
Organization size (ref. = small)							
Medium	+	0.10**	0.03	0.01	0.04	0.03	0.02
Large	+	0.10**	0.03	0.05	0.04	0.02	0.02
Collective labor agreement	+	0.03	0.03	0.06	0.04	0.04	0.02
Control variables							
Young children		–0.04***	0.01	–0.03	0.01	–0.04***	0.01
Part-time work		–0.00	0.02	–0.04*	0.02	–0.04**	0.01
% female in organization		0.05**	0.02	0.03	0.02	–0.01	0.01
Variance terms							
Female (slope)		0.70	0.60	0.20	0.80	0.00	0.00
Team (intercept)		0.45	0.70	0.43	0.60	0.19	0.50
Organization (int.)		0.51	0.90	0.55	0.90	0.18	0.40
Individual (error)		3.29		3.29		3.29	
Deviance (df.)		10,910 (28)		11,577 (28)		10,363.93 (28)	
N of employees		9,489		9,489		9,489	
N of teams		811		811		811	
N of organizations		240		240		240	

Notes
The variables years of education, age, and percentage females are standardized.
* $p<0.05$, ** $p<0.01$, *** $p<0.001$ (2-sided).

organizational characteristics relate to training participation. Results show that women's chances of participating in training are 4 percent lower than those of men, thereby confirming Hypothesis 1. The results additionally show that training participation is related to employees' level of education and age. The highest educated employees, who have had 20 years of education, are 3 percent more likely to be trained by a co-worker than employees with an average of 14 years of education. Similarly, for each ten year increase in employees' age, their chances of participating in this type of training decrease by almost 5 percent. Employees with a permanent contract are 10 percent less likely to participate in training given by a co-worker than employees with a fixed-term contract. Therefore, we can confirm Hypothesis 2 regarding the role employees' education and age plays in training opportunities, but have to reject the hypothesis based on contract type.

Whether the organization resides in the public or the private sector and whether collective labor agreements are in place does not significantly affect employees' training opportunities. The size of the organization does, however: employees are 10 percent more likely to be trained by a co-worker in medium-sized organizations and 9 percent more likely to be trained in large organizations, compared to small organizations. Therefore, the results of Model 1 indicate that in line with Hypothesis 4, employees are more likely to be trained when they work in large organizations. However, this relationship is not linear: employees who work in medium and large organizations do not differ significantly in their likelihood of being trained.

Employees with young children living at home are 5 percent less likely to be trained by a co-worker than employees without young children living at home. There are no significant differences in training participation between employees who work full-time and employees who work part-time. Employees also become significantly more likely to participate in training when the percentage of females in the organization increases.

Training given by a professional from outside the organization

Model 2 presents the logistic multi-level models estimated to test the hypothesis regarding participation in training given by a professional from outside the organization. In contrast to the results regarding participation in training by a co-worker, the results of Model 2 indicate no significant differences between men and women's participation in training. Therefore, we cannot confirm Hypothesis 1 regarding this type of training. Confirming Hypothesis 2, employees are more likely to be trained when they are higher educated and more likely to be trained when they have a permanent rather than a fixed-term contract. Employees are also less likely to be trained by a professional when they are older. More specifically, for each additional three years of education, employees become almost 7 percent more likely to be trained by a co-worker. Whereas Model 1 illustrates that employees with a permanent contract are less likely to participate in training given by a co-worker, Model 2 shows that these employees are 8 percent more likely to participate in training given by a professional than employees with a fixed-term contract. Age has a small but significant effect on training participation: for every ten years of employee age, the likelihood of their participating in training decreases by 3 percent.

Regarding training by a professional, organizational characteristic such as whether the organization operates in the public or the private sector and whether collective labor agreements are in place do not significantly affect employees' participation in training. Moreover, the size of the organization and the percentage of females employed do not significantly relate to employees' training participation. Employees with young children living at home are not significantly less likely to participate in this type of training than employees without young children. However, employees who work part-time are 5 percent less likely to participate in training given by a professional than employees who work full-time.

Participating in an educational program

Model 3 presents the logistic multi-level models regarding participation in an educational program. The results from Model 3 illustrate that women are less likely to participate in an educational program than men. More specifically, women are 3 percent less likely to participate in this type of training than men. This is in line with Hypothesis 1. Consistent with the results for the other types of training, Model 3 illustrates that employees become 4 percent more likely to participate in training with each additional three years of education, and become almost 5 percent less likely to participate in training for every ten years they age. In contrast to the results for the other types of training, employees with a permanent contract do not differ significantly from those with a fixed-term contract in their likelihood to participate in an educational program. Therefore, we can partly confirm Hypothesis 2: education relates positively to employees' likelihood of participating in an educational program, while age relates negatively to the likelihood of such participation.

Based on Model 3, Hypothesis 4 cannot be confirmed: employees who work in public sector organizations or organizations where collective labor agreements are in place do not differ significantly in their likelihood of participating in an educational program from employees working in private sector organizations or organizations where there are no collective labor agreements. Employees who work in large organizations are more likely to be enrolled in an educational program than those who work in small organizations.

Employees with young children are 4 percent less likely to participate in an educational program than those without young children. Working part-time also negatively influences the likelihood of employees participating in an educational program: those who work part-time are 4 percent less likely to participate in this type of training than those who work full-time.

Differential influence on men and women's training participation

In the next step, we include the interaction terms in the model to examine whether employee and organizational characteristics have a differential influence on men and women's likelihood of participating in training. The results are shown in Figure 4.1 to provide a more intuitive interpretation of the interaction effects (the full results are reported in Appendix 2).[1]

In Figure 4.1, the panel for training by a co-worker shows that the positive relationship between level of education and employees' likelihood of being trained by a co-worker is stronger for women than for men. Although men and women are both less likely to be trained when they grow older, Figure 4.1 illustrates that this negative effect is significantly less for women than for men. Therefore, we can confirm Hypothesis 3 regarding level of education and age. The results provide no indications to confirm Hypothesis 3 regarding contract type. Figure 4.1 seems to illustrate that working in the public sector has a positive effect on women's likelihood of being trained by a co-worker, but a negative effect on men's likelihood of participating in this type of training. However, this difference is not statistically significant. Similarly, although Figure 4.1 seems to illustrate that the positive effect of working in medium or large organizations (as compared to small organizations) is greater for women than for men, these differences are not statistically significant. The effect of working in an organization where collective labor agreements are in place does not differ significantly for men and women. Therefore, we find no support for Hypothesis 5 regarding the differential influence of organizational characteristics on men and women's likelihood of being trained by a co-worker.

The second panel in Figure 4.1 depicts the interaction effects regarding employees' likelihood of being trained by a professional. In line with the results regarding training by a co-worker, the panel for training by a professional shows that the positive relationship between education and employees' likelihood of being trained by a professional is stronger for women than for men. However, age and contract type do not seem to have a differential influence on men and women's likelihood of being trained. We can therefore only partly confirm Hypothesis 3 for this type of training. Based on Figure 4.1, we can also only partly confirm Hypothesis 5: although on average employees who work in organizations in the public sector are less likely to be trained than employees who work in the private sector, this negative effect is weaker for women than for men. Size of organization and whether collective labor agreements are in place do not seem to have a differential influence on men and women's participation in training.

Lastly, the third panel in Figure 4.1 depicts the interaction effects regarding employees' likelihood of participating in an educational program. Consistent with the models regarding the other types of training, the results illustrate that the positive relationship between level of education and likelihood of participating in an educational program is stronger for women than for men, thereby partly confirming Hypothesis 3. Hypothesis 3 cannot be confirmed regarding

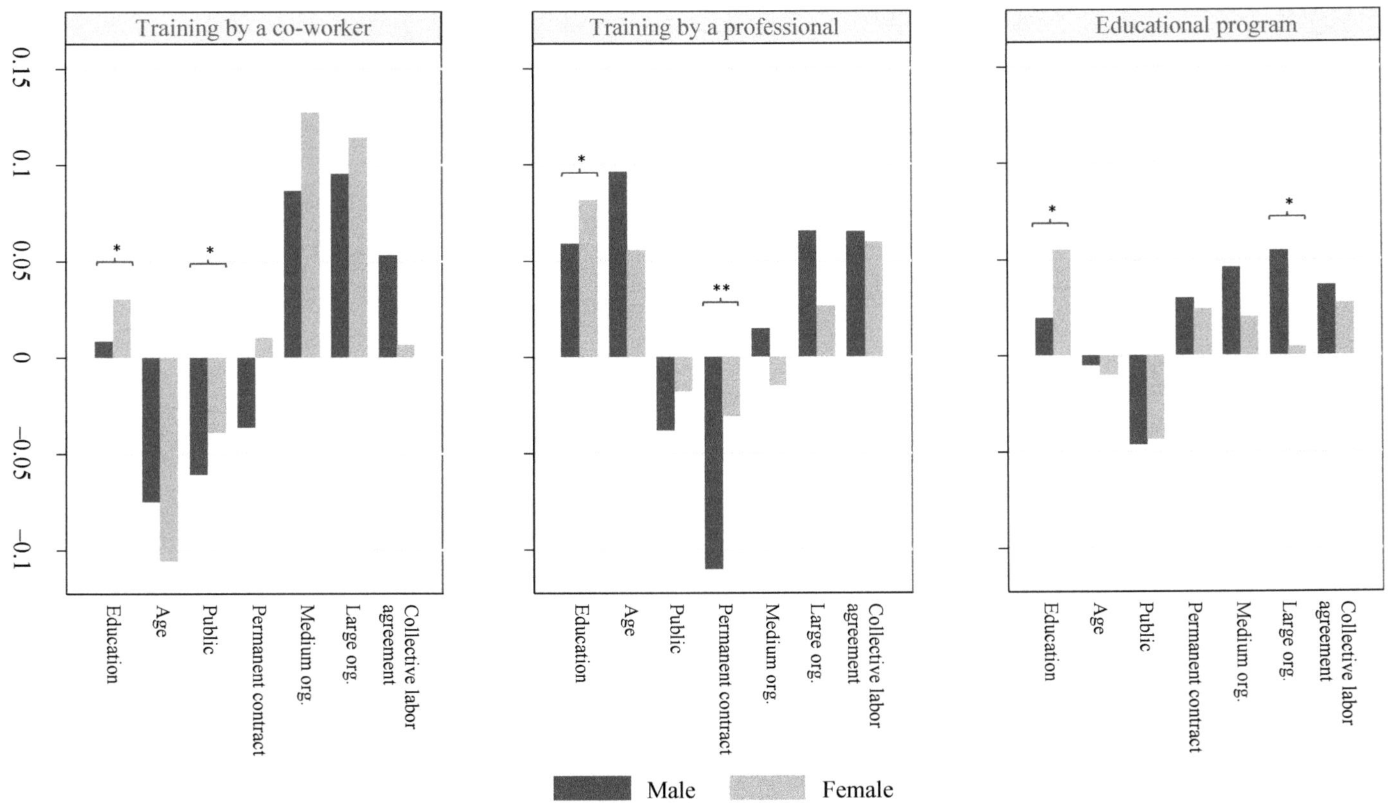

Figure 4.1 Plotted average marginal effects, separately for men and women.

any of the other employee characteristics. Age and contract type do not have a differential influence on men and women's chances of participating in an educational program. With regard to organizational characteristics, the results indicate that the positive effect of working in a large organization is weaker for women than for men. This contrasts with Hypothesis 5, which predicts that women profit more from working in a large organization than men. Hypothesis 5 cannot be confirmed or rejected for the other organizational characteristics.

Conclusion and discussion

This chapter has examined the differential influence of employee and organizational characteristics on men and women's participation in training. In doing so, it has made two important contributions to the literature. First, empirical research on differences in training participation between men and women has yielded inconclusive evidence. The chapter has added to the ongoing debate in the literature regarding differences in participation in training between men and women. Whereas previous research has mainly focused on how employee or organizational characteristics relate to employees' training participation, this chapter has moved forward by examining whether these characteristics have a differential influence on men and women's training opportunities. Second, the inconclusive results from previous work on this topic might be partially attributed to differences in the type of training studied. This chapter contributes to the literature by studying men and women's chances of participating in three different types of training. Few earlier studies have been able to study training participation in such a complex way. Our approach has resulted in three substantive conclusions.

The first conclusion pertains to the ongoing debate in the literature regarding gender differences in training participation. Are women less likely to participate in training than men? We conclude that women *are* less likely to participate in training given by a co-worker and less likely to be enrolled in an educational program than men. However, we do not find a difference for participation in training provided by a professional. The findings of this chapter illustrate the importance of specifying the type of training that is being studied. Part of the reason for the inconclusive results in previous research might be due to ambiguities in the definition of training. For example, the studies by Grund and Martin (2012), O'Halloran (2008), and Renaud et al. (2004) all asked respondents whether they participated in "further training." O'Halloran (2008) and Renaud et al. (2004) conclude that women are more likely to be trained than men, while Grund and Martin (2012) suggest that women are less likely to be trained than men. None of these studies specified whether respondents participated in training by a co-worker or by a professional. Our finding that women are equally as likely to be trained by a professional as men, but less likely to be trained by a co-worker, might be explained by the "nature" of the training. Being trained by a co-worker might happen on a more casual basis, whereas participation in training by a professional is often more institutionalized. Due to the more formalized nature of the latter type of training, employers might take more steps to ensure the inclusion of all groups of employees and so gender differences are less likely to occur. Also, other research on gender differences in organizations has concluded that more formal rules and regulations reduce gender differences between men and women (for an example on earnings, see Abendroth et al., 2017).

Our second conclusion is that some employee characteristics have a differential influence on men and women's participation in training, but organizational characteristics mostly do not. Although we already know from previous research that level of education promotes training opportunities (Bassanini et al., 2005; Carmichael & Ercolani, 2014; Connell & Byrne, 2010; Grund & Martin, 2012; Van Dalen et al., 2009), we show that being higher educated promotes women's training opportunities more than it does for men. Moreover, we are among the first to show that this holds for each type of training. This finding is in line with our theoretical argument that employers rely on level of education as a signal for determining the risk of the investment. In line with a plethora of research (Carmichael & Ercolani, 2014; Fleischmann et al., 2015; Remery et al., 2003), we conclude that employees become less likely to participate in each type of training as they age. This relationship between age and training participation shapes men and women's opportunities to participate in training provided by a professional or an education program in a similar manner. In respect of participation in training provided by a co-worker, however, we conclude that being older harms women's training opportunities less than it does men's. We furthermore conclude that while contract type does not have a differential influence on men and women's training participation, interesting differences exist between employees with a permanent contract and those with a fixed-term contract when looking at each type of training. The results of this chapter illustrate that employees with a fixed-term contract are more likely to be trained by a co-worker, but less likely to be trained by a professional compared to employees with a permanent contract. Besides the explanation that employers are less willing to invest in the training of employees with a fixed-term contract than in that of those with a permanent contract (Arulampalam et al., 2004; Leuven & Oosterbeek, 1999), this difference might also simply be attributed to differences in help of an informal nature that is needed. Employees with fixed-term contracts, especially when they are still rather new to the organization, might need more help from co-workers than employees with permanent contracts.

Lastly, we conclude that of all three organizational characteristics studied, only the size of an organization relates to men and women's participation in training. In line with previous research (Black et al., 1999; Carmichael & Ercolani, 2014; Hoque & Bacon, 2006; O'Halloran, 2008; Tam & Chiu, 2010), we conclude that employees working in large organizations are more likely to participate in training by a co-worker than those who work in small organizations. However, we also conclude that size of organization does not relate to employees' likelihood of participating in training by a professional or in an educational program. This is interesting, as the argument that large organizations can spread their training costs over more employees than small organizations would especially hold for these costlier types of training. A possible explanation for this result might be that smaller organizations nowadays have a fixed training budget per employee.

Besides these contributions to the literature, this chapter has at least two limitations. First, although we paid attention to supply- and demand-side arguments in theorizing why certain groups of employees can be expected to be more likely to be trained than others, we could not disentangle these processes empirically. Having more information about whether employees want to participate in training could be particularly helpful when studying differences in participation in educational programs between men and women. Being enrolled in an educational program requires a substantive time investment from the employee, especially as employers often expect employees to continue their normal work tasks. Previous research has shown that when studying differences in career aspirations between men and women, women more often consider that spending additional time at work detracts from time spent with family, whereas men are more fully concentrated on their careers (Van der Horst, Van der Lippe, & Kluwer, 2014). Future research may help us understand gender differences in training participation even further by including more information on employers' and employees' choices regarding participation in training. Second, although one of the contributions of this chapter lies in its ability to study three types of training, the results still rely on a rather "vague" concept of training. There is no information on the content of the training available. When women are mostly participating in training aimed at updating their skills and knowledge for their current job, while men are being trained for new jobs, this seemingly subtle difference might promote inequalities between men and women. Future research could sharpen the conclusions of this chapter by including information regarding the content of training.

Overall, this chapter has showed the existence of differences in men and women's participation in training. Women are less likely to be trained by a co-worker or to be enrolled on an educational program than men. Furthermore, we conclude that women's training opportunities are mostly affected by other employee characteristics, such as level of education or age, and less so by characteristics of the organizations in which they work. This implies that women do not self-select into specific organizations in which the need for training is less prominent, and that differences in training participation between men and women might be partially due to differences in, for example, level of education. Organizations seeking to improve gender equality between men and women might do so by specifically targeting lower-educated women.

Note

1 In order to obtain this figure we first ran the models from Table 4.2 separately for men and women. The results from these models were stored and displayed in the graph. To obtain the significance levels for the differences, we ran the models from Table 4.2 (on the entire sample) including the interaction terms.

5 Investments in working parents

The use of parental leave

Leonie van Breeschoten, Katia Begall, Anne-Rigt Poortman, and Laura den Dulk

Introduction

Both national governments and organizations increasingly invest in working parents by offering them work–family policies such as part-time work, childcare support, or family leave policies (maternity, paternity, and parental leave) (Abendroth & Den Dulk, 2011; Den Dulk, Peters, & Poutsma, 2012; Organisation for Economic Co-operation and Development [OECD], 2017b). These policies are designed to help employees with young children to better combine work and family life, and can potentially increase employees' work–family balance as well as their work performance (Kossek & Friede, 2006; Wheatley, 2017). However, despite these potentially positive outcomes, there is a huge discrepancy between work–family policy *availability* and work–family policy *use*, especially for men (Beauregard, 2011; OECD, 2016). Research has suggested that this is not just due to a lack of interest – there are also many people who have access to work–family policies and would like to use these, but who still refrain from doing so (Adams et al., 2016; McDonald, Brown, & Bradley, 2005). This suggests that there are structural constraints that restrict the utilization of work–family policies that are officially available. We will focus on one central player: the organization.

Research on the relation between organizations and work–family policy utilization is relatively scarce and scattered, with the majority of studies focusing on work–family policy *availability* (Den Dulk, 2001; Den Dulk & Peper, 2007). These studies mostly look at whether organizations provide additional work–family policies on top of the statutory policies they are obliged to provide by law. However, organizations are also gatekeepers to the statutory work–family policies; even though employees are officially entitled to the provisions contained in these policies, organizations can in practice, through informal means, strongly discourage or encourage employees from utilizing work–family policies (Boon, Paauwe, Boselie, & Den Hartog, 2009; Goodstein, 1994; Lewis & Smithson, 2001). Most of what we know about the relationship between organizations and work–family policy utilization comes from qualitative studies, which have provided valuable insights into people's perceptions of organizational restraints and support for utilization (e.g., Kaufman, 2017; Lewis & Den Dulk, 2008; Ter

Hoeven, Miller, Peper, & Den Dulk, 2017). Few quantitative studies focus on organizations and policy utilization, and those that exist rarely study the individual and the organization at the same time, either relying on samples of individuals, who provide limited information on their organizational context (e.g., Thompson, Beauvais, & Lyness, 1999), or on case studies conducted among the employees or managers of one or a few organizations (e.g., Blair-Loy & Wharton, 2002; Den Dulk & Peper, 2007; Haas, Allard, & Hwang, 2002; Pasamar, 2015; Pettigrew, 2014; Smith & Gardner, 2007).[1] The European Sustainable Workforce Survey (ESWS) allows us to be among the first to make a large-scale, systematic study of the relationship between organizations and work–family policy utilization in multiple European countries. The survey's multilevel nature allows us to combine reports from individual employees with reports from managers and the organization (as represented by the HR manager), which limits common-method bias (the bias that occurs when the same respondent reports on multiple variables) and controls for unobserved organizational characteristics that might affect employee outcomes (Podsakoff, MacKenzie, Lee, & Podsakoff, 2003).

In this chapter we will focus on how organizations relate to the use of one type of work–family policy: parental leave.[2] In doing so, we will combine two ways of looking at organizations: the family-supportiveness of their organizational culture, and by treating them as actors that make strategic choices to invest in policies. Although few studies have looked at organizations and work–family policy use, those that do focus almost exclusively on the role of organizational support, reasoning that employees are more likely to use work–family policies when they receive support from the organizational culture and their manager (Allen, 2001; Thompson, Beauvais, & Lyness, 1999). We combine these ideas on organizational support with institutional theory (DiMaggio & Powell, 1983) and business-case argumentation (Den Dulk, 2001; Kossek & Friede, 2006), both of which maintain that organizations make the strategic choice to adopt work–family policies when this is in their own interest. We will explore whether this argument can also be extended to policy use, because it is likely that the strategic choices of organizations extend to utilization – for example, through increased access. Lastly, we will pay special attention to gender. Gender norms impose different expectations regarding participation in work and family on men and women (Kanji & Samuel, 2017; Munn & Greer, 2015), and it is known that work–family policy utilization is more frequent among women than among men in all European countries (European Parliament, 2015; Moss, 2011). However, it remains unclear whether organizational aspects also affect men and women differently. All in all, this chapter contributes to the understanding of work–family policy utilization by studying the following question: *To what extent do organizational support and/or organizational characteristics explain the utilization of parental leave, and does this differ for men and women?*

Parental leave in Europe

Parental leave can be distinguished from maternity and paternity leave by its aim and characteristics – though this distinction is not clear-cut in all countries. Maternity leave is generally aimed at protecting the health of mother and child, and limited to the period directly before and after the delivery of the child. Paternity leave is generally short (2–15 days), directly surrounding the delivery, and well-compensated. Parental leave varies in length, can often be taken when the child is a bit older, and is rarely fully compensated (Moss, 2017; Van Belle, 2016).

Following the 2010 Parental Leave Directive of the European Union (Directive 2010/18/EU), all EU member states are to provide employees with at least four months parental leave. The directive leaves it to countries to decide on the specifics of the parental leave, including eligibility, possibilities for part-time take-up, and whether the leave is a "family right" (meaning that the couple is jointly entitled to a period of leave and can decide which partner takes it) or an individual right (both partners are individually entitled to leave). According to the EU directive, at least one of the four months is to be non-transferable

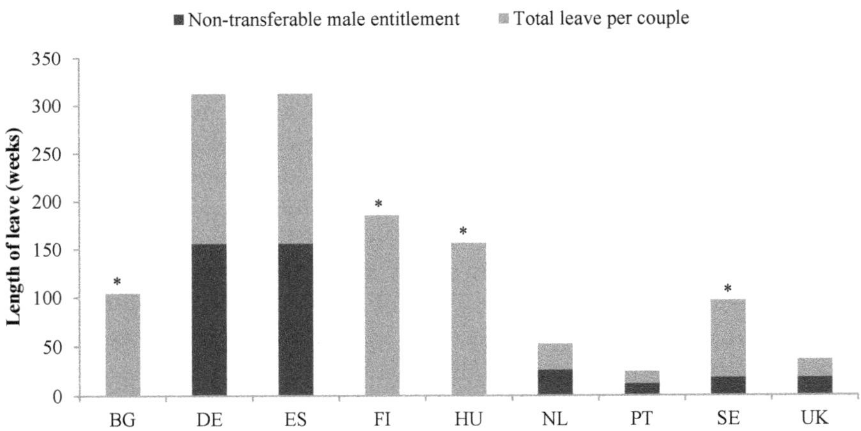

Figure 5.1 Length of parental leave in the ESWS countries, total leave per couple[a] and non-transferable male entitlements.[b]

Source: Based on information from the International Network on Leave Policies and Research (2016), complemented with data from the European Parliament (European Parliament, 2015).

Notes

BG – Bulgaria; DE – Germany; ES – Spain; FI – Finland; HU – Hungary; NL – Netherlands; PT – Portugal; SE – Sweden; UK – United Kingdom.

* Parental leave is awarded as a family right (i.e., the couple can divide it among themselves), not an individual right.

a The total leave per couple is in 'family right' countries the period that is awarded to the couple jointly; in countries with individual entitlements it includes the individual right twice.

b The non-transferable male entitlement refers to the period that is exclusively reserved for the male partner. Although in the 'family right' countries men could take more leave – as the partners can divide it between them – in practice this is mostly used by the female partner (van Belle, 2016).

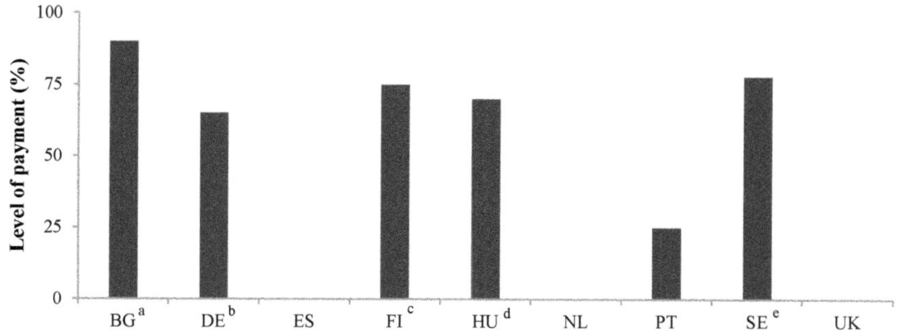

Figure 5.2 Level of payment of parental leave in the ESWS countries.

Source: Based on information from the International Network on Leave Policies and Research (2016), complemented with data from the European Parliament (European Parliament, 2015).

Notes

BG – Bulgaria; DE – Germany; ES – Spain; FI – Finland; HU – Hungary; NL – Netherlands; PT – Portugal; SE – Sweden; UK – United Kingdom.

There is no guaranteed level of payment for parental leave in Spain, the Netherlands, and the UK.

a For 26 weeks, then flat-rate.

b For 52 weeks (up to a ceiling), with an extra 8 weeks if both partners take at least 8 weeks, then unpaid.

c For 4 weeks, then 70 percent (both up to a ceiling).

d For 108 weeks (up to a ceiling), then flat-rate; non-insured parents only get the flat-rate.

e For 56 weeks, then 13 weeks at flat-rate.

between partners, in order to incentivize men to partake in childrearing. This, however, has not been implemented in all countries (European Parliament, 2015; International Network on Leave Policies and Research, 2016). In countries with a family right where no period of leave is specifically reserved for male use, all leave is frequently taken by the female partner (Van Belle, 2016). Figures 5.1 and 5.2 show the length of parental leave (as a family entitlement and as a male entitlement), and the level of payment in the nine ESWS countries. It can be seen that countries differ strongly on all dimensions.

Theory and hypotheses

The family-supportiveness of the organizational culture

Though few studies have taken a systematic, multilevel approach to studying the utilization of parental leave (or work–family policies more broadly), theoretical (e.g., McDonald et al., 2005), qualitative (e.g., Kaufman, 2017; Lewis & Den Dulk, 2008; Ter Hoeven et al., 2017), and small-scale quantitative studies (e.g., Blair-Loy & Wharton, 2002; Den Dulk & Peper, 2007; Haas et al., 2002; Pettigrew, 2014; Smith & Gardner, 2007; Thompson et al., 1999) have stressed the importance of a family-supportive organizational culture for employees' use of work–family policies. Organizations have a distinct organizational culture which supports or discourages the integration of employees' work and family lives (Thompson et al., 1999). This, in turn relates to the sense of entitlement that employees feel regarding the use of available policies (Lewis & Smithson, 2001). Many organizations that are unsupportive towards employees' family responsibilities adhere to "ideal worker" culture (Acker, 1990). The notion of an "ideal worker" is based on the traditional male breadwinner: an employee who exists only for the job, and has no other (family) responsibilities that are interfering (for example, because he has a homemaker spouse). Organizations with a strong ideal worker culture expect their employees never to prioritize family, and when employees do (for example, by using leave) they are seen as less committed to their job, which often has consequences for their career progression (Acker, 1990; Haas & Hwang, 2016; Lyonette, 2015; Munn & Greer, 2015). Other organizations, however, adhere less to ideal worker culture, and actively support employees who want to use work–family policies, either because they believe that it will result in better employee productivity, or because they feel a social or moral responsibility to do so (Been, Den Dulk, & Van der Lippe, 2017a), meaning that employees do not need to fear repercussions and feel more free to use work–family policies.

In addition to the general organizational culture, employees' direct managers are important agents that influence their work–life decisions, and managers can independently withhold or provide support. Managers may adhere to the (ideal worker) norms of the organizational culture, but they are independent actors who can also convey a different message, namely, that choosing family over work is or is not acceptable in their team (Allen, 2001; Den Dulk & De Ruijter, 2005, 2008). Because managers hold a key position in shaping the future career of an employee, employees are likely to want to live up to their manager's expectations (Allen, 2001; Perlow, 1995), making employees more likely to use work–family policies if their manager is supportive than if (s)he is not. Therefore, we expect that employees in an organization with a more family-supportive organizational culture (Hypothesis 1a) and those who have a manager who is more family-supportive (Hypothesis 1b) are more likely to use parental leave.

Institutional theory and business-case argumentation

There are two main theories that treat organizations as actors that make strategic choices to invest in work–family policies: institutional theory and business-case argumentation. Institutional theory (DiMaggio & Powell, 1983) maintains that organizations *adopt* work–family policies – and human resource practices more broadly – in response to institutional pressures. Organizations with certain characteristics face more institutional pressures and thus experience a stronger need to obtain legitimacy than other organizations (Goodstein, 1994). We rely on three organizational characteristics which are commonly perceived as indicative of high institutional pressures for the adoption of work–family policies, and which have frequently been found to be of importance in predicting work–family policy adoption, namely: organization size, ownership (i.e., public or private ownership), and proportion of women within an organization (Den Dulk, Groeneveld, Ollier-Malaterre & Valcour, 2013; Goodstein, 1994; Ingram & Simons, 1995). Larger organizations and organizations in the public sector are deemed to be more susceptible to external, societal pressures, while organizations with a higher proportion of women face greater pressures from within, as women would be more likely to call for the adoption of work–family policies than men (Goodstein, 1994; Ingram & Simons, 1995).

Institutional theory has repeatedly been applied to the adoption of additional work family–policies (Den Dulk et al., 2013; Goodstein, 1994; Haas & Hwang, 2009; Ingram & Simons, 1995), but whether it can also be extended to the *utilization* of work–family policies is unclear. For a long time scholars maintained that greater institutional pressures would only lead to policy adoption, but not to utilization, because the policies would be adopted for symbolic rather than substantive reasons (Blair-Loy & Wharton, 2002). However, we argue that institutional theory could also extend to policy use, because when organizations face institutional pressures and adopt work–family policies this may increase both practical accessibility and awareness and entitlement among employees.[3] For example, when policies are adopted an organization's human resource department formalizes how employees can request utilization and how this will be managed in terms of finances and personnel replacement. This will substantially ease applying for utilization. Similarly, organizations with more institutional pressures are more likely to take their statutory obligation seriously and increase access to work–family policies. Formalized infrastructure will further create enhanced awareness of the available policy as well as a higher sense of entitlement among employees (Beauregard & Henry, 2009; Lewis & Smithson, 2001), both of which will lead to higher utilization.

Business-case argumentation also sees organizations as actors that make strategic choices, but focusses more on a financial cost–benefit analysis. In this line of reasoning, organizations are likely to adopt policies when they believe this will be in their own financial interest – for example, because it will attract or retain desirable employees, or because it increases the performance of current employees – but set this off against the expected costs of the policy (Been, 2015; Den Dulk, 2001; Kossek & Friede, 2006; Wheatley, 2017). Following this line of reasoning, larger organizations would be more likely to provide work–family policies, because it is easier to redistribute work to other employees or to hire temporary replacements, i.e., the costs of having these policies is lower (Bygren & Duvander, 2006; Haas & Hwang, 2009). Moreover, because public organizations are less profit-oriented, they would be less opposed to employee absences that might cause production loss (Bygren & Duvander, 2006), making it easier for employees to use such policies. Lastly, employees in public organizations might feel more entitled to use work–family policies as these are seen as "compensating differentials" to the lower salaries in the public sector; people have *chosen* to work in the public sector, knowing that it will pay less but provide better access to secondary employment conditions, such as work–family policies

(Groeneveld, Steijn, & Van der Parre, 2009; Rosen, 1986). Thus, they feel more entitled to use these policies. We therefore expect that employees who work in organizations that are large (Hypothesis 2a), that are in the public sector (Hypothesis 2b), and have a higher proportion of female employees (Hypothesis 2c) are more likely to use parental leave.

Gender

Parental leave policies are frequently aimed at women, and women tend to have better access to them, or are entitled to longer periods of leave. Thus, it is not surprising that women use parental leave more frequently and for longer periods than their male counterparts (European Parliament, 2015; Moss, 2011). This is in line with prevailing normative prescriptions regarding gender norms, which continue to hold that women shoulder the main responsibility for home and childcare, and men for paid labor (Kanji & Samuel, 2017; Munn & Greer, 2015). Using work–family policies violates ideal worker norms (Acker, 1990), but for women it is in line with gender norms that still oppose full-time maternal employment (Booth & Van Ours, 2009; Roeters & Craig, 2014). This means that it is not only more acceptable for women to use work–family policies, but that they are also more expected to do so, and that this has a price in that they are taken less seriously at work (Evertsson & Duvander, 2011). For men, on the other hand, using work–family policies clearly violates expectations regarding masculinity and being an ideal worker (Acker, 1990; Kanji & Samuel, 2017), making men less inclined to use these policies. We thus expect the utilization of parental leave to be higher among women than among men (Hypothesis 3a).

Having outlined how using work–family policies is a stronger violation of gender norms for men than for women, we can expect organizational support factors to play a larger role in the utilization decisions of men than in those of women. After all, women feel they have access to the use of work–family policies even when they are not actively supported in this. Men, however, need to violate 'normal' behavior, which is costly, but it becomes less costly when they experience organizational support. Similarly, we can expect that organizational characteristics will play a larger role for men than for women, considering that these can lead to easier and more institutionalized access to policies. In other words, the relationship between organizational support factors (Hypothesis 3b) and organizational characteristics (Hypothesis 3c) and the utilization of parental leave is stronger for men than for women.

Method

Sample

For the purpose of this chapter we rely on a sub-sample of parents with a child under four years old, because we wanted to make sure their leave use was recent in order to minimize the risk that organizational factors had changed over time (e.g., if people were assigned to a different manager between their parental leave use and the time they completed the survey). We also excluded people who did not work for their current employer at the time they became parents, as the characteristics of their current workplace would not be related to their past use of leave policies. This led to a sample of 1,211 people. We then excluded employees with missing values on gender ($n = 4$), but used multiple imputations with regression switching (Van Buuren & Oudshoorn, 1999) for missing cases on all other variables. Our total sample consists of 1,207 employees in 521 teams and 232 organizations.

Measures

Use of parental leave

Our dependent variable *use of parental leave* (0 = no use, 1 = use) is measured by asking respondents, "Did you use parental leave in connection with the birth of your youngest child?" Note that this refers to whether respondents took *any* leave at all, but says nothing about the duration of the leave. We chose to measure this variable in this way for country comparability; using, for example, a month of parental leave is a long period in some countries, but very short in others. By looking at use dichotomously we use a more crude, yet more comparable, measure.

Organizational support

In this chapter we use both a subjective and an objective measure for organizational support and managerial support. Subjective measures capture whether employees *perceive* their organization and manager to be supportive, reasoning that the *perception* of employees influences their behavior. However, using two self-reported measures (perceived organizational support and the leave used) introduces common-method bias which can be limited using objective measures, especially when these are reported by different actors such as managers or HR managers (Podsakoff et al., 2003). Therefore, we also include two objective indicators as proxies for cultural and managerial support, namely, collegial use of work–family policies and managerial use of work–family policies. Collegial use of work–family policies is a proxy for the supportiveness of the organizational culture, because in a supportive culture employees are more likely to use leave. Moreover, managerial use of work–family policies can be seen as a proxy of a managerial support for two reasons: (1) managers who value work–family integration are more likely to have used parental leave themselves; and (2) because of their personal experiences they are likely to be more supportive of employees wanting to use leave, and can serve as role models.

Our subjective measure for cultural support and managerial support is based on a reduced scale using Thompson et al.'s (1999) measure of organizational work–family culture. The scale consists out of nine items to which respondents could respond on a 5-point Likert scale, ranging from strongly disagree to strongly agree. We conducted a factor analysis which showed two clear factors both consisting of three items. Based on this, we constructed two variables: *perceived cultural support*, and *perceived managerial support*. Perceived cultural support is based on three items: "employees are often expected to take work home at night or during the weekend"; "to turn down a promotion or transfer for family-related reasons will seriously hurt one's career progress in this organization"; and "to get ahead in this organization, employees are expected to work overtime." It has a Cronbach's alpha of 0.67. Perceived managerial support is also based on three items: "my manager is understanding when I have to put my family first"; "higher management encourages supervisors to be sensitive to employees' family concerns"; and "my manager is very accommodating of family-friendly needs." It has a Cronbach's alpha of 0.79.

Our objective measure for cultural support is measured as the *use of parental leave by colleagues*, as reported by the HR manager. HR managers reported on a 7-point scale what proportion of male and female employees who became parents used parental leave. They thus reported this separately for male and female employees, but we took the mean of these two. Additional analyses were conducted where we in turn included use by male and use by female colleagues, but this did not make any difference to the results.

Objective managerial support is measured as *use of parental leave by manager* (no = 0, yes = 1), as reported by the manager. If the manager was childless this was also coded as not having taken leave, as they would not have experienced the benefits of using leave, nor would they have set an example for their subordinates.

Organizational characteristics

Studies vary in their measurement of organizational size, with the majority using either two or three categories or including the log of the number of employees (e.g., Been et al., 2017a; Been et al., 2017b; Den Dulk et al., 2013; Goodstein, 1994; Haas & Hwang, 2009; Ingram & Simons, 1995). In this study we include size of the organization (as reported by the HR manager) dichotomously – because we expected that only large organizations (>1,000 employees) would be susceptive to institutional pressures – rather than as linear increase by organization size. Additional analyses were conducted where we included the log, linearly and quadratically, and used different cut-off points, which can be found in the sensitivity analyses.

Whether an organization is private (0) or public (1) was also reported by the HR manager. Mixed organizations were coded as private, as they would also have a commercial goal, while charities were coded as public. Additional analyses were conducted where this was reversed, which did not change the results.

Lastly, we included the *proportion of women* in an organization, as reported by the HR manager, on a 9-point scale. The range was: "none," "1 percent to less than 10 percent," "10 percent to less than 20 percent," "20 percent to less than 40 percent," "40 percent to less than 60 percent," "60 percent to less than 80 percent," "80 percent to less than 90 percent," "90 percent to less than 100 percent," and "all." Values were recoded by taking the mid-value for each percentage interval.

Gender and control variables

We include gender as 0 = female and 1 = male. Moreover, we control for age of the youngest child, because this can be seen as a proxy for how long ago the leave was taken, as it is often taken relatively close to childbirth.

Moreover, we include the sex of the manager as a control variable, as male and female managers might differ in their support for work–family issues due to their different experiences of managing and (not) having a family. We also include whether the manager has children (0 = no, 1 = yes), as not having used parental leave is different for managers with and without children.

Sector and country fixed effects

We include sector and country dummies as controls, because both the sector and the country in which an organization is situated are likely to influence the organizational context, as well as how common it is for employees to use parental leave.

Descriptive statistics

Figures 5.3 and 5.4 show parental leave use by gender, country, and sector in our sample. Further descriptive statistics are presented in Table 5.1. We see that there is much variation between countries in how much leave men and women use, while the variation between sectors is more limited. Moreover, we see that in our sample, men use parental leave more often than women (46 percent vs 41 percent), which might appear odd considering that register data and representative samples show that women use parental leave more often than men (European Parliament, 2015; Moss, 2011). It should be noted, however, that we do not have a representative sample, and that it is likely that there is a selection effect, which entails that many young mothers will be absent from our organization sample. Moreover, our measure captures whether people used parental leave *at all*, but does not distinguish between the length of the leave. Further reflection on this is included in the discussion.

The correlations between the independent variables were moderate-to-low. Support is measured in a variety of ways, including attitudes and co-worker behavior, which explains some of the low correlations. Correlations between perceptions of managerial and organizational support are moderate ($r = 0.34$), suggesting that these are indeed distinct concepts.

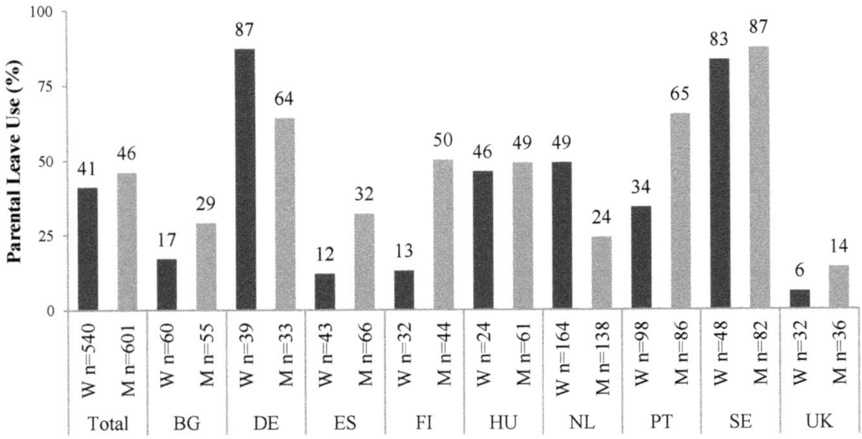

Figure 5.3 Use of parental leave in the ESWS sample, by gender and by country.

Notes
BG – Bulgaria; DE – Germany; ES – Spain; FI – Finland; HU – Hungary; NL – Netherlands; PT – Portugal; SE – Sweden; UK – United Kingdom.
W – Women; M – Men.
Figure calculated based on the non-imputed dataset.

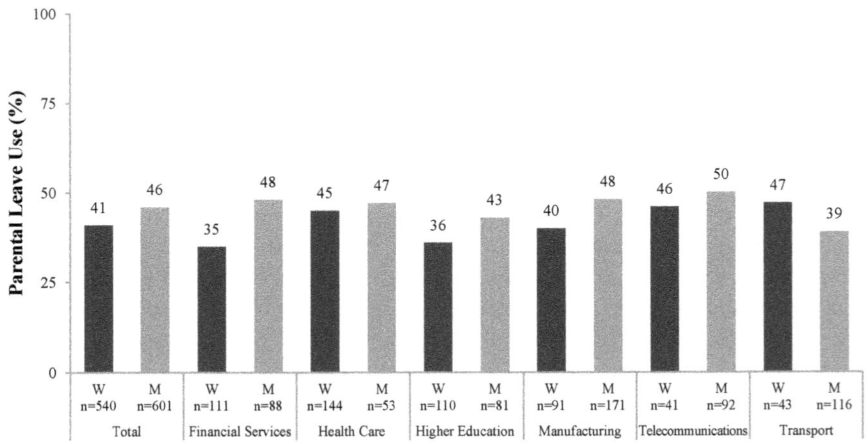

Figure 5.4 Use of parental leave in the ESWS sample, by gender and by sector.

Notes
W – Women; M – Men.
Figure calculated based on the non-imputed dataset.

Table 5.1 Descriptive statistics for men, women and the pooled sample

			Total		*Women*		*Men*	
	Min	*Max*	*Mean*	*Std.*	*Mean*	*Std.*	*Mean*	*Std.*
Dependent variable								
Use parental leave	0	1	0.43		0.41		0.46	
Independent variables								
Organizational support								
Perceived cultural support	0	1	0.56	0.17	0.55	0.17	0.57	0.17
Perceived managerial support	0	1	0.47	0.16	0.48	0.16	0.46	0.16
Use by colleagues	0	1	0.58	0.34	0.57	0.33	0.60	0.34
Use by manager	0	1	0.17		0.13		0.21	
Organizational characteristics								
Large (>1000 employees)	0	1	0.24		0.28		0.20	
Public	0	1	0.35		0.44		0.27	
Proportion of women	0	1	0.48	0.23	0.55	0.22	0.41	0.22
Controls								
Male	0	1	0.52					
Age youngest child	0	4	2.06	1.27	2.17	1.27	1.96	1.26
Supervisor is male	0	1	0.63		0.51		0.75	
Supervisor has a child	0	1	0.53		0.47		0.59	
Sector								
Financial services			0.17		0.20		0.14	
Health care			0.17		0.26		0.08	
Higher education			0.16		0.19		0.13	
Manufacturing			0.24		0.17		0.29	
Telecommunications			0.12		0.08		0.15	
Transportation			0.15		0.10		0.19	
Country								
Bulgaria			0.11		0.13		0.09	
Finland			0.06		0.05		0.07	
Germany			0.06		0.07		0.05	
Hungary			0.08		0.05		0.10	
Netherlands			0.26		0.29		0.23	
Portugal			0.16		0.18		0.15	
Spain			0.10		0.09		0.12	
Sweden			0.11		0.08		0.13	
UK			0.06		0.06		0.06	
N			1,207		583		624	

Note
Means and standard deviations reported using the non-imputed dataset.

Analytical strategy

All measures were recoded to range from 0–1 to ease interpretation. We used linear probability models with clustered standard errors to predict the probability of using parental leave. Linear probability models constitute the use of a regular ordinary least squares (OLS) regression for predicting a dichotomous variable. As set out by Hellevik (2009) this is an acceptable alternative to using a logistic regression as long as the dependent variable is not too skewed. Linear probability models have the additional advantage of easier interpretation (Hellevik, 2009). Results from a linear probability model can be interpreted as the increase in probability of the dependent variable being 1 (i.e., one uses leave) as the independent variable changes from 0 to 1. In other words, if, for example, the use by a manager has a coefficient of 0.20, this means that people with a manager who used parental leave are 20 percent more likely to use parental leave than people with a manger who did not use parental leave. As a robustness check we also ran logistic regression models, which led to the same results.

In addition, we used clustered standard errors on the organization-level to account for the fact that our observations are not independent, as employees are nested within organizations. Additional analyses were run where we included a multilevel model, which led to similar results. It was not possible to use clustered standard errors on the department-level – or a multilevel model which includes both the department- and the organization-level – as too few people per department are included in our selected sample (i.e., too few people had a child within the past four years).

Results

Figure 5.5 shows the increase in one's probability of using leave, both with and without country and sector fixed effects. Starting at the results without country and sector controls, we see a positive significant effect of the two objective measurements of organizational support, namely, use of parental leave by colleagues and use of parental leave by one's manager. This indicates that when an employee's colleagues have used leave, (s)he is 21 percent more likely to have used parental leave as well. Similarly, when an employee's manager has used leave, the probability that the employee uses leave increases by 20 percent. No significant effect of the subjective support variables (perceived cultural and managerial support), organizational characteristics (size, public sector, and proportion of women), or gender was found.

Sector and country fixed effects

As can be seen in Figure 5.5, the effects of both collegial and managerial use of parental leave are fully explained by the inclusion of country dummies. This probably stems from the fact that there are vast policy and cultural variations between countries, which can explain a respondent's own use of parental leave,

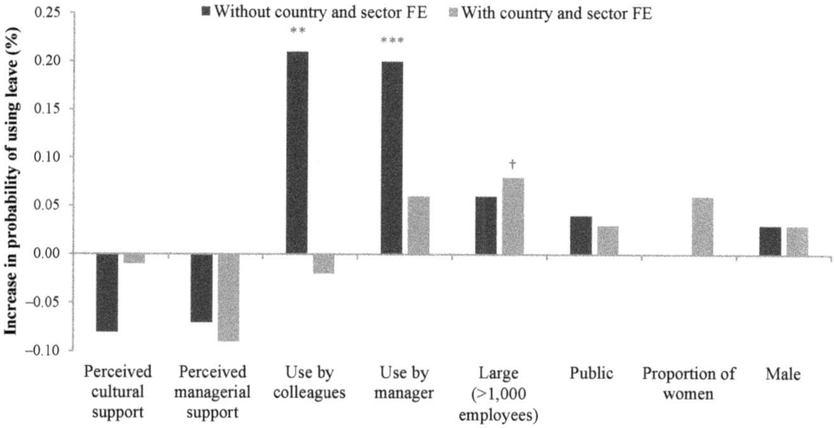

Figure 5.5 Probabilities of using leave without and with sector and country fixed-effects.

Notes
$N = 1207$.
Estimates based on linear probability model with clustered standard errors for the organization.
Control variables: age youngest child, gender manager, whether manager has children.
† $p < 0.10$, * $p < 0.05$, ** $p < 0.01$, *** $p < 0.001$ (2-sided tests).

collegial use, and managerial use – after all, in some countries it is either very common or very uncommon to use leave. When we include country and sector dummies, we do find an effect of the size of the organization, indicating that employees in a larger organization have an 8 percent higher probability of using leave than employees in a smaller organization, which supports Hypothesis 2a. No support was found for Hypothesis 1a and Hypothesis 1b, regarding supportive organizational culture and managerial support, nor for Hypothesis 2b and Hypothesis 2c regarding organizations in the public sector or with a higher proportion of women.

When we include country and sector fixed effects separately, we see that the change in the effects of the independent variables results from the inclusion of country dummies, but that no such change occurs when only sector dummies are included. Country differences contribute significantly to the probability of using parental leave, while sector does not. For this reason, we will explore country differences further in the sensitivity analyses.

Gender differences

Based on Figure 5.5 we rejected the hypothesis that the use of parental leave would be higher among women than among men (Hypothesis 3a). We want to further test whether the importance of the independent variables is different for men and for women, as hypothesized in Hypothesis 3b and Hypothesis 3c. Figure 5.6 shows the same model as Figure 5.5 with sector and country fixed

Figure 5.6 Probabilities of using leave, separately for women and men.

Notes

N women = 624, *N* men = 583.

Estimates based on linear probability model with clustered standard errors for the organization.

Control variables: age youngest child, gender manager, whether manager has a child, sector, country.

† $p<0.10$, * $p<0.05$, ** $p<0.01$, *** $p<0.001$ (2-sided).

⁀ indicates that the estimates significantly differ between women and men.

effects, but this time conducted separately for men and women. Starting with women, we see that none of the included variables affect women's parental leave use. For men, we see that three variables relate to their parental leave use, namely, perceived managerial support, use of leave by the manager, and the proportion of women in the organization. It should be noted, however, that perceived managerial support relates *negatively* to male parental leave use (-23 percent), while we expected this to have a positive effect. The other two effects are in the expected direction, i.e., men are 11 percent more likely to use parental leave if their manager did so as well, and 24 percent more likely to use parental leave if they work in an organization with a higher proportion of women. However, when we test the difference between the effects for men and for women, we see that only the effect of proportion of women in the organization is significantly different for men and for women. This is not the case for perceived managerial support and use by manager. Therefore, we reject Hypothesis 3b, as we find that for none of the organizational support variables is there evidence that they have a greater effect on the utilization of parental leave for men than for women. We partially reject Hypothesis 3c, as we find only for one organizational characteristic – the proportion of women – a stronger effect for men than for women, but no difference for organization size and public sector.

Sensitivity analyses

In order to better understand the effect that was found of size of the organization, organizational size was included in a number of ways to see if the effect was linear, quadratic (i.e., first increases and then decreases or vice versa), or occurred at different cut-off points than the one currently included (1,000 employees or more). No linear or quadratic effect was found. When including different categories, we see that the effect really occurs among the largest category compared to smaller categories, indicating that (as is theoretically expected) parental leave use is higher in really large organizations than in smaller organizations, rather than that it linearly increases as organizations become larger.

Additional country analyses

Previously, we saw that including country fixed effects substantially changed our results, and that there were large significant effects of the country dummies. This suggests that the prevalence of using parental leave differs strongly between countries, and that these country differences are of greater importance than most organizational factors or sector differences. Although we were not able to conduct analyses separately per country, we did conduct a jackknife procedure (i.e., exclude each country in turn), as well as clustered analyses for countries that were similar in the length of time or level of pay offered for parental leave. These show quite similar results: we find an effect of size of the organization. Although this effect sometimes falls short of conventional statistical significance, it is always in the same direction and point estimates are comparable in size. When we cluster countries based on the duration of the leave, we have two groups: countries with relatively long leave (Bulgaria, Finland, Germany, Hungary, Spain, and Sweden), and countries with relatively short leave periods (the Netherlands, Portugal, and the UK). We find no effects in either group. When we cluster countries based on level of pay for parental leave, we have, on the one hand, countries where leave is substantially paid (Bulgaria, Finland, Germany, Hungary, and Sweden) and, on the other hand, countries where parental leave is (largely) unpaid (the Netherlands, Portugal, Spain, and the UK). It is notable that we find two effects in the countries where leave is largely paid: a negative effect of perceived managerial support (25 percent) and a positive effect of organization size (15 percent), while no effects are found in the lesser-paying countries (though it should be noted that the difference between the two clusters is only statistically significant for organization size). Based on this, we would cautiously suggest that organizational factors are of greater importance for parental leave use in countries where parental leave is relatively well paid than in countries where it is not.

Discussion

In this chapter we examined how far organizations relate to the utilization of parental leave, and whether this differed for men and women. The ESWS, with its multi-country and multi-organization design, allowed us to be the first to make a large-scale, systematic study of the relationship between organizations and work–family policy use. In doing so we combined two ways of looking at organizations: the family-supportiveness of their organizational culture, and by treating them as actors that make strategic choices to invest in policies. We found few systematic effects of organizations on employees parental leave use over and above the variation in institutional settings. Only one, out of a total of seven organizational aspects that were included, was shown to be related to leave utilization: namely, the size of the organization. No gender differences were found in parental leave use, but we did find some variation in how organizational factors affect the use of parental leave between men and women.

Our most important finding is that organizational aspects played a smaller role than we expected, and that much of the variation is explained by country differences. On the one hand, this may perhaps seem unsurprising: considering the wide array of variations in country-level parental leave provisions and cultural norms surrounding leave utilization, it is to be expected that leave utilization varies strongly between countries. On the other hand, numerous qualitative and small-scale quantitative studies have found that parents use of work–family policies is affected by organizational factors, especially organizational support (e.g., Allen, 2001; Blair-Loy & Wharton, 2002; Den Dulk & Peper, 2007; Haas et al., 2002; McDonald et al., 2005; Smith & Gardner, 2007; Thompson et al., 1999). This had led us to expect that even in varying contextual settings the effect of certain organizational factors would function similarly; i.e., while in some countries it might be more or less common to use work–family policies, there will always be some people for whom this decision is not clear-cut, and whose decision is influenced by the organizational context. This, in our study, did not prove to be the case. Although sample-size restrictions prevented us from conducting in-depth country comparative analyses, our results suggest that organizational aspects might only be relevant in countries where parental leave use is relatively well paid. We maintain that this would theoretically make sense: only once employees have the (financial) freedom to choose between using and not using parental leave, do organizational aspects become important. Previous research has also shown that when income replacement of parental leave is low, employees are less likely to use leave but find other alternatives instead, such as dropping out of employment or switching to part-time work (Brinton & Mun, 2016; Pettigrew, 2014).

While country variations proved most important, we still found evidence that one organizational characteristic relates to parental leave use: organization size. Employees in larger organizations were more likely to use parental leave than employees in smaller organizations. This can be explained through the strategic choices made by larger organizations in comparison to smaller ones.

According to institutional theory, larger organizations face more societal pressures than smaller organizations, and wish to obtain social legitimacy through the adoption of additional work–family policies or the implementation of statutory work–family policies (DiMaggio & Powell, 1983; Goodstein, 1994). Additionally, business-case argumentation maintains that larger organizations would be more likely to adopt and implement work–family policies because it is cheaper for them to do so than smaller organizations – for example, because it is easier to redistribute work to other employees, or to hire temporary replacements (Bygren & Duvander, 2006; Haas & Hwang, 2009). Simultaneously, organizations would deem these policies to have benefits such as the attraction and retention of employees, and higher productivity (Been, 2015; Den Dulk, 2001; Kossek & Friede, 2006; Wheatley, 2017). It is notable, however, that we do not find a similar effect for public organizations and organizations with a greater proportion of women, although these are theoretically expected to experience similar institutional pressures as large organizations. This might suggest that the observed effect for large organizations can be explained by business-case considerations rather than institutional pressures: the costs of making work–family policies available are lower for large organizations, but are not necessarily lower for public organizations or for those with a large proportion of women. Additionally, large organizations might be particularly focused on attracting desirable employees, which is not necessarily the case for public organizations or those with a large proportion of women. Thus, large organizations would attach greater value to the benefits of having work–family policies, which extends to higher levels of policy utilization.

Turning to gender differences, we found no significant difference between men and women's likelihood of using parental leave, while we know that this is the case in reality (European Parliament, 2015; Moss, 2011). This probably stems from our measure, which captures whether people used parental leave *at all*, but does not distinguish between the length of the leave. Moreover, as we sampled people in their workplace, there might be a selection effect where many young mothers who had used parental leave were absent from our sample, because they were not at work during the time of the survey. This is less likely to be an issue for men, who tend to take shorter leave (OECD, 2016).

We do find that organizations affect the utilization decisions of men, but not of women. This suggests that the organizational context is not only *more* influential for men's utilization decisions than for women's, but that it hardly plays a role for women at all. Possibly, this stems from the fact that gender norms prescribe that men are primarily responsible for work and women for family (Acker, 1990; Kanji & Samuel, 2017; Munn & Greer, 2015). This means that it is often *expected* that women will be active caregivers, by using work–family policies or perhaps even dropping out of employment altogether. Men, on the other hand, are workers first, and base the extent of their involvement at home partially on pressures from the organizational context at work.

For men, we found an effect of perceived managerial support, use of leave by manager, and proportion of women in the organization. It should particularly be noted that, contrary to what we expected, having a manager who is supportive related to men using *less* rather than more parental leave. This might stem from the fact that we measure *general* support for work–family issues, rather than specific support for parental leave use (Den Dulk, Peper, Kanjuo Mrčela, & Ignjatović, 2016). This might entail that male employees with supportive managers are more able to accommodate work and family without needing to use formal arrangements, such as using parental leave. For women, this might function differently, because managers are more likely to accommodate men informally, while encouraging women to use formal arrangements that help them with childcare (Booth & Van Ours, 2009; Roeters & Craig, 2014).

Limitations and implications

Although this study makes some important contributions to the literature, there are at least three important limitations from which future research could learn. First, our results show the importance of studying in-depth country variations, but unfortunately we were not able to do this because of sample-size restrictions. These issues warrant further investigation, but the complexities in obtaining a multi-country dataset that includes large samples per country suggest that perhaps smaller studies that focus on one or a few countries may be a more realistic approach. Our findings suggest that utilization decisions function differently across European countries, and therefore we caution researchers about extrapolating the results regarding work–family policy use from one country to another.

Second, in this study we used a rather crude measure of parental leave, through which we could only dichotomously distinguish whether employees used any parental leave, and not include any information on the duration of the leave. This was done in order to ease comparing parental leave over countries, as the differences in national leave provisions substantially complicate comparing whether a certain period of leave constitutes long or short parental leave. However, the crudeness of our measure obviously prevented us from capturing the depth of variations in parental leave. Similarly, as mentioned above, the measure used for perceived support was not specific to support for parental leave. Using such a specific measure might lead to very different results (Den Dulk et al., 2016).

Third, we use cross-sectional multilevel organization data, which has the huge advantage of including information on employees, their managers, *and* the organization, but has the disadvantage of excluding people who were not present in the organization to be sampled, particularly women who were using parental leave at the time the survey was carried out.

Conclusion

All in all, this chapter shows that the influence of organizations on employees' parental leave use is limited – we only find this for organization size – and that, instead, country variations play a very large role. We therefore underline the importance of conducting country-specific research, and stress the importance of taking caution when extrapolating findings from one country to another in the field of work–family policy research – this might not function as universally as is sometimes assumed. Moreover, our findings indicate that organizations play a role in the utilization decisions of men but not in those of women, suggesting that while women are expected to use parental leave, men base the extent of their involvement at home partially on pressures from the organizational context at work. Although we were unable to conduct country-specific analyses, our findings suggest that organizational aspects are of greater importance for utilization decisions in countries where parental leave is (partially) paid than in countries where it is not, suggesting that organizational aspects come into play when the national conditions create a situation where people have the (financial) freedom to choose between using and not using parental leave.

Notes

1 For a notable exception see Bygren and Duvander (2006), who rely on Swedish register data regarding individuals and workplaces to predict fathers' parental leave use.
2 In this study we look specifically at parental leave, although we extrapolate from research on other work–family policies, such as paternity or maternity leave, part-time work, childcare support, and flexibility. Studies that look specifically into parental leave policies are scarce (Mulvaney, 2014), yet they provide good cases because parental leave policies are "employee serving" rather than "organization serving"; they are instigated at the request of the employee and do not directly serve the organization – in contrast to, for example, flexible working hours, which can also be used to make employees work flexible hours that suit the company. This makes it not clear-cut that organizations want to increase utilization (Leslie et al., 2012; Wheatley, 2017).
3 Note that Pasamar and Alegre (2015) also applied institutional theory to policy utilization, but they focus more on disentangling different types of external pressures and do not explicitly set out how these pressures would not only lead to adoption but also to utilization.

6 Which older workers participate in which personnel policies?

Jelle Lössbroek, Joop Schippers, Bram Lancee, and Stefan Szücs

Introduction

The workforce is aging in all Western countries, and governments throughout Europe aim to improve the sustainability of their economies by promoting the lengthening of working lives. Organizations employing older (50+) workers are central actors in this ambition, as they have a wide range of human resource (HR) policy options at their disposal to support prolonged working lives. The most frequently mentioned tool in this field is on-the-job training. However, a wide range of research indicates that older workers participate less often in on-the-job training compared to their younger colleagues, due to a combination of older workers' lower motivation to do so and employers' lower inclination to offer it (Arulampalam, Booth, & Bryan, 2004; Carmichael & Ercolani, 2014; Taylor & Urwin, 2001). Hence, this chapter analyses participation in two other types of arrangements that are used to support older workers: flexibility policies (such as the option to work from home) and phasing out arrangements (such as a reduced workload for older workers). Indeed, several studies suggest flexibility policies (Moen, Kojola, Kelly, & Karakaya, 2016; Shacklock & Brunetto, 2011) and phasing out measures (Göbel & Zwick, 2013) potentially contribute to the goal of prolonged working lives.[1]

Flexibility and phasing out policies are among those most frequently offered by organizations to their older personnel (Lössbroek, 2018). There have been several studies on the average level of participation of older workers in phasing out policies (e.g., Tros, 2010). However, little is known about which employees are most likely to use the phasing out measures that are available to them. The field on the use of flexibility policies is far more developed, but the argumentation is often strongly tied to childcare and career planning (Den Dulk & Peper, 2007; Dikkers et al., 2007; Kossek, Lautsch, & Eaton, 2006). Evidently, these considerations are less relevant for older workers than for the prime-age workers that are central to most of these studies. In order to understand the impact of personnel policies on prolonged working lives, it is essential to understand which older workers are covered and which are not. Additionally, a study on engagement of older workers has shown that phasing out arrangements may be beneficial for some workers, but may contribute to disengagement for others

(Bal, Kooij, & De Jong, 2013). To understand the relevance of older-age adaptation policies, and to enable organizations to reach older workers currently overlooked by their policies, it is vital to know the extent to which employability arrangements reach the workers who could benefit from them. Therefore, this chapter studies which older workers use which policies.

Participation may be influenced both by older workers and by their managers for a combination of two reasons. On the one hand, participation in personnel policies is known to be influenced by cost–benefit calculations (Carmichael & Ercolani, 2014), based on the extent to which a job is compatible with using certain personnel policies and an employee's age. On the other hand, participation may be influenced by the attitudes held by workers and managers, namely, gender role socialization (Courtenay, McCreary, & Merighi, 2002; Kristiansen, 1990) and agism. The central research question is thus: How is the participation of older workers in flexibility and phasing out policies influenced by cost–benefit considerations and attitudes?

The chapter contributes to our current knowledge in three ways. First, many organizations have implemented policies specific to older workers, such as semi-retirement and reduced workloads. A growing body of research has studied which organizations implement which older-age adaptation policies (Armstrong-Stassen & Cattaneo, 2010; Conen, Henkens, & Schippers, 2012; Lössbroek, Lancee, Van der Lippe, & Schippers, 2017; Principi, Fabbietti, & Lamura, 2015; Van Dalen, Henkens, & Wang, 2015). Yet, none of these studies also analyses the extent to which policies which have been implemented and are used by older workers. Second, the role of age in participation in personnel policies is usually studied in the context of a focus on training participation (Armstrong-Stassen & Cattaneo, 2010; Fleischmann, Koster, & Schippers, 2015; Martin, Dymock, Billett, & Johnson, 2014). This chapter analyzes the extent to which theories about training and older workers also apply to other arrangements. Third, we use data from the European Sustainable Workforce Survey (ESWS) (Van der Lippe et al., 2016) which allows us to pay attention to the fact that participation in personnel arrangements is strongly clustered within departments inside organizations, leading to more reliable results than purely employee-based surveys. Theoretically, this allows us to test hypotheses that recognize that participation in personnel arrangements is the result of an interplay between employers and older employees.

Flexibility and phasing out arrangements

Organizations can offer a variety of personnel policies that aim to improve the employability of their older workers. In the academic literature, studies tend to focus on training arrangements (Fouarge & Schils, 2009; Leppel, Brucker, & Cochran, 2012; Picchio & Van Ours, 2013). To further cater for the needs of older workers, organizations are known to offer other types of arrangements as well. Two of the most frequently offered types of personnel policies that may aid older workers in prolonging their working lives until an increased retirement age are flexibility and phasing out arrangements.

Flexibility policies give employees, old and young, greater responsibility and freedom in deciding when, where, and how they spend their working hours. This greater control enables employees to improve the relationship between work and private obligations and needs[2] and is found to contribute to greater work–life balance (Peters, Den Dulk, & Van der Lippe, 2009; Szücs, Drobnič, Den Dulk, & Verbiede, 2011). ESWS data includes three of the most common types of flexibility policies: freedom to decide when one's working day starts; freedom to work from home; and freedom to work during the commute and count this as working time.

In addition to arrangements that are in principle open to workers of all ages, many organizations have implemented policies that particularly target their older workforce, such as extra leave or a reduced workload for older workers. While a broad variety of policies has been documented, scholars have frequently distinguished two categories of policies, which have been called phasing out policies and activating policies (Bal et al., 2013; De Grip, Fouarge, & Montizaan, 2015; Kotiso & Lokhorst, 2009; Lössbroek et al., 2017; Van Dalen, Henkens, & Schippers, 2007; Ybema, Geuskens, & Oude Hengel, 2009). In this chapter, we study phasing out arrangements, which reduce the role older workers have within an organization and are built around making working life easier by lowering the demands placed on them; these have therefore been labeled "accommodating" or "comforting" policies (Perek-Białas & Turek, 2012; Van Dalen et al., 2015). Based on ESWS data, we study three phasing out polices: additional leave from work, lighter workload, and semi-retirement. These are among the most frequently implemented measures for older workers in Europe, particularly additional leave (Lössbroek, 2018), and are assessed at the employee level (unlike, for instance, a policy of mixed-age working teams).

Explaining older workers' participation in personnel policies

To understand participation in personnel policies, the perspectives of both the employer and the employee should be considered. Employers will expect less beneficial outcomes from policy participation if it is involuntary. Therefore, employers will not be eager to force employees to work during their commute or take extra leave (although this may to some extent depend on the measure). Employees have an active interest in maintaining good relations with their manager and may be persuaded to take the employer's preferences into account. They may be less eager to participate in arrangements if their manager disapproves of their doing so, even if they are formally entitled to participate. Hence, participation in a policy is assumed to signal mutual agreement. It has been found that implementation of *policies* for older workers is the result of an interplay between employers and employees (Armstrong-Stassen, 2008; Lössbroek et al., 2017). We believe this holds true for participation in implemented *arrangements* as well. Previous studies give empirical support to the theory that both managers' and employees' characteristics influence, for instance, (mostly) younger workers' participation in flexibility arrangements (Den Dulk & Peper, 2007; Dikkers et al., 2007) and older workers' participation in on-the-job training (Carmichael & Ercolani, 2014; Fleischmann & Koster, 2017; Lössbroek & Radl, 2018). This theoretical section studies four drivers of policy use, relying on arguments from both the employee's perspective and the manager's perspective. Two arguments are based on the costs and benefits that employees and employers derive from policy participation; these relate to employee age and the compatibility of the job with policy use. The final two arguments are attitudinal and based on the views that employees and employers may have regarding employee gender roles and managerial agism.

Employee age

The first characteristic that may influence the costs and benefits of participation is an employee's age. Although the sample of 50+ workers already comprises a selective subgroup of an organization's personnel, age differences are still expected to influence policy use. Although older workers are less likely to need flexibility for childcare than their younger peers, new reasons for a desire for flexibility arise. For instance, working from home may be less stressful for persons with lower stamina or health, and flexible working hours can be tailored to biorhythms to make working life more comfortable. Studies indeed show that older workers attach greater value to flexibility policies (Armstrong-Stassen & Ursel, 2009), that older workers in particular become more engaged when they can use the flexibility policies they prefer (Pitt-Catsouphes & Matz-Costa, 2008), and that the presence of flexibility policies can contribute to being able and willing to work longer (Shacklock & Brunetto, 2011). It comes as no surprise, then, that many organizations have implemented flexibility programs specifically for their older workers (Conen, Van Dalen, Henkens, & Schippers, 2011; Oude Mulders, Henkens, & Van Dalen, 2018; Van Dalen, Henkens, & Schippers, 2009, 2010a; Vidovićová, 2014; Žnidaršič & Dimovski, 2009). Therefore, older workers are, plausibly, interested in general flexibility policies as well. The reasons that many older workers appreciate flexibility are likely even stronger for 'older' older workers, as preferences tend to shift gradually over time rather than abruptly at the threshold of becoming 50 years of age.

A comparable trend is expected for phasing out arrangements. These policies are specifically designed to cater for older workers' needs. Phasing out arrangements accommodate the gradual shift from being a 'core worker' to eventual retirement. As retirement is closer for 'older' older workers than for those who have just passed the threshold of being 50+, these workers are more likely to start scaling down responsibilities and burdens. Such considerations are presumably reflected in managerial attitudes toward policy uptake: managers may more readily expect workers close to retirement age to use phasing out arrangements, contributing to more positive responses to requests to use them. Therefore, our first hypothesis is:

Hypothesis 1 Among 50+ workers, age is positively associated with the likelihood of using flexibility and phasing out policies.

Job compatibility

A second cost–benefits-based mechanism influencing the likelihood of using personnel policies is the extent to which these are compatible with one's job. Flexibility policies are highly dependent on the job tasks that employees perform, including characteristics such as physical activity, team interdependence, and managerial control. Physical presence at the workplace is not required for some jobs, but others are hard to perform from home. Additionally, in some teams, colleagues may be highly dependent on each other's work in jobs that involve close cooperation. In this case, the time and place of the job may in principle be flexible, but only for the team as a whole, e.g., starting later in the morning would only be possible if everyone else decided to do so as well. Finally, employees whose jobs are characterized by high levels of skill and professionalism are generally more trusted and less directly controlled by managers. If the (perceived) managerial need to monitor is lower, they will be more supportive toward workers desiring to use flexibility policies.[3] For these reasons, use of flexibility policies is hypothesized to be greater in jobs that are more compatible with such policies, characterized by higher educated workers, high occupational class, and a low degree of physical work.

In respect of participation in phasing out policies, we expect the opposite relationship. Compared to flexibility, phasing out policies rely less on the ambition to maintain a situation in which an older worker continues to perform all the current tasks. Instead, such policies may be implemented from the perspective that a more comfortable job can support working longer, at a slower pace (Lössbroek et al., 2017). This change may even increase productivity per hour even though the number of hours worked may be lower. This 'comfort' may be particularly appealing to workers whose work involves heavy physical or mentally demanding labor, who may want to reduce their workload and increase their recovery time through extra leave or partial retirement.

A cost–benefit analysis from the employer's perspective also leads us to expect a relationship between job characteristics and policy use. An important perspective within cost–benefit analyses is that of human capital, the dominant argument in the literature on employers' considerations concerning personnel policies (Carmichael & Ercolani, 2014). From this perspective, employers aim to maximize the value and applicability of the human capital of their staff. Generally, it is harder to replace workers who are higher educated and in a job of a high occupational class, than it is to replace workers who are low educated and in a job of low occupational class. Therefore, employers are more likely to (informally) support the use of flexibility by the former groups of workers, as they still perform the same job tasks, and less likely to support the use of phasing out, as it is harder to reallocate the tasks that a worker no longer performs to a colleague or to a new recruit. For all these reasons, our second hypothesis is:

> *Hypothesis 2* Among 50+ workers, higher educated, higher occupational class workers with less physical jobs are more likely to use flexibility policies and less likely to use phasing out policies.

Employee gender roles

Third, it may be expected that participation in these arrangements for older workers is associated with attitudes, such as the way workers are socialized into certain gender roles. Among older cohorts, in particular, traditional gender roles may be relatively influential in shaping behavior. In respect of flexibility arrangements, this concerns the still influential gender role that assigns women the primary responsibility for care-related and household tasks. Although the burden of child care plausibly wanes for women over the age of 50, this demographic group tends to become increasingly involved in providing informal care to parents, relatives, or friends. Compared to men, women, on average, spend more hours on informal care (Principi et al., 2014), and this unequal distribution of household tasks is perpetuated among older couples (Hank & Jürges, 2007). Moreover, the content of tasks differs: women more often perform tasks that are time-inflexible, such as cooking, whereas men more often perform tasks that are more time-flexible, such as financial administration (Shelton, 1990). Since gender roles contribute to greater private sphere responsibilities for older women, and flexibility policies are known to potentially reduce work–family conflict (De Sivatte & Guadamillas, 2013; Peters et al., 2009), women may have more to gain from flexibility arrangements. Conversely, men may have more to lose, as studies on gender roles indicate that men experience 'chronic presenteeism': a strong pressure to spend many hours at the workplace (Sheridan, 2004). Both older and younger men may feel that they should live up to these gender roles; indeed, previous studies indicate that men, particularly, are stigmatized and penalized for utilizing family leave (Rudman & Mescher, 2013) or flexibility policies (Vandello, Hettinger, Bosson, & Siddiqi, 2013). Therefore, we expect that compared to older men, older women will more often ask to make use of existing flexibility arrangements.

With regard to phasing out policies, the same mechanisms plausibly apply. Household production may also induce participation in certain arrangements that provide the employee with more time to attend to these tasks; a reduced workload may prevent overburdening at work, leaving more energy for private sphere activities. Additionally, the normative gender roles are expected to nudge older men into continued full-time work. This gives older women a greater incentive to apply for phasing out arrangements than older men. A counterargument is that, generally, the financial position of men is better that of women (Christofides, Polycarpou, & Vrachimis, 2013). To the extent that using phasing out policies may affect (future) wages, it is easier for older men to bear these costs than older women.

From the employer's perspective, ingrained gender attitudes possibly contribute to a more supportive attitude toward female use than toward male use. If managers are more likely to approve a request from women to use a certain personnel policy than from men, that would also support the expectation that women are more likely to use flexibility and phasing out policies. On balance, these arguments support the expectation of greater use among older women than among older men. Therefore, our third hypothesis is:

Hypothesis 3 Among 50+ workers, women are more likely to use flexibility and phasing out policies than men.

Employer's agism

Finally, managers may be driven by agist stereotypes in their behavior toward their employees. Studies on the use of flexibility policies for working parents suggest that managerial support influences uptake (Den Dulk & Peper, 2007) and agism plausibly influences the support experienced. Many studies indicate that employers predominantly hold negative agist stereotypes concerning older workers' motivation (Ng & Feldman, 2012) and productivity (Conen et al., 2012; Van Dalen, Henkens, & Schippers, 2010b). To some extent, negative agist stereotypes can be counterbalanced by positive agist stereotypes, such as those that maintain that older workers score higher on interpersonal skills, patience, and commitment (Loretto & White, 2006). However, particularly for employees in non-managerial positions, negative stereotypes tend to be dominant. Previous studies indicate that employer agism contributes to a disadvantaged position for older workers in various aspects of HR, including job applications (Büsch, Dahl, & Dittrich, 2009; Oude Mulders, Henkens, Liu, Schippers, & Wang, 2018; Taylor & Walker, 1998), training availability (Gray & McGregor, 2003; Lössbroek & Radl, 2018; Taylor & Walker, 1998), and promotion opportunities (Taylor & Walker, 1998).

Considering the central role of managers in these arrangements, it is plausible that managerial agism also influences participation in flexibility and phasing out arrangements. This builds on the previous argument that managers prefer phasing out rather than flexibility policies for workers who are less central to the organization. In the same way, it may be expected that managers are less likely to promote these arrangements among older workers if they hold negative, agist ideas about them. For phasing out arrangements, the influence of agism is plausibly different. If a manager thinks of an older worker as someone about to retire rather than as someone who is a worker like any other worker, this is rather compatible with arrangements that gradually phase a worker out from work and into retirement. Hence, our final hypothesis is:

> *Hypothesis 4* Among 50+ workers, use of flexibility policies is less likely and use of phasing out policies is more likely for workers with more agist managers.

Data and methods

Operationalization

This chapter uses data from the ESWS (Van der Lippe et al., 2016). The design and fieldwork for the data collection can be found in Chapter 3. Below, the operationalization of each variable used in this chapter is discussed. The precise phrasing of each question and the descriptive statistics are presented in Table 6.1.

For the dependent variables, participation is measured by asking whether a certain policy was available to the respondent and, if so, whether they had or had not used it in the past 12 months. For both flexibility and phasing out, these items were combined into a single variable. For flexibility, if a respondent used one or more flexibility policies (working from home, working during their commute, deciding their own working times), they scored 1; if a respondent had not used any flexibility policies, they scored 0; if no flexibility policies were offered by their organization, they were coded as 'missing.' The same procedure was used for phasing out policies (extra leave, reduced workload, partial retirement).

In respect of employee gender, a question was asked whether a respondent was female (1) or male (0); employee age was asked in years, and we followed common practice by placing the threshold for older workers at age 50. To capture job compatibility, three characteristics were included: the extent to which the job involves physical activity, ranging from (almost) never (0) to (almost) always (4); educational attainment, which was recoded into years of education; and proxies potential for flexibility and occupational class, which were generated by recoding answers to the open-ended question of what occupation the employee had into the European Socio-economic Classification (ESeC) (Rose & Harrison, 2007). Manager agism was proxied by asking managers the extent to which they agreed or disagreed that older workers are biding their time until retirement, a measure that has been used to predict older workers' training participation (Lössbroek & Radl, 2018).

We controlled for employee health, working hours, tenure period, hours of household production, manager age, manager gender, and whether the employee works for a 'core' or a 'supporting' department. Full descriptive statistics and question phrasing can be found in Table 6.1.

Table 6.1 Descriptive statistics

	mean	*std.*	*min*	*max*
Dependent variables				
Flexibility policies				
Decide working hours	0.40		0	1
Work from home	0.26		0	1
Work during commute	0.10		0	1
Use of flexibility	0.49		0	1
Phasing out policies				
Additional leave	0.54		0	1
Lighter workload	0.37		0	1
Semi-retirement	0.13		0	1
Use of phasing out	0.43		0	1
Independent variables (employee)				
Age	55.74	4.26	50	77
Female	0.54		0	1
Years of education	12.97	3.24	3	21
Physical job	2.24	1.42	0	4
Occupation				
Routine worker	0.09		0	1
Higher salariat	0.23		0	1
Lower salariat	0.27		0	1
Intermediate occupations	0.17		0	1
Higher blue collar	0.06		0	1
Lower sales and service	0.09		0	1
Skilled workers	0.04		0	1
Working hours	36.43	8.23	3	80
Tenure	18.44	12.14	0.08	52
Supervisory position	0.20	0.40	0	1
Health	2.76	0.75	0	4
Immigrant	0.07		0	1
Household hours	24.55	19.85	0	80
Employment contract type				
Permanent contract	0.95		0	1
Fixed-term contract	0.04		0	1
Other type	0.01		0	1
Independent variables (manager)				
Managerial ageism	1.37	1.01	0	4
Manager age	48.90	8.12	25	71
Manager is female	0.37		0	1
Supporting department	0.26		0	1

Notes
N = 2,202.
Mean scores of individual policy participation refer to the subsample of organizations offering the policy.

Estimation strategy

To estimate which older workers are most likely to participate in older-age adaptation policies, multilevel regression is used. Evidently, the availability of the arrangements discussed in this chapter is strongly dependent on organizational characteristics. Additionally, among organizations which offer certain arrangements, participation is still strongly clustered. Intraclass correlations are >0.10 for both flexibility and phasing out use, at both the organization and the department level. Therefore, we use a three-level regression analysis with mixed effects at the organization and department level. As there seems to be no consensus about the optimal choice between linear probability models and logistic regressions for binary dependent variables with non-extreme probabilities (Hellevik, 2009), both approaches are used.

Results

In Table 6.2, the three-level regressions are displayed for the use of flexibility and phasing out policies.

There are no indications of the expected higher female participation in flexibility or phasing out policies. Surprisingly, being female even has a significant negative effect on the use of flexibility policies, although this is only significant in the linear probability model. This counterintuitive finding for flexibility policies may be due to a 'survivor bias': older women, on average, tend to retire earlier than older men. Older women who wish to reduce work strain or who struggle to combine work with giving informal care may be more likely to retire early and drop out of the workforce than an older man in the same situation. This could generate higher participation in flexibility options among older male workers. There is no effect of gender on the use of phasing out policies. Hypothesis 1 is rejected for both policies.

Age has no effect on the use of flexibility measures. In respect of the use of phasing out policies, however, age has a robust positive effect. As expected, phasing out is more popular among 'older' older workers. Hypothesis 2 is rejected for flexibility and supported for phasing out.

Job characteristics have the expected influence on the use of flexibility policies: uptake is greater among workers who are higher educated and have a job in a higher occupational class. The extent to which the job involves physical work is not significant for flexibility. It is significant in the expected direction for phasing out: the more physical the work someone does, the more likely they are to use phasing out measures. However, educational attainment and occupational class of the job do not influence uptake of phasing out. Therefore, Hypothesis 3 is supported for flexibility and rejected for phasing out.

Finally, the coefficients for managerial agism are in the expected direction, but not significant for either policy. Models with fewer control variables show a significant positive effect on phasing out, but this is not robust. Hence, Hypothesis 4 is rejected for both flexibility and phasing out.

Table 6.2 Coefficients from mixed-effects linear probability models and logistic regression predicting use of flexibility and phasing out policies

	Flexibility	*Flexibility*	*Phasing out*	*Phasing out*
	Logistic	*LPM*	*Logistic*	*LPM*
Female	–0.30	–0.05*	0.03	0.00
Age	–0.03	–0.00	0.13***	0.02***
Physical job	–0.09	–0.01	0.22**	0.004**
Years of education	0.14***	0.02***	0.01	0.00
Occupation (ref. = routine workers)				
Higher salariat	1.81***	0.26***	0.54	0.10
Lower salariat	1.02***	0.16***	0.70	0.13
Intermediate occupations	1.28***	0.19***	0.58	0.11
Higher grade blue collar	0.75*	0.11*	1.12*	0.22*
Lower sales and service	0.73*	0.10*	0.62	0.12
Skilled workers	–0.24	–0.00	0.83	0.17
Managerial ageism	–0.10	–0.02	0.17	0.03
Working hours	–0.01	–0.00	0.01	0.00
Hours of household work	0.00	0.00	–0.00	–0.00
Supervisory position	0.48*	0.06*	–0.47	–0.08
Health	0.10	0.01	–0.19	–0.04
Immigrant	0.27	0.04	–0.66	–0.12
Employment type (ref. = permanent contract)				
Temporary contract	0.25	0.02	0.29	0.06
Other contract	–0.19	–0.01	–1.86*	–0.37*
Tenure	–0.01	–0.00	–0.01	–0.00
Manager age	–0.00	–0.00	–0.01	–0.00
Manager is female	–0.47*	–0.07*	–0.32	–0.06
Supporting department	0.95***	0.14***	0.04	0.01
Constant	–0.81	0.41*	–7.77***	–1.03***
N employee	2,202	2,202	929	929
N department	479	479	285	285
N organization	214	214	148	148

Note
* $p < 0.05$, ** $p < 0.01$, *** $p < 0.001$ (2-sided).

Discussion and conclusion

It is widely recognized that personnel policies potentially support older (50+) workers in prolonging their working lives (Göbel & Zwick, 2013; Moen et al., 2016; Shacklock & Brunetto, 2011). However, a substantial proportion of older workers does not use these policies, even in organizations that implement them. Moreover, the usefulness of such policies depends in part on which older workers are using them (Bal et al., 2013). Therefore, this chapter analyzed which older workers participate in two of the most frequently offered types of policies: flexibility and phasing out policies. Using the employee and employer characteristics available in the ESWS data, we tested two cost–benefit considerations, related to employee age and job compatibility, and two attitudinal considerations, related to gender roles and managerial agism.

We found that employers' cost–benefit considerations are more important than the attitudinal considerations in explaining policy participation. Most predictably, the phasing out policies implemented for older workers are most frequently used by 'older' older workers. It should be noted that our findings reflect the situation of employees working in organizations that offer particular arrangements, and should be generalized with caution. For instance, age did not influence participation in flexibility arrangements in our study, and additional analyses comparing workers aged 50+ to those aged 49 or under also showed comparable participation rates. However, these within-organization comparable rates obscure the fact that older workers are over-represented in organizations that do not offer any flexibility arrangements. Moreover, as expected, we found that high-end older workers more frequently use flexibility policies. In respect of more physical jobs, we expected that phasing out would be more likely, which is indeed the case.

Concerning the 'attitudinal' theoretical framework, neither managerial agism nor gender roles had the expected influence on policy participation. Managerial agism did not influence participation in any policy. Possibly, agist managers could consider participation in these arrangements as a double-edged sword: on the one hand, participation reduces the role of older workers in the organization if they work fewer hours and are less often present at the workplace. On the other hand, these arrangements potentially delay retirement. Managers with agist attitudes could plausibly accept either of these two arguments, which may, overall, cancel each other out. A comparable argument has been made in a study about implementation of phasing out measures: managerial age norms strongly influenced implementation of activating arrangements, but not of phasing out arrangements (Lössbroek et al., 2017).

The expected higher female participation in flexibility and phasing out measures was not found; older women may even use flexibility policies less often than older men. A study on Dutch older workers found that older men experienced more workplace flexibility than older women, because they worked more hours, were more highly educated, and worked in different occupations in different sectors, compared to older women (Damman & Henkens, 2018). Models without these variables indeed show wider gender differences, thus supporting this argument. However, as presented in our model, some differences remain. This could be the result of selection into labor market exit (a 'survivor bias'): some workers are more likely to continue working until the statutory pension age than others. It is possible that 50+ women with the greatest informal care burden have already left the labor market, which could explain the lack of support for our expectations regarding this group. Also, it should be noted that because older women more often ask for policies that can improve their work–life balance, this does not necessarily mean that older men do not need these policies as well. To some extent, the conclusions tacitly support the argument that participation is most likely in situations of mutual agreement between employer and employee. The more frequent use of phasing out by 'older' older workers and flexibility use by more high-end workers was hypothesized based on both employer and employee considerations. For the hypothesis on gender difference in the use of phasing out policies, employers' gender attitudes would suggest more frequent use by women, whereas older workers' cost-benefit considerations would suggest that the financial costs could more easily be borne by older men. However, alternative explanations cannot be ruled out.

In addition to the previously mentioned selection issue, two other limitations of this study should be kept in mind. The data is cross-sectional rather than longitudinal, which means that participation in certain arrangements could, in theory, influence other employee characteristics. Fortunately, it is highly unlikely that participation in specific personnel policies would influence employee gender, level of education, or agist attitudes that their manager may have. Occupational class could in theory be influenced by participating in the arrangements studied here, but this generally stabilizes before an employee turns 50. Nevertheless, it would be interesting to replicate this study using longitudinal data. Lastly, the availability of arrangements varied substantially between organizations, so the sample was not the same for different subsamples of employees. Future researchers are invited to gather data including a sufficiently large number of organizations that offer (nearly) all arrangements, in order to be able to assess the extent to which participation in the various arrangements substitutes or complements each other. This would also involve taking into account that job hunters may base their decisions on where to work partially on an organization's personnel policies.

The lack of importance of managerial agism appears to be hopeful: even if managers hold discriminatory ideas about older workers, they still participate in different types of arrangements. The group of older workers with incompatible jobs, however, appear to be more restricted in their usage of flexibility measures. To the extent that this is driven by employers' desire to spend limited HR budgets on the most valuable employees, governments could explore options that would make spending HR budgets on more peripheral workers more attractive. It should be emphasized that job compatibility with certain policies is not 'fixed' and may change over time. Technological changes have had a major impact on both occupations themselves and the possibilities of working flexibly with regard to time and place, and will probably continue to expand the options available to combine work with the use of desired personnel policies. Finally, the role of gender socialization in combining work with informal caregiving may be hard to change. Yet, the need to combine these two, for both older men and women, is increasing due to the shift from a demographic pyramid to a demographic pillar and growing labor participation among female older workers. It is therefore in the interests of older workers, employers, and governments to continuously develop personnel policies and to support the use of these options.

Notes

1 We emphasize that the contribution is potential rather than automatic, as other studies find preferred or actual retirement age is not affected by participation in flexibility policies (Van Solinge & Henkens, 2014) or phasing out policies (Hermansen, 2015; Midtsundstad, Hermansen, & Nielsen, 2012; Van Solinge & Henkens, 2014).
2 These include both social duties, such as informal care for elderly parents or relatives, and health-related needs, such as working at times that match one's biorhythm.
3 Technology could reduce the complications, such as through digital monitoring or an administrative system through which workers with comparable skills can swap working hours (e.g., Intus, www.intus.nl/online-ruilen). Still, we expect that employees and employers prefer policy use with as few complications as possible.

7 Worksite health promotion in European organizations

Availability according to employers and employees

Anne van der Put and Jornt Mandemakers

Introduction

Owing to the health implications of an aging workforce and sedentary work, a growing number of organizations invest in the health of their employees in the form of offering worksite health promotion (WHP) (Goetzel & Ozminkowski, 2008). For example, organizations can provide employees access to onsite fitness facilities, make financial contributions towards gym membership, and offer healthier catering options on the canteen menu. Previous studies suggest that employees benefit from WHP: they are more physically active (Conn, Hafdahl, Cooper, Brown, & Lusk, 2009) and have healthier diets (Maes et al., 2012), lower weight (Anderson et al., 2009) and better health in general (Rongen, Robroek, Van Lenthe, & Burdorf, 2013). Employers stand to benefit as well: WHP has been associated with increased productivity (Goetzel & Ozminkowski, 2008) and decreased absenteeism (Parks & Steelman, 2008). Furthermore, employers who offer WHP are seen to take social responsibility seriously by caring about their employees (Nöhammer, Stummer, & Schusterschitz, 2014). Finally, WHP has the potential to narrow existing socio-economic differences in health in Europe (Huijts et al., 2017; Mackenbach et al., 2017). People spend a large part of their lives at work, making it possible to involve less resourceful workers who participate little in society outside of work. However, if access to WHP is limited to higher echelons of the working population, it could also widen socio-economic differences.

The benefits of WHP can only be reaped when employees make use of WHP, but average participation hovers around 30–50 percent of employees and rates of WHP participation vary widely between workplaces; from almost zero to almost maximum participation (Bull, Gillette, Glasgow, & Estabrooks, 2003; Robroek, Van Lenthe, Van Empelen, & Burdorf, 2009). WHP participation depends on the extent to which employees know about WHP availability at their workplace and on the match between actual workplace implementation of WHP and the demands of employees. Employee perceptions are crucial for WHP participation (Grawitch, Gottschalk, & Munz, 2006). When employees do not know WHP is available or deem the offer to be inadequate, they will not make use of it; yet little is known about the factors that determine whether employees perceive their organization to offer (adequate) WHP (Kilpatrick, Blizzard, Sanderson, Teale, & Venn, 2015). In our study we bridge this gap in the literature by studying both organizational reports of WHP provision and employee perceptions of availability.

We investigate both WHP availability according to organizational reports and employees' perceptions thereof using the European Sustainable Workforce Survey (ESWS). We first explore the European organizational landscape in terms of four WHP interventions: healthy nutrition, sports facilities, ergonomic facilities and health checks. These four types of WHP cover the broad spectrum of possible interventions by employers to improve employee health, as they differ in whether they directly prevent the onset of ill health or contribute to an earlier detection of potential health problems. Also, the extent of intrusion in employee day-to-day (work) lives differs between these forms of WHP, as does the timeframe of their (health) consequences (McEachan, Lawton, & Conner, 2010). Finally, healthy nutrition and ergonomic facilities can be considered as environmental strategies towards health promotion, meaning that employees do not need to consciously decide to make use of them and they are generally available across the organization as a whole (Engbers, Van Poppel, Chin, Paw, & Van Mechelen, 2005).

In the second part of this chapter, we study which organizational and employee factors contribute to employees' perceived availability of these four WHP interventions. We take both employee characteristics and the role of the organizational context into account. Most studies of WHP are limited to a single organization or a few organizations from one country and/or sector (Bull et al., 2003), which makes it hard to investigate the organizational context. Moreover, very little is known about European patterns in WHP availability as most studies have been carried out in the US (Fielding & Piserchia, 1989; Magnavita et al., 2017). Unlike in the US, universal health care is available in Europe and so WHP complements the provisions of the existing health-care system. European countries differ in health-related lifestyle issues such as smoking and obesity levels (Huijts et al., 2017) and health legislation (Eikemo, Bambra, Huijts, & Fitzgerald, 2017), which may affect whether companies implement WHP. The European context therefore offers ample variation in factors that may affect WHP availability and employee perceptions.

We first examine country and sectoral differences in organizational WHP provision. Little is known about WHP in Europe given that it is not a statutory requirement of occupational health and safety management (European Agency for Safety and Health at Work, 2015). To our knowledge there are no representative datasets of organizations in Europe that cover WHP. The European Working Condition surveys do contain information on health and safety standards and occupational hazards but do not inquire about the existence of organizational WHP (Eurofound, 2017c). The ESWS is not representative but it does include 259 organizations across 6 sectors in 9 countries and can thus give a first impression of the level and variation in WHP availability in these sectors. It should be noted that various sectors that face high health risks (such as retail and hospitality) are unfortunately not covered by the ESWS, so we continue to lack information regarding WHP provision in these sectors. We map availability according to both human resource (HR) managers and employee perceptions. Various organizational studies have pointed to the discrepancy between organizational and employee reports in the availability of HR practices (McCleary et al., 2017; Wright & Nishii, 2007), and we show that this is also the case with regard to WHP.

Employees cannot benefit from WHP if they are not aware of its existence, but neither can organizations. In the second part of this chapter we examine employee perceptions of the availability of the four WHP arrangements in the subset of organizations that offer WHP. Perceptions of availability indicate employee awareness of certain policies, but they also indicate how successful the implementation of a certain health policy by organizations is. In cases where employees perceive that WHP is not available, the policy does not reach them and possible beneficial effects are called into question. So, it is important to take a detailed look at employee perspectives in organizations that claim to offer WHP.

We apply information theory and motivation theory to explain variations in employee perceptions of WHP availability. In line with research on other employee-friendly benefits such as pension plans (Mastin, 1998) and work–family policies (Prottas, Thompson, Kopelman, & Jahn, 2007), we argue that employees are more likely to report WHP to be available when the costs of acquiring this information are lower and the information is useful to them. In addition, employee perceptions may also signal the extent to which organizational policies and/or implementation of policies match employees' values (Rothbard, Phillips, & Dumas, 2005).

Background: worksite health promotion in Europe

Within the European union, there is no statutory WHP requirement. Statutory requirements with regard to Occupational Health and Safety (OHS) exist, but this mainly concerns worker protection and the prevention of occupational risks (European Agency for Safety and Health at Work, 2015). Although health promotion is covered by OHS, organizations in European countries are not required or bound to implement health arrangements (Verra, Benzerga, Jiao, & Ruggeri, 2019). The few existing studies show that organizations mainly offer arrangements targeted towards nutrition and physical activity (European Agency for Safety and Health at Work, 2015) with some notable differences between European countries. Finnish establishments offer the most WHP (European Agency for Safety and Health at Work, 2015; European Network for Workplace Health Promotion, 2009), and Central and Eastern European organizations tend to invest less in WHP than Western European ones (Magnavita et al., 2017). Some countries have developed an extensive strategy for promoting employee health subsidized by the government (e.g., the Netherlands), while others have less funding available for health promotion (e.g., Bulgaria) as a result of the economic crisis (Magnavita et al., 2017). In certain countries national governments have developed nationwide policies that require action from organizations to promote healthy lifestyles at work (e.g., the UK, Germany and the Nordic countries), but others (e.g., Portugal and Hungary) have not (Verra et al., 2019).

Employee perceptions of WHP availability: theory and hypotheses

Beyond making WHP arrangements formally available, the extent to which employees perceive these arrangements to be available is crucial for the uptake and success of WHP for both employees and the organization. Employee perceptions of availability may also indicate how well WHP policies are implemented in the workplace, which remains hidden if one only analyzes the formal availability of policies.

Previous studies explaining employee perceptions of HR practices have used information theory and motivation theory (Prottas et al., 2007).

Information theory suggests that acquiring information is costly and individuals will seek information until the marginal cost of acquiring new information exceeds the benefits (Stigler, 1961). For some employees, the costs of gathering information on WHP outweigh the potential benefits, and therefore they will not actively seek out this information. The frequency of using and processing information at work plays an important role in the evaluation of the costs and benefits of acquiring information. The costs may be lower for those who frequently use information as a means to solve problems or enhance knowledge in their work (Tichenor, Donohue, & Olien, 1970).

The expectancy theory of motivation holds that people will make an effort to acquire information when they feel that it is useful to them (Vroom, 2005). This would mean that employees gather information on policies if they are interested in the content of these policies or if this is more salient to their daily life. For example, working parents are more likely to be aware of the existence of work–family policies within their organization because they combine paid work with caring for their children (Baird & Reynolds, 2004). We argue this also applies to WHP. For some employees, information about WHP is more relevant, and therefore they are more likely to actively search for information. For example, health conscious employees may seek information on how their organization contributes to their goal of a healthy lifestyle, for example, in the form of paying for their gym subscription.

Both workplace characteristics, including dispositions and actions of the manager, and the employee's own characteristics affect the costs of acquiring information and the salience of it. Based on the literature, we identified characteristics of organizations and employees that may affect employee perceptions of WHP availability, namely, aspects of the organizational context, the employee's human capital, working hours, tenure, contract type and health. We discuss each of these in turn below.

Organizational context

First, organizations differ in the emphasis on and attention paid to health and safety (Aldana et al., 2012). Employees might be more likely to perceive WHP to be available when they work in an organization where health is deemed important, and where this importance is clearly expressed. WHP may also be better implemented in such organizations. Organizations that provide employees with the resources needed to initiate or maintain healthy lifestyles are interested in ensuring their employees are aware of this (McCleary et al., 2017). There are several ways in which organizations can communicate about WHP availability, for example, through posts on the intranet, distributing flyers or hosting awareness events (European Network for Workplace Health Promotion, 2009; Grawitch et al., 2006). If information about WHP is readily available and employees can access it through several means, the costs of finding out about WHP availability are lower. Smaller organizations might lack the means necessary to implement a comprehensive WHP program and inform their employees about it (Goetzel & Ozminkowski, 2008; Linnan, Sorensen, Colditz, Klar, & Emmons, 2001; Williams & Snow, 2012). We therefore hypothesize that employees in larger organizations are more likely to perceive WHP to be available (*H1*).

Second, comprehensive WHP strategies target multiple aspects of health and well-being, given that a variety of arrangements is important to successfully improve the health and lifestyle of employees (European Network for Workplace Health Promotion, 2009; Kilpatrick et al., 2015). Employees might have different preferences with regard to WHP, but with more alternatives on offer the likelihood increases that they come into contact with WHP directly or are informed about it through their colleagues. This lowers the costs of finding out about WHP. Having a larger number of WHP offers also indicates that organizations have set aside more resources for WHP and may indicate a more extensive WHP implementation (Grawitch et al., 2006). In addition, an inclusive WHP strategy also signals that organizations are more concerned with employee health (Aldana et al., 2012). Employees might embrace these norms and also come to see the usefulness of targeting a healthy lifestyle at work (McCleary et al., 2017), making WHP more salient to them. For these reasons, we predict that employees who work in organizations with more extensive WHP will be more likely to report WHP to be available (*H2*).

A third element within the organizational context is the extent to which management embraces WHP (Passey, Brown, Hammerback, Harris, & Hannon, 2018). Without management support, WHP cannot be successful (Hammer, Liebherr, Kersten, & Haas, 2015). Managers can contribute to employee perceptions of WHP by endorsing WHP and allocating resources, for example, providing employees with time during work for WHP (Passey et al., 2018), but also by simply telling employees that there are health arrangements they are entitled to use (Dejoy et al., 2011). This also lowers the costs of finding out about the existence of WHP. Team managers are especially important in supporting employees' healthy lifestyles (Linnan, Weiner, Graham, & Emmons, 2007;

McCleary et al., 2017; Olson & Chaney, 2009). Team managers' awareness of WHP is a key aspect of its implementation and forms a precondition for managers to promote it to their employees. We therefore predict that team managers' perceptions of WHP availability positively influence employee perceptions of WHP availability (*H3*).

Employee characteristics

Human capital

There are two mechanisms for how human capital influences employee perceptions of WHP: the costs of acquiring information and the importance attached to health-related information (Mastin, 1998). For employees with more human capital, reflected in their educational or job-skill level, the costs of acquiring information about WHP are lower because they are more used to dealing with information in their jobs. Previous studies have shown that higher educated employees are more often aware of information regarding pension plans (Mastin, 1998; Mitchell, 1988) and work–life practices (Baird & Reynolds, 2004). Kilpatrick et al. (2015) found that this also applies to WHP: higher educated employees perceived more WHP activities to be available to them. In addition, employees with more human capital tend to have higher health literacy, the ability to obtain, process and understand health information (Nutbeam, 2008), which lowers the costs of acquiring information as well. Other research suggests that because those with greater human capital have invested more during their lifetime, exemplified by a higher level of human capital, they have more reason to invest in future longevity and thus have more to lose by behaving unhealthily (Cutler & Lleras-Muney, 2006). This means that knowing about WHP is more useful to them. We hypothesize that employees with more human capital are more likely to report WHP to be available (*H4*).

Working hours, tenure, flexibility

The extent to which employees are part and parcel of their organization, reflected in working hours, tenure and the flexibility of their contract, may increase perceptions of WHP availability. Employees who have been working for the organization for a longer period of time or spend more hours at work have had more exposure to organizational information through official and informal channels, such as discussing WHP with colleagues (Baird & Reynolds, 2004). Organizations might also make it easier for workers that are more bound to the organization to become aware of HR policies (Liao, Toya, Lepak, & Hong, 2009). Employees with flexible contracts may be less interested in WHP programs because they may not expect to stay with the organization for long (Wright & Nishii, 2007). Also, organizations do not necessary need flexible workers to know about health promotion initiatives, as the organization will likely not reap the benefits from their investments. To our knowledge no studies exist that examine whether these factors are related to WHP perceptions, but research on knowledge about work–family policies shows that employees with longer tenure (Prottas et al., 2007) and permanent employment (Kopelman et al., 2006) are more likely to know about the existence of these policies. We expect this also to be the case for perceptions of WHP availability and so we hypothesize that employees with more working hours (*H5a*), longer tenure (*H5b*) and those with a permanent contract (*H5c*) are more likely to perceive WHP to be available.

Health status

There are conflicting expectations of how employee health affects the perception of WHP availability. On the one hand, WHP often includes prevention aimed at individuals who are at high risk because of an unhealthy lifestyle, for example, those who have poor nutrition and who engage little in physical activity (Goetzel & Ozminkowski, 2008). This may reduce the information costs for unhealthy employees. Some evidence suggests this to be the case, as those with more sedentary behaviors reported greater perceived availability of WHP (Kilpatrick et al., 2015). In addition, Meng et al. (2017) found that less healthy employees attached more value to learning about health-related information. On the other hand, research also shows that healthier people are more willing to take care of their health and thus may be more likely to actively seek out information regarding health promotion initiatives (Dutta-Bergman, 2004). It is important for WHP to be targeted at the needs and preferences of employees (Rongen et al., 2014b). Healthier employees may perceive the availability of, for example, fruit at work as part of an organization's WHP strategy because this is in line with their own values to eat healthily, and thus they are more likely to perceive health-related initiatives in the organization as WHP (Dailey & Zhu, 2017). Despite conflicting views regarding health and WHP perceptions, we think that the perception enhancing aspects dominate and therefore expect healthier employees to have increased perceived WHP availability (*H6*).

Methods

Sample

We present two analyses based on the first wave of the ESWS. The first descriptive analysis on the availability of four WHP arrangements (healthy nutrition, sports participation, ergonomic facilities and health checks) uses all organizations present in the ESWS that had valid reports from the HR manager with regard to the presence of these arrangements in the organization (for healthy nutrition, 10,636 employees/249 establishments; for sports participation, 10,673 employees/250 establishments; for ergonomic facilities, 10,673 employees/250 establishments; and for health checks, 10,710 employees/251 establishments).

The analysis of employee perception of WHP availability includes establishments that offered WHP. Only in these establishments can we test under which conditions employees know about availability. We selected establishments based on the reports of the HR managers assuming that they know best what kind of policies are offered. Establishments that did not offer any WHP arrangements were excluded ($N = 301$ employees in 8 establishments). We analyzed each WHP separately. Note that the sample size differs between WHP arrangements as not all establishments offered all four arrangements. We also excluded employees with missing values on any of the variables ($N = 2{,}799$, mainly missing on team manager reports – see below for sensitivity checks). This resulted in a total sample of 7,911 employees in 695 teams across 242 establishments.

Variables

We measured perception of WHP based on employee self-reports of whether four types of WHP (healthy nutrition, sports participation, ergonomic facilities and health checks) were available within their establishment. Employees could indicate that these were "available" (1), "not available" (0) or that they "did not know." In the latter case, these were coded as not available (0). We performed additional analyses to evaluate whether the results were sensitive to our decision to combine the "not available" and "don't know" categories (see section on sensitivity analysis).

To account for the influence of the team manager, we used that manager's report on availability for each of the four types of WHP. Team managers' reports were coded in a similar way to those of employees (1 = available, 0 = not available).

The two other measures of organizational context were the extent of WHP in the establishment and establishment size. For each type of WHP, we totaled the number of other WHP arrangements available within the establishment, as reported by the HR manager, to measure the extent of WHP. For example, in the case of healthy nutrition, this would mean that we totaled whether sports facilities, ergonomic facilities and health checks were available. Size was based on the number of employees working within the establishment. Small establishments employed up to 100 employees, medium establishments between 100 and 249 and large establishments over 250.

To measure the influence of human capital, we included the highest completed level of education and skill level of the job. Education was measured as the highest level of completed education using the cross-country standardized International Standard Classification of Education (ISCED) coding scheme (Schneider & Kogan, 2008). Skill level of the job was based on occupation. Employees were asked to provide a full description of their occupation which was coded in native coding systems and mapped onto the International Standard Classification of Occupations (ISCO) 2008 (International Labour Office, 2012). Because some groups were very small, we combined these into categories based on skill level in the job (Tijdens, 2012). We distinguished between highly skilled (professional, ISCO = 2); skilled (managers, technicians and associate professional, ISCO = 1 or 3); and semi-skilled or unskilled workers (ISCO = 4 to 9).

Employees without a permanent contract (e.g., on call or on a trainee contract or doing seasonal work) were dummy-coded as having a non-permanent contract. The number of working hours was assessed by asking how many hours employees actually worked per week. When employees did not answer this question, they were assigned the value of their contracted hours if available. For employees who reported to be working more than 90 hours, the variable was top-coded at 90 hours (this did not influence the results). Tenure was measured by employee self-reports of how many years they had been working for their organization. Both working hours and tenure were standardized.

To measure health, we used self-rated health. Self-rated health was measured by asking employees how they rated their health on a 5-point scale ranging from "very good" to "very poor." Those who indicated their health to be "very good" or "good" were dummy-coded as having good health (versus fair/poor health).

We controlled for gender (female = 1), age in years, economic sector and country. Descriptive statistics of all variables can be found in Table 7.1.

Analytical approach

First, we examined availability per type of WHP based on HR manager reports and compared this to average employee reports of availability. Employee reports were based on average perceptions of employees per establishment (i.e., the proportion of employees that reported a WHP arrangement to be available). We then examined WHP availability per country and sector based on HR manager reports.

The second part examines employee perceptions of WHP availability using multilevel models in the subset of establishments that offer WHP. Employees are nested in teams which are nested in establishments, and the outcome variables are dichotomous, so we employed multilevel logistic regression models. Without this multilevel structure we cannot account for the clustering of employees, resulting in an underestimation of the standard errors of parameters (Hox, 2010). We estimated models for each type of WHP separately. Results are shown as average marginal effects. Given that we have four different dichotomous outcome variables, average marginal effects allow for the comparison between models (Mood, 2010). The average marginal effects show how the average probability that an employee reports that a particular type of WHP is available changes as the independent variable increases by one unit, keeping everything else constant.

Table 7.1 Descriptive statistics

	Mean	*s.d.*	*Min*	*Max*
WHP availability according to HR manager				
Healthy nutrition	0.45		0	1
Sports facilities	0.54		0	1
Ergonomic facilities	0.86		0	1
Health checks	0.64		0	1
WHP availability according to team manager				
Healthy nutrition	0.38		0	1
Sports facilities	0.45		0	1
Ergonomic facilities	0.80		0	1
Health checks	0.66		0	1
WHP availability according to employee				
Healthy nutrition	0.38		0	1
Sports facilities	0.40		0	1
Ergonomic facilities	0.64		0	1
Health checks	0.53		0	1
Employee characteristics				
Highest completed education	5.39	1.41	1	8
Skill level of job				
Highly skilled job	0.32		0	1
Skilled job	0.35		0	1
Semi-skilled or unskilled job	0.33		0	1
Contract type				
Permanent contract	0.89		0	1
Non-permanent contract	0.11		0	1
Working hours	39.42	9.47	0	90
Tenure	10.70	9.84	0.08	52
Health				
Poor/fair health	0.28		0	1
Good health	0.72		0	1
Age	42.02	10.99	16	74
Sex				
Male	0.43		0	1
Female	0.57		0	1
Organisation characteristics				
Extent of other WHP				
Healthy nutrition	2.04	0.88	0	3
Sports facilities	1.95	0.86	0	3
Ergonomic facilities	1.63	0.99	0	3
Health checks	1.85	0.92	0	3
Size				
Small	0.23		0	1
Medium	0.29		0	1
Large	0.48		0	1

Note
N (employees) = 7,911.

Results

WHP availability in Europe

We first show the overall availability of four types of WHP within the ESWS according to the HR managers and employee reports averaged per establishment. Figure 7.1 shows that 42 percent of the establishments have healthy nutrition arrangements available according to the HR manager; sports facilities are present in 52 percent; ergonomic facilities are available in 88 percent; and health checks can be found in 69 percent of the establishments. The figure also shows employee reports of availability of each type of WHP based on the average levels of employees that report that WHP is available: 35 percent of employees report healthy nutrition is offered in their establishment; 40 percent report sports facilities; 63 percent report ergonomic facilities; and 53 percent report that their establishment offers health checks. The figure also shows that (perceptions of) availability of WHP are similarly high or low for both the HR manager and employees, but overall employees report lower availability than HR managers.

We next examine the availability of WHP per country and sector based on HR manager reports. Figure 7.2 shows country differences in WHP availability. In line with previous findings (European Network for Workplace Health Promotion, 2009), Finland is among the countries that offer the most WHP for each type, while in Bulgarian establishments the least WHP is generally available. All Spanish establishments offer ergonomic facilities and health checks, as a focus on the prevention of health risks is compulsory by law (Anaya, Ayuso,

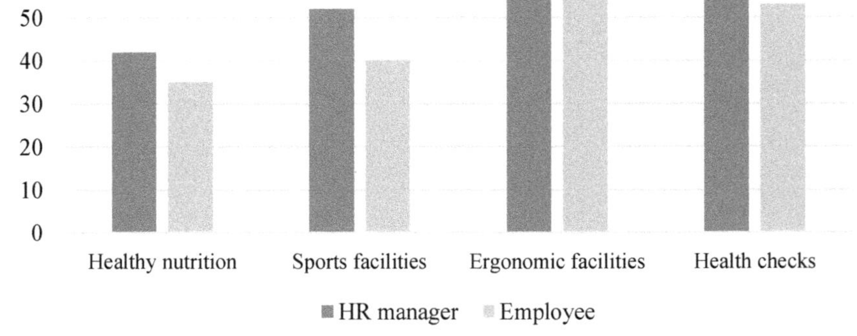

Figure 7.1 Availability of Worksite Health Promotion (WHP) according to HR managers and employee reports.

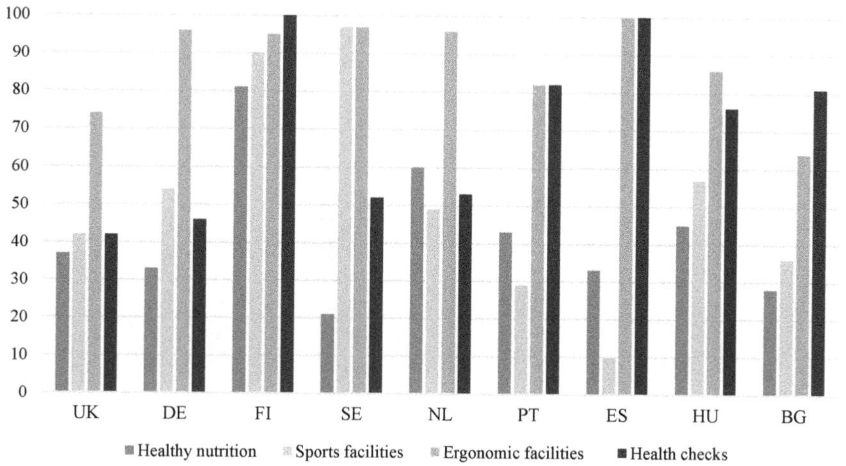

Figure 7.2 Worksite Health Promotion (WHP) availability by country according to HR managers.

Note
UK – United Kingdom; DE – Germany; FI – Finland; SE - Sweden; NL – Netherlands; PT – Portugal; ES – Spain; HU – Hungary; BG – Bulgaria.

& Fries-Tersch, 2015). However, the availability of healthy nutrition arrangements (33 percent) and sports facilities (10 percent) is low compared to other countries. Some other patterns are also discernible. For example, sports facilities are offered most often in the Nordic countries. Ergonomic facilities are available to a large extent in most countries, but less so in Eastern European countries – for example, only 64 percent of Bulgarian establishments offer this arrangement. With the exception of Finland, health checks are most often present in Southern and Eastern European countries.

Finally, we turn to differences between sectors, as shown in Figure 7.3. At first glance the higher education sector appears to offer the most WHP: 60 percent have healthy nutrition arrangements, 71 percent have sports facilities and 95 percent have ergonomic facilities. However, health checks are offered more often in the manufacturing and banking sectors. Compared to other sectors the transport sector seems to lag behind in availability: only 28 percent of organizations have healthy nutrition, 33 percent have sports facilities and 59 percent have health checks. Overall, the patterns are less clear than for country differences.

Employee perceptions

Although in the previous paragraphs we took the HR manager's perspective, Figure 7.1 clearly shows that there are discrepancies between reports made by the HR managers and by employees. We therefore investigate employee perceptions

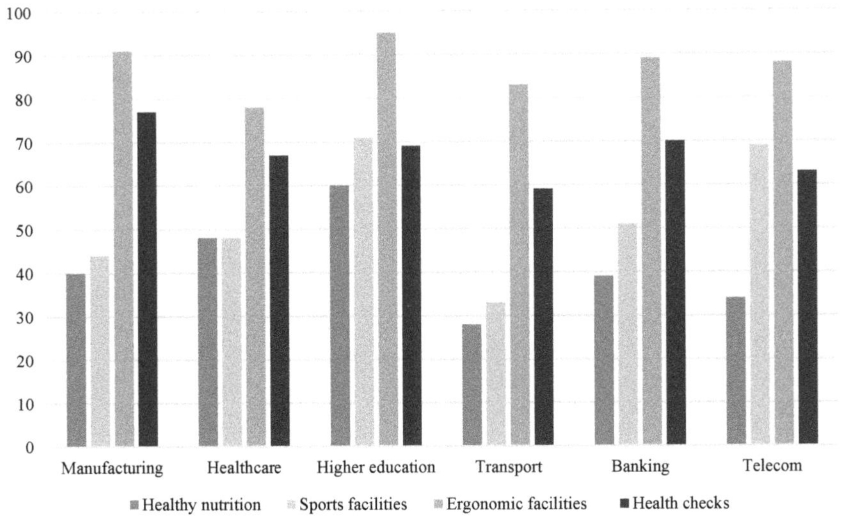

Figure 7.3 Worksite Health Promotion (WHP) availability by sector according to HR managers.

in more detail. Table 7.2 shows the results of multilevel logistic regression models of employee perceptions of WHP availability for the subset of organizations that offer WHP according to the HR manager. The top panel of Table 7.2 shows that mean availability hovers between 38 percent and 64 percent, which indicates that the employee perspective is very different from that of the HR manager.

Table 7.2 shows the average marginal effects predicting WHP availability according to employees for healthy nutrition, sports facilities, ergonomic facilities and health checks separately. We first turn to aspects of the organizational context (*H1* to *H3*). We find that the organizational context influences the extent to which employees report WHP availability, but not all aspects play a role and not all types of WHP were affected equally. Contrary to expectation, the size of an establishment (*H1*) only increased perceptions of availability of ergonomic facilities: employees in small establishments were 7 percentage points less likely to report availability and employees in medium establishments 6 percentage points less likely. For other WHP arrangements, organization size did not matter. *H2*, which predicted that perceptions of availability increased in establishments that offer more arrangements, turns out to hold for all but one type of WHP. Employees in establishments that offer more WHP were more likely to report healthy nutrition arrangements, ergonomic facilities and health checks, but not sports facilities. *H3*, which examined the role of the team manager, received the most support of the three relating to organizational context. In cases where the team manager reports that a specific WHP is available, this increases the likelihood of employees reporting WHP for all types: 7 percentage points for healthy

Table 7.2 Average marginal effects from multilevel logistic regressions predicting employee perception of WHP availability

	Healthy nutrition	*Sports facilities*	*Ergonomic facilities*	*Health checks*
Availability according to employees	38%	40%	64%	53%
Organizational context				
Establishment size (ref. = large)				
Small	–0.04	–0.06	–0.07*	–0.03
Medium	0.04	–0.05	–0.06*	0.00
Availability of other WHP	0.08***	0.04	0.05***	0.05*
WHP available according to team manager	0.07*	0.10**	0.10***	0.14***
Employee characteristics				
Highest completed education (std.)	–0.02	0.01†	0.02**	–0.01
Skill-level job (ref. = semi/unskilled)				
Highly skilled	0.05*	0.01	–0.01	–0.01
Skilled	0.002	0.05**	0.04*	0.002
Non-permanent contract (ref. = permanent)	0.04	–0.08***	–0.01	–0.05**
Working hours (std.)	0.01	–0.01	–0.00	0.00
Tenure (std.)	0.02†	0.02*	0.03***	0.03***
Good health (ref. = poor/fair health)	0.07***	0.04**	0.06***	0.03**
Control variables				
Female (ref. = male)	0.06***	0.01	0.02	–0.01
Age (std.)	–0.01	–0.02**	–0.01	0.01
Sector (ref. = healthcare)				
Manufacturing	0.03	–0.05	0.01	0.01
Higher education	–0.09	0.01	0.01	–0.04
Transport	0.09	0.08	0.02	0.12*
Banking	–0.01	0.04	0.09*	–0.01
Telecommunications	0.19**	0.17**	0.15***	–0.03
Country (ref. = Netherlands)				
UK	0.01	0.07	–0.05	0.10
Germany	0.06	0.20*	–0.06	0.11
Finland	0.16**	0.28***	0.04	0.44***
Sweden	–0.23**	0.34***	0.08*	0.26**
Portugal	–0.04	–0.15	–0.26***	0.36***
Spain	–0.41***	–0.08	–0.13*	0.55***
Hungary	–0.07	–0.13	–0.05	0.31***
Bulgaria	–0.20**	–0.11	–0.24***	0.41***
N employees	3,586	4,238	6,800	5,073
N teams	282	344	610	466
N organizations	101	126	212	167

Notes
*** $p < 0.001$, ** $p < 0.01$, * $p < 0.05$, † < 0.1.
Sample differs between WHPs because the analyses were limited to organizations that offer a specific WHP according to the HR manager's report.

nutrition, 10 percentage points for both sports and ergonomic facilities and 14 percentage points for health checks.

Next, we move to the individual characteristics of employees. We found some support for the positive role of human capital (*H4*). Higher educated employees reported ergonomic facilities more often, but no significant differences were found for the other arrangements. Highly skilled employees were more likely to report healthy nutrition arrangements than semi-skilled or unskilled employees, while skilled employees were more likely to report sports participation and ergonomic facilities compared to those who were semi-skilled or unskilled.

A mixed view emerges with respect to job characteristics (*H5a–c* on type of contract, working hours and tenure). We find that employees with a non-permanent contract were less likely to report sports participation and health checks, but contract permanency did not affect the reporting of healthy nutrition arrangements or ergonomic facilities. Working hours appear to play no role at all. We find tenure to be related to awareness of each type of WHP but effects were minor: for every standard deviation increase in tenure, employees were 2 percentage points more likely to report nutrition arrangements and sports participation, and 3 percentage points more likely to report ergonomic facilities and health checks.

Finally, as expected by *H6* we find that healthier employees more often reported each type of WHP to be available in their establishment.

Sensitivity analysis

Here we describe the results of two sensitivity analyses. First, our analytical sample consisted of all employees who had a valid team manager report for the availability of WHP. Excluding cases for which the team manager's report was not available resulted in a large deduction of sample size; we therefore also ran the analyses without the team manager's report. The results were very similar. Only in respect of healthy nutrition did the perception differences by employee skill level disappear.

Second, the analyses contrasted employees who reported WHP to be "available" versus "not available" or "don't know." It could be that reports of "don't know" are driven by substantially different processes than reports of "not available." We therefore reran the analysis contrasting "available" versus "not available" and excluded the "don't know" answers. The results of this sensitivity analysis were very similar to the presented results (not shown, but available upon request).[1] We find differences with regard to the contract and tenure indicators for three of the four WHP indicators (all but healthy nutrition). The main analyses showed that employees on a non-permanent contract were less likely, and longer tenure workers more likely, to report WHP availability. These effects disappeared in the sensitivity analyses, which fits with our theoretical reasoning that these findings were driven by non-permanent and shorter tenure workers reporting "don't know" more often. The substantial interpretation was therefore not affected by our decision to collapse the "not available" and "don't know" answer categories.

Discussion

The aim of this chapter was twofold: first, to offer an impression of the availability of WHP in European organizations where there has been no previous research; and second, to study WHP availability from the point of view of employees. The multilevel design of the ESWS allowed us to compare the availability of WHP as indicated by the organization and by employees.

First, our results show that there are large differences between countries and economic sectors in WHP availability. We find that, overall, ergonomic facilities are available in 86 percent of establishments and offered the most, while healthy nutrition arrangements were least reported (45 percent). Compared to the US where the availability of these arrangements hovers around 30 percent, European establishments more frequently offer WHP (Fielding & Piserchia, 1989; Linnan et al., 2008). Our results show that, in general, employers in Northern Europe offer more WHP and those in Eastern European the least, which is in line with previous findings (Magnavita et al., 2017). We also find differences between economic sectors in terms of WHP availability, with most WHP available for employees in higher education and the least in the transport sector. In summary, the substantial difference to the US and variation across European countries in WHP provision justify our claim that a distinct European perspective is needed in WHP research.

The second aim of our study was to examine employee perceptions of WHP availability. In line with research on other HR practices (McCleary et al., 2017; Wright & Nishii, 2007), we find large discrepancies between organizational WHP and employee perceptions of its availability. The second part of our study therefore focused on which employee and organizational characteristics contribute to employee perceptions. To our knowledge, we are among the first to study this question. We argue that the costs of acquiring information and its salience influences the perceptions employees hold of WHP.

WHP is not just a health activity but also an organizational activity (Sloan & Gruman, 1988). We find that when organizations offer a more comprehensive WHP plan, employees are more likely to perceive WHP to be available. Organizations would thus do better to offer more forms of WHP rather than just one, in order to increase the salience of the policies. Organizations might communicate information about WHP centrally, but these initiatives may not reach all parts of the organization equally (Robroek et al., 2009). We find that when the team manager reports WHP to be available, employees are more likely to report WHP to be available too. Our results imply that managers are crucial when it comes to informing employees about WHP. Alternatively, it could also be the case that differences between team managers indicate that WHP was rolled out differently across an organization. Furthermore, organizational size was hardly related to the reported availability of WHP. Smaller organizations are less likely to offer WHP (Williams & Snow, 2012), but once the arrangements are in place employees are not less likely to report that health policies are available. Given that most people work in small or medium-sized organizations and this will continue to be the case (Guazzi et al., 2014), efforts should be made to ensure that all employees have access to WHP equally.

Our results show that also characteristics of employees themselves affect whether they perceive WHP to be available, both in terms of lowering the costs of seeking information about WHP as well as the evaluation of the usefulness of this information. We expected that human capital would be related to both, but find that generally human capital only plays a modest role in the perception of WHP availability. Previous studies have shown that human capital is related to knowledge about health (Pampel, Krueger, & Denney, 2010), but our results show that this might not necessarily be the case in the workplace. This could have implications for the relationship between WHP and health inequalities because the lack of a social gradient in awareness of WHP increases the importance of the formal provision of WHP to reduce inequalities in health. There are, of course, large differences between sectors and organizations in the composition of the workforce (Nabe-Nielsen, Garde, Clausen, & Jørgensen, 2015); this might have implications for existing inequalities in health, especially if those with unhealthy lifestyles more often work in organizations with less WHP available.

The type of contract and employment history of employees also played a role, but the number of working hours did not. Employees with a non-permanent contract report less WHP compared to employees with a permanent contract. We found longer tenure to increase awareness of each type of WHP. This suggests that organizations should bring WHP to the attention of employees when they start a job so as to create awareness among new employees as well.

Finally, our results indicate that healthier employees are more likely to be aware of WHP. Because we used cross-sectional data, we cannot rule out the possibility that healthier employees are more likely to be aware of WHP because they more often make use of it; so knowing about WHP is a precondition to its use and possible better health. However, earlier research has shown that healthier individuals have higher self-efficacy with regard to health (Rongen, Robroek, & Burdorf, 2014a). Knowledge about healthy lifestyle opportunities (including what the organization offers in the form of WHP) is closely attached to, if not a prerequisite for, having control over one's own health. We leave it to future studies to examine the relationship between awareness, use and effect of WHP on employee health.

Other limitations of our study should also be noted. Our theoretical discussion relied on information and motivation theories, but we did not empirically distinguish the different underlying mechanisms. Studies on perception of other HR practices (see, for example, Prottas et al., 2007 for a discussion on work–life policies) do not typically investigate these mechanisms in detail either. However, understanding which underlying mechanisms are at play in bringing about employee awareness helps organizations to decide how to target employees. For example, is it sufficient to provide information about WHP or is it also necessary to emphasize and embrace shared responsibility (organization and employee) for health and well-being in communications about WHP (Aldana et al., 2012)? Future research should pay attention to this.

Another limitation is that although we tried to map the availability of WHP within European organizations, we could only do so for nine countries across six sectors. Although this is a much-needed first step, we suggest that future studies build upon our findings by offering a more comprehensive overview.

Our results show that organizational characteristics matter for employee perceptions of WHP availability. Focusing on formal characteristics, we did not explicitly address the impact of workforce composition. Part of the variation at the organizational level may be due to employee composition effects rather than contextual effects. It should be noted that this problem also applies, in part, to the effects of individual employee characteristics, which may reflect organizational compositional aspects (e.g., higher educated people working at universities where most other employees are also highly educated).We partly account for this by including both employee characteristics and economic sector in our analyses, as well as restricting our sample to organizations that offer WHP.

Finally, we assumed employee perceptions of availability to be a reflection of the extent to which employees know about the WHP offered in their organizations. However, perceptions are not completely neutral, as they also reflect the extent to which employees evaluate the implementation of WHP. Organizations may offer WHP, but if employees do not conceive what is on offer as useful or as part of HR practices, they may not report WHP to be available. We unfortunately did not have detailed information on WHP implementation in organizations. However, the strong effects of organizational context indicate that perceived WHP closely links to WHP implementation. For instance, the positive effect on WHP of team managers' knowledge could indicate that implementation and communication about WHP differs across teams within the organization.

This chapter shows that characteristics of both organizations and employees impact employee perceptions of WHP. Our findings show that employee awareness of WHP is not bestowed merely by implementing the programs. Organizations that experience under-utilization of their WHP programs may find our findings useful in respect of targeting employees who are less aware of WHP. A healthy workforce contributes to a sustainable workforce, but without awareness of how to tackle unhealthy behavior in the work environment, both employees and organizations miss out on the advantages WHP may bring to the workplace.

Note

1 Full results are available on request from the first author: a.c.vanderput@uu.nl.

8 Immigrants' access to employer-provided professional training within firms

An analysis for the United Kingdom, Germany, Sweden and the Netherlands

Silvia Maja Melzer

Introduction

The wage disadvantages of immigrants are well documented in the sociological and economic literature (e.g., Algan, Dustmann, Glitz, & Manning, 2010; Kogan, 2006; Melzer, Tomaskovic-Devey, Schunck, & Jacobebbinghaus, 2018; Tomaskovic-Devey, Hällsten, & Avent-Holt, 2015). Much less attention has been paid to immigrants' access to employer-provided training (Barret, McGuinness, O'Brien, & O'Connell, 2013), although training increases wage growth (e.g., Brunello, 2001; Lechthaler & Snower, 2008; for immigrants, see Yoshida & Smith, 2005; for a meta-analysis, see Haelermans & Borghans, 2012), employment stability (Kampkötter & Marggraf, 2015; Lynch, 1991) and opportunities for permanent employment (Frazis & Loewenstein, 2005; McVicar, Wooden, Leung, & Li, 2016). Moreover, employer-provided training provides employees with the new skills that are necessary at a time of perpetual technological change and creates a sustainable workforce. Access to employer-provided training is related to various aspects of employment advantage, as well as increasing immigrants' chances of integrating successfully into the host country's labor market. It is therefore important to identify the factors that restrict immigrants' access to training.

This study examines access to employer-provided formal (off-the-job) training[1] and how firms' resources, training costs and training intensity influence immigrants' opportunities to participate in training. Although training enhances employees' human capital, decisions regarding training are not individual decisions: they depend on the employer or firm as much as on the employee (Tomaskovic-Devey, Thomas, & Johnson, 2005).

Previous research investigating wage inequality and labor market segregation has long underlined the importance of firms and their characteristics for individual outcomes (Avent-Holt & Tomaskovic-Devey, 2012a; Baron & Bielby, 1980; Tomaskovic-Devey, Thomas, & Johnson, 2005). Moreover, this research conclusively demonstrated that establishment characteristics affect various groups such as natives or immigrants differently. Establishments and their characteristics (e.g., size, sector, workforce composition) can reinforce or mute the effects of salient individual characteristics, such as immigrant status, on social inequality (for an empirical analysis of immigrant–native wage gaps, see Melzer et al., 2018; Tomaskovic-Devey et al., 2015). In addition, previous research on (in-)formal training has shown that establishments' characteristics, such as size or work practices, influence the incidence and duration of training (Frazis, Gittleman, & Joyce, 2000; Green, Machin, & Wilkinson, 1999; Halldén, 2015; Méndez & Sepúlveda, 2015; Waddoups, 2011, 2014). However, to the best of this author's knowledge, no study has investigated the interrelation between establishment resources and immigrant status in the context of employer-provided training and how specific establishment characteristics moderate immigrants' opportunities to participate in training.

This study aims to close this gap. Analyses are conducted using the unique European Sustainable Workforce Survey (ESWS) data for four immigration countries, namely, the United Kingdom, Germany, Sweden and the Netherlands. The linked employer–employee data allow us to investigate not only which individual and job-related characteristics influence employees' likelihood of participating in training, but also how employees' embedment within establishments with certain resources, training costs and training may impact immigrants' likelihood of participating in training.

The determinants of employer-provided training

Access to training is highly stratified by age, gender, ethnicity and immigrant status. Employees who are younger (Frazis et al., 2000; Shields & Wheatley Price, 1999a, 1999b; Waddoups, 2014), male (Boye & Grönlund, 2018; Evertsson, 2004; Grönlund, 2017; Halldén, 2015) and white (Duncan & Hoffmann 1979; Gibson, 2002; Shields & Wheatley Price, 1999a, 1999b; Sexton & Olsen, 1994) are more likely to participate in employer-provided training and to receive it for longer periods. Access to training depends strongly on employees' education. The Organization for Economic Cooperation and Development (OECD) indicates that Sweden, with a training incidence only twice as high for employees with tertiary education as for those with a lower secondary education, has relatively moderate differences between low-educated and highly-educated individuals in the likelihood of receiving training compared with other European countries; the United Kingdom has 4.2-fold higher likelihood and Germany a 6-fold higher likelihood (O'Conell & Jungblut, 2008, p. 112, based on Organisation for Economic Co-operation and Development, 2005). Employees who have received training before – for example, those who have participated in vocational training – are more likely to receive it again (Bellman & Düll, 2001). Full-time employees and those with permanent contracts are also more likely to receive training (Arulampalam & Booth, 1998; Cutuli & Guetto, 2013).

Among the few studies that have investigated immigrants' access to training, there is a broad consensus that immigrants are less likely to receive it (Barrett,

McGuinness, O'Brien, & O'Connell, 2013; Hum & Simpson, 2003; Kennedy, Drago, Sloan, & Wooden, 1994; Miller, 1994; Van den Heuvel & Wooden, 1997). The typically lower average levels of education of immigrants compared to natives (e.g., Kogan, 2004) may in part explain this difference. At the same time, immigrants may be more motivated to participate in training, as the potential financial returns from training is highest among people with the lowest likelihood of receiving it (Bartell, 1995; Blundell, Dearden, & Meghir, 1996). Nevertheless, returns from immigrants' general human capital or, more precisely, labor market experience in the host country are lower than that of natives, which might be related to their reduced participation in employer-provided training (Blackaby, Clark, Leslie, & Murphy, 1994; Shields & Wheatley Price, 1999a, 1999b).

At the establishment level, one of the most discussed and best established factors that influence training provision is establishment size (e.g., Barrett et al., 2013; Holtmann & Idson, 1991; Shields & Wheatley Price, 1999a, 1999b). Larger establishments provide training to their employees more often than smaller establishments (e.g., Barrett et al., 2013; Frazis et al., 2000; Green et al., 1999; Holtmann & Idson, 1991; Jacobs, Lukens, & Useen, 1996; Lynch & Black, 1998; O'Conell & Byrne, 2012; Shields & Wheatley Price, 1999a, 1999b). This is often explained by the greater financial resources of larger establishments that allow them to absorb possible losses in production due to employee training better than smaller establishments (Lynch & Black, 1998). In addition, larger establishments have lower 'fixed costs' per employee because more employees can simultaneously participate in a training (Lynch & Black, 1998). Finally, larger establishments are more likely to provide attractive long-term career options to their employees, reducing the incentive for employees to advance their careers by changing employers (Lynch & Black, 1998) and ensuring that the establishment profits from investing in training their employees. Other factors found in previous research to influence employees' likelihood of receiving training are work practices, union coverage, being in the private or public sector and competition (Green et al., 1999; Royalty 1996; Waddoups, 2014; Xu & Lin, 2011).

Bigger firms face less pressure to minimize labor and training costs and they have more financial resources to allocate to training; such firms, in general, therefore train more employees. Training is thus likely to be more broadly accessible to employees. Due to the wide accessibility of training as an organizational resource, workplace competition in which native workers usually hold a more advantageous position is less likely to occur. Therefore, it less likely that large firms differentiate between immigrants and natives when providing training, compared to smaller firms.

Firms that finance longer training programs for employees are also likely to produce less inequality between native and immigrant workers in access to training. Given the larger investments these firms make in training, selection processes are likely to be more formalized, centralized and more achievement-based. While formal selection and evaluation procedures are not unsusceptible to stereotype bias (see Castilla & Benard, 2010), in formalized allocation procedures there is less room for such biases to influence decisions compared to those solely based on supervisory discretion. Hence, the immigrant disadvantage in training should be lower in bigger firms, those with greater financial resources and training-intensive firms. Moreover, it is not only the current size or current financial resources that may be be decisive for access to training, but also recent changes in the situation of the firm. For example, recent increases in a firm's size probably also increase the need to train recently hired employees. Recent increases in firms' financial situation, in turn, might provide the financial means for broad – and inclusive – training participation.

Aim and research questions

The aim of this analysis is to investigate the relationship between immigrant status and formal employer-provided training. This study aims to answer the following questions:

1 To what extent do immigrants receive less formal employer-provided training than natives?
2 Are immigrants treated in a more similar way to natives and less disadvantaged in bigger establishments, establishments with more financial resources and training-intensive workplaces?

Data, variables and methods

This study used unique linked employer–employee data from the ESWS project. For this study, a subsample of immigration countries, namely, the United Kingdom, Germany, Sweden and the Netherlands, was selected. After the exclusion of employees and employers with missing information, and firms that did not employ any immigrants, the analytical sample consists of 4,362 employees in 101 establishments.

The dependent variable, employer-paid formal *training* (also referred to as off-the-job training), was measured using the following question: "In the past 12 months, have you been trained by a professional instructor from outside your organization?"

The variable of main interest at the individual level is *immigrant* status, based on country of birth. In the pooled sample, 14.2 percent of employees were born abroad (see Table 8.1). The highest percentage of immigrants was interviewed in the United Kingdom sample (31.3 percent), while the lowest percentage was 10.3 percent in the Netherlands. *Education* was measured on the International Standard Classification of Education (ISCED) scale which differentiates between higher tertiary, lower tertiary, higher secondary or, at most, lower secondary education. Level of education was included as dummy indicators in the models. *Tenure* (in years) is used as a proxy for firm-specific human capital. Control variables for job characteristics are: *full-time vs part-time*, and *permanent vs temporary employment*, and whether the position included *supervisory* responsibilities. As immigrants are over-represented in occupations that require less initial training (Barrett et al., 2013), 1-digit International Standard Classification of Occupations (ISCO) *occupation* codes were included in the models. Finally, there were also controls for demographic characteristics such as *age* (in years), *age squared* and *gender* (women = 1).

Across all countries, 33 percent of immigrants and 45 percent of natives received employer-provided formal training (see Table 8.1). The gap in access to formal training was highest in the United Kingdom, with a 17.6 percent difference between immigrants and natives, and lowest in Sweden, with only a 4.8 percent difference. Compared with natives, immigrants more often had lower secondary or even lower levels of education, were less likely to be employed on a permanent contract and had, on average, lower tenure than natives.

At the establishment level, *size* was measured by the number of employees. The establishments included in the data had an average of 557 employees, but size varied considerably among the countries studied; larger establishments were more common in the United Kingdom, while smaller establishments were predominant in Germany and Sweden (see Table 8.2). A second measurement examined change in establishment size, which was measured with a set of dummy variables based on the question: "Has the total number of employees at your establishment increased, stayed about the same, or decreased?" In the pooled sample, size increased in 57 percent of establishments, while it remained the same in 23 percent and decreased in 20 percent of establishments. Establishments' financial situation was measured with the question: "How would you rate the financial situation of your establishment?" Responses ranged from "very good" (17 percent), "good" (50 percent) and "neither good nor bad" (29 percent) to "rather bad" (5 percent). Changes in establishments' financial situation was based on the question: "Has the financial situation of your establishment improved (55 percent), stayed the same (25 percent), or worsened (20 percent) in the past three years?"; this indicator was also operationalized with a set of dummy variables. Initially, the question could be answered on a 5-point scale. However, because the categories "improved a lot" and "worsened a lot" were sparsely populated, the responses were combined on a 3-point scale. The final indicator at the establishment level, training intensity, was accounted for by the average number of days spent in formal training within an establishment and aggregated to the establishment level from individual responses.

On average, employees in the sample spent 1.8 days in training, but the duration of days varied considerably across establishments. At some establishments, employees spent on average only 0.1 days in training, while at others they spent 7.4 days in training (see Table 8.2). The average amount of time employees spent in formal training also varied across countries, with 1.3 days in Sweden, 1.6 days in the Netherlands, 1.7 days in the United Kingdom and Spain and 2.9 days in Germany (see Table 8.2).

To investigate immigrant–native differences in training and variation by establishment characteristics (such as establishment size), multilevel regression

Table 8.1 Descriptive statistics of employee characteristics (percent) for natives (nat.), immigrants (mig.) and the pooled sample (all) by country

	All			*UK*			*DE*			*SE*			*NL*		
	All	*Nat.*	*Mig.*	*All*	*Nat.*	*Mig.*	*All*	*Nat.*	*Mig.*	*All*	*Nat.*	*Mig.*	*All*	*Nat.*	*Mig.*
Individual characteristics															
Formal employer-provided training	42.8	44.6	32.5	37.0	42.5	24.9	44.1	44.6	40.0	40.3	41.0	36.2	45.1	46.4	33.6
Immigrant	14.2			31.3			11.3			14.5			10.3		
Women	52.4	52.2	53.5	55.2	55.0	55.7	57.3	57.0	58.9	47.6	49.3	36.9	51.7	50.9	59.3
Age	42.6	42.9	40.6	39.4	40.3	37.6	42.5	42.8	39.9	44.9	44.9	45.5	42.5	42.7	40.7
Education and qualification															
Lower secondary education or less															
Higher secondary education	42.6	43.2	39.1	35.3	34.4	37.3	37.3	36.3	44.4	52.2	53.3	46.2	42.6	43.5	34.1
Lower tertiary education	23.1	23.3	22.0	32.8	36.4	24.9	4.6	4.5	5.6	22.2	22.0	23.1	27.9	28.1	25.7
Higher tertiary education	21.0	20.9	21.6	11.8	13.8	7.6	35.1	36.1	27.8	21.2	20.6	24.6	18.2	16.9	29.4
Tenure in years	11.1	11.5	8.4	7.7	8.6	5.6	10.5	10.6	10.0	11.4	11.6	10.0	12.1	12.5	9.2
Job characteristics															
Full time employment	70.7	68.7	83.0	88.5	85.3	95.7	74.1	74.2	73.3	92.4	92.6	91.5	54.9	53.0	71.0
Fixed-term employment	86.9	87.1	85.9	94.1	93.4	95.7	79.1	79.0	80.0	93.3	93.6	91.5	85.1	86.1	76.6
Supervisory position	16.1	15.4	20.2	27.4	27.8	26.5	21.0	20.6	24.4	20.0	19.8	21.5	9.3	8.9	12.1
ISCO occupations															
Professionals, legislators	5.5	5.7	3.9	8.1	11.1	1.6	5.5	5.5	5.6	9.2	9.6	6.9	3.0	3.0	3.3
Senior officials, manager	28.1	28.6	24.9	32.6	39.3	17.8	25.9	26.6	20.0	21.7	21.6	22.3	30.4	29.9	34.6
Technicians, associate professional	30.4	31.2	26.2	25.8	26.3	24.9	26.1	24.6	37.8	31.6	33.1	23.1	32.9	33.9	24.3
Clerks	14.6	14.9	12.4	11.1	13.5	5.9	13.8	14.1	11.1	13.9	14.5	10.8	16.2	15.8	19.6
Service workers, shop, market sales	5.9	6.1	4.7	3.5	4.2	2.2	3.9	3.7	5.6	6.3	7.2	1.5	7.2	7.1	8.4
Skilled agricultural, fishery workers	0.1	0.1	0.0	0.0	0.0	0.0	0.1	0.1	0.0	0.0	0.0	0.0	0.1	0.2	0.0
Craft, related trades workers	1.9	2.0	1.8	2.0	1.0	4.3	3.8	3.9	2.2	1.4	1.7	.0	1.4	1.5	0.5
Plant, machine operators, assembler	6.3	4.2	18.4	12.0	2.2	33.5	2.8	2.3	6.7	13.0	9.8	32.3	3.0	3.2	1.9
Elementary occupations	2.2	2.0	3.6	1.2	0.5	2.7	1.0	0.8	2.2	0.0	0.0	0.0	3.9	3.5	7.0
N	4,362	3,743	619	592	407	185	800	710	90	898	768	130	2,072	1,858	214

Note
UK – United Kingdom; DE – Germany; SE – Sweden; NL – Netherlands.

Table 8.2 Descriptive statistics of organizational characteristics in the pooled sample (all) and by country

	All				*UK*	*DE*	*SE*	*NL*
	Mean	*Sd.*	*Min*	*Max*	*Mean*	*Mean*	*Mean*	*Mean*
Establishment size	556.6	857.7	9	4286	988.1	371.8	430.3	571.3
Number of employees (%) increased	57.4				73.3	52.6	53.6	56.4
Number of employees (%) stayed the same	22.8				13.3	26.3	17.9	28.2
Number of employees (%) decreased	19.8				13.3	21.1	28.6	15.4
Average days of formal training in firm	1.8	1.4	0.1	7.4	1.7	2.9	1.3	1.6
Establishment's financial situation (%) very good	16.8				20.0	10.5	28.6	10.3
Establishment's financial situation (%) good	49.5				46.7	57.9	25.0	64.1
Establishment's financial situation (%) neither good nor bad	28.7				26.7	21.1	39.3	25.6
Establishment's financial situation (%) rather bad	5.0				6.7	10.5	7.1	0.0
Establishment's financial situation (%) improved	55.4				60.0	36.8	64.3	56.4
Establishment's financial situation (%) stayed the same	24.8				20.0	36.8	10.7	30.8
Establishment's financial situation (%) worsened	19.8				20.0	26.3	25.0	12.8
N	101				15	19	28	39

Note
UK – United Kingdom; DE – Germany; SE – Sweden; NL – Netherlands.

models with random slope were estimated (Wooldridge, 2010, p. 481). Multi-level regression made it possible to account for the nested structure of the data, and the fact that employees working within one establishment are more similar to each other than employees across establishments. To analyze the likelihood of participation in training, which is a binary variable, linear probability models were estimated, which allowed us to compare the influence of factors across models when entering them stepwise (Mood, 2010). Linear probability models provide unbiased and consistent estimates of average effects (Mood, 2010).

Results

Table 8.3 displays the results from the linear probability models with random intercept and random slopes for immigrant status estimating the likelihood of participating in employer-provided training. Models I to V test the first research question and sequentially include controls for demographic characteristics (Model II), human capital (Model III) and occupations (Model IV). Model V includes establishment-level characteristics, while Model VI tests the second research question including interaction terms between immigrant status and establishment-level characteristics. Model I indicates that immigrants are, on average, 7.2 percent less likely to participate in training. Adding demographic variables in Model II did not further explain immigrants' lower access to training; nor did including education and tenure in Model III.

The relationship between age and training was nonlinear. At first, the likelihood of receiving training increased with every year an employee ages, but the effect decreases once the employee reaches age 37[2] (for similar results regarding age, see e.g., Frazis et al., 2000; Waddoups, 2014). Moreover, in line with the previous literature, employees with higher education are more likely to participate in training (Barrett et al., 2013; Gibson, 2002; O'Connell & Byrne, 2012).

A common theoretical argument is that immigrants are (self)-selected into jobs that require less initial training (Barrett et al., 2013). To control for such selection effects, Model IV included ISCO 1-digit occupations and other job characteristics, such as full-time vs part-time employment, jobs with or without supervisory responsibilities or fixed vs permanent working contracts. Although immigrant workers did indeed differ from natives with respect to occupations and were less likely to have permanent work contracts (see Table 8.1), controlling for occupation or type of contract did not further explain the immigrant disadvantage in training. Rather, Model IV indicates that despite the net effect of individual characteristics, immigrants working in the same job and at the same establishment are still 8.5 percent less likely to receive employer-provided formal training.

Model V reveals that even after controlling for establishment characteristics, immigrants are 8.7 percent less likely to receive training. In addition, Model V captures the direct effects of establishment characteristics on the likelihood of receiving training for all employees. As expected, training participation is higher in training-intensive establishments that provide longer periods of training.

Table 8.3 Random slope regressions of individual, job and firm characteristics on the likelihood of participation in formal training

Model	*I*	*II*	*III*	*IV*	*V*	*VI*
Demographic characteristics						
Immigrant	–0.072**	–0.082***	–0.088***	–0.085***	–0.087***	–0.080
	(0.024)	(0.024)	(0.023)	(0.023)	(0.023)	(0.066)
Women		0.002	0.001	0.009	0.005	0.005
		(0.016)	(0.016)	(0.016)	(0.016)	(0.016)
Age		0.020***	0.019***	0.012*	0.012*	0.012*
		(0.005)	(0.005)	(0.005)	(0.005)	(0.005)
Age squared		–0.000***	–0.000***	–0.000**	–0.000**	–0.000**
		(0.000)	(0.000)	(0.000)	(0.000)	(0.000)
Human capital						
Education (ref. = lower secondary education and lower)						
Higher secondary education			0.099***	0.089***	0.095***	0.094***
			(0.024)	(0.024)	(0.024)	(0.024)
Lower tertiary education			0.151***	0.123***	0.129***	0.126***
			(0.027)	(0.028)	(0.027)	(0.027)
Higher tertiary education			0.163***	0.118***	0.117***	0.115***
			(0.029)	(0.031)	(0.031)	(0.031)
Tenure in years			0.000	–0.001	–0.001	–0.001
			(0.001)	(0.001)	(0.001)	(0.001)
Job characteristics						
Full-time employment				0.005	–0.000	–0.001
				(0.019)	(0.019)	(0.019)
Fixed-term employment				0.107***	0.105***	0.108***
				(0.025)	(0.025)	(0.025)
Supervisory position				0.058**	0.057**	0.058**
				(0.022)	(0.022)	(0.022)
ISCO occupations (ref. = professionals)						
Legislators, senior officials, manager				0.033	0.038	0.039
				(0.036)	(0.036)	(0.036)
Technicians, associate professional				–0.033	–0.028	–0.026
				(0.021)	(0.021)	(0.021)
Clerks				–0.092***	–0.084**	–0.083**
				(0.026)	(0.026)	(0.026)
Service workers, shop, market sales				–0.053	–0.038	–0.037
				(0.037)	(0.036)	(0.036)
Skilled agricultural, fishery workers				–0.381	–0.375	–0.371
				(0.239)	(0.238)	(0.238)
Craft, related trades workers				–0.166**	–0.180**	–0.174**
				(0.057)	(0.056)	(0.056)
Plant, machine operators, assembler				–0.042	–0.017	–0.016
				(0.039)	(0.038)	(0.038)
Elementary occupations				–0.122*	–0.109*	–0.112*
				(0.057)	(0.055)	(0.055)
Organizational characteristics						
Establishment size/100					0.002	0.003†
					(0.001)	(0.001)
Number of employees (ref. = increased)						
Stayed the same					0.032	0.025
					(0.032)	(0.033)
Decreased					0.027	0.005
					(.034)	(.036)
Average days of formal training in establishment					0.064***	0.069***
					(0.009)	(0.009)
Establishment's financial situation (ref. = very good)						
Good					.0035	0.025
					(0.037)	(0.038)
Neither good nor bad					–0.026	–0.033
					(0.042)	(0.044)

Table 8.3 Continued

Model	I	II	III	IV	V	VI
Rather bad					–0.105	–0.122†
					(0.070)	(0.072)
Establishment's financial situation (ref. = improved)						
Stayed the same					–0.024	–0.023
					(0.030)	(0.031)
Worsened					0.025	0.024
					(0.036)	(0.037)
Interaction terms with immigrant						
× establishment size/100						–0.003
						(0.003)
× *number of employees (ref. = increased)*						
Stayed the same						0.056
						(0.064)
Decreased						0.143*
						(0.062)
× average days of formal training in establishment						–0.040*
						(0.017)
× *establishment's financial situation (ref. = very good)*						
Good						0.059
						(0.071)
Neither good nor bad						0.012
						(0.079)
Rather bad						0.081
						(0.125)
× *establishment's financial situation (ref. = improved)*						
Stayed the same						0.008
						(0.055)
Worsened						0.042
						(0.070)
Intercept	0.420***	0.067	–0.041	0.071	–0.080	–0.069
	(0.017)	(0.099)	(0.100)	(0.104)	(0.108)	(0.109)
Variance terms						
Immigrant (slope)	0.004***	0.003***	0.002*	0.001†	0.002*	0.000***
	(0.003)	(0.002)	(0.002)	(0.002)	(0.002)	(0.000)
Establishment (intercept)	0.022***	0.022***	0.020***	0.020***	0.008***	0.008***
	(0.002)	(0.002)	(0.002)	(0.002)	(0.001)	(0.001)
Individual (error)	0.224***	0.223***	0.221***	0.218***	0.218***	0.218***
	(0.002)	(0.002)	(0.002)	(0.002)	(0.002)	(0.002)
N employees	4,362	4,362	4,362	4,362	4,362	4,362
N establishment	101	101	101	101	101	101
Log-likelihood	–3,006.5	–2,991.0	–2,971.8	–2,943.6	–2,915.1	–2,908.3

Notes
Standard errors in parenthesis.
† $p<0.1$, * $p<0.05$, ** $p<0.01$, *** $p<0.001$ (2-sided).

In Model VI, interaction terms were added to investigate whether immigrants are treated more or less similarly to natives when the establishment was bigger, and the resources available to the establishment or the training intensity were higher. Contrary to expectations, the results indicate that immigrants employed in establishments that had decreased in size in the last three years were more likely to receive training than natives.

Also contrary to the expected pattern, a statistically significant negative effect was found between training-intensity, measured as average number of days

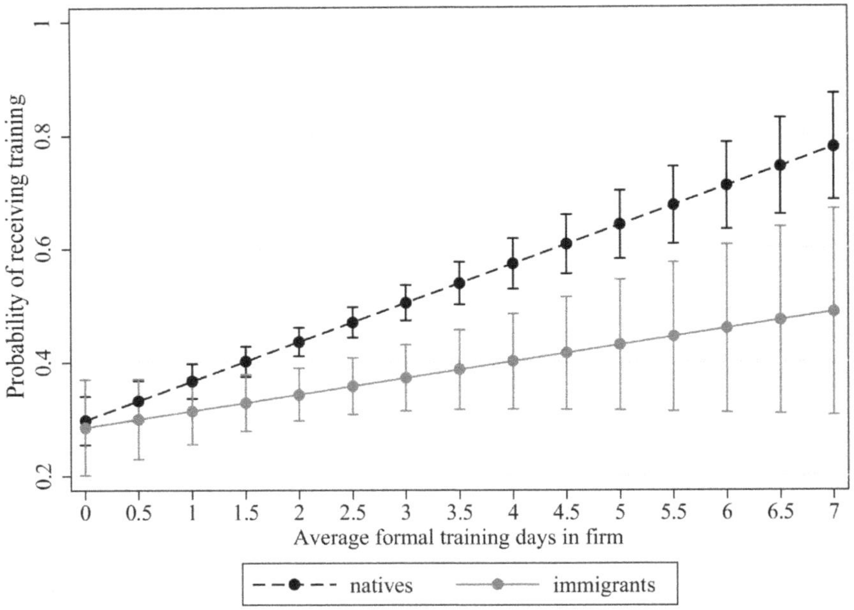

Figure 8.1 Interaction effect between firms' average training duration and immigrant status influencing the likelihood of receiving training.

of formal employer-provided training, and immigrant status, indicating that immigrants are less likely to receive training compared to natives the more training-intensive the establishment is. To facilitate the interpretation of this interaction, marginal effects are plotted in Figure 8.1. Training-intensive establishments indeed offer more training to immigrants. At the same time, training-intensive establishments were also the ones in which the immigrant disadvantage in training was highest. As the likelihood of training increased with the average number of training days, the likelihood of receiving training was highest at training-intensive establishments for both natives and immigrants. However, as the likelihood of training increased much more rapidly for natives than for immigrants, the disadvantage in access to training was also highest among immigrants employed at training-intensive establishments.

Discussion and conclusion

Using unique linked employer–employee data from the ESWS project for four immigration countries (United Kingdom, Germany, Sweden and the Netherlands), this study investigated immigrants' access to formal employer-provided training. The results indicate that limited access to such training among immigrant employees is not explained by individual or job-related characteristics. This result is in line with the previous literature which shows, using variance decompositions, that the disadvantage of immigrants with regard to training cannot be explained by differences in average characteristics between immigrants and natives (e.g., Gibson, 2002; Shields & Wheatley Price, 1999b). More importantly, even after controlling for establishments' size and financial resources, the changes in these factors and training intensity, the immigrant training disadvantage still prevails.

This study showed not only that establishment resources influence the likelihood of employee training, but also that establishment characteristics can exacerbate or mitigate immigrant–native gaps in training. Thus, this research underlines once again the importance of studying the impact of establishments and their characteristics when examining social inequality in the labor market (cf. Avent-Holt & Tomaskovic-Devey, 2012a; Baron & Bielby, 1980; Melzer et al., 2018; Tomaskovic-Devey et al., 2005; Tomaskovic-Devey et al., 2015).

Immigrants who are employed by establishments after they have undergone a reduction in size are more likely to receive training. However, immigrants are usually hired last and fired first (Kogan, 2004); therefore, immigrants who remain working for the establishment after size reduction are very likely to be a selective group that might occupy key positions or to be otherwise privileged. Working at a training-intensive establishment increases immigrants' likelihood of receiving training. Paradoxically, the immigrant–native gap in training is also the highest in these establishments. This contradicts the expectation that training-intensive establishments would differentiate less between immigrants and natives when choosing who to train. A possible reason for this comes from job queuing processes: training-intensive establishments are likely to be highly selective, based on expected productivity and employee resourcefulness because they invest heavily in workers; being an immigrant puts these workers at a disadvantage in applying for jobs in training-intensive firms, irrespective of other factors, compared to the most resourceful native applicants. As a consequence, otherwise very capable migrants may be pushed into establishments that invest less in training their workers; however, in these establishments they may be more competitive compared to the natives working there, which increases their training chances.

Dynamic changes in the contemporary labor market increase not only the demand for highly qualified employees, but also the need for all employees to adapt to new technologies throughout their working lives. Formal or informal employer-provided training might moderate these challenges, which underlines the importance of access to training and lifelong learning opportunities for all employees. Immigrants, whose qualifications from abroad might be more difficult for potential employers to evaluate, might especially profit from training and its signaling effect, as formal training certificates might reduce future employers' doubts regarding the quality of immigrants' qualifications received from abroad. The ongoing reduced access to training for immigrants decreases their chances of successfully integrating into the host country's labor market. Moreover, as training is mostly offered to qualified employees, it is not possible for immigrants who have potentially less formal education to catch up with natives through formal training. Instead of reducing the differences between immigrants and natives, participating in training seems to strengthen pre-existing differences in access to training. As many European labor markets already face skill shortages, it seems short-sighted to abandon the huge potential of this employee population.

Notes

1 Formal (off-the-job) training refers to an employer-provided courses by a professional instructor.
2 Estimation based on Model VI.

Part III

Returns on investments in a sustainable workforce for employers and employees

9 HR investments in an employable workforce

Mutual gains or conflicting outcomes?

Jasmijn van Harten, Zoltán Lippényi and Paul Boselie

Introduction

The relevance of a sustainable workforce is receiving increasing attention from organizations (Kossek, Valcour, & Lirio, 2014; Pfeffer, 2010). Because of developments such as an aging population, ongoing technological advances, globalization and increased competition, there is an apparent need for a workforce that is resilient, productive, innovative and, accordingly, able to continuously deal with change. Therefore, employability, individuals' ability and willingness to work productively (Van Harten, Knies, & Leisink, 2015) or, put differently, to gain and maintain employment (Rothwell & Arnold, 2007) is attracting growing scholarly attention (Forrier, Verbruggen, & De Cuyper, 2015; Van Harten et al., 2017). Management theory and practice both assume that employability mutually benefits employees and employers. Organizations would benefit in terms of, for instance, increased work performance that may create competitive advantage (Van der Heijde & Van der Heijden, 2006), while employees experience enhanced well-being (Kirves, Kinnunen, De Cuyper, & Mäkikangas, 2014).

Organizations can stimulate their workers' employability through, among other things, human resources (HR) policies and practices that typically aim to support the growth and development of employees through training, and the successful management of the work–life interface through flexible work arrangements. However, whether such investments truly pay off in terms of increased performance and employee well-being remains unclear, as research on the effectiveness of human resource management (HRM) aimed at stimulating employability is still very limited (Van Harten et al., 2017).

As well as the lack of empirical evidence, the mutual benefits assumption can be questioned based on a broader debate in the HRM literature. On the one hand, literature reviews by Van de Voorde, Paauwe and Van Veldhoven (2012) and Peccei, Van de Voorde and Van Veldhoven (2013) support the mutual gains perspective by showing that HRM is generally associated with higher performance and employee happiness. On the other hand, reviews are also supportive of what is known as the conflicting outcomes perspective: while HRM boosts performance, it could simultaneously lead to work intensification, increasing employee stress and the likelihood of burn out. In the context of HR practices that aim to boost employability, HR development practices could, for instance, improve employee performance while at the same time negatively affecting well-being due to strain from employees' development activities and inherent performance expectations.

The mutual gains and conflicting outcomes perspectives are often presented as contradictory. However, many existing studies make use of a composite index of HR practices instead of examining the impact of different sorts of HR policies and practices (Guest, 2017). Putting highly heterogeneous HR practices together overlooks the fact that they target different areas, and some practices may yield more conflicting outcomes than others. It therefore remains unclear which specific sets of HR practices contribute to performance and well-being (Ogbonnaya & Messersmith, 2018). Adjudicating between the two perspectives is nevertheless highly relevant for advancing successful HRM.

The aim of this chapter is to examine the extent to which two different sets of HR investments in employability relate to both employee performance and well-being. We study multiple performance and well-being variables, acknowledging the multidimensionality of these constructs (Guest, 2017) and provide a nuanced insight into the possible mutual gains and/or trade-off effects. We use data collected in multiple industries (both public and private) across nine countries in Europe to provide more robust and generalizable findings on the effects of employability investments in European organizations.

Theoretical background

HRM: state-of-the art research insights

HRM refers to management decisions on policies and practices that together shape the employment relationship in and around organizations (Boselie, 2010). A vast body of literature aims to identify the mechanisms that determine how HRM ultimately affects organizational performance (Boxall, Guthrie, & Paauwe, 2016). The AMO-model is commonly used to explain the mediating mechanisms and states that employees show positive attitudes and desired behaviors (in other words, perform) when they have the abilities (A) in terms of skills and competences to do their job, are motivated (M) toward their job and have the opportunities (O) to perform or contribute. A meta-analysis by Jiang, Lepak, Hu and Baer (2012) has shown that HR practices designed to enhance employees' abilities, motivations and opportunities increase organizational performance. Two underlying psychological mechanisms explain this pattern. The human capital mechanism or the "cognitive path" explains that HRM stimulates employees' skills and abilities to solve work problems more effectively, resulting in better performance (Boxall and Macky, 2009). The "motivational path" suggests that HRM increases workers' satisfaction and other affective reactions and, in this way, ensures that employees want to perform and to continue to take responsibility for this, which will then lead to increased performance (Boxall and Macky, 2009).

Recently, Guest (2017) argued that the HRM literature is dominated by a performance focus. The main concern with such a one-sided approach is that "the search for a link between HRM and performance has been pursued at the expense of a concern for employee well-being" (Guest, 2017, p. 22), while changes in the nature and context of work call for an approach to HRM that stimulates both employee well-being and performance. In this contribution, we examine whether these outcomes can be achieved through HR investments in employees' sustainable employability.

HR investments in employability

Employability can be defined as the extent to which workers are able and willing to work productively. The term 'productive work' refers to adequately performing one's current job or, in the event of change, other tasks or jobs (Van Harten, Knies, & Leisink, 2015). Careers are extended because of an aging population and, in combination with other developments such as ongoing technological innovation, it is of vital importance that employees do not only have the ability to perform their current job, but are motivated to continue working in constantly changing work environments as well (Van den Broeck et al., 2014). This means that employability consists of up-to-date expertise or competences together with a willingness to continually develop and adapt to changes in the work environment. Such attributes help employees survive in contemporary turbulent labor markets (Thijssen, Van der Heijden, & Rocco, 2008).

It is argued that employability has benefits for both organizations and employees, and research shows the positive effects of employability on individuals' job performance (Kinnunen, Mäkikangas, Mauno, Siponen, & Nätti, 2011), commitment (De Cuyper & De Witte, 2011) and health (Berntson & Marklund, 2007). Many organizations therefore develop and implement practices aimed at increasing their employees' employability (Fleischmann, Koster, & Schippers, 2015; Veld, Semeijn, & Vuuren, 2015). However, research examining the effectiveness of these practices is largely lacking (Van Harten et al., 2017).

In addition, employability studies tend to focus merely on HR practices aimed at training and development, as such practices can stimulate the growth and maintenance of employees' capabilities and motivations. Although development investments have been shown to contribute to employability, other sets of HR practices could be important as well (Van Harten et al., 2017). Development practices can be expected to primarily boost individuals' capabilities and development motivations; however, as described above, employability consists of more than just these aspects. Offering flexible work arrangements could be another important way to boost employability as it enhances employee flexibility and adaptability by, among other things, providing employees with the opportunity to balance work and family demands (Stavrou, 2005).

In this study we aim to expand the focus on development HR in employability research and examine the performance and well-being effects of two different sets of HR practices that are likely to stimulate employability: (1) training and development opportunities; and (2) flexible work arrangements. The two sets are included in this chapter as they are directly linked to the two elements of our definition of employability. As illustrated above, both sets can be expected to relate to these two elements; essentially, training and development opportunities can be expected to primarily stimulate abilities and development motivations, while flexible work arrangements are likely to primarily stimulate flexibility/adaptability motivations.

Two perspectives on outcomes of HR investments in employability: mutual gains vs conflicting outcomes

Before explaining how HR investments in workers' employability impact performance and well-being, we need to make clear that we focus on performance and well-being effects on the employee level as it is suggested that organizational outcomes are too distal for assessing the impact of HRM (Ogbonnaya & Messersmith, 2018; Takeuchi, Chen, & Lepak, 2009). We regard employee well-being as the overall quality of an employee's experiences and functioning at work and further conceptualize this into a happiness and health dimension (Van de Voorde et al., 2012). We narrow the concept of performance to employee performances, which refers to optimal functioning at work reflected in employee in-role and extra-role behaviors that contribute to organizational functioning (De Cuyper et al., 2014).

Regarded from the mutual gains perspective, HRM is assumed to have positive outcomes for both the organization and its workers: what is good for the employee is also good for the employer, and the other way around. First, performance benefits arise as HR practices provide the necessary operational control for employees to improve their skills and perform their jobs in line with organizational goals (Guest, 2017; Takeuchi et al., 2009). In line with this, research shows that HR investments boost employability skills and competences (Van Harten et al., 2015; Veld et al., 2015) and a positive link between employability and job performance has also been established (Kinnunen et al., 2011). Next, based on social exchange theory it is argued that employees interpret HR investments as indicative of their employer's supportiveness and care and reciprocate by showing higher levels of trust and organizational commitment, ultimately leading to better in-role and extra-role performance (Ogbonnaya & Messersmith, 2018). The social exchange argument has been corroborated in employability research as well, and studies have found positive links between HRM, employability, commitment and job performance (Camps, Oltra, Aldás-Manzano, Buenaventura-Vera, & Torres-Carballo, 2016; De Cuyper & De Witte, 2011; Solberg & Dysvik, 2015). Next to performance benefits, the mutual gains perspective argues, among other things, that HRM leads to employees experiencing greater well-being – for example, in terms of job satisfaction – as they feel valued by their employer. HR investments in employability could improve well-being as well, as employable individuals are likely to be able to cope with the changes and uncertainty in current labor markets better than workers with low levels of employability, which could lead to them experiencing less stress and being more satisfied (Berntson & Marklund, 2007; Kirves et al., 2014). The most optimistic view of the mutual gains perspective regards HRM as directly impacting well-being and performance, and to have an additional mediated effect on performance via increased employee well-being (Van de Voorde et al., 2012). The 'happy workers are productive workers' thesis further supports this view (Wood, Van Veldhoven, Croon, & De Menezes, 2012).

The conflicting outcomes perspective in turn holds that well-being and performance are two distinct goals that are influenced by different sets of HR practices. This means that high-performance investments do not significantly influence employee well-being (Van de Voorde et al., 2012). The most pessimistic view of the conflicting outcomes perspective even claims that increased performance is achieved at the cost of reduced employee well-being, implying that organizations must make trade-offs as to which outcomes to invest in (Peccei et al., 2013). More specifically, it is argued that employees may experience work intensification resulting in increased stress in an organization that invests in high performance (Ogbonnaya & Messersmith, 2018). Some authors go further, referring to high expectations or demanding practices, the sole purpose of which is that employees internalize norms regarding high levels of effort. Such criticisms of the exploitative nature of HRM (Legge, 1995) claim that HRM may increase performance, while at the same time having negative consequences for employee well-being (Wood et al., 2012). HR investments in employability could also produce trade-off effects. For example, intensive training or development programs could help to improve employability and subsequently increase job performance, but at the same time they can intensify work, resulting in stress and decreased satisfaction with work–life balance.

Reviews by Van de Voorde et al. (2012) and Peccei et al. (2013) show that HRM is generally associated with higher organizational performance and employee happiness (mutual gains), yet is negatively related to employee health (conflicting outcomes); however, the latter needs to be further researched as the empirical evidence is lacking. Moreover, there is a need for research that investigates the performance and well-being effects of different sets of HR practices instead of treating HRM as a composite measure, as the effects could differ depending on the specific set of HR practices (Ogbannaya & Messersmith, 2018). Taken together, we expect the employability HR sets of (1) training and development opportunities and (2) flexible work arrangements to positively relate to employee performance (Hypothesis 1). In line with the mutual gains perspective, we also expect a positive relationship between the sets of HR practices and the happiness dimension of employee well-being (Hypothesis 2a). Based on the conflicting outcomes perspective, we expect the HR sets to non-significantly or even negatively (pessimistic view) relate to the health dimension of well-being (Hypothesis 2b). Finally, in line with the optimistic view of the mutual gains perspective, we expect the HR sets to have an indirect positive performance effect through increased

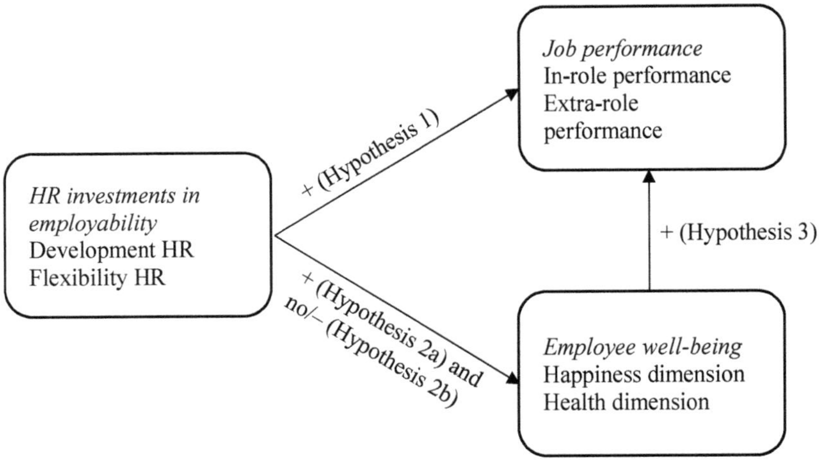

Figure 9.1 Conceptual model.

well-being on the happiness dimension (Hypothesis 3). This results in the research model in Figure 9.1.

Methods

Data

For our analyses we used the Employee Questionnaire from the European Sustainable Workforce Survey (ESWS) dataset. The sampling and data collection are described in detail in Chapter 2 of this book. As HR practices are typically accessible to employees, we excluded workers who were not formally employed by the organization (e.g., agency workers, interns, n = 266). Analyses are based on 10,654 employees from 259 organizations in nine countries (UK, Germany, Finland, Sweden, Netherlands, Portugal, Spain, Hungary and Bulgaria) and six industries (manufacturing, healthcare, higher education, transport, finance and telecommunications).

Measurements

Independent variables

The set of *flexible work arrangements* was measured through respondents' perceptions of whether telecommuting, flexible work schedules and commuting time could be counted as working time. Items were measured by asking for "yes," "no" and "do not know" answers, and were dichotomized by collapsing the "no"/"do not know" answers. For the analysis, we created a composite scale by performing principal component analysis on the polychoric correlation matrix of the dichotomous items (Kolenikov & Angeles, 2004). All polychoric correlations have correlations above 0.4. The *training and development* set was measured with a single item – the number of training days provided by an external trainer in which the respondent participated in the last 12 months. Items measuring perceptions of training availability were not measured in the Employee Questionnaire; we therefore resort to the participation measure.

Dependent variables

Well-being. We distinguished two dimensions of well-being, happiness and health. The happiness dimension was first captured using a 3-item affective organizational commitment scale (Allen & Meyer, 1996) (alpha = 0.85) and, second, with a single-item scale measuring overall job satisfaction measure (see Knies, Leisink, & Van de Schoot, 2017). Third, happiness with the work–life interface was added because it is increasingly argued that comprehensive evaluations of employee happiness should consider the employee as a whole, and therefore include the balance of work and non-work demands (Brough et al., 2014). The variable was measured with a single work–life balance satisfaction item ("How satisfied are you with the time you spend on paid work versus the time you spend on other parts of your life?") taken from the scale developed by Valcour (2007), ranging from 1 (extremely dissatisfied) to 10 (extremely satisfied). The health dimension was measured using a 4-item scale of perceived time pressure adapted from Garhammer's (2002) index of time pressure (alpha = 0.85), as an early indicator of burn out risks, and a single item self-reported general health measure (Pejtersen, Kristensen, Borg, & Bjorner, 2010).

Job performance. To measure this construct, we used the Individual Work Performance scale developed to measure different dimensions of self-evaluated performance. The instrument has good psychometric properties as well as invariance to cultural context and job type (Koopmans, Bernaards, Hildebrandt, De Vet, & Van der Beek, 2014). Our scale consists of two dimensions: task performance (five items, alpha = 0.86) and extra-role behavior (four items, alpha = 0.79).

Control variables

To account for worker and workplace characteristics that may correlate with the utilization of HR investments and are likely to influence employee well-being and performance, we included respondents' years of education, gender, age, years of firm tenure, salary and supervisory position as controls. Moreover, following Guest (2017), we included a 4-item scale of self-reported work autonomy (alpha = 0.86) as this variable is found to be a key job characteristic that has a vital impact on employee well-being and performance.

Results

Descriptives

Table 9.1a shows that there were significant differences between industries in the perceived availability of HR sets. Notably, employees in the higher education and telecommunications industries perceived significantly more flexible work arrangements compared to manufacturing, transport, financial services and health care. Next, employees perceived quite significant autonomy, with the same pattern that employees in higher education and telecommunications perceived more autonomy in comparison to the other industries. Turning to our dependent variables, employees were rather positive about their own level of task performance but reported slightly less extra-role behavior. The well-being scores (Table 9.1b) were quite positive; employees were, for instance, quite satisfied with their jobs and assessed their general health as rather good, yet they were less satisfied with their work–life balance. Table 9.2 shows the correlations between this study's variables, which are small to medium-sized and mostly positive.

Hypotheses 1 and 2: direct effects on performance and well-being

We tested our hypotheses using multivariate regression analyses. Slightly under half of the HR sets' direct effects on the performance and well-being variables were positive and significant (Table 9.3). One effect was negative and significant, and the other half of the effects were non-significant. To further elaborate, we analyze the effects separately. The HR set of flexible work arrangements was positively related to extra-role behavior ($\beta = 0.06$) and to most of the well-being variables, but at the expense of task performance ($\beta = -0.06$). Participation in training and development opportunities positively impacted affective commitment ($\beta = 0.04$) but had no significant effect on the remainder of the well-being variables, nor on the performance variables. These results only weakly support Hypothesis 1, as only the HR set of flexible work arrangements had a positive performance effect (extra-role behavior), but it also had a negative performance effect (task performance). Training and development did not directly affect performance. We found more robust support for Hypothesis 2a as flexible work arrangements had positive effects on the happiness well-being variables and training and development practices had a positive effect on affective commitment. However, the non-significant effects of training and development practices on most happiness well-being variables (except commitment) contradicted Hypothesis 2a. We also found some support for Hypothesis 2b – for instance, we found that the development HR set was non-significantly related to health outcomes – yet flexible work arrangements positively impacted general health perceptions, which contradicts Hypothesis 2b.

Table 9.1a Sample estimated means of scale measures: full sample and sector comparisons

	Full sample		*I*	*II*	*III*	*IV*	*V*	*VI*
	Mean	*Min/max*	*Mean*	*Mean*	*Mean*	*Mean*	*Mean*	*Mean*
Flexible work	0.82	0/3	ref.	–1.04***	0.71***	–0.11†	0.17***	0.77***
Extra-role behavior	8.82	0/16		–0.13***	0.18***	–0.21***	0.19***	0.22***
Task performance	13.86	0/20		0.03	–0.003	–0.05	–0.004	0.03
Affective commitment	8.29	0/12		–0.13***	0.03	–0.07†	0.13**	0.0001
Time pressure	7.20	0/16		0.05*	0.12***	0.06*	0.18***	0.15***
Job autonomy	11.05	0/16		–0.12***	0.18***	–0.17***	–0.02	0.14***

Notes
N = 10,654.
Full-information ML estimates of means.
Sectors: I – Manufacturing; II – Health care; III – Higher education; IV – Transport; V – Finance; VI – Telecommunications.
Scale measures are calculated as a sum of constituting items for total sample descriptions.
Sector comparison results are from multi-group analysis. Intercepts/thresholds and factor loadings of indicators constrained equal across groups and the means of latent scales are constrained to be zero for identification purposes in sector I (manufacturing).
† $p<0.1$, * $p<0.05$, ** $p<0.01$, *** $p<0.001$ (2-sided).

Table 9.1b Sample estimated means of single-item measures: full sample and by sector

	Full sample		*I*	*II*	*III*	*IV*	*V*	*VI*
	Mean	*Min/max*	*Mean*	*Mean*	*Mean*	*Mean*	*Mean*	*Mean*
Training AND development	2.45	0/365	2.67	2.57	2.09	2.02	2.85	2.41
Job satisfaction	5.98	0/9	5.89	5.95	6.16	5.84	6.00	6.12
Work–life balance	5.22	0/9	5.17	5.22	5.36	5.04	5.20	5.38
General health	2.88	0/4	2.85	2.82	2.89	2.88	2.94	2.94
Hourly wage (euro)	11.95	0.01/339	11.28	1.42	13.57	11.28	13.53	13.49
Contracted working hours	36.42	2/58	38.20	34.19	34.98	38.31	36.50	38.28
Female gender	0.56	0/1	0.38	0.80	0.63	0.38	0.64	0.39
Age	42.42	14/81	42.49	44.16	44.37	42.47	39.25	38.16
Tenure	11.01	0.08/55	11.53	12.55	11.35	1.08	9.72	7.98
Temporary contract	0.09	0/1	0.05	0.09	0.24	0.06	0.05	0.04
Supervisory position	0.20	0/1	0.23	0.15	0.22	0.23	0.14	0.20
Years of education	14.24	6/20	13.31	13.96	16.22	13.35	14.46	14.55

Notes
N = 10,654; full-information ML estimates of sample means.
Sectors: I – Manufacturing; II – Health care; III – Higher education; IV – Transport; V – Finance; VI – Telecommunications.

Table 9.2 Bivariate correlations between the main study variables

		1	2	3	*4*	5	6	*7*	8	9
1	Flexible work HR									
2	Training & development HR	0.04								
3	Job autonomy	0.26	0.03							
4	Extra-role behavior	0.25	0.05	0.34						
5	Task performance	–0.01	0.02	0.32	0.29					
6	Affective commitment	0.12	0.05	0.27	0.26	0.25				
7	Job satisfaction	0.14	0.01	0.21	0.14	0.26	0.42			
8	Work–life balance	0.16	0.02	0.28	0.19	0.27	0.54	0.69		
9	Time pressure	0.00	0.02	–0.12	0.08	–0.22	–0.22	–0.42	–0.30	
10	General health	0.09	0.02	0.13	0.10	0.15	0.18	0.21	0.22	–0.21

Note
N = 10,654; full-information ML estimates; scale variables are calculated as sum of standardized factor scores.

Table 9.3 Results from structural equation models – standardized direct effects

	Extra-role behavior	*Task performance*	*Affective commitment*	*Job satisfaction*	*Work–life balance*	*Time pressure*	*General health*
Affective commitment	0.17***	0.10***					
Job satisfaction	0.001	0.07***					
Work–life balance	0.04**	0.06***					
Time pressure	0.17***	–0.11***					
General health	0.03**	0.06***					
Flexible work HR	0.06***	–0.06***	0.08***	0.05***	0.05***	0.01	0.03**
Training & development HR	0.02	0.00	0.04***	0.02	0.02†	0.00	0.01
Job autonomy	0.26***	0.28***	0.24***	0.27***	0.21***	–0.16***	0.11***

Notes

N = 10,564; full-information ML estimates using cluster-robust standard errors (adjusting for organizational clustering of employees).

Additional controls: years of education, supervisory position, employment contract type, company tenure, age, gender, contracted working hours, log hourly wage, public sector employer, log organization size, industry x country.

† $p<0.1$, * $p<0.05$, ** $p<0.01$, *** $p<0.001$ (2-sided).

Table 9.4 Indirect, direct and total effects of HR investments and job autonomy on extra-role behaviour and task performance

	Flexible work	*Training AND development*	*Job autonomy*
Extra-role behavior			
Total indirect effect	0.02***	0.01***	0.03***
Indirect effect via happiness	0.02***	0.01***	0.06***
Indirect effect via time pressure	0.001	–0.001	–0.03***
Indirect effect via general health	0.002***	0.001†	0.004***
Direct effect	0.04***	0.02*	0.26***
Total effect	0.07***	0.03***	0.30***
Task performance			
Total indirect effect	0.02***	0.01***	0.08***
Indirect effect via happiness	0.02***	0.01***	0.05***
Indirect effect via time pressure	–0.001	0.001	0.02***
Indirect effect via general health	0.004***	0.001†	0.01***
Direct effect	–0.08***	–0.003	0.26***
Total effect	–0.06***	0.008	0.34***

Notes

Statistical inferences on indirect, direct, and total effects are based on bootstrapped standard errors (N of bootstrap samples = 500); bootstrap sampling was performed on cases with complete data within organizational strata (N = 7,197).

Robustness tests of the original sample comparing complete case and full-maximum likelihood analyses produced close to identical estimates.

Additional controls: years of education, supervisory position, employment contract type, company tenure, age, gender, contracted working hours, log hourly wage, public sector employer, log organization size, industry x country.

† $p < 0.1$, * $p < 0.05$, ** $p < 0.01$, *** $p < 0.001$ (2-sided).

Hypothesis 3: Mediation of well-being

To simplify interpretation, we performed mediation tests by combining job satisfaction, work–life balance and affective commitment on a scale measuring the happiness well-being dimension (alpha = 0.78). The two variables tapping into the health dimension, self-reported general health and perceived time pressure, had a small-to-moderate but significant correlation (r = –0.25), and we decided against combining these items. Table 9.3 shows that most of the well-being variables were positively related to job performance; although work pressure was negatively related to task performance, it was positively related to increased extra-role behaviors. Our mediation results (Table 9.4) show that both HR sets had positive indirect effects on extra-role behavior and task performance via the happiness well-being dimension, supporting Hypothesis 3. In addition, the mediation effects of flexible work arrangements through the general health construct were also positive though substantially weaker. The mediation effects through time pressure were non-significant.

Control variables' effects

Job autonomy had substantive positive effects on the outcome variables. As can be seen from Table 9.3, job autonomy was the main driver of extra-role behavior ($\beta = 0.26$, $p < 0.001$), task performance ($\beta = 0.28$, $p < 0.001$) and work–life balance ($\beta = 0.21$, $p < 0.001$). Table 9.4 indicates that job autonomy also had positive indirect effects on the performance variables mediated through well-being, and these effects were generally stronger than those of the HR sets.

Besides job autonomy, the control variables working hours, hourly wage, supervisory function, age and education had significant positive effects on extra-role behavior. Women reported higher, and older workers lower, task performance. The regression models reveal notable sectoral effects. Workers in higher education, financial services and telecommunications exhibited higher levels of extra-role behavior than workers in the other sectors. Workers' commitment, as well as their experienced time pressure, was higher in the financial sector.

Conclusions and discussion

This chapter has examined whether HR investments in employability are able to fulfill the promise of enhancing both employee performance and employee well-being or whether there are trade-off effects. We found much more convincing evidence for the mutual gains perspective, but also found some instances of conflicting outcomes (in line with Van de Voorde et al., 2012). This means that HR investments in employability generally contribute to both employee performance and employee well-being while at the same time – and depending on the HR set under investigation – they can have trade-off effects as well, meaning that either performance or well-being is sometimes non-significantly or even negatively affected.

The mutual gains perspective was corroborated by the mediation results. These demonstrate that both HR sets contribute to the happiness and health dimensions of well-being and indirectly (mediated through most of the well-being variables) to employee performance. It is important to point out that the positive performance effects were to a considerable extent indirect, mediated through well-being. This means that employee well-being and employee performance are not contradictory but mutually enforcing (optimistic mutual gains view).

In line with the conflicting outcomes perspective, we found, for example, that flexible work arrangements had a direct negative effect on in-role performance, while positively contributing to happiness-related well-being. While this trade-off effect has not been suggested by the conflicting outcomes HRM perspective so far, conflicting effects of flexible work arrangements have been demonstrated elsewhere. For instance, studies have found contradictory effects of telecommuting on different outcome domains: telecommuting has been shown to increase job satisfaction (Golden & Veiga, 2005), but it can also lead to an extension of working hours into employees' own time (Glass & Noonan,

2016) and increased work–family conflict, while it has no positive or negative impact on task performance (Van der Lippe & Lippényi, 2018). For flextime and compressed workweeks, the meta-analysis of Baltes, Briggs, Huff, Wright, and Neuman (1999) reveals mostly positive effects on job satisfaction, but positive effects on absenteeism and performance ratings were very modest and, in most studies, non-significant. These findings strengthen our initial message to HR scholars that a multi-dimensional analysis of HR investments is needed to understand how HR investments produce mutual gains and conflicting outcomes.

Next, the results regarding the development HR set provide support for the skeptical conflicting outcomes view in which it is thought that the set of HR practices that stimulates performance is not necessarily the same set that impacts well-being (Van de Voorde et al., 2012). That is, participation in training and development only contributed to affective organizational commitment and indirectly to employee performance, while it was not significantly related to the other well-being variables. The positive relationship with commitment is interesting to note, though, as it falsifies the so-called employability management paradox which states that employees are likely to leave the organization when they perceive their employability to have increased as a result of development investments (De Cuyper & De Witte, 2011).

Finally, our findings indicate that the control variable of job autonomy appeared crucial for both employee performance and employee well-being. This variable is often seen as a key job resource that employees need to be able to properly function in the workplace (Guest, 2017). Also, employability studies (Van Emmerik, Schreurs, De Cuyper, Jawahar, & Peeters, 2012) have found that job autonomy is an important driver. This means that besides stimulating workers' employability by providing them with supportive HR practices, employers should ensure that employees have sufficient autonomy in their jobs to benefit from employability in terms of increased performance and well-being, possibly leading to more workplace productivity and cohesion.

Our study makes several scientific contributions. First, we add rigorous empirical evidence to the topical HRM debate on mutual gains vs conflicting outcomes. Our results show a mutual gains dominance, but also show that these effects should not be overestimated. While HR investments in employability generally boost employee performance and their affective commitment or job satisfaction – perhaps because of more challenging work – in some instances this could lead to employees experiencing more stress at work as well. Recently, Ogbonnaya and Messersmith (2018) have drawn similar conclusions, but pointed out that stressful work need not always carry a negative connotation. Indeed, short-term stress need not be problematic, but once it leads to long-term negative health reactions (e.g., burn out), the sustainability of the workforce could be in danger. Our results provide the first indications on such negative health reactions, but further research is needed to investigate this issue further.

Second, by showing that the HR sets we distinguished had different effects, this chapter provides sophisticated empirical support for the call that HRM research should not simplify HRM into an index measure, but instead distinguish multiple sets of HR practices (Guest, 2017). The concept of HR sets acknowledges that HR policies can be bundled based on their purpose (HR system approach) and, at the same time, it provides the opportunity to detect nuanced effect patterns that would not have been found using a composite measure of one HRM system. In addition, our results are quite generalizable as we used multiple industries data across nine European countries.

Third, by distinguishing different outcome domains, analyzing both in-role and extra-role performance and happiness and health well-being, we were able to show that HR investments in employees' employability have domain-specific effects, which is a significant step toward understanding the mechanisms behind mutual gains and conflicting outcomes.

Our research is not without its limitations, however. First, we used cross-sectional data based on self-reported measures. This presents the possibility of common-method bias and means that one should be careful when drawing definitive conclusions on the causality of the relationships between HRM, performance and well-being. Second, we assumed that the HR sets stimulate employees' employability and consequently boost their performance and well-being. However, we did not measure employability in itself and can only argue that the concept acts as a mediating mechanism based on theoretical arguments and other research (Van Harten et al., 2015). Third, only in the case of the HR development set did we have data on the level of training participation for the whole sample, while for flexible work arrangements, participation was only asked about in respect of those who perceived their availability. For further research, the intensity of participation in HR sets, and under which circumstances they are implemented, could be important explanatory mechanisms and provide additional insight into the performance and well-being effects.

In conclusion, this chapter's mutual gains results show the relevance for employers of investing in their workers' employability by providing them with ample development opportunities and the space to work flexibly. Benefits do materialize for performance, but they generally do so indirectly by improving employee well-being. Our results suggest that it is important for organizations to offer a diversified HR system to improve both employee well-being and employee performance.

10 Temporary contracts, job uncertainty, and work–life balance

A multilevel study across European organizations

Zoltán Lippényi, Alessandra Gasparotto, and Jouko Nätti

Introduction

There is an increasing understanding of the ways in which work organizations can facilitate the reconciliation of work and private life. Current studies in work–life balance research, however, predominantly focus on work arrangements, such as working from home or organizational culture (see Greenhaus, 1988; Jones, Burke, & Westman, 2013; Van der Lippe & Lippényi, 2018). We know much less about how various employment relationships influence workers' capacity to reconcile work and family. This question is relevant to address as economic competition and uncertainty in Europe and North America pressurizes work organizations to invest less in durable employment relations. As a result, organizations often substitute long-term, stable employment – the dominant employment form until the 1980s – with flexible and temporary contracts (Kalleberg, 2000). Temporary workers account for between 9 percent and 25 percent of the labor force in Europe; on average, one in seven European workers have a temporary affiliation with their employer, exceeding the number in the US where one in ten workers have a temporary affiliation with their workplace (Organisation for Economic Co-operation and Development, 2017c).

The sustainability of temporary employment arrangements is subject to debate. On the one hand, organizations prefer short-term commitment to workers as it provides greater flexibility; but temporary employment is highly unpopular among workers, with the exception of a minority of highly-skilled freelancers (Amuedo-Dorantes, 2000). Existing research underlines employees' concerns with temporary contracts, showing that temporary workers perceive higher levels of job insecurity and are less satisfied with their jobs (De Cuyper et al., 2008; Kauhanen & Nätti, 2014; Kalleberg, 2012; Saloniemi & Zeytinoglu, 2007; Wilkin 2013). Most research focuses on outcomes at work, and we know little about the outcomes of temporary jobs for well-being outside work (see Scherer, 2009). The few existing studies that address consequences beyond the organizational domain focus on material and behavioral consequences. They show that having a temporary job influences everyday consumption patterns (Lozza, Libreri, & Bosio, 2013), the accumulation of wealth (McGrath & Keister, 2008), and decisions regarding the timing of raising children among female workers (Central Bureau voor de Statistiek, 2017). However, besides material and behavioral outcomes, we know very little about how temporary employment contracts influence personal life.

In this chapter we aim to fill this gap by studying the differences in perceived work–life balance of temporary and permanent workers in European organizations. We focus on work–life balance as it has been shown to influence overall well-being: numerous studies suggest that a positive work–life balance contributes to life satisfaction (Greenhaus Collins, & Shaw, 2003; Haar, Russo, Suñe, & Ollier-Malaterre, 2014) and imbalance is associated with higher levels of stress, lower effectiveness and efficiency at work, and even burn-out (Kofodimos, 1993; Shanafelt et al., 2012). The growing recognition of the importance of work–life balance is manifested in policy initiatives, such as the European Commission's 'New Start' initiative in 2016–2017 which addresses the challenges faced by working parents and careers in combining work and family.

This chapter also addresses how organizations' strategic considerations regarding the use of temporary workers matters for these workers' perceived work–life balance. Specifically, we focus on two common strategies: using temporary workers as incidental labor or using temporary contracts as a recruitment tool for permanent positions. The reasons for using temporary workers have been shown to be relevant to the wages and training opportunities of such workers (Lautsch, 2003). A US study shows that the adoption of a temporary employment strategy is also relevant to the attitudes of permanent staff (Way, Lepak, Fay, & Thacker, 2010). The authors document that permanent workers are more likely to withdraw supportive behaviors in organizations that hire temporary workers with the aim of decreasing labor costs. The context of the employing organization is, however, mostly missing in research on the well-being of temporary workers. Our study contributes to a better understanding of how organizational strategies with regard to flexible employment are relevant to the psychological outcomes of workers.

As is the case with most of the chapters in this book, our study uses the European Sustainable Workforce Survey (ESWS), focusing on organizations in countries where the use of temporary work arrangements is prolific: Finland, the Netherlands, Germany, Portugal, and Spain.

Theoretical background

Temporary employment, job uncertainty, and work–life balance

Work–family border theory argues that work and private life (leisure, family, household) are perceived to be in balance when the borders between the two different domains are strong (Clark, 2000). Borders could be physical, but may also be psychological. Psychological borders are rules self-created by individuals that dictate which thinking patterns, behaviors, and emotions are appropriate for one domain but not the other. The theory suggests that high permeability of the borders between work and family negatively affects the capacity to maintain a work–life balance. This can occur in the instance of strong negative emotions at work which are difficult to keep outside the family domain and have a tendency to permeate home life (Evans & Bartolome, 1980). Research on the work–life experiences of workers who work at home support these theoretical notions: permeations between work and family experienced by these workers makes it difficult to maintain physical borders between the two domains (Guest, 2002).

We argue that such permeations may occur in the case of temporary workers due to the job insecurity they experience. Although there are many terms to denote such employment relationships, such as nonstandard work (Ashford, George, & Blatt, 2007; Broschak, Davis-Blake, & Block, 2008), fixed-term employment (De Cuyper & De Witte, 2005), or as contingent employment (Green & Heywood, 2008; Wilkin, 2013), we prefer to refer to these arrangements as temporary employment to denote the temporary scope of the employment relationship. Numerous studies have documented that temporary employment generates perceptions of job insecurity (De Cuyper & De Witte, 2005; Green & Heywood, 2008; Guest, 2004; Virtanen, Kivimäki, Elovainio, Vahtera, & Ferrie, 2003). Job insecurity may affect work–life balance by keeping workers' thoughts involved with their work situation even during their leisure time (Sora, Caballer, & Hoege, 2012). Associated with the threat of job loss, feelings of deprivation of needs such as a stable income and the structuring of time, along with unpredictability about the future, are likely to permeate the mental borders and enter the private sphere. Research by Lozza et al. (2013) supports this contention: they found that *perceptions* of job insecurity rather than objective job insecurity led to a lowered capacity among workers to take part in entertainment activities or day-to-day activities such as grocery shopping – it even impacted their intention to take on long-term projects, such as getting a mortgage or buying a house.

In contrast to this argument, a few studies report that temporary workers are more satisfied with their jobs than permanent workers (De Witte & Näswall, 2003; Parker, Griffin, Sprigg, & Wall, 2002). These studies argue that temporary workers have reduced demands and experience less conflict at work compared to permanent workers because their jobs involve less responsibility and have lower performance expectations (Parker et al., 2002). However, both studies that find higher levels of job satisfaction among temporary workers report that temporary workers do experience higher levels of job insecurity compared to those on permanent contracts.

Job insecurity associated with temporary employment may also affect work–life balance indirectly, through job strain. Feelings of job insecurity have been shown to include a sense of lack of control, or the feeling of being powerless (Greenhalgh & Rosenblatt, 1984), as the reasons for job insecurity, such as age or health, are beyond the individual's control. The job insecurity experiences of temporary workers are likely to be associated with a lack of control too (see

Parker et al., 2002), as these workers typically have a minor direct influence on the employer's decisions regarding their future employment (Pearce, 1993; Rogers, 2000; Smith, 2002). Lack of control, in turn, is a highly important factor in job strain and stress (Karasek, 1979). Following the work–family border theory, the experience of high job strain, and associated feelings of stress, are likely to spill over from the work sphere and permeate the family domain.

Next to lack of control, strain can also be brought about by work exhaustion owing to the workplace behaviors that workers in precarious positions engage in. Job uncertainty has been shown to prompt workers to actively search for a new job while still employed in their current job (Bryson, 2004; Kahn, 2012), as well as to increase their efforts at work in order to improve their chances of getting a stable employment contract or a good referral (Engellandt & Riphahn, 2005; McDonald & Makin, 2000). In addition, job insecurity felt by temporary workers could also contribute to fear and anxiety about making mistakes at work and feelings of the need to perform well (Rogers, 2000). Researching temporary agency workers, Giunchi, Emanuel, Chambel, and Ghislieri (2016) found that these workers took on high workloads, mainly to show effort and have a chance of keeping their jobs, but at the same time this led to feelings of exhaustion.

Based on these mechanisms, we hypothesize that temporary employment has a negative effect on work–life balance. This negative effect is mediated through job uncertainty. We do not expect any direct effect of temporary employment on work–life balance. We expect job uncertainty to negatively influence work–life balance – in part, indirectly, through job strain. The lower part of Figure 10.1 presents this mediation model. In this model we also account for a potential negative direct effect of temporary contracts on job strain (see Parker et al., 2002).

Organizational strategy with hiring temporary workers

Perceptions of uncertainty may vary across organizations as their reasons for using temporary workers are not alike. One of the most common uses of temporary work

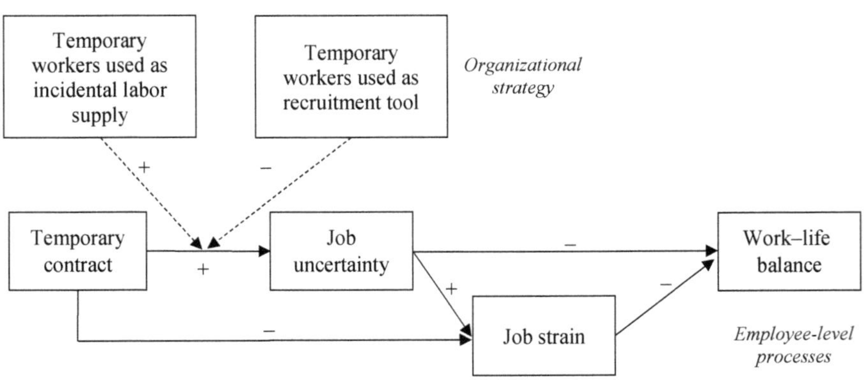

Figure 10.1 Conceptual model and hypotheses.

is to accommodate a temporary need for labor. Due to the short-term nature of the employment relationship, firms seldom hire workers on temporary contracts for functions which are constantly needed by the firm and central to their production (Atkinson, 1984). 'Core' functions require a high specificity of human capital, a high chance of repetition, and high monitoring costs, which makes it more efficient for employers to bind workers performing these tasks to their company (Masters & Miles, 2002). At the same time, tasks that are only temporarily relevant and thus marginal to core production can be filled with cheaper temporary labor; typical examples are low-skilled jobs in business services, such as photocopying or office cleaning (Rogers, 2000). High-skilled occupations with a similar temporary demand, such as IT maintenance or project management, are also filled using a temporary workforce (Barley & Kunda, 2001). Firms also use temporary workers to fill in during periods of peak demand or when there is a shortage of permanent staff because of sickness (Hakim, 1990).

In the US and Canada in particular, savings in direct labor costs are an important motivation for companies to hire temporary workers (Davis-Blake & Uzzi, 1993). Companies realize cost-savings by using externalized forms of employment, such as agency work, instead of direct hiring; this requires less investment in benefits and training (Houseman, Kalleberg, & Erickcek, 2003). In European labor contexts, externalized employment is less common, partly because regulation of co-employment does not allow employers to differentiate in benefits and training between direct employees and external workers. While direct cost-savings may be less important in Europe than in the North American context, cost considerations are likely to enter European employers' hiring strategies, as employment protection legislation (e.g., severance pay, job protection in case of sickness) makes dismissal of permanent workers costly for the enterprise (see Polavieja, 2003).

A different strategic option is to use temporary labor as a channel to recruit permanent staff (Von Hippel, Mangum, Greenberger, Heneman, & Skoglind, 1997). Using a temporary contract as a probation period during which the employer and the employee could evaluate the quality of the 'match' or 'fit' has numerous advantages for companies. First, probation periods are typically short, only a few of months, whereas temporary contracts are usually longer, which extends the period of evaluating the employee and thus reduces the risk of a mismatch. In addition, management may anticipate performance gains from such a recruitment strategy, because the prospect of permanent employment motivates temporary workers to be involved at the workplace, to maintain good workplace relations, and to increase their effort (Van Dyne & Ang, 1998). When organizations employ this strategy, they also integrate temporary and permanent workers on similar tasks, and invest more in the training and supervision of temporary workers (Lautsch, 2003). These investments signal to temporary workers that the employer is interested in extending the employment relationship, which reduces the insecurity associated with having a temporary contract. In contrast, when organizations hire temporary workers on an ad hoc basis, they are unlikely to profit from such benefits or feel that their employer is interested in a long-term employment relation. Therefore, when the company strategy in hiring temporary workers is to access ad hoc labor, the actual and perceived position of these workers will be more precarious. We expect temporary contracts to lead to lower perceived job uncertainty in organizations where recruiting for permanent positions is an important reason for hiring temporary workers, and to lead to higher perceived job uncertainty in organizations where gaining ad hoc labor through hiring temporary workers is of higher importance (see upper part of Figure 10.1).

Method

Data

This study draws on the ESWS, and covers the Netherlands, Spain, Portugal, Germany, and Finland. Surveys from Bulgaria, Hungary, and the UK were excluded because fixed-term contracts are quite atypical in these contexts (Eurostat, 2013). We also excluded Sweden because a number of Swedish companies participated in the survey with a sample of 'core' workers from a team or department and therefore fixed-term employees were not in their samples.

The total number of respondents in the five countries was 6,388 employees. We excluded 12 organizations (367 employees) that did not have temporary workers, as well as respondents that were not employed by the organization, such as interns, agency workers, and freelancers (in total 222 cases). While the outcomes of non-employee workers is certainly relevant, our survey – focusing on organizational investments in employees – had limited means to reach and adequately represent the non-employee population of workers. The analytical sample comprises 5,799 employees from 133 organizations. Most respondents were Dutch ($n = 2{,}400$), followed by Portuguese ($n = 1{,}099$), Germans ($n = 880$), Spanish ($n = 692$), and Finnish ($n = 728$) employees. We weighted the data to equalize the number of cases per country in order to avoid the dominance of a single country.

Measures

In line with studies in the work–life balance literature (Hill, Hawkins, Ferris, & Weitzman, 2001; Lyness & Kropf, 2005; Sturges & Guest, 2004), we captured the subjective perception of respondents have about their *work–life balance* with a single-item measure: "How satisfied are you with the time you spend on paid work versus the time you spend on other parts of your life?" Responses ranged from 1, "extremely dissatisfied" to 10, "extremely satisfied."

Temporary contract was identified through the question: "What kind of employment contract do you have?" The possible answers distinguished between permanent contract and different types of temporary employment. We only included directly hired fixed-term workers in the analysis ($n = 781$). A dummy variable (coded 1 = yes and 0 = no) was created to indicate temporary employment status.

The item "I worry about keeping my job" was used to measure the perception of *job insecurity*. This item is often used in research on job insecurity (e.g., Burgoon & Dekker, 2010; Richter, Näswall, & Sverke, 2010). Response possibilities ranged from 1, "strongly disagree" to 5, "strongly agree."

Job strain was measured using four items from the job inventory questionnaire (Karasek, 1979), to capture the perceived demands of work ($\alpha = .75$).

Two items capturing organizational reasons for hiring temporary employees were reported by the organization's HR manager. The first item asked whether the reason for hiring employees for a fixed term was "to assess performance before granting a permanent contract," capturing *hiring temporary workers for recruitment*; the second item asked whether it was "to replace employees who are absent temporarily," capturing *hiring temporary workers for incidental labor*. For both items, response possibilities ranged from 1, "strongly disagree" to 5, "strongly agree." The correlation between the two items is $r = -.21$.

We included as control variables the characteristics of workers in our analysis. We incorporated demographic characteristics (female gender, age, years of education, indicators for being partnered and having children at home), job characteristics (occupational status measured as Standard International Socio-Economic Index of Occupational Status [ISEI] scores, years of organizational tenure, indicators for supervisory position, part-time work status, telecommuting, flexible starting and finishing times), job quality indicators (level of job autonomy measured using a scale of four items, $\alpha = 0.86$, and a single-item measure of overall job satisfaction), a measure of job involvement (using a four-item organizational citizenship behavior battery, $\alpha = 0.75$), and partner job characteristics (indicators for working and permanently employed partner). At the level of the organization, we included sector, country, and organizational size as controls. Table 10.1 provides descriptive statistics of the study variables.

Analytic approach

We specified multilevel structural equation models (MSEM) to estimate the proposed structural model. The first model estimates the direct, indirect, and total effects of temporary contract on work–life balance. Based on this model we test the hypothesized structural relations between temporary contract, uncertainty, job strain, and work–life balance. This model includes organization random intercepts for the endogenous constructs uncertainty, job strain, and work–life balance. The second model incorporates a random slope parameter (impact of temporary contract on job uncertainty) and cross-level interactions between temporary contract and organizational goals in hiring temporary workers to test the hypothesized moderation. The three endogenous variables – work–life balance, job uncertainty, and job strain – are regressed on all individual and organizational control variables. We used full-information maximum likelihood estimation to utilize all the available data in the sample.

Table 10.1 Descriptive statistics

	Mean	*Var.*	*Min*	*Max*
Employee-level variables				
Work–life balance	5.27	4.27	0	9
Job uncertainty	1.92	1.66	0	4
Job strain	9.51	7.09	0	16
Temporary contract (0/1)	0.14			
Organizational strategy				
Temporary workers as recruitment tool	2.02	1.85	0	4
Temporary workers as incidental labor supply	2.28	1.42	0	4
Control variables				
Job autonomy	10.98	10.63	0	16
Job satisfaction	6.10	3.59	0	9
Organizational citizenship	8.99	14.92	0	16
Supervisory position (0/1)	0.23			
Female	0.57			
Age (in years)	42.60	106.94	16	77
Tenure (log)	3.15	2.16	0.29	7.41
Education (ISCED)	4.42	5.86	0	7
Occupational status (ISEI)	58.44	313.18	11.56	88.70
Part-time status (0/1)	0.25			
Flexible working hours (0/1)	0.50			
Working from home (0/1)	0.21			
Having a partner (0/1)	0.75			
Having a working partner (0/1)	0.62			
Having a permanently employed partner (0/1)	0.49			
Having a child at home (0/1)	0.51			
Sector				
Manufacturing	0.19			
Health care	0.23			
Higher education	0.20			
Transportation	0.14			
Financial services	0.14			
Telecommunications	0.10			
Organization size (log)	5.23	1.65	2.77	9.21

Notes
N = 5,799; means and variances are estimated using full-informational maximum likelihood. Post-stratification weighting is applied to balance the sample sizes per country.

Results

Figure 10.2 shows the standardized coefficients for the employee-level part of our conceptual model. As expected, we find that workers with a temporary contract experience higher levels of job uncertainty, and job uncertainty leads to higher levels of experienced job strain. Temporary workers experience less job strain than permanent workers, as has been shown by other studies. With respect to work–life balance, we find that higher levels of job strain lead to

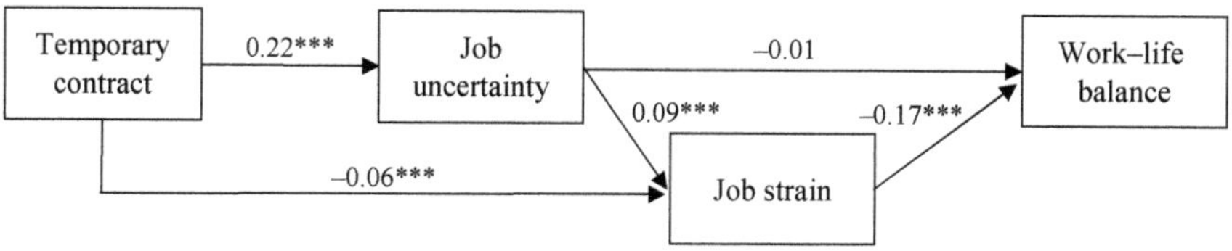

Figure 10.2 Estimates from multilevel structural equation model – employee-level processes.

Notes
N of workers = 5,799. N of organizations = 133. Restricted maximum-likelihood estimates (standardized) including random intercept components for endogenous variables. Chi2 (145) = 7786. Data are weighted and stratified by country.
All endogenous variables are regressed on control variables at the individual level (female gender, age, years of education, partner status, having children at home, occupational status scores, organizational tenure, supervisory position, part-time work status, telecommuting, flexible starting and finishing times, job autonomy, overall job satisfaction, part-time and permanently employed partner) and organizational level (sector, country, and organizational size). Full results can be obtained from the first author on request: z.lippenyi@rug.nl.
† $p < 0.1$, * $p < 0.05$, ** $p < 0.01$, *** $p < 0.001$ (2-sided).

lower perceived work–life balance but, against our expectations, job uncertainty does not have a direct negative effect on work–life balance.

Given these structural relationships, what conclusions can be drawn on the impact of temporary employment on work–life balance? Table 10.2 shows the total effect of temporary employment on work–life balance, as well as the direct and multiple indirect effects calculated from the MSEM model.

The results show that when indirect and direct effects are taken together, temporary employees experience greater work–life balance than permanent workers. The strongest explanatory mechanism in our mediation model is job strain: temporary workers experience less strain than permanent workers, which results in increased work–life balance. Job uncertainty perceptions do not directly explain differences in work–life balance between temporary and permanent workers.

Table 10.2 Standardized total direct and indirect effects of temporary employment on work–life balance – employee-level processes

	β
Total effect	0.03*
Total indirect	0.01
Specific indirect effects	
Through job uncertainty	–0.00
Through job strain	0.01**
Through job uncertainty and strain	–0.003***
Direct effect	0.03

Notes
† $p < 0.1$, * $p < 0.05$, ** $p < 0.01$, *** $p < 0.001$ (2-sided).
Additional details about the model are provided in the Notes to Figure 10.2.

However, job uncertainty perceptions do explain the differences indirectly, via job strain: temporary workers experience higher levels of uncertainty which induces strain and this strain diminishes work–life balance. The direct effect of having a temporary contract is positive, but not statistically significant.

Taken together, temporary workers perceive more balance between their work and private lives than permanent workers, and it is because they experience less strain in their jobs. However, temporary workers experience more uncertainty which, through the mediation of job strain, negatively influences work–life balance. This mediation mechanism supports our expectations based on work–life border theory, but the effects are weaker insofar as they do not offset the work–life benefits of the lower job strain temporary workers experience compared to permanent workers. In summary, our assertions about the negative effect of temporary employment on work–life balance (through job uncertainty and job strain) has only limited support, because the significantly lower strain temporary workers experience weighs more heavily than the indirect negative influence of job uncertainty and job strain on work–life balance.

Our next question pertains to whether organizational strategies in respect of hiring temporary workers influence the relationship between temporary contract and work–life balance. Our expectations found partial support (see Figure 10.3). When organizations engage more with the strategy of recruiting future permanent employees through the hiring of temporary workers, the latter experience less job uncertainty. At the same time, it is not relevant to the experienced job uncertainty of temporary employees whether incidental hiring is an important or less important organizational goal. In summary, we find moderate support for our assertion that organizational strategic goals send signals to these workers

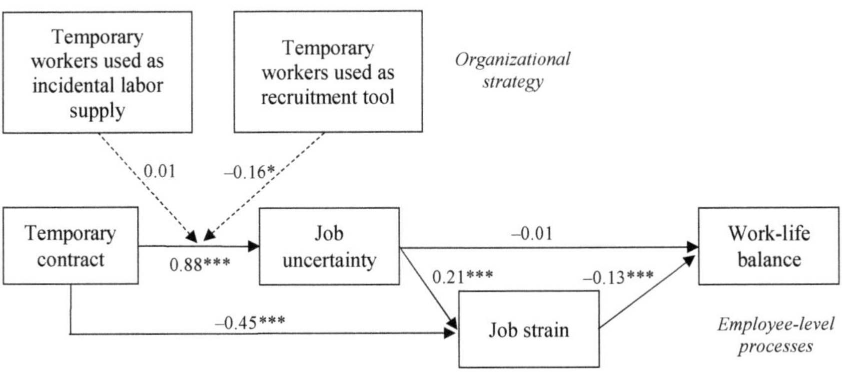

Figure 10.3 Estimates from multilevel structural equation model – moderation effects of organizational strategy.

Notes

N of workers = 5,799. N of organizations = 133. Restricted maximum-likelihood estimates (unstandardized) incorporating random intercepts of endogenous variables, and a random slope for the effect of temporary contract on job uncertainty. Data are weighted and stratified by country.

All endogenous variables are regressed on control variables as in Figure 10.2. Standardized coefficients are currently not available in Mplus for random slope models.

† $p < 0.1$, * $p < 0.05$, ** $p < 0.01$, *** $p < 0.001$ (2-sided).

about their future job prospects, mitigating the negative consequences of temporary contracts on job insecurity and work–life balance.

It is possible that temporary workers experience higher strain when they are in contention for a permanent job, offsetting the benefits of higher job certainty. For instance, they may be putting more effort into their jobs to convince organizational decision-makers to give them a permanent contract (McDonald & Makin, 2000). The strain effects of increased effort could then lead to lower perceived work–life balance. We specified a model in which we included parameters capturing organizational-level variation in the direct effect of temporary contract on job strain. We do not, however, find either recruitment or incidental hiring goals to be relevant to how much job strain temporary workers experience relative to permanent workers.

Discussion

The use of temporary employment in organizations has generated much public debate about the potential risks for employee well-being. While the literature extensively discusses work-related outcomes, less attention has been paid to the impact of temporary employment at the work-life interface. This chapter contributes to the literature by studying the relationship between temporary employment and work–life balance.

Contrary to the critical voices, we found that temporary workers experience more balance between work and family life than permanent workers. This finding echoes earlier research which has shown that permanent workers experience greater time pressure at work than temporary workers (Van der Lippe, 2007). Our results suggest that temporary workers' more favorable perceptions of work–life balance can be attributed to experiencing relatively less strain in their jobs. This is not unexpected, as permanent workers usually have more responsibilities and face higher expectations at work than those employed on temporary contracts (Vough, Broschak, & Northcraft, 2005). The fact that temporary workers are present in the workplace may even negatively impact permanent workers' work–life balance, as it can lead to higher workload and the overburdening of permanent workers with additional tasks, for instance, the supervision of temporary workers.

When we looked into the mechanisms explaining the link between temporary employment and work–life balance, we found that temporary workers experience greater job uncertainty than permanent workers, inducing job strain that has a negative effect on work–life balance. Although this chain mediation effect was not as strong as the job strain associated with permanent employment, it has a number of relevant implications. First, it lends additional support to the theoretical perspective that negative experiences in the work domain – job uncertainty and job strain – have detrimental consequences for other life domains (Clark, 2000). Second, it conveys the message to work–life balance scholars that employment arrangements matter. The work–life literature mostly studies the impact of work arrangements (e.g., work–life policies) as a means through which organizations can contribute to work–life balance. The mechanism we unearthed shows that employment arrangements are also relevant to perceived work–life balance. Finally, the chapter contributes to a new avenue in scholarship about employment arrangements focusing on outcomes outside work. Our results indicate that the psychological consequences of different employment arrangements reach further than the work domain, influencing the perceived interface of work and private life.

Our study found that the outcomes of temporary and permanent workers differ: while the former group reports higher job insecurity, the latter experiences higher levels of job strain and lower work–life balance. The fact that the two groups distinguished by employment contract face different challenges at work holds relevant implications for workplace cohesion and cooperation in flexible organizations. Earlier research argued that workplace cohesion may deteriorate in flexible organizations because temporary and permanent employees have differing formal, contractual and informal, motivational attachment to the organization (Vough et al., 2005). An additional theoretical mechanism distinct from formal and informal organizational attachment may exist, namely, that temporary and permanent employees also differ in the consequences and challenges they face in being employed in a flexible organization. The bifurcation of everyday workplace problems and experiences, rooted in differences in employment form, can impede joint effort, cooperation, and solidarity among workers. In the current state of contingent employment research, this is merely a theoretical suggestion worth studying for its implications for labor performance, as well as for the potential for mobilization and representation of employee interests.

A further contribution of our study is the investigation of the interplay between employment form and organizational context – strategic goals in hiring temporary workers – in influencing the work–life balance of workers. We focused on organizational variation in the extent to which job uncertainty perceptions mediate the impact of temporary employment and found less difference in job uncertainty perceptions between temporary and permanent workers in contexts where the organization's strategic goal with temporary employment is to recruit long-term permanent staff. We did not, however, find evidence that the job uncertainty gap would be greater in organizations that use temporary workers for ad hoc incidental labor. One reason may be that the use of the wording "to replace employees who are absent temporarily" does not best capture hiring temporary workers for ad hoc incidental labor. For example, in Finland, replacement of absent employees typically means the use of substitutes to replace, for example, workers on family leave, especially in female-dominated sectors where temporary contracts are common (see Eurofound, 2007). Furthermore, the job quality of substitutes is much better compared to those recruited, for example, for seasonal or other incidental work.

Nevertheless, the finding that the organizational strategy is relevant supports assertions that organizational context intersects with employee and job characteristics in influencing work experiences and worker outcomes (Kristal, 2017).

Addressing the organizational context is of course not new in scholarship on contingent work. Earlier studies on employment systems engaged with the systemic features of contingent employment (Lautsch, 2002), and recent scholarship in the strategic HRM literature has addressed the workplace-level consequences of different contingent employment strategies (Way et al., 2010). However, the literature on individual-level outcomes of temporary work has paid little attention so far to the role of organizational context. With the availability of multilevel organizational surveys such as the ESWS we hope that there is movement in the direction of incorporating organizational context and the interplay between context and individual in discussions about the psychological and behavioral consequences of contingent work. While this chapter has looked at organizational strategy, future research could investigate the consequences of the normative organizational context, such as organizational culture, for the outcomes of temporary workers. For instance, a familial organizational culture (see Cameron & Quinn, 2006) can trigger supportive behavior by co-workers and supervisors, which could buffer the uncertainty and strain of temporary employment (Voydanoff, 2005).

We should note some limitations of the present study as well. First, due to the organizational survey design, we were not able to analyze the work–life balance of temporary workers whose administrative control lay with another employer (temporary work agency) or themselves (freelance contractors). While this group of external temporary workers is much smaller in Europe than in the US, it is growing. Their workplace experiences are likely to differ from those of directly hired temporary workers: temporary agency workers have dual commitments – to the employing organization and to the organization they work for (Liden, Wayne, Kraimer, & Sparrowe, 2003). In addition, due to their outsider status, agency workers may receive less support from managers and supervisors (Parker, 1994) and may even be stigmatized by their co-workers (Boyce, Ryan, Imus, & Morgeson, 2007). Freelance contractors probably have greater time pressures: as case studies aptly describe, they are simultaneously working on jobs, integrating into workplace communities, and searching for the next client (Barley & Kunda, 2006; Osnowitz, 2010). Current research has yet to explore the consequences of being an 'itinerary worker' and 'outsider' at the workplace for work–life balance, and we encourage future studies to take on this task.

In our discussion, we implicitly assumed that temporary employment is involuntary. However, there are temporary workers who chose their contract in order to be loosely attached to the domain of work or to a particular employer (see Broschak, Davis-Blake, & Block, 2008; Kauhanen & Nätti, 2014; Origo & Pagani, 2008). As temporary contracts are their preferred form of employment, they are likely to experience lower levels of uncertainty and job strain, making it easier to maintain borders with the family domain. While such considerations are important for part-time work, labor market research shows that preferences for temporary employment are very rare: most temporary workers, with the exception of freelancers, would prefer to have a permanent work contract (Amuedo-Dorantes, 2000; Forrier & Sels, 2003). In addition, temporary jobs are popular only among certain employee demographics – mainly young workers who value flexibility in taking a new direction in their careers – while they are much less appreciated among older workers (Bardasi & Francesconi, 2004). It is worth noting that our study excluded freelancers who have the highest preference among all temporary workers for their form of employment.

Another limitation concerns the cross-sectional design of our data. While we adjusted to a wide range of confounders in our analyses, the cross-sectional nature of our dataset prevents causal claims about the impact of temporary contract on work–life balance. In particular, negative selection into temporary contract based on unobserved productivity could be problematic, as it may explain away the contract effect on uncertainty and strain. However, it is unlikely that unobserved confounders explain away our findings concerning the negative impact of temporary contract on job uncertainty, as studies based on longitudinal survey design have identical findings to ours (e.g., Bardasi & Francesconi, 2004; Buddelmeyer, McVicar, & Wooden, 2015; Parker et al., 2002, Virtanen et al., 2003). An advantage of using longitudinal data is that one could investigate temporal changes in the workplace outcomes of temporary workers. In particular, the 'honeymoon-hangover effect' – workers' high levels of satisfaction when starting a new job (Boswell, Boudreau, & Tichy, 2005) – may have implications for job satisfaction differences between permanent and temporary workers (Chadi & Hetschko, 2013). We could expect temporal dynamics in the work–life balance of temporary workers as well, if temporary workers receive a greater number and more significant tasks from their employer as their contract period advances. By using job tenure as a covariate, we could only partially control this honeymoon-hangover effect. A final limitation is that we were able to use only single-item questions for job uncertainty and work–life balance, although similar items have been used in earlier studies.

Despite these limitations, our research fills an important gap in the literature regarding the interplay between employment relationships and the work–life interface. With regard to current discussions about the long-term sustainability of temporary employment, we would like to emphasize the importance of balancing the diffuse and sometimes contradictory interests of workers and organizations. For workers, temporary employment may have negative psychological consequences but, at the same time, it could be a stepping stone at the start of a career (Gash, 2008). For organizations, temporary work benefits labor flexibility, but it may come at the cost of low commitment (Van Dyne & Ang, 1998), leading to high turnover, sickness, and productivity concerns. One of the implications of the findings of our study is that organizations may be able to combine both flexibility and good performance by seeking temporary employment strategies that provide better outlooks for temporary workers to attain permanent employment. For societal equity, the balance between flexibility and security should be judged by how the costs, such as individual well-being and organizational productivity, measure up to the benefits in terms of job opportunity and firms' labor flexibility. Temporary work is here to stay, so it is important to have a good understanding of the benefits and risks for sustainable employment.

11 Human capital investments and the value of work

Comparing employees and solo self-employed workers

Wieteke Conen and Paul de Beer

Introduction

At the turn of the nineteenth century, self-employment was much more common than it is today and could especially be found among farmers, tradesmen, craftspeople and freelance professionals. Throughout the twentieth century, paid employment increased substantially and went hand-in-hand with technical change that favored capital-intensive, large-scale production; the rise of the 'Fordist model'; and the emergence of the 'standard' employment contract (Organisation for Economic Co-operation and Development [OECD], 2000; Supiot, 2001). Over recent decades, the nature, structure and organization of work transformed once again (as a result, among other things, of technological development and globalization), and many European labor markets have become more flexible. Various forms of 'non-standard' employment contracts appeared and since the 1970s the long-term historical decline in self-employment has slowed in many European economies and, in some countries, even reversed (Broughton et al., 2016; Eurofound, 2017a, 2017b; OECD, 2000).

For a long time, organizations have invested in employees in order to enhance individual and organizational performance, for instance, through various human resources (HR) policies such as training, health and work–family policies. Solo self-employed workers typically lack access to organizational policies – including formal training opportunities inside corporations – and must procure them themselves (Smith, 2010). This raises the question: what happens to human capital accumulation if there is no 'organization' that invests in the worker? Previous research in this area seems to indicate that the *amount* of training or the percentage of self-employed people who receive training is lower than that of employees (e.g., Broughton et al., 2016, p. 89, 93; Van Echtelt, Croezen, Vlasblom, De Voogd-Hamelink, & Mattijssen, 2016). On the one hand, this may indicate that self-employed people are lacking in a sufficient training investment (due to monetary constraints, time or access) to pursue sustainable careers. On the other hand, it may also mean that relatively highly skilled individuals opt into self-employment or that self-employed people are more effective or rational in choosing the training they really need. Against this background, we will first address the question whether solo self-employed workers differ from employees in their self-assessed skills: do they think their skills correspond well with their own work duties, or would they require further training? Next, we examine how and to what extent solo self-employed workers – as compared to employees – invest in their employability or in their careers through training.

In addition, we will distinguish between employees on permanent and on temporary contracts. As found in previous research, a temporary employment relationship may adversely affect the willingness of both employers and workers to invest in training, due to the short payback period for the investment. Studies in this field indeed indicate that workers on temporary contracts undergo less formal training than permanent employees (Arulampalam, Booth, & Bryan, 2004; Forrier & Sels, 2003; Fouarge, De Grip, Smits, & De Vries, 2012; Sequeda, De Grip, & Van der Velden, 2015). From the literature it is unclear how the training of solo self-employed workers relates to both permanent and temporary employees.

Finally, in addition to our analysis of differences in human capital investments between various groups of workers, we study how investments are related to self-assessed work valuations. We hypothesize that workers with different types of contracts vary in how human capital investments are associated with work engagement and career prospects. Career theorists have argued that organizationally bounded linear careers (or unidimensional advancement on career ladders within organizational hierarchies) are increasingly being replaced by independent employment relationships and flexible career patterns. Not only did written contracts change when permanent contracts and lifetime employment were replaced by temporary and external contracts, but the psychological contract or implicit agreement between employers and employees also began to shift from an essentially relational agreement to a more transactional agreement (Cappelli, 1999; Clarke, 2008). We hypothesize that the human capital investments of permanent workers are positively related to both the current and future value of their work through this relational agreement, whereas for temporary and self-employed workers human capital investments are part of the transactional framework. The transactional nature thus refers to "specific, short-term and monetizable obligations entailing limited involvement of the parties" (Morrison & Robinson, 1997, p. 229).

Earlier research has typically focused on the value of work in terms of job satisfaction, finding that self-employed individuals are on average significantly more satisfied with their work than are organizational employees (e.g., Benz & Frey, 2008; Blanchflower, 2000; Hundley, 2001). However, it is increasingly acknowledged that such 'general' findings need further development through a more differentiated approach. That is, various authors have stressed the need for a more detailed examination of individual work facets (for example, distinguishing between the valuation of content, pay or job security) and among different types of workers (Brown, Forde, Spencer, & Charlwood, 2008; Clark, 2005; Millán, Hessels, Thurik, & Aguado, 2013; Rose, 2005; Warr & Inceoglu, 2018).

In this chapter we study workers' valuations by examining *work engagement* and self-assessed *prospects for career advancement*, two individual work facets which are potentially affected by investments in employability.[1] Work engagement is defined as "... a positive, fulfilling, work-related state of mind that is characterized by vigor, dedication, and absorption" (Schaufeli, 2017, p. 3). Whereas work engagement captures the current value of work, prospects for career advancement provide insight into a worker's expected future valuation of work. In addition, we study workers' valuations by examining different types of workers, i.e., by making distinctions between workers in terms of skill level, occupational class and grade of job (Broughton et al., 2016; Warr & Inceoglu, 2018). Moreover, in the 'traditional' literature on self-employment, the self-employed are framed as a category of independent entrepreneurs who voluntarily seek to gain higher utility from income, autonomy, flexibility and other working conditions attributed to self-employment. However, the structure and the nature of occupations carried out by those who are self-employed have changed substantially over recent decades (Conen, Schippers, & Schulze Buschoff, 2016) and a new branch of literature has emerged, emphasizing the heterogeneity among the 'new' solo self-employed. This heterogeneous group also includes the 'involuntary' self-employed and those operating at the fuzzy boundary between being an employee and employee-like self-employment (or bogus self-employed), a distinction increasingly made in the literature (Conen, 2018; Kautonen et al., 2010; Schulze Buschoff & Schmidt, 2009; Stone, 2006; Westerveld, 2012). In our study, the (in)voluntariness of the transition into solo self-employment will also be included as a predictor of training investments as well as of a worker's valuation of work.

Theoretical background

The theoretical background for our study lies in human capital theory, as developed half a century ago by Becker (1962, 1964) and others. According to this theory, a worker can accumulate human capital either through (formal) education and training or through learning-by-doing or (informal) on-the-job training. The advantage of learning by doing and on-the-job training is that it is cheap and it generally does not interfere with working time, since it is part of the working process itself. However, not all knowledge and skills can be acquired while working and sometimes formal training is necessary. Becker (1964) distinguished further between two kinds of training, namely, general training and specific training. General training is also useful in other firms besides the current firm of the worker, whereas (wholly) specific training is only useful in the current firm. Since the productivity of a worker who has followed general training increases in all firms, their market wage will rise and the current employer will have to pay a higher wage in order to prevent the worker from quitting. Therefore, the firm will not be prepared to pay for training and the worker will have to pay for it themselves. Since specific training only raises the productivity in the current firm, the market wage of the worker does not rise and the current employer can reap the return on the training. Consequently, the firm has to pay for the training. However, if the worker who received the specific training nevertheless quits, the firm incurs a loss. The firm may therefore try to shift part of the costs of specific training onto the worker in return for a slightly higher wage to discourage quitting.

This theoretical approach applies first of all to employees with a permanent contract, who are expected to stay in the firm for a considerable time. Since employees on a temporary contract are expected to stay in the firm only temporarily, firms will be less willing to invest in specific training as the period available to recoup the returns will in general be too short. Since temporary workers are generally more frequently active on the open labor market than permanent employees, they are expected to invest more in general training themselves to remain attractive to other employers.

Solo self-employed workers have no durable or exclusive relationship with any firm, so firms, in general, will not be willing to pay for training as competitors would also benefit from that investment. To maintain or increase productivity self-employed workers have to invest in (general) training themselves. Therefore, we expect them to follow training paid by themselves more frequently than permanent employees.

Based on this theoretical reasoning we hypothesize that:

1 Permanent employees receive more training paid by the employer than temporary employees and solo self-employed workers.
2 Solo self-employed workers undergo more training paid by themselves than temporary employees and temporary employees undertake more self-financed training than permanent employees.
3 There is no difference in the amount of (informal) on-the-job training received by permanent employees, temporary employees and solo self-employed workers.

As mentioned in the introduction, employees with a permanent contract, on the one hand, and temporary workers and solo self-employed workers, on the other, may differ in how they experience the relationship with the organization they work for. Permanent workers who have a long-term relationship with their employer may develop a relational perspective on their employment relationship. This a based on the (implicit) psychological contract between the worker and the firm, that is, "an individual's system of beliefs, based on commitments expressed or implied, regarding an exchange agreement with another" (Rousseau, 2011, p. 191). When the employer offers the employee the opportunity of training, paid by the employer, this reinforces mutual expectations. Hence, the psychological contract is confirmed, and this may enhance both the current work engagement and the future career prospects of the worker.

However, for a worker on a temporary contract the psychological contract is likely to be based on the idea of a transactional agreement. Since the employer does not commit to any future prospects for the worker (unless this is part of the labor contract), the worker will also not commit to the employer. Hence, any training, whether it is paid by the employer or not, will only have instrumental value for the worker, in the sense that it may improve their future career prospects. We therefore do not expect that training paid by the employer will increase the current work engagement of a temporary worker, although it may improve their career prospects.

The relationship between a solo self-employed worker and a company is even more transactional and has a strong instrumental purpose. If self-employed people invest in training themselves, this is expected to be done to increase future career opportunities, while it has less of an impact on their current work engagement.

Hence, we hypothesize that:

4 On-the-job training increases (a) the work engagement and career prospects of permanent workers and (b) the career prospects of temporary workers and solo self-employed workers.
5 Training paid by the employer increases (a) the work engagement and career prospects of permanent workers and (b) the career prospects of temporary workers.
6 Training paid by workers themselves increases the career prospects of all types of workers but not their work engagement.

Methodology

Data

To address the research questions, we used data from the sixth European Working Conditions Survey (EWCS) (Eurofound, 2015a), a cross-sectional dataset providing unique and detailed information on work in Europe. The EWCS is a questionnaire-based survey, based on interviews with approximately 1000 individuals in each EU country. The sample is representative for those aged 15 years and older who are in employment. Further details about EWCS and its methods are available online (Eurofound, 2015b). For the sake of comparability with other chapters in this book, we selected the same countries covered in the European Sustainable Workforce Survey (ESWS), i.e., Bulgaria, Finland, Germany, Hungary, the Netherlands, Portugal, Spain, Sweden and the United Kingdom. The countries included are geographically dispersed across Europe and cover all types of European welfare state regimes (Arts & Gelissen, 2002; Esping-Andersen, 1990).

Measures

Dependent variables

Self-assessed skill adequacy was based on the question, "Which of the following statements would best describe your skills in your own work?" (answer categories: "I need further training to cope well with my duties," "My present skills correspond well with my duties" and "I have the skills to cope with more demanding duties"). Type of training and training days were assessed by asking respondents:

- whether they had undergone any of the following types of training to improve their skills over the past 12 months: training paid for or provided by the employer, training paid by the worker himself/herself and informal on-the-job training (i.e., informal training at work, for instance, learning from co-workers or supervisors)
- how many days they spent in training over the past 12 months on a scale between 1 (1 day or less) and 6 (20 days or more).

Work engagement was assessed based on the three-item Utrecht Work Engagement Scale (UWES-3) (Schaufeli, 2017), containing the items "At my work I feel full of energy," "I am enthusiastic about my job" and "Time flies when I am working" ($\alpha = 0.74$). Measurement of prospects for career advancement was based on the statement, "My job offers good prospects for career advancement" (answer categories range between 1, strongly disagree and 5, strongly agree). Descriptive statistics of the variables used in the analyses are presented in Table 11.1.

Independent variables

For employed workers, employment form was measured by the questions: "Are you working as an employee or are you self-employed?" and "What kind of employment contract do you have in your main job?" Answer options for the latter were: "Contract of unlimited duration/permanent," "Contract of limited duration/fixed-term" and "A temporary employment agency contract." For solo self-employed workers, employment form was based on the questions: "Are you working as an employee or are you self-employed?" and "Regarding your business, do you have employees (working for you)." Heterogeneity among solo self-employed workers was assessed by the question: "When you became self-employed, was it mainly through your own personal preference or because you had no other alternatives for work?" Answer options were: "Mainly through own personal preference," "No other alternatives for work," "A combination of both (spontaneous)" and "Neither of these reasons (spontaneous)." In the analyses, the distinction between voluntary and involuntary self-employment was incorporated with an interaction term.

Control variables

In our analyses we controlled for the following work characteristics: working hours per week, occupational class (International Standard Classification of Occupations) and sector (NACE rev.2). We also included socio-demographic characteristics: gender, age, educational attainment level (International

Table 11.1 Descriptive statistics

	Mean	*Std.*	*Min*	*Max*
Dependent variables				
Self-assessed skill adequacy (ref. = correspond well)				
need further training	0.13		0	1
have skills to deal with more demanding duties	0.28		0	1
Training paid by worker (0/1)	0.07		0	1
Training paid by employer (0/1)	0.42		0	1
On-the-job training (0/1)	0.41		0	1
Training days paid by worker (ref. = no training)				
1–3 days	0.03		0	1
4–9 days	0.02		0	1
10–19 days	0.01		0	1
20+ days	0.01		0	1
Training days paid by employer (ref. = no training)				
1–3 days	0.18		0	1
4–9 days	0.17		0	1
10–19 days	0.06		0	1
20+ days	0.04		0	1
Work engagement (1 = never, 5 = always)	3.86	0.70	1	5
Prospects for career advancement (1 = strongly disagree, 5 = strongly agree)	2.95	1.34	1	5
Independent variables				
Employment form (ref. = permanent contract)				
solo self-employed	0.08		0	1
employee with fixed-term/temporary contract	0.12		0	1
Motives (ref. = through personal preference)				
no other alternatives for work	0.02		0	1
other	0.01		0	1
Control variables				
Working hours/week	35.83	11.40	1	100
Occupation (ref. = managers, professionals, technicians, associate professionals)				
clerical support workers, service and sales workers	0.30		0	1
skilled agricultural, forestry/fishery and craft workers	0.13		0	1
plant/machine operators and assemblers, elementary occupations	0.16		0	1
Sector of employment (ref. = public sector)				
private sector	0.70		0	1
other	0.09		0	1
Gender (ref. = male)	0.48		0	1
Age	42.47	12.17	15	87
Educational level	4.90	1.73	1	9
Country (ref. = Finland)				
Sweden	0.05		0	1
Germany	0.35		0	1
Netherlands	0.07		0	1
Spain	0.15		0	1
Portugal	0.03		0	1
United Kingdom	0.27		0	1
Bulgaria	0.03		0	1
Hungary	0.04		0	1

Source: Eurofound, 2015a.

Note
N = 10,682.

Standard Classification of Education) and country. Since the number of countries in our analyses is too small to perform multilevel analyses (Maas & Hox, 2005; Stegmueller, 2013), we controlled for country characteristics by including dichotomous country indicators.

Results

Self-assessed skill adequacy

We first address the question whether paid employed workers differ from solo self-employed workers in their self-assessed skills: do they think their skills correspond well to their work duties, or would they require further training? Table 11.2 presents results from the multinomial logistic regression model explaining self-assessed skill adequacy (the base outcome is "My present skills correspond well with my duties") by employment form and control variables.

The results show that compared to the reference group (paid employed workers with a permanent contract) paid employed workers on temporary contracts relatively often report that they are in need of further training. Solo self-employed workers, on the other hand, relatively often report that they have the skills to deal with more demanding duties; the interaction term with those who became self-employed because they had no other alternatives for work is not significant.

Post-school training

The next step is to examine how employability is taken care of by employed workers and solo self-employed workers. Table 11.3 shows the type of training workers underwent over the past 12 months in order to improve their skills. Table 11.3 shows that 6 percent of all employed workers (both those with permanent and those with temporary contracts) underwent training which was paid for by themselves. This percentage is significantly higher among solo self-employed people: 20 percent of all solo self-employed workers underwent training which was paid for by themselves. On the other hand, employed workers more often participated in training paid for or provided by their employer and on-the-job training (e.g., by co-workers or supervisors); almost half of the employed workers with a permanent contract had undergone these types of training over the past 12 months. Employees on temporary contract participated in training paid for or provided by their employer and on-the-job training less often than those with permanent contracts. These results partly confirm our hypotheses 1, 2 and 3. However, contrary to hypothesis 2, temporary workers do not invest more in training themselves than permanent workers and, contrary to hypothesis 3, self-employed workers significantly less often participate in (informal) on-the-job training than employees.

Although solo self-employed workers engage in training less often than employees, the intensity and efficiency of these trainings may also differ, which

Table 11.2 Multinomial logistic regression analysis of self-assessed skill adequacy

	Need further training (ref. = correspond well)	*Have skills to deal with more demanding duties (ref. = correspond well)*
Employment form (ref. = permanent contract)		
Solo self-employed	0.11	0.34**
Solo self-employed, no other alternatives for work	–0.40	–0.36
Employee with fixed-term/temporary contract	0.41**	0.07
Work characteristics		
Working hours/week	0.01**	0.00
Occupation (ref. = managers, professionals, technicians)		
Clerical support, service, sales workers	–0.52**	0.12
Skilled agricultural and craft workers	0.62**	–0.01
Operators, assemblers, elementary occupations	–0.97**	–0.07
Sector of employment (ref. = public sector)		
Private sector	–0.38**	–0.01
Other	–0.08	–0.04
Socio-demographic characteristics		
Gender (ref. = male)	0.12	–0.11
Age	–0.05	–0.02
Age squared/1000	0.38	0.12
Educational level	0.05	0.07**
Countries (ref. = Finland)		
Sweden	0.59**	0.53**
Germany	1.29**	0.49**
Netherlands	0.58**	0.33*
Spain	0.56**	0.59**
Portugal	–0.36	–0.24
United Kingdom	0.22	0.58**
Bulgaria	–0.53*	0.13
Hungary	0.057**	0.76**

Source: Eurofound, 2015a.

Notes
N = 10,682.
*$p < 0.05$; **$p < 0.01$ (2-sided).

Table 11.3 Type of training received (percentage of respondents), by employment form

	Employees with permanent contract	*Employees with temporary contract*	*Solo self-employed*
Training paid by worker	6	6	20**
Training paid by employer	48	33**	–
On-the-job	45	37**	15**

Source: Eurofound, 2015a.

Note
** (*) = significant difference compared to employees with permanent contract at the 1 percent (5 percent) level.

may be partly reflected in the number of training days and in the effect of their investments in employability on work engagement and prospects. Table 11.4 presents results from the multinomial logistic regression model, explaining the number of training days by employment type, self-assessed skill adequacy and control variables (the base outcome is "no training").

The results show that compared to the reference group (employed workers with a permanent contract) solo self-employed workers more often report all durations of training periods paid for by the worker. Thus, the fact that self-employed workers undergo more self-financed training than employees is not restricted to short – and therefore likely relatively cheap – trainings, but to training of all durations. Temporary and permanent staff do not significantly differ in their distribution of the number of training days paid for by the worker himself/herself. When training days paid for by workers and by employers are taken together, the solo self-employed and employees with temporary contracts participate significantly less in almost all durations of training than permanent staff. This shows that self-employed workers do not fully bridge the gap with training paid for by employers by making higher investments in training themselves. Workers who indicated they would require further training to cope well with their duties more often engaged in training.

Work engagement and prospects

Table 11.5 presents results from the ordered logistic regression analyses, examining whether human capital investments and control variables affect individuals' work engagement and prospects for career advancement.

Columns 1 and 2 of Table 11.5 show that employees with permanent contracts who had participated in training paid for or provided by the employer and in on-the-job training have significantly higher work engagement levels and more often think their job offers good prospects for career advancement. For employees with temporary contracts (columns 3 and 4) none of the training types is related to engagement with work, but training paid for or provided by the employer and on-the-job training are positively associated with *prospects* for

Table 11.4 Multinomial regression analyses of training days paid by worker and employer

	Days paid by worker (base outcome = no training)				*Days paid by worker or employer (base outcome = no training)*			
	=<3 days	*4–9 days*	*10–19 days*	*20+ days*	*=<3 days*	*4–9 days*	*10–19 days*	*20+ days*
Employment form (ref. = permanent contract)								
Solo self-employed	1.15**	1.95**	1.68**	0.97*	–1.70**	–1.62**	–2.10**	–1.30**
Solo self-employed, no other alternatives for work	0.25	0.07	0.26	0.01	0.24	–0.38	0.71	0.22
Employee with fixed- term/temporary contract	–.046	0.15	0.24	0.16	–0.54**	–0.79**	–0.71**	–0.19
Self-assessed skill efficacy (ref. = need further training)								
Correspond to skills	–0.87**	–1.08**	–1.07**	–1.40**	–1.22**	–1.66**	–1.53**	–2.12**
Have skills to deal with more demanding duties	–0.84**	–1.13**	–0.40	–0.76**	–1.28**	–1.49**	–1.33**	–1.49**
Work characteristics								
Working hours/week	0.01	0.02*	0.01	–0.01	0.00	0.02**	0.03**	0.01
Occupation (ref. = managers, professionals, technicians)								
Clerical support, service, sales workers	–0.35	–0.36	–0.44	–0.40	–0.20	–0.53**	–0.70**	–0.49**
Skilled agricultural and craft workers	0.00	0.16	0.11	–0.67	–0.46**	–0.68**	–1.07**	–0.60*
Operators, assemblers, elementary occupations	–0.19	–0.51	–1.87**	–0.83*	–0.55**	–1.12**	–1.86**	–1.41**
Socio-demographic characteristics								
Gender (ref. = male)	0.49**	0.46*	0.31	0.31	0.08	0.15	–0.10	0.15
Age	–0.03	0.02	–0.03	0.00	0.03	0.03	0.02	–0.03
Age squared/1000	0.25	–0.11	0.18	–0.52	–0.38	–0.46	–0.30	–0.04
Educational level	0.28**	0.29**	0.33**	0.26**	0.10**	0.19**	0.14**	0.23**
Countries (ref. = Finland)								
Sweden	–0.48	–1.43**	–0.9	–0.19	–0.55**	–0.52**	–0.78**	–0.76**
Germany	–0.37	–0.31	–1.31*	–1.24*	–0.64**	–0.51**	–1.08**	–1.08**
Netherlands	–0.42	–0.26	–1.13*	–0.23	–0.16	0.02	–0.31	–0.11
Spain	–0.56*	–0.26	0.21	0.83**	–1.06**	–0.70**	–0.69**	0.19
Portugal	–1.01*	–0.15	0.54	–0.30	–1.01**	–1.04**	–1.04**	–0.70*
United Kingdom	–0.45	–0.65*	–1.41*	–0.56	–0.21	–0.15	–0.23	–0.35
Bulgaria	–2.47**	–2.27**	–1.00	–0.32	–2.06**	–2.18**	–2.11**	–1.27**
Hungary	0.37	0.02	–0.19	0.08	–0.99**	–1.85**	–1.72**	–0.84**

Source: Eurofound, 2015a.

Notes
1 N = 10,682.
2 * $p < 0.05$; ** $p < 0.01$ (2-sided).

Table 11.5 Ordinal logistic regression analyses of work engagement and employment prospects

	Employees, permanent		*Employees, temporary*		*Solo self-employed*	
	Engagement	*Prospects*	*Engagement*	*Prospects*	*Engagement*	*Prospects*
Training types						
Training paid by worker	–0.11	0.02	–0.17	–0.48	0.91	1.02**
Training paid by employer	0.60**	0.40**	0.22	0.51**	–	–
On-the-job	0.29**	0.29**	0.49	0.45**	1.39*	0.42
Motives (ref. = through personal preferences)						
No other alternatives for work	–	–	–	–	–0.85**	–0.90**
Other	–	–	–	–	–0.93**	–.083**
Work characteristics						
Working hours/week	0.01	0.02**	–0.01	0.01	–0.01	0.01*
Occupation (ref. = managers, professionals, technicians)						
Clerical support, service, sales workers	–0.36**	–0.34**	–0.51	–0.55**	–0.44	–0.53
Skilled agricultural and craft workers	–0.15	–0.55**	–0.15	–0.24	–0.13	–0.66*
Operators, assemblers, elementary occupations	–0.98**	–1.15**	–0.66*	–0.76**	–1.14*	–1.23**
Sector of employment (ref. = public sector)						
Private sector	0.02	0.13	–0.26	–0.03	–0.50	–0.73
Other	0.06	0.14	–0.27	0.13	0.25	–0.29
Socio-demographic characteristics						
Gender (ref. = male)	0.21	–0.14*	–0.11	–0.23	0.49	0.22
Age	0.04	–0.09**	–0.02	–0.04	–0.05	–0.05
Age squared/1000	–0.37	0.70**	0.34	0.15	0.58	0.25
Educational attainment	–0.37	0.06*	0.04	0.02	0.06	–0.06
Countries (ref. = Finland)						
Sweden	–0.15	–0.07	–0.41	–0.33	0.65	0.30
Germany	–0.31	–0.07	–0.47	–0.42	–0.88	–0.70*
Netherlands	1.01**	0.10	0.53	–0.25	1.53	–0.28
Spain	–0.26	0.21*	–0.17	–0.41	–0.52	–0.76**
Portugal	–0.24	0.52**	–0.61	–0.24	–1.77**	–0.81*
United Kingdom	–0.36*	0.36**	–0.24	0.34	–0.77	–0.25
Bulgaria	0.17	0.48**	0.26	0.68*	–0.80	–0.51
Hungary	–0.59**	0.51**	–0.40	0.15	–0.29	0.65
N	8107	8107	1583	1583	992	992

Source: Eurofound, 2015a.

Notes
N = 10,682.

career advancement. Solo self-employed workers (columns 5 and 6) who indicated they had participated in on-the-job training over the past 12 months are more likely to feel engaged with work. Training paid for by the worker has a positive and significant effect on prospects for career advancement for self-employed workers. Solo self-employed people who became self-employed by personal preference are more likely to experience higher levels of work engagement and to think their job offers good prospects for career advancement than those who became self-employed because they had no other alternatives for work.

These results largely confirm hypothesis 4, in the sense that on-the-job training seems to increase both the work engagement and the career prospects of permanent workers, and the career prospects of temporary workers. However, contrary to hypothesis 4, on-the-job training does not increase the career prospects of solo-self-employed workers, although it does increase their work engagement. The results also confirm hypotheses 5, i.e., training paid by the employer increases the work engagement and the career prospects of permanent workers, and the career prospects of temporary workers. However, contrary to hypothesis 6, training self-financed by the worker does not increase the career prospects of permanent or temporary employees. This is rather surprising, and it raises the question why employees invest in self-financed training at all.

Robustness check

Since we estimated the effects of variables based on nine countries, it is possible that the results were driven by one, very influential country. We therefore also performed a robustness check by deleting every country once from the various analyses (jackknife procedure). The results show that the findings as described in the previous section are quite stable. The effects of employment forms and self-assessed skill adequacy on training days remain significant and changes in the sizes of the effects are minor. Similarly, the effects of training types and motives on work engagement and career prospects remain significant and changes in the sizes of the effects are minor here as well. An exception is the effect of informal on-the-job training on career prospects, which becomes significant only at the 10 percent level when Spain is excluded. Moreover, taking Germany out has a relatively strong effect on the relationship between self-assessed skill adequacy and self-employment; in Germany, relatively speaking, many solo self-employed workers seemed to indicate that they had the skills to deal with more demanding duties.

Conclusion and discussion

Studies on the training of workers usually focus on employees and rarely on self-employed workers. However, as the number of solo self-employed workers has risen in a number of countries, the relevance of training for the self-employed increases. Moreover, the rise in other types of non-standard employment – in particular, temporary contracts – raises issues regarding the training opportunities for workers with a short-term relationship with an organization. Put differently, if an increasing share of workers cannot count on the organization they work for to invest in their employability, will they be able and willing to invest in their own training? Moreover, will the effect of this training on workers' valuation of their current work – in terms of their work engagement – and on their future career prospects be different depending on whether the employer or the worker himself/herself paid for the training? These questions were examined in this chapter for different types of workers in the nine countries that are the focus of this volume.

First, we found that solo self-employed workers more often than permanent employees say that they have skills to deal with more demanding duties and, hence, are probably not in need of further training. Temporary employees, however, state more often than permanent employees that they need further training. This last finding is in line with findings from earlier studies (Arulampalam et al., 2004; Forrier & Sels, 2003; Fouarge et al., 2012; Sequeda et al., 2015) and has been noted by policy makers, highlighting the risk of underinvestment currently looming among this group (Broughton et al., 2016).

Second, solo self-employed workers do indeed participate less often in training than permanent employees and receive less on-the-job training, although they undergo more training that they pay for themselves. Temporary employees also receive less training paid by their employer and less on-the-job training, but this is not compensated for by more training paid by themselves. These differences are not explained by differences in the intensity of the training, since they still exist when we look at training of various durations.

Third, for permanent employees training paid by the employer and on-the-job training increase both their work engagement and their career prospects, but for temporary workers such training increases only their prospects. Surprisingly, training paid by the worker himself/herself increases neither work engagement nor career prospects for employees. This may be due to endogeneity, in the sense that those with lower career prospects more often have to pay for training themselves rather than getting it from the employer, cancelling out a positive effect. Training paid by the worker does increase the career prospects for solo self-employed people.

Although we find that solo self-employed workers invest less in training than permanent employees, we cannot conclude from this that the self-employed in general invest too little since they, more often than permanent employees, report that their skills are sufficient to tackle more demanding duties. Moreover, the solo self-employed who do invest in training believe this improves their career prospects.

Perhaps more worrisome is our finding that temporary employees undergo less training than permanent workers – even though they state more often that they need further training. Since temporary workers who receive training are more optimistic about their career prospects, a potentially important and fruitful role may be reserved for organizations in terms of training temporary workers.

We conclude that workers with non-standard employment relationships less often participate in both formal and informal forms of post-school training.

Various scholars have stated that the emphasis on individual responsibility needs re-examination and encourage a greater role for organizations in their support for all workers, in order to adequately manage their careers and sustain their employability; in this way workplace productivity would also increase (Clarke, 2008; Forrier & Sels, 2003). Others plead for a more 'universal' approach, for instance, in the form of universal funds for post-school education (The Netherlands Scientific Council for Government Policy [WRR], 2013). Our findings indicate that these suggestions deserve further discussion, although we would recommend distinguishing between employees with a temporary contract and solo self-employed people: underinvestment in terms of training seems to be more of a problem for the former group than for the latter, and both groups differ in the strategies open to them for enhancing employability (Smith, 2010). Finally, our general findings regarding the training investments of solo self-employed workers do not rule out the possibility that for specific groups of solo self-employed a danger of underinvestment may be looming as well. For future research, it may be worth examining skill adequacy and training investments among various classes of solo self-employed in more depth.

Acknowledgments

The European Working Conditions Surveys are sponsored and owned by the European Foundation for the Improvement of Living and Working Conditions and distributed by UK Data Archive, University of Essex. These institutions bear no responsibility for the present analysis and interpretation of the data.

Note

1 Although pay satisfaction may also be affected by investments in employability, this relationship is likely to be less immediate/have a longer time lag; it is not possible to study this effect with the survey data we used.

12 Do female managers improve women's promotional opportunities?

Margriet van Hek and Anja-Kristin Abendroth

Introduction

Empowering women in the labor market has been a central issue on the political agenda of the European Union as well as of many European member states (European Commission, 2015). Even though women are still underrepresented in positions of power, the number of women occupying managerial positions is rising (Bygren, Gahler, Elisabeth, Morris, & Magnus, 2012; Jacobs, 1992; Mintz & Krymkowski, 2010; Van der Lippe, Van Doorne-Huiskes, & Blommaert, 2014). Managers play a key role in organizations as they decide, among other things, on the hiring, promotion and wages of workers (Briscoe & Kellogg, 2011; Elvira & Graham, 2002; Reskin, 2000). The question therefore arises of what the consequences are of the growing number of women in managerial positions (Cohen & Huffman, 2007). Do female managers in the workplace enhance promotional opportunities for women, or are they limited in their opportunities or motivation to do so? This chapter specifically focuses on whether women's representation in management affects gender inequality in *perceived* promotional opportunities in organizations.

A growing body of literature relates male overrepresentation in management to gender inequality in promotional opportunities. Many studies, predominantly from psychology, managerial studies and public administration, have assessed the in-group preferences of small samples of managers and found that managers do have a preference for workers with similar characteristics (Blum, Fields, & Goodman, 1994; Castilla & Benard, 2010; Hoobler, Wayne, & Lemmon, 2009). Large-scale assessments, almost all from the United States, have mostly compared the promotional opportunities of women working in organizations with high and low proportions of women in management (Cohen & Broschak, 1998; Cook & Glass, 2015; Kurtulus & Tomaskovic-Devey, 2012; Skaggs, Stainback, & Duncan, 2012; Stainback, Kleiner, & Skaggs, 2016). These studies, overall, show that women have better promotional opportunities in organizations with a high proportion of female managers. Huffman (2016) however, noted that an important drawback of the existing large-scale assessments is that they do not identify whether women in their studies actually work under a female manager. As such, it remains unclear whether the association found in these studies was due to: female managers improving the opportunities of the women who work for them; to female managers improving the opportunities of all female workers in the organization; or to organizational characteristics influencing both the proportion of female managers and the promotional opportunities of female workers. Srivastava and Sherman (2015) noted that studies linking the presence of female managers in an organization to the promotional opportunities of female workers therefore run the risk of ecological fallacy.

Notable exceptions are Elliott and Smith (2004) and Maume (2011). Employing survey data from three large cities in the United States, Elliott and Smith (2004) found that white women have a greater chance of advancing to a supervisory position when they have a female manger, but their chances of being promoted to a managerial position are actually lower when they report to a female manager. Maume (2011) used employee-reported data from the United States to assess the perceived promotional prospects and job-related support of women and men who were asked to indicate whether they reported to a female or to a male manager. Interestingly, he found that men, rather than women, perceive more promotional opportunities when they have a female manager. The findings of organizational-level studies that focus on the proportion of female managers in the organization, and of individual-level studies that look at whether workers have a female or a male manager thus seem to differ.

In this chapter we will investigate whether the *perceived* promotional opportunities of women and men are affected by (a) the proportion of female managers in the organization and (b) reporting directly to a female manager. We contribute to existing research in several ways. First, whereas most previous studies in this field employed organizational-level data to link the gender composition of an organization's management to women's promotional opportunities – and a few studies used worker-level data to assess whether workers' chances of advancing depend on the sex of their manager – the European Sustainable Workforce Survey (ESWS) data allow us to simultaneously assess the influence of the proportion of female managers in the organization *and* the impact of reporting directly to a female manager on the perceived promotional opportunities of female and male workers. This combined approach is vital since it provides insight into the mechanisms through which female managers influence the opportunities of other women in the organization. Scholars have proposed that female managers may either improve the opportunities of all female workers in the organization (e.g., through promoting gender equality enhancing policies), or improve the opportunities of their female subordinates (e.g., by giving them better performance evaluations) or both (Huffman, 2016). As the ESWS provides information on workers, their managers and the organizations for which they work, we can assess both aspects, providing more insight into the ways in which female managers influence workplace inequality, while controlling for possible confounding factors on the worker- and the organizational-level – such as the number of workers and the proportion of female workers in the organization.

Second, very little is known about how the gender composition of management or the sex of a manager impact differences in the perceived job opportunities of men and women. Perceptions about promotional opportunities may differ from *actual* opportunities because the presence of female managers can signal better job opportunities for women, irrespective of whether female managers are able or willing to change the actual job opportunities of female workers.

Third, the ESWS holds information on a wide range of organizations in nine European countries, making it possible to test our hypotheses in a wide range of contexts. In this regard, almost all research on the importance of women in management for women's promotional opportunities has been in the United States, and many used very selective samples (e.g., Fortune 500 or Fortune 1000 firms) (Cook & Glass, 2015; Kurtulus & Tomaskovic-Devey, 2012; Maume, 2011; Skaggs et al., 2012; Stainback et al., 2016). With this in mind, we will present analyses combined and separately for the nine countries in the ESWS. We pose the following research question: *To what extent are women's and men's perceived promotional opportunities affected by the proportion of female managers in their organization, and by being supervised by a female manager?*

Theory

Prior research indicates that female managers enhance the promotional opportunities of female workers in their organization, but scholars have also proposed that female managers may not have the power or the motivation to do so. Like previous research in this field, we formulate opposing hypotheses arguing that female managers are either change agents that actively enhance the promotional opportunities of female workers, or cogs in the machine, limited in terms of power or motivation to help other women advance in the organization (Maume, 2011; Stainback et al., 2016).

Change agents

First, female managers might improve the promotional opportunities of female workers in the organization because of their tendency for homophily, a preference for people with similar characteristics (Elliott & Smith, 2004; Kanter, 1977). Kanter (1977) described homophily in organizations as a consequence of the need for clear communication and trust between co-workers. People expect others like them to "speak the same language" and share the same values and, as a result, prefer them as co-workers. Kanter (1977) argues that this need increases as one goes higher up the organizational ladder. Higher up in the organization, work situations are more uncertain and, consequently, clear communication and trust is more important. A key characteristic for making social distinctions is sex: people attach meaning to the fact that somebody is a woman or a man (England, 2010; Reskin, 2000). Accordingly, managers likely foresee a smoother cooperation with workers of the same sex and are therefore more inclined to hire and promote them to higher positions in the organization (Elliott & Smith, 2004). Homophily is linked to several indirect mechanisms that are expected to result in better promotional opportunities for people with the same sex as their manager. First, homophily leads to sex-segregated networks which makes managers more likely to socialize with co-workers of the same sex. Many studies have shown that informal networks are important for job outcomes such as hiring and promotion (Huffman & Torres, 2002; McPherson, Smith-lovin, & Cook, 2001). A second and related consequence of homophily is that managers are more likely to befriend and to function as a mentor to subordinates of the same sex (Ehrich & Kimber, 2015; McPherson et al., 2001; Tsui & Gutek, 1999). Third, homophily is said to influence managers' performance evaluations of subordinates. Castilla (2011) found that managers rate subordinates of the same sex higher and argues this is because they have more positive views of people belonging to the same social categories.

A second reason why female managers might foster women's promotional opportunities is because of shared experiences of sex-based stereotyping and discrimination (Maume, 2011). Research has shown that women, especially mothers, are perceived as less devoted workers and, as a result, are less often considered for promotion (Cuddy, Fiske, & Glick, 2004). Female managers are likely more aware of (often subtle forms of) sex-based discrimination, and therefore might practice it less. Many diversity training programs are, in fact, based on the notion that increased stereotype awareness counteracts discriminatory behavior (Bezrukova, Jehn, & Spell, 2012). Moreover, experiences of discrimination could motivate female managers to actively counter the discrimination of female workers. In line with these arguments, Halpert, Wilson and Hickman (1993) showed that men give more biased performance evaluations of pregnant workers than women do. Shared experiences of sex-based stereotypes and discrimination in the work–family domain may also mean that female managers are more able to sympathize with and more willing to support female subordinates in these situations (Maume, 2011). Previous research has established that women experience more work–family conflict than men (Rothbard & Dumas, 2006; Valcour, 2007); female managers might be more accommodating than male managers because they experience more work–family conflict themselves (Linehan & Walsh, 2000). Research has also shown that emotional support in the workplace for workers' family responsibilities helps employees to establish a healthy work–life balance (Abendroth & Den Dulk, 2011) which leads to higher job satisfaction (Butts, Casper, & Yang, 2013). Female managers may therefore influence female workers' perceived promotional opportunities by being more accommodating of their family responsibilities.

Homophily and awareness of stereotyping and discrimination can help the promotional opportunities of women who work directly to a female manager. The presence of female managers in an organization may, however, also induce mechanisms that help *all* women in the organization to advance, even when they do not themselves work to a female manager. First, female managers can alter social cognitions related to sex. In other words, they challenge stereotypes about women. Prior studies have shown that women are perceived as less ambitious and committed workers than men (Acker, 1990), and most people's preexisting schema of leaders (i.e., managers) is that they are men (Schein,

Mueller, Lituchy, & Liu, 1996). It is well established that this hurts women's promotional opportunities (Blau, Ferber, & Winkler, 2006). The presence of a higher proportion of women in management positions in an organization may alter people's stereotypes about the commitment and capability of women and change perceptions of what a leader looks like (Ridgeway, 1997). Importantly, this may be relevant to both managers' and other workers' perceptions. Managers may be more inclined to promote female workers, but female workers may also more actively pursue higher positions in such organizations. In line with this argument, Ely (1995) found that the proportion of women in management is negatively related to stereotypical sex roles in organizations. Moreover, following status value belief concepts (Ridgeway, 1997) female managers and supervisors in the workplace might change women's status value beliefs in relation to the way they perceive that it is legitimate and possible for women to be promoted at work.

Lastly, female managers can improve the promotional opportunities of female workers by promoting the implementation of gender equality enhancing policies in the organization. Female managers may be stronger supporters of such policies because they are more likely to have experienced sex-based discrimination than male managers, but also because the implementation of policies that enhance gender equality may be in their own interest (i.e., by increasing their own opportunities for promotion). Empirical research in this field is scarce, but there are indications that female managers are stronger supporters of such policies than male managers. Cohen and Huffman (2007) found that female managers more often agreed with the statement that organizations should make a special effort to hire and promote women. Dobbin, Kim and Kalev (2011) found that there were more diversity policies in organizations with a higher proportion of female managers. Organizational policies that target sex-based discrimination can directly enhance the promotional opportunities of female workers and, in addition, they might signal organizational concern with diversity and gender equality to managers and workers alike (Butts et al., 2013; Grover & Crooker, 1995; Spence, 1973). This, in turn, could motivate managers to promote women more often, but it could also be a motivation for female workers to actively pursue higher positions in the organization.

In sum, we expect female managers to improve the promotional opportunities of women working directly to them because of mechanisms of homophily and awareness of stereotypes and discrimination. We also expect female managers to improve the promotional opportunities of all women in the organization because they challenge gender stereotypes and are more in favor of gender equality enhancing policies. As a consequence, women's *perceived* promotional opportunities should improve when there are more female managers in the workplace. In general, these mechanisms point to opposite effects for men, such that men who work for a female manager, or in an organization with a high proportion of female managers, have less promotional opportunities, which in turn affects their perceived promotional opportunities. We therefore hypothesize that: *women's perceived promotional opportunities positively relate to the proportion of female managers and men's perceived promotional opportunities negatively relate to the proportion of female managers in the organization* (hypothesis 1a); and *women's perceived promotional opportunities are higher when they have a female manager compared to a male manager and men's perceived promotional opportunities are higher when they have a male manager compared to a female manager* (hypothesis 2a).

Cogs in the machine

Some scholars propose that female managers may not have the power or the motivation that the "change agent" perspective attributes to them to improve promotional opportunities of female workers in the organization. The "weak" version of this perspective suggests that the lack of power and adherence to gender stereotypes prevent female managers from enhancing women's promotional opportunities. The "strong" version goes further in suggesting that female managers may be socialized into the role of "queen bee," which results in lower promotional opportunities for women when female managers are present (Staines, Tavris, & Jayaratne, 1974). Accordingly, we will formulate a weak and strong version of the "cogs in the machine" hypothesis.

Lack of organizational power may prevent female managers from improving women's promotional opportunities (Cohen & Huffman, 2007; Maume, 2011). Blair-Loy and Wharton (2002) showed that male supervisors were more likely than female supervisors to have access to resources that benefit their subordinates. Cohen and Huffman (2007) argue that the assumption that (all) managers having organizational power is doubtful. Organizations, especially those that are more bureaucratic, enact regulations and procedures that limit managers' power. Charles and Grusky (2004) demonstrated that the influx of women into management was accompanied by a rise of bureaucratization; they argue that this has led to women's limited managerial power. In a similar vein, Jacobs (1992) noted that women's entry into management was accompanied by "title-inflation," a general increase in workers with a managerial title but without actual power. In addition, women are disproportionally more likely to be situated in lower level managerial positions (Acker, 2006; Dobbin, 2009) where they are more restricted by the procedures, routines and demands of managers higher up the hierarchy. Maume (2011) argued, in this regard, that organizational elites might withhold power from women through the use of rules and procedures.

Furthermore, female managers may not affect women's promotional opportunities because they have the same stereotypes about female workers as male managers. Derks, Ellemers, Van Laar and De Groot (2011) showed that female managers also adhere to the stereotype that women are less committed and have weaker leadership abilities. If female managers act according to the stereotype that women are less devoted and ambitious workers, they might not support the promotional opportunities of their female subordinates or gender equality enhancing policies in the organization (Acker, 2006; Ridgeway, 2001, 2011).

Based on these two arguments, we expect managers' sex to be unrelated to women's and men's perceived promotional opportunities. So, female managers do not improve, but also do not harm, the promotional opportunities of other women in the organization. We formulate a "weak" version of the "cogs in the machine" hypothesis: *women's and men's perceived promotional opportunities are unrelated to the proportion of female managers in an organization* (hypothesis 1b); and *women's and men's perceived promotional opportunities are unrelated to their managers' sex* (hypothesis 2b).

The "strong" version of the "cogs in the machine" hypothesis argues that women who are in management positions are likely to accept the status quo (Cohen & Huffman, 2007). This is in part because of selection (i.e., women for whom gender equality is not a concern are more likely to be promoted to managerial positions) and partly because of socialization (women in management positions adopt the views of male managers). Due to these mechanisms, they are also not likely to contribute to better promotional opportunities for female workers. "Queen bee" theory suggests a similar mechanism: in order to get and keep positions of power, women have to subject themselves to the masculine culture higher up in the organization (Ely, 1995; Kanter, 1977; Ridgeway, 2001; Staines et al., 1974). To do so, they have to act as queen bees and distance themselves from associations with femininity. Queen bees will therefore not help other women to advance, or show involvement with gender equality in the organization. Some scholars argue that queen bees even openly counter opportunities for other women and initiatives to promote gender equality to show adherence to masculine organizational cultures (Derks, Van Laar, & Ellemers, 2016; Ellemers, Van den Heuvel, de Gilder, Maass, & Bonvini, 2004). If this is the case, it could explain Maume's (2011) finding that men experience more job-related support from female managers than from male managers. Our strong version of the "cogs in the machine" hypothesis is as follows: *women's perceived promotional opportunities relate negatively to the proportion of female managers and men's promotional opportunities relate positively to the proportion of female managers in the organization* (hypothesis 1c); and *women's perceived promotional opportunities are higher when they have a male manager compared to a female manager and men's promotional opportunities are higher when they have a female manager compared to a male manager* (hypothesis 2c).

Data and measurements

Data selections

From the ESWS dataset, we removed workers whose manager had not filled in the questionnaire, workers in organizations that employed only women or only men and workers who younger than 18 years old. There were 2,937 workers who had one or more missing values on our variables; most missing values concerned the sex of the worker's manager (1,353 workers). We listwise-deleted respondents with missing values from the data, which left us with 7,669 workers, working for 669 managers in 231 organizations for our analyses.

Measurements

Dependent variable

Our dependent variable is workers' *perceived promotional opportunities* in the organization. We asked respondents to indicate whether they agreed with the following statement: "I am likely to get a better job in this organization in the next three years." Respondents could strongly disagree (0), disagree (1), neither agree nor disagree (2), agree (3) or strongly agree (4). We include this variable linearly in the analyses; dichotomizing it (0 and 1 recoded into 0; 2 to 4 recoded into 1) produces highly similar results and identical conclusions.

Independent variables and controls: worker level

Most importantly, we include whether the worker is *female* (1) or male (0). At the worker level, we controlled for *age* and respondents' educational level (as a linear measure ranging from primary education or first stage of basic education (0) to doctoral degree (7). We controlled for two household characteristics: living with a partner and having dependent children (children under the age of 18 and children living at home). Three job characteristics were included in the models. The variable *tenure* indicates how many years the worker had worked for the organization. We controlled for *contract hours* and for workers who work non-fixed hours; we used the hours respondents actually worked for the organization. We controlled for workers' occupational class by constructing dummy variables using International Standard Classification of Occupations (ISCO) codes on the 1-digit level.

Independent variables: team manager level

We measured whether the *team manager is female* (1) or male (0). The multilevel structure of the ESWS data allowed us to directly link team managers to workers.

Independent variables and controls: organizational level

We used organizational representatives' reports on *the percentage of female managers in the organization*. If the representative did not know the exact figure, they were asked to estimate. At the organizational level we controlled for organizational size, indicated by *the number of workers* in the organization. To deal with the non-normal distribution and possibly non-linear effect of this variable, we included both the main effect and the natural log of this variable in our analyses. We controlled for the *percentage of female employees* in the organization. Organizational representatives were asked to indicate the percentage on a 9-point scale ranging from "there are no female employees" (0) to "all employees are female" (8). We assigned values of 0 percent and 100 percent to these categories and took the median of the categories in-between to convert it into a linear variable. Descriptive statistics can be found in Table 12.1.

Table 12.1 Descriptive statistics

	Mean	*Std.*	*Min*	*Max*
Employee variables				
Perceived promotional opportunities	1.53	1.07	0	4
Female	0.56		0	1
Age	41.99	10.93	18	74
Educational attainment	4.41	1.42	0	7
Living with partner	0.74		0	1
Dependent children	0.50		0	1
Tenure (years)	10.49	9.70	0.08	52
Contract hours	37.06	7.63	0	60
Occupation (ISCO)				
Managers	0.06		0	1
Professionals	0.32		0	1
Technicians and associate professionals	0.29		0	1
Clerical support workers	0.17		0	1
Services and sales workers	0.05		0	1
Skilled agricultural workers	0.00		0	1
Craft and related trades workers	0.04		0	1
Plant and machine operators and assemblers	0.05		0	1
Elementary occupations	0.02		0	1
Department variables				
Female manager	0.38		0	1
Organizational variables				
Proportion female managers	0.36	0.25	0	1
Proportion female employees	0.50	0.24	0.05	1
Number of employees	767.51	1,547.59	9	10,000
Number of employees (natural log)	5.59	1.43	2.20	9.21
Sector				
Manufacturing	0.25		0	1
Health care	0.24		0	1
Higher education	0.16		0	1
Transport	0.12		0	1
Financial services	0.14		0	1
Telecommunications	0.10		0	1
Country				
UK	0.07		0	1
Germany	0.08		0	1
Finland	0.08		0	1
Sweden	0.10		0	1
The Netherlands	0.24		0	1
Portugal	0.10		0	1
Spain	0.08		0	1
Hungary	0.13		0	1
Bulgaria	0.14		0	1

Note
N = 7,669.

Analyses

Methods and models

To accommodate the three-level structure of the ESWS data we performed three-level linear regression models in R (LME). We allowed the intercept and the effect of female to vary over teams and organizations (Schmidt-Catran & Fairbrother, 2016). With the exception of the null-model, we included dummy variables for country and sector to control for the nesting of organizations within countries and sectors. The sector "transport" and the country "Hungary" are the reference categories.

We first estimated a null-model that shows how much of the variance in perceived promotional opportunities is due to workers' nesting in teams and organizations. Model 1 includes only the effect of female, indicating the uncontrolled difference between women's and men's perceived promotional opportunities. In Model 2, personal and human capital indicators were added to the model; this tells us whether the sex difference in perceived promotional opportunities is due to such indicators. We then separately added job characteristics to Model 3 for the same reason. In Model 4 we also included the main effects of all team and organizational characteristics. We tested our hypotheses in Model 5, in which interactions of female with having a female manager and the percentage of female managers in the organization show the extent to which women's perceived promotional opportunities are (differently) affected by these characteristics. Model 5 is presented and discussed separately for all countries in Appendix 3. As a sensitivity analysis, we further performed team fixed effect models which control for all unobserved heterogeneity at the team level and which only report gender differences in the perceived promotional opportunities of men and women working in the same team.

Results

The null-model in Table 12.2 shows considerable variation in perceived promotional opportunities between teams and organizations, validating multilevel analyses. The intraclass correlation, which indicates the variance in perceived promotional opportunities at the different levels, is 10 percent for teams and 24 percent for organizations. Model 1 shows the difference in perceived promotional opportunities between women and men, uncontrolled for personal, job or organizational characteristics (but controlled for country and sector). Although the direction of this uncontrolled effect is in the expected direction (women perceiving fewer promotional opportunities than men), it does not reach statistical significance. In Model 2, where personal and human capital characteristics are included, the effect of female (b = –0.07) is negative and statistically significant, indicating that, as expected, women perceive fewer promotional opportunities than men when personal and human capital differences are taken into account. Model 2 furthermore shows that older workers (b = –0.02) and workers

Table 12.2 Hierarchical linear regression models on perceived promotional opportunities

	Model 0	*Model 1*	*Model 2*	*Model 3*	*Model 4*	*Model 5*
Employee variables						
Female		–0.04	–0.07*	–0.05†	–0.05†	–0.09†
		(0.03)	(0.03)	(0.03)	(0.03)	(0.05)
Age			–0.02***	–0.02***	–0.02***	–0.02***
			(0.00)	(0.00)	(0.00)	(0.00)
Educational level			0.03***	0.02†	0.02†	0.02†
			(0.02)	(0.01)	(0.01)	(0.01)
Partner			–0 .05†	–0.05†	–0.05†	–0.05†
			(0.03)	(0.03)	(0.03)	(0.03)
Dependent children			0.04†	0.04	0.04†	0.04†
			(0.02)	(0.02)	(0.02)	(0.02)
Tenure				–0.02***	–0.02***	–0.02***
				(0.00)	(0.00)	(0.00)
Contract hours				0.00*	0.00*	0.00*
				(0.00)	(0.00)	(0.00)
Department variables						
Female manager					0.04	0.06
					(0.03)	(0.05)
Organizational variables						
Proportion female managers					0.02	–0.08
					(0.11)	(0.14)
Proportion female employees					–0.22†	–0.22
					(0.13)	(0.13)
Number of employees					0.00	0.00
					(0.00)	(0.00)
Number of employees (natural log)					0.01	0.01
					(0.02)	(0.02)
Interactions with female						
× proportion female managers						–0.03
						(0.06)
× female manager						0.14
						(0.11)
Intercept	1.60***	1.22***	2.13***	1.93***	1.97***	1.98***
	(0.03)	(0.09)	(0.11)	(0.14)	(0.18)	(0.19)
Random variance terms						
Organization (intercept)	0.37	0.32	0.27	0.25	0.25	0.25
Female (slope organizations)		0.13	0.09	0.10	0.09	0.09
Department (intercept)	0.19	0.20	0.20	0.17	0.18	0.18
Female (slope departments)		0.06	0.06	0.00	0.03	0.03
Employee variance	0.10	1.00	0.97	0.97	0.96	0.96

Notes
†$p<0.1$, *$p<0.05$, **$p<0.01$, ***$p<0.001$ (2-sided); standard errors in parentheses.
Country and sector dummies are included in all models except Model 0; Occupation (ISCO) indicators are included in all models except Model 0 and Model 1, but are not shown in the table.

with a partner (b = –0.05) perceive fewer promotional opportunities, whereas higher educated workers (b = 0.03) and workers with dependent children (b = 0.04) perceive more promotional opportunities overall. Model 3 shows that the longer workers are employed by an organization, the less positive they are about their promotional opportunities (b = –0.02). Workers who are contracted to work more hours perceive more promotional opportunities (b = 0.004). Differences in working hours between men and women, in particular, partly explain the difference between women's and men's perceived promotional opportunities (b = –0.05), but the effect of female stays negative and significant at a 0.1 level. In Model 4, the main effects of the team's and organizational characteristics are included. Only the proportion of female workers affects workers' perceived promotional opportunities (b = –0.22); workers employed in an organization with a high proportion of female workers perceive fewer promotional opportunities than workers employed in predominantly male organizations. In Model 4 the effect of female stays negative and significant at a 0.1 level.[1]

Our hypotheses concern the extent to which the proportion of female managers and having a female manager exert differential effects on women's and men's perceived promotional opportunities. These differential effects are indicated by the cross-level interactions in Model 5. The main effects of proportion of female managers and having a female manager apply to men in this Model (scoring 0 on *female*). The interaction term indicates the difference between the effect for women and for men; adding the interaction term to the main effects results in the effect for women (scoring 1 on *female*).[2] Model 5 shows that women and men are not (differently) affected by either the proportion of female managers, or by having a female manager themselves.[3] This supports hypotheses 1b and 2b (the weak versions of the "cogs in the machine" hypothesis).

Conclusions and discussion

Increasing the number of women in powerful positions in the labor market has been discussed in research and in public debate as a way to reduce workplace gender inequalities (e.g., Cohen & Huffman, 2007; European Commission 2015). In this chapter we investigated the implications of the proportion of women in management and having a female manager for women's and men's perceived promotional opportunities. To this end, we employed manager–worker linked data from the ESWS that includes nine European countries. We argued that female managers can either promote women's promotional opportunities in the organization, or that female managers may not be able or willing to do so. Theoretical arguments on the ability and willingness of female managers to promote equal opportunities led to contradictory hypotheses on the implications of female managers for women's and men's perceived promotional opportunities in the organization.

Our main finding is that women and men do not perceive more or fewer promotional opportunities depending on the proportion of female managers in their organization or the sex of their manager. This finding is in line with the weak version of the "cogs in the machine" hypothesis that managers' sex does not affect women's or men's perceived promotional opportunities. It seems that the presence of women in positions of power in organizations does not compellingly improve the opportunities of female workers. More precisely, as sensitivity checks showed, the gender gap in perceived promotional opportunities is mainly driven by the sorting of men and women into different teams; female managers and supervisors seem not to be powerful enough to eradicate this segmentation within the organization, which leads to certain workplace outcomes. This finding is in line with previous research which shows that female managers lack the power to change gendered workplace practices (e.g., Blair-Loy and Wharton 2002; Cohen & Huffman, 2007; Maume, 2011). However, it could also be that female managers and supervisors are not willing to change gender segregation in the workplace – an allusion to the "queen bee" argument (e.g., Ely 1995; Kanter 1977; Ridgeway, 2001; Staines et al., 1974). The results further underscore the consequences of occupational segregation within organizations for gender gaps in job outcomes (Charles & Grusky, 2005). Considering that our study focuses on *perceived* promotional opportunities, it further seems that female managers do not even function as role models, signaling good promotional opportunities for women within the team or organization irrespective of their ability to improve women's actual promotional opportunities.

The finding that female managers are not powerful enough, or willing, to enhance women's careers contrasts with the findings of previous organizational-level studies that have found women's promotional opportunities to be better in organizations with a high proportion of female managers (Kurtulus & Tomaskovic-Devey, 2012; Skaggs et al., 2012; Stainback et al., 2016). There are considerable differences between previous studies and ours that may explain this difference in findings. First, relating to the sample studied, previous research often employed data on large, highly visible commercial firms (i.e., Fortune 1000 firms) from the United States, whereas the ESWS data contain information on a broad scope of commercial and non-commercial organizations from nine European countries. Scholars have contended that social context may be relevant to the amount of influence female managers exert on the opportunities of women in the organization (Maume & Ruppanner, 2015). The ESWS data is not suited to testing hypotheses on whether country characteristics affect the influence female managers have on the job outcomes of female workers, but a task for future research may be to use international datasets that include more countries. As our robustness analyses (see Note 2) and country-specific results revealed similar patterns for all types of workers, managers and organizations, as well as for all countries, there is no indication that our results are strongly dependent on country context. Second, it could be that women's perceived and actual promotional opportunities differ. Whereas the proportion of female managers shapes women's actual promotional opportunities in the workplace, women may be unrealistically optimistic about their chances of advancing in the organization because they are not aware of the discriminatory mechanisms at play that will eventually prevent them from reaching higher-status positions.

Future research should compare perceptions with actual promotional opportunities to understand whether perceptions and actual opportunities match.

Findings of previous individual-level studies that examined whether (perceived) promotional opportunities depended on the sex of the worker's manager were more mixed; whereas Maume (2011) found clear support for the strong version of the "cogs in the machine" hypothesis, Elliott and Smith's (2004) results were more ambiguous. Considering that Maume (2011) also studied perceived promotional opportunities, our studies both point in the direction that women at least do not perceive better promotional opportunities when their direct manager is female. A similar result was found by one of the few individual-level European studies in this field: Abendroth, Melzer, Kalev and Tomaskovic-Devey (2017) show that in Germany women's earnings are also not affected by the sex of their manager.

We concur with the call made by Huffman (2016) that more data collection efforts are needed in order to determine whether and how female managers affect inequality in organizations. In depth investigations of female managers' motives and obstacles may provide more insights into the applicability of the mechanisms that underlie the hypotheses formulated in this and other studies in this field. Longitudinal data is needed as changes in women's power within the workplace might produce implications after a certain time period, or it may be that female managers who want to create change may (be forced to) quit before they have a chance to do so. Lastly, international datasets may enable researchers to investigate the interplay between social context and the possibilities of female managers affecting gender inequality in their organization.

Overall, this chapter highlights that simply increasing the representation of women in managerial positions does not lead to more equal perceptions of women and men concerning their chances of achieving promotion in the organization. On the one hand, it can be considered good news that we found that managers' sex does not affect workers' perceived promotional opportunities; it could indicate that female and male managers do not promote workers of their own sex more often than others. On the other hand, it could be that institutional and organizational factors prevent women in positions of power from appealing to the same mechanisms their male counterparts practice in order to enhance the opportunities of their female subordinates. Endeavors to achieve gender equality in organizations through equalizing access to managerial positions may not therefore be pointless; they may help break down gendered structures in organizations and lead to organizational cultures in which gender equality in job outcomes is established.

Notes

1 The sensitivity analysis based on fixed effect analysis produced no significant gender effect across all models. This indicates that gender differences in perceived promotional opportunities are due to the sorting of men and women into different teams which have different promotional opportunities. Country-specific fixed effect analyses produced more nuanced results. For Hungary, the results show a significant gender

effect on perceived job opportunities, irrespective of job characteristics and the sorting of men and women in different establishments. For the Netherlands, gender inequalities in perceived promotional opportunities within organizations are visible, but they can be explained by differences in working hours between men and women.

2 We performed several robustness analyses. The results were similar to when the interactions were included separately. The three-way interaction between female, female manager and proportion of female managers is not statistically significant. We examined variation in results between high- and low-educated workers (Abendroth et al., 2017), large and small organizations and different organizational sectors. Results did not vary significantly between these subgroups, nor did they show significant interaction effects for any of the subgroups, with the exception of the interaction of female with percentage of female managers in the financial sector. This interaction effect indicated that women in the financial sector benefit more from working in an organization with a high level of female managers than men. We also tested whether results differed when controlling for or differentiating between high- and low-status managers based on the managers' educational level, income (Cohen & Huffman, 2007), the time she/he had been managing the team and the number of workers in her/his team. This did not appear to be the case. Unfortunately, the ESWS does not provide more specific data to determine managers' status, nor does it report information on respondents' ethnicity so we could not investigate its influence on the associations we examined. We checked for influential cases using the jackknife procedure, but no influential cases were found.

3 The results are the same in the fixed effect analyses, indicating that women in management and having a female supervisor does not moderate perceived promotional opportunities.

13 Technology implementation within enterprises and changes in the educational and age composition of enterprise workforces

Jannes ten Berge and Maarten Goos

Introduction

Recent studies indicating that large numbers of human work tasks could be automated in the near future have sparked scientific research into the effects of technological change on work (Frey & Osbourne, 2017; Manyika et al., 2017; World Bank, 2016). Feasibility studies estimate that advances in robotics, machine learning and artificial intelligence can automate or partially automate around 47 percent of US jobs in the coming decades (Frey & Osbourne, 2017), and almost 60 percent of jobs in the Organisation for Economic Co-operation and Development (OECD) (World Bank, 2016). As technology advances, it poses a challenge to the creation of sustainable workforces: technological change can destroy a large number of job tasks (Acemoglu & Autor, 2011). More specifically, recent empirical labor market studies show that technology is associated with decreased employment in middle-skill jobs and increased employment in high- and low-skilled jobs, leading to a polarization of labor markets (Acemoglu & Autor, 2011; Autor, Levy, & Murnane, 2003; Goos & Manning, 2007; Goos, Manning, & Salomons, 2009, 2014).

What is underexposed in these studies is how organizations, in which the process of technological advancement plays out, adapt their workforces to technological changes. There are four major advantages of taking an organizational perspective on how technological change impacts jobs that macro-level studies which focus on aggregate labor flows are unable to recognize.

First, organizations are the sites where workers' jobs are created and distributed (Baron & Bielby, 1980). What remains unclear is for which workers technological changes within enterprises create job opportunities, and which workers face increasing difficulties in finding and maintaining employment within enterprises when technology is implemented. In the current chapter we contribute to the small but emerging literature on how technological change impacts work within organizations (Bauer & Bender, 2004; Beckmann, 2007; Cortes & Salvatori, 2016; Fernandez, 2001; King, Reichelt, & Huffman, 2017; Nedelkoska, 2013; Siegel, 1998).

Second, for the sustainability of workforces, the relation in organizations between technology implementation, education and age is highly important. Previous literature has shown that technology is skill biased, meaning that it provides opportunities for higher educated workers in particular, while posing challenges for middle and lower educated workers (Autor et al., 2003). In addition, technology is found to lead to a growing pace of skill depreciation and the increased importance of adaptability of workers and organizations (Beckmann, 2007; Fernandez, 2001; Siegel, 1998). In the current study we contribute to the literature by studying whether workforces change with regard to the level of education and age, and how technology implementation relates to changes in the education and age composition of workers entering and leaving enterprises.

Third, an advantage of investigating organizations is that it allows a closer inspection of how institutional contexts influence the impact of technological change (Fernandez, 2001; Kalleberg, Wallace, & Althauser, 1981; Kristal, 2013). As shown in previous studies, organizational decision making is strongly influenced by institutional context, such as unionization and collective bargaining (Fernandez, 2001; Kalleberg et al., 1981; Kristal, 2013). To clarify how the institutional contexts of enterprises shape the effects of technological change, we compare changes in the education and age composition of the workforce and worker flows as a consequence of technological change across industries varying in the degree of unionization.

Finally, macro-level studies imply, rather than directly measure, technological change. Previous research has mainly used a proxy measure of technology, namely the level of routineness of a job (Autor et al., 2003; Goos & Manning, 2007; Goos, Manning, & Salomons, 2009, 2014; Spitz-Oener, 2006). It is argued that only job tasks that follow an exact routine can be effectively codified and computerized. When a decline in routine jobs is observed, it is assumed that technology is the main driver of this change. However, testing this assumption, Nedelkoska (2013) finds little evidence that higher occupational change among routine workers and wage losses for those leaving routine jobs were the result of the implementation of code-based technologies, thus stressing the importance of employing direct measures of technology. Using a large-scale survey of (technological) innovation within Dutch enterprises, we measure technology implementation as the investment of enterprises in advanced machinery, equipment or computer hardware/software specifically purchased to implement new or significantly improved products (goods/services) and/or processes.[1] To examine the relationship between technology implementation, the flow of workers in and out of enterprises and changes in workforce composition, we match this firm-level data to Dutch register data on employees. This allows us to follow over three million employees within over 30,000 enterprises over a period of fourteen years (2000–2014).

Theory

Technology implementation and the educational composition of workers entering enterprises

A leading hypothesis within the literature on the effects of technology is the Skill-Biased Technological Change (SBTC) hypothesis, which proposes that technology increases the marginal productivity of highly skilled workers, such as engineers, scientists and consultants (Autor, Katz, & Krueger, 1998; Berman, Bound, & Griliches, 1994; Card & DiNardo, 2002; Katz & Murphy, 1992; Krueger, 1993; Michaels, Natraj, & Van Reenen, 2014). This increased marginal productivity increases the demand for highly skilled workers (Acemoglu & Autor, 2011; Autor et al., 2003; Fernandez, 2001; Spitz-Oener, 2006). Education increases problem-solving capability, analytical capacity, inductive reasoning and communication skills (Becker, 1964), which are central to high-skill work tasks (Acemoglu & Autor, 2011; Autor et al., 2003; Spitz-Oener, 2006). It can therefore be expected that as the demand for more highly skilled workers increases with technological change in enterprises, it also increases the demand for higher educated workers (Autor et al., 2003). Thus, we expect that:

> Hypothesis 1: When technology is implemented, the proportion of higher educated workers entering the enterprise increases while the proportion of lower educated workers entering the enterprise decreases.

A critique of the SBTC framework is that it falls short in explaining the relative decrease of workers in middle-skill jobs, such as clerical and production, evident in recent labor market developments (Acemoglu & Autor, 2011; Autor et al., 2003; Goos & Manning, 2007; Goos, Manning, & Salomons, 2009, 2014). This relative decline in middle-skill work is explained as resulting from the automation of work, particularly of middle-skilled tasks such as record-keeping or repetitive assembly. Technology mainly substitutes work tasks that are routine intensive, such as repetitive assembly, because these tasks are codifiable in programming language (Autor et al., 2003). Because technology reduces the demand for middle-skilled workers performing routine tasks within organizations we expect that:

> Hypothesis 2: When technology is implemented, the proportion of middle educated workers entering the enterprise decreases relative to the proportion of lower educated workers and higher educated workers entering the enterprise.

Technology implementation and the educational composition of workers exiting enterprises

With the automation of middle-skilled work tasks, the demand for middle-skilled workers already working in the enterprise also decreases. Within assignment models of technological change, the automation of work tasks is argued to lead to a reallocation of middle-skilled workers to high- or low-skill work tasks depending on the comparative advantage of workers in performing either high- or low-skilled tasks, as well as the relative demand and supply of workers' skills (Acemoglu & Autor, 2011). Based on the SBTC hypothesis, we expect that the demand for higher-skilled workers increases. However, assuming that in most cases middle-skilled workers are unable to perform high-skill work tasks, we do not expect middle-skilled workers to reallocate to perform high-skill job tasks. Furthermore, we have little cause to suspect that middle-skilled workers reallocate to perform low-skill job tasks. There are two reasons for this. First, employers cannot easily lower wages, and since middle educated workers on average have higher earnings than lower educated ones, it is more cost-efficient to keep lower educated workers and have them perform tasks that require lower skills rather than reallocating middle educated workers into low-skill jobs. Furthermore, assuming that skills are to some degree transferrable, middle-skilled workers may choose to find work in another enterprise with similar skill requirements and pay, rather than switching to a low-skill job. Second, a reason to retain and reallocate middle educated workers would be their higher productivity in low-skilled job tasks, but it is not clear whether these workers are in fact more productive in performing low-skilled job tasks than low-skilled workers (Acemoglu & Autor, 2011). In conclusion, we expect that the implementation of technology decreases both the demand for middle-skilled work tasks as well as for middle-skilled workers. We therefore expect that:

> Hypothesis 3: When technology is implemented the proportion of middle educated workers leaving the enterprise increases.

Technology implementation and the educational composition of enterprise workforces

Thus, on the one hand, we predict that under circumstances of technological change the proportion of higher educated workers entering an enterprise increases. On the other hand, we predict that the proportion of middle educated workers entering an enterprise decreases and the proportion of middle educated workers leaving it increases. Based on these predictions we expect that:

> Hypothesis 4: When technology is implemented the proportion of higher educated workers in enterprise workforces increases relative to the proportion of middle and lower educated workers.

Technology implementation and the age of workers entering enterprises

From the human capital literature, we know that within enterprises a large amount of a worker's productivity stems from experience gained within their current and previous jobs. As a result, for an enterprise, experienced workers are generally the more valuable workers (Crook, Todd, Combs, Woehr, & Ketchen, 2011; Gathmann & Schönberg, 2010; Jovanovic, 1979; Lazear, 2009; Topel, 1991). Technological change, however, alters skill requirements and increases the pace at which certain skills and knowledge become outdated. New technologies often require some form of adaption – for example, in how to organize a new production process, or how to use new technology. Consequently, experience with the old process, or knowledge about the old product (unless a prerequisite of the new product) decreases in importance with the implementation of new products or processes (Beckmann, 2007).

Skill obsolescence and human capital depreciation is likely to affect younger and older workers differently. The depreciation of existing human capital and the increase in demand for new types of skills are likely to increase the appeal of employing younger workers for two reasons. First, because younger workers have attained their education more recently, they are more likely to offer the necessary state-of-the art skills than older workers (Beckmann, 2007). Second, even if retraining can help workers to attain the necessary skills, enterprises are more likely to invest in retraining younger rather than older workers (Arulampalam, Booth, & Bryan, 2004; Bartell & Sicherman 1993; Beckmann, 2007; Carmichael & Ercolani, 2014; Guerrazzi, 2014; Taylor & Urwin, 2001). The reason for this is that retraining younger workers is more profitable because there is more time for training costs to be recouped. Furthermore, older workers have a shorter time horizon in the labor market, making them reluctant to invest in training themselves (Beckmann, 2007). We therefore expect that:

> Hypothesis 5: When technology is implemented the proportion of younger workers entering an enterprise increases.

Technology implementation and the age of workers leaving enterprises

As workers gain experience within the firm – for example, via job training about current production processes – their productivity increases (Dearden, Reed, & Van Reenen, 2006), resulting in higher wages (Brown, 1989). For employers, wages are a cost that is worth paying as long as this cost is compensated for by the high productivity of an employee. When technology implementation changes a production process, however, the productivity premium resulting from experience decreases. Thus, technology implementation negatively affects the productivity premium of having on-the-job experience, resulting in wage costs that are out of balance with the productivity of tenured workers. One way to recover the balance between costs and worker productivity is to reduce wages, but in the European context this is often unfeasible as wages are subject to wage regulation by the state, unions or through collective labor agreements. Another way to recover the balance between wage costs and productivity is to lay off or incentivize tenured workers to leave the enterprise.

Some studies argue that rather than facing actual problems with work performance, older workers suffer from negative stereotyping and discrimination, which influences managerial expectations and decision making (Posthuma & Campion, 2009). The stereotype that older workers are less adaptable than younger workers leads to lower training participation among older workers as well as early retirement arrangements (Posthuma & Campion, 2009; Shore & Goldberg, 2013). We expect that discriminatory practices and experiencing managerial favoritism, on the one hand, and actual difficulties with skill adaption and lack of retraining, on the other, will lead to increases in both workers leaving and lay-offs. We therefore expect that:

> Hypothesis 6: When technology is implemented the proportion of older workers leaving an enterprise increases.

Technology implementation and the age composition of enterprise workforces

As a result of increases in both the proportion of younger workers entering and the proportion of older workers leaving enterprises under circumstances of technological change, we expect that:

> Hypothesis 7: When technology is implemented the proportion of younger workers in enterprise workforces increases while the proportion of older workers decreases.

Technology implementation and the role of institutions

The behavior of organizational actors is strongly influenced by the institutional context of the organization (Scott, 2014). How organizations adapt their workforces is likely to depend on how they enable and constrain the actions of both employers and employees (Avent-Holt & Tomaskovic-Devey, 2014; Orlikowski & Barley, 2001). Employers are constrained by laws, unions and collective agreements that, at the same time, 'empower' employees in negotiation with the employer. Studying the adaption process to technological innovation of a food processing plant, Fernandez (2001) finds that the effects of technology implementation are strongly shaped by bargaining processes between the employer and the workers' union. In return for no-lay-off and wage guarantees, the union agreed to relax seniority and work rule requirements and to support retraining efforts by the enterprise (Fernandez, 2001). While the supply and demand framework aids us in hypothesizing how the implementation of new technologies changes employers demands for skills, the decisions that employers make to adapt to these changing skills demands are constrained by regulative institutions (Avent-Holt & Tomaskovic-Devey, 2014). More specifically, the degree to which employers can use churning as a way of adapting an enterprise's workforce to new technologies seems to be less when workers can rely on institutions to bargain for enterprise resources such as jobs, training and wages.

To study the role of institutions we compared more and less unionized industries. In 2016, out of all wage-earning workers in the Netherlands, 17 percent were union members – similar to the average for OECD countries (Organisation for Economic Co-operation and Development [OECD], 2018). In the Netherlands, however, unions are more influential than their membership suggests because they bargain at the company or industry level concerning collective labor agreements, which thereby also includes workers who are not members of a union. In the Netherlands, 79 percent of wage earners are covered by collective bargaining agreements, ranking ninth among 36 countries included in OECD data.

Looking at different industries we find substantial variation in union coverage. In manufacturing, union coverage was 31 percent (in 2011), whereas in business services only 11 percent of workers were covered by unions (Statistics Netherlands, 2012). We expect that in unionized industries, employers are less able to use worker churning to adapt their workforces to technology. We therefore expect that:

> Hypothesis 8: The effects of technology implementation on the age and educational composition of workforces, and on workers entering–leaving enterprises, are less in unionized industries.

Data

Our study makes use of the combination of a large-scale enterprise survey and social micro-register data. Data on company investment in technology is taken from the Community Innovation Survey (CIS). The CIS is a large-scale cross-national panel survey of innovation activity in enterprises, repeated every two years. In the Dutch survey used in this study, the sample is stratified by sector and establishment size, excluding enterprises with less than ten workers (Mortensen & Bloch, 2005). Due to the longitudinal design, we are able to study changes in technology implementation within enterprises over time. We focus on the period 2000–2014, during which a total of 36,230 enterprises participated in the Dutch CIS survey. Because enterprises do not always participate in the survey follow-ups, we generally did not observe enterprises for the full period 2000–2014. The average number of years that enterprises are observed in the data is 4.64 years. Of the total 36,230 enterprises that participated in the survey, 26,273 (72.52 percent) did not implement technologies during the period of observation, while 5,820 (16.06 percent) were observed during periods both with and without technology implementation. The remaining 4,137 enterprises (11.42 percent) implemented new technologies during all periods of observation. We linked these enterprises to register data on workers' jobs and demographic characteristics from the System of Social Statistics Databases (SSB) of the Dutch Central Bureau of Statistics, creating a longitudinal matched employer–employee dataset.[2] Having linked information about workers' jobs, educational attainment and age with the enterprises in the CIS, we were able to track how many workers entered and left the enterprise and what the composition of job entrants, job leavers and workforces looked like, with regard to educational attainment and age.

To study how the implementation of technologies within enterprises affects the composition of entrants, leavers and workforces with regard to educational attainment and age, we selected only the 5,820 enterprises that were observed in contexts both with and without technology being implemented. Furthermore, we exclusively analyzed enterprises in which we, over time, observed a shift from a period without technology implementation (0) to a period with technology implementation (1). Because the effects of technology implementation on the age and education composition of workforces are likely to last after the technology has been implemented, we did not include observations of time periods without technology implementation that follow time periods with technology implementation. This selection of observations excluded 2,243 enterprises (38.54 percent) in which we only observed a shift from technology being implemented (1) to technology no longer being implemented (0). Furthermore, this means that we excluded the observations that came after the observed periods of no technology implementation (0) to technology implementation (1). The remaining analytical sample consists of 3,577 enterprises and 23,156 observations. Table 13.1 provides descriptive statistics for enterprises when implementing and not implementing technologies.

Measurement

Dependent variables

Educational composition of enterprise workforces was measured as the proportion of the workforce with low, high and middle educational attainment within an enterprise, at the end of a year. Level of education was measured according to the International Standard Classification of Education (ISCED). Eight educational levels are distinguished. We recoded the levels into low, middle and high education following guidelines in the ISCED 2011 manual (Organisation for Economic Co-operation and Development/Eurostat/UNESCO Institute for Statistics, 2015): low education, including those who attained less than primary education, primary education and lower secondary education; medium education, including employees who attained upper secondary education and post-secondary non-tertiary education; and high education, including employees who attained short-cycle tertiary, bachelor's, a master's or doctoral equivalent education.

Table 13.1 Descriptive statistics of enterprises by context of technology implementation

	No technology implementation		*Technology implementation*		*All enterprises*	
	Mean	*s.d.*	*Mean*	*s.d.*	*Mean*	*s.d.*
Education of workers entering (%)						
Low	19.76	18.00	17.50	16.49	18.55	14.98
Middle	43.00	19.08	45.87	19.99	44.45	16.73
High	37.24	24.58	36.63	25.38	37.00	23.09
Education of workers leaving (%)						
Low	20.48	17.96	19.34	17.05	19.87	15.49
Middle	42.59	18.84	45.16	19.41	44.09	16.39
High	36.93	24.65	35.50	24.60	36.04	22.87
Education of workforce (%)						
Low	24.53	17.38	23.11	16.40	23.76	16.44
Middle	44.26	15.60	45.32	15.54	44.77	14.95
High	31.20	22.38	31.57	22.17	31.47	21.91
Age of workers entering (%)						
Below 30	51.61	20.24	53.17	21.33	52.64	17.88
Between 30 and 50	41.34	18.57	39.06	19.01	40.03	15.80
Above 50	7.05	8.96	7.77	9.78	7.33	7.52
Age of workers leaving (%)						
Below 30	44.68	21.55	42.05	21.67	43.24	19.60
Between 30 and 50	41.51	18.75	39.85	18.43	40.53	16.11
Above 50	13.81	13.90	18.10	15.37	16.22	12.80
Age of workforce (%)						
Below 30	25.43	16.32	21.69	15.65	23.54	15.43
Between 30 and 50	55.81	13.13	55.23	13.05	55.52	12.28
Above 50	18.75	11.37	23.08	12.44	20.94	11.41
Organizational innovation (%)	33.60	43.78	46.26	44.27	40.18	44.48
Industry union density (%)	56.00	49.65	56.00	49.65	56.00	49.64
Size enterprise	240	887	287	1,528	263	1,250

Source: Results based on calculations by Utrecht University using non-public microdata from Statistics Netherlands.

Note
N enterprises = 3,577.

Educational composition of enterprise entrants was measured as the proportion of low, middle and high educated entrants within the enterprise in a given year.

Educational composition of workers leaving an enterprise was measured as the proportion of low, middle and high educated employees who left the enterprise in a given year.

Age composition of the workforce was measured as the proportion of younger, middle-aged and older employees within an enterprise, at the end of the year. Following Beckmann's (2007) study on the age composition of workforces, we differentiated between three age categories: workers aged below 30, workers aged between 30 and 50 and workers aged above 50.

Age composition of workers entering the enterprise was measured as the proportion of workers aged below 30, between 30 and 50 and above 50, entering the enterprise in a given year.

Age composition of workers leaving the enterprise was measured as the proportion of workers aged below 30, between 30 and 50 and above 50, leaving the enterprise in a given year.

Independent variables

Implementation of technology was measured using an item from the CIS. A higher manager from the enterprise was asked to indicate whether, over the past two to three years (depending on the survey date), the enterprise had purchased machinery, equipment and/or software with the aim of significantly improving products, services and/or production processes.

Industry unionization was captured by differentiating between industries with higher and lower union densities. Union density is defined as the number of unionized employees younger than 65 years of age with paid work for at least 12 hours a week, as a percentage of the total number of employees with paid work for at least 12 hours per week. We treated industries where union density is over 25 percent as more unionized. Industry and mining, energy and water management, manufacturing, transport and communication fall in this category: their union densities range from 26 percent (industry and mining) to 37 percent (manufacturing). Trade, retail, financial services and business services are less unionized: their union densities range from 12 percent in trade to 14 percent in financial services (Statistics Netherlands, 2012).

We controlled for *organizational innovations* to capture changes in the organization of an enterprise which can be related to worker flows in and out of enterprises (Bauer & Bender, 2004; Bresnahan, Brynjolfsson, & Hitt, 2002). A higher manager from the enterprise was asked to indicate whether, over the past two to three years (depending on the survey date), the organization had introduced new business procedures, new methods for the organization of professional responsibilities and decision making or new methods for external relations with other companies or institutes.

Furthermore, we controlled for *enterprise size*, which is measured as the number of employees that worked in the enterprise at the beginning of the year.

Because the distribution of enterprise size is strongly right skewed, indicating the presence of several very large enterprises, we use the log of enterprise size in the analyses.

Method

To test the relationship between technology implementation within enterprises and changes in the composition of enterprise workforces and worker flows in and out of enterprises with regard to educational attainment and age, we took the following steps. First, we calculated the proportions of workers, with regard to educational attainment and age, entering and leaving an enterprise, on the one hand, and the workforce total, on the other, for the years 2000–2014. Second, we identified periods in which a change from no technology implementation to technology implementation could be observed – for example, the selected period 2002–2010, during which, between 2002 and 2008 the enterprise did not implement technology, while between 2008 and 2010 it did. Third, having selected periods of change we took the average of the proportions of workers, with regard to education and age, entering, working in and leaving the enterprise. These averages were subtracted from the observed proportions per year, such that observed proportions per year then represented deviations from the enterprise-period specific mean. The advantage of using these deviations from the enterprise-period mean is that when analyzing the data we only analyzed within-enterprise variation, allowing us to control for time-invariant unobserved heterogeneity.

As the dependent variables are compositions that together always add up to 1, there is covariation between the variables. We used seemingly unrelated regression (SUR) estimation to account for the correlation between error terms that arose when analyzing the proportions of entrants, leavers and workforces, with regard to education and age. Furthermore, we included dummies for years to control for over time trends in the composition of workers with regard to education and age. Finally, we added weights to the analyses. The measurement of educational attainment was taken from a combination of surveys. Consequently, the coverage of educational attainment varied per enterprise. To partially account for the error this missing data incurred, we added weights indicating the percentage of entrants, leavers and enterprise workforces with data on educational attainment. Furthermore, we added weights for the log of enterprise size to allow larger enterprises to influence the results more strongly than small enterprises, leading to more generalizable results. To test whether technology implementation continues to affect the education and age composition of enterprise entrants, leavers and workforces after periods of technology implementation we performed an additional analysis in which we included one-, two- and three-year lagged effects of technology implementation to the model (results not shown). We found the directions of the effects of technology implementation to remain the same for all models including one-, two- or three-year effects.

Results

Table 13.2 provides the results for the seemingly unrelated regression of technology implementation on the educational composition of workers. We find that the implementation of technology is associated with an increase in the proportion of middle educated workers entering enterprises, relative to higher and lower educated workers. These results are only partly in line with our first hypothesis. Corroborating Hypothesis 1, we find the relative inflow of lower educated workers to decrease. However, contradicting Hypothesis 1 we find the relative proportion of higher educated workers to decrease, rather than increase. We find that the relative proportion of middle educated workers entering enterprises increases, rather than decreases, when technology is implemented; we therefore reject Hypothesis 2. With respect to the educational composition of workers leaving enterprises, we find support for Hypothesis 3: the proportion of middle educated workers leaving enterprises increased relative to the proportions of higher and lower educated workers. The results on the effect of technology implementation on the educational composition of the enterprise do not correspond with our expectations: we do not find the proportion of higher educated workers to increase. Instead, we find that the proportion of middle educated workers increases, primarily at the expense of lower educated workers. Nevertheless, this relative increase in middle educated workers is in line with the hypothesis that technology is associated with educational upgrading of the workforce. However, we expected this upgrading to occur through an increase in the proportion of high educated workers; we therefore reject Hypothesis 4.

Table 13.3 shows the effects of technology implementation on the age composition of workers. Contrary to our expectations, we find that the proportion of workers aged 50+ entering the enterprise increases relative to the proportion of workers aged between 30 and 50. We therefore reject Hypothesis 5. Turning to the effects of technology implementation on the age composition of workers leaving enterprises, we find that, in accordance with Hypothesis 6, technology implementation is associated with an increased proportion of workers aged 50+ leaving the enterprise. Finally, changes in the age composition of enterprise workforces do not support our expectations: we find technology implementation to be associated with an increase, instead of a decrease, in the proportion of workers aged 50+.

To investigate the role of the institutional context, we included interaction effects between technology implementation and unionization within an industry. We do not find unionization to unequivocally be associated with weaker effects of technology on the education composition of enterprise workforces, entrants and leavers (see Table 13.4). Changes in the composition of high educated workers entering, leaving and working in enterprises do appear to be significantly smaller in unionized industries. However, the decrease in the proportions of lower educated workers entering, leaving and working in enterprises appear to be more pronounced in unionized industries. With respect to changes

Table 13.2 Seemingly unrelated fixed-effects regressions of technology implementation on educational composition of workers in enterprises

	Education entrants			*Education leavers*			*Education workforce*		
	% low	*% mid*	*% high*	*% low*	*% mid*	*% high*	*% low*	*% mid*	*% high*
Technology implementation	–0.013***	0.025***	–0.013***	–0.011***	0.022***	–0.010***	–0.008***	0.010***	–0.002*
	(0.002)	(0.003)	(0.003)	(0.003)	(0.003)	(0.003)	(0.001)	(0.001)	(0.001)
Organizational innovation	0.000	0.003	–0.003	0.001	0.003	–0.004	–0.001	0.001	0.001
	(0.003)	(0.003)	(0.003)	(0.003)	(0.003)	(0.003)	(0.001)	(0.001)	(0.001)
Log enterprise size	–0.000	0.001	–0.001	–0.000	0.001	–0.001	–0.000	0.001***	–0.001*
	(0.001)	(0.001)	(0.001)	(0.001)	(0.001)	(0.001)	(0.000)	(0.000)	(0.000)
Constant	0.018***	–0.002	–0.017**	–0.002	–0.003	0.006	0.006***	–0.002	–0.004*
	(0.005)	(0.007)	(0.006)	(0.005)	(0.007)	(0.006)	(0.002)	(0.002)	(0.002)
Observations		21,731			21,049			22,494	

Source: Results based on calculations by Utrecht University using non-public microdata from Statistics Netherlands.

Notes
All models are weighted with the log of enterprise size*proportion of non-missing data for education and include year dummies.
* $p < 0.05$, ** $p < 0.01$, *** $p < 0.001$ (2-sided); standard errors in parentheses.

Table 13.3 Seemingly unrelated fixed-effects regressions of technology implementation on age composition of workers in enterprises

	Age entrants			*Age leavers*			*Age workforce*		
	% <30	% 30–50	% 50+	% <30	% 30–50	% 50+	% <30	% 30–50	% 50+
Technology implementation	0.002	–0.010***	0.008***	–0.020***	–0.009**	0.029***	–0.027***	–0.005***	0.032***
	(0.003)	(0.003)	(0.002)	(0.003)	(0.003)	(0.002)	(0.001)	(0.001)	(0.001)
Organizational innovation	–0.004	0.003	0.001	–0.007*	0.007*	0.001	0.001	–0.001	0.000
	(0.003)	(0.003)	(0.002)	(0.003)	(0.003)	(0.003)	(0.001)	(0.001)	(0.001)
Log enterprise size	0.000	–0.000	0.000	0.000	0.000	–0.000	–0.000	–0.000	0.000
	(0.001)	(0.001)	(0.001)	(0.001)	(0.001)	(0.001)	(0.000)	(0.000)	(0.000)
Constant	–0.006	0.005	0.002	0.016*	0.007	–0.024***	0.027***	–0.009***	–0.018***
	(0.007)	(0.006)	(0.004)	(0.006)	(0.006)	(0.005)	(0.002)	(0.002)	(0.002)
Observations		21,935			21,386			22,495	

Source: Results based on calculations by Utrecht University using non-public microdata from Statistics Netherlands.

Notes
All models are weighted with the log of enterprise size*proportion of non-missing data for education and include year dummies.
* $p < 0.05$, ** $p < 0.01$, *** $p < 0.001$(2-sided); standard errors in parentheses.

Table 13.4 Seemingly unrelated fixed-effects regressions of technology implementation on educational composition of workers in enterprises – interaction effects of industry unionization

	Education entrants			*Education leavers*			*Education workforce*		
	% low	*% mid*	*% high*	*% low*	*% mid*	*% high*	*% low*	*% mid*	*% high*
Technology implementation	–0.003	0.025***	–0.021***	–0.007*	0.024***	–0.017***	–0.003***	0.011***	–0.008***
	(0.003)	(0.004)	(0.004)	(0.003)	(0.004)	(0.004)	(0.001)	(0.001)	(0.001)
Technology × unionized industry	–0.017***	0.001	0.016***	–0.008*	–0.005	0.013**	–0.009***	–0.003*	0.012***
	(0.004)	(0.005)	(0.005)	(0.004)	(0.005)	(0.005)	(0.001)	(0.001)	(0.001)
Observations		21,935			21,386			22,495	

Source: Results based on calculations by Utrecht University using non-public microdata from Statistics Netherlands.

Notes
All models are weighted with the log of enterprise size*proportion of non-missing data for education, include year dummies and control for organizational innovation and enterprise size.
* $p < 0.05$, ** $p < 0.01$, *** $p < 0.001$ (2-sided); standard errors in parentheses.

in age composition, we find a mixed pattern of weaker and stronger associations in unionized industries (see Table 13.5). In summary, although the effects of technology differ significantly between industries, the pattern of findings do not support our expectation of weaker associations in unionized contexts. We therefore reject Hypothesis 8.

Conclusion and discussion

In this study we investigated how the implementation of new technologies affects the education and age composition of workers entering, leaving and working in enterprises. Using a large-scale survey of (technological) innovation within Dutch enterprises, linked with register data, we created a longitudinal (2000–2014) employer–employee dataset to study the effect of technology implementation on enterprise workforces.

We did not witness an increase in the proportion of higher skilled workers, as expected, based on the skill biased technological change hypothesis. Recent empirical work, however, documents a decrease in demand for high-skilled, cognitive work tasks from the 2000s onwards (Beaudry, Green, & Sand, 2016; Mishel, Schmitt, & Shierholz, 2013). Beaudry et al. (2016) argue that during the key investment stage in technology there is high and growing demand for skilled cognitive tasks to build up new technological capital. However, they expect a reduction in demand for these tasks relative to the peak investment stage, and argue that the turn of the twenty-first century marked a turning point from peak investment to a stage of maturity. Although this argument may explain why we see decreased demand for cognitive skills, it is less clear how this dynamic may affect the demand for labor in enterprises that are implementing new technologies. One possible scenario is that when technologies enter a 'phase of maturation,' their applicability to standardized tasks increases, complementing the skills of middle educated workers (Autor, 2015; Holzer, 2015). At the same time, when technologies are in their 'revolutionary stage,' there may be a higher demand for the cognitive skills of high educated workers. If the advancement of technology indeed shows such cyclical trends, this may imply that advances in artificial intelligence (AI), machine learning and robotics will lead to a surge in technology investments, increasing the demand for high educated workers, followed by a maturation of these technologies, complementing middle educated workers.

Our findings lend mixed support for the routine biased technological change hypothesis (Acemoglu & Autor, 2011; Autor et al., 2003). While the proportion of middle educated workers leaving enterprises increased as predicted by the theory, we also find the relative number of middle educated entrants as well as the proportion of middle educated workers to increase following technology implementation. The organizational-level patterns in our study do not correspond with labor market findings of polarization in earlier research (see Acemoglu & Autor, 2011; Autor et al., 2003; Goos & Manning, 2007; Goos, Manning, & Salomons, 2009, 2014). An explanation may be that technology increases

Table 13.5 Seemingly unrelated fixed-effects regressions of technology implementation on age composition of workers in enterprises – differences by industry unionization

	Age entrants			*Age leavers*			*Age workforce*		
	% <30	% 30–50	% 50+	% <30	% 30–50	% 50+	% <30	% 30–50	% 50+
Technology implementation	0.003	–0.009***	–0.006**	–0.021***	–0.002	–0.023***	–0.031***	0.008***	0.023***
	(0.004)	(0.004)	(0.002)	(0.004)	(0.004)	(0.003)	(0.001)	(0.001)	(0.001)
Technology × unionized industry	–0.002***	–0.002	0.004	0.001	–0.013**	0.012**	0.008***	–0.023***	0.015***
	(0.005)	(0.005)	(0.003)	(0.005)	(0.005)	(0.004)	(0.001)	(0.002)	(0.001)
Observations		21,935			21,386			22,495	

Source: Results based on calculations by Utrecht University using non-public microdata from Statistics Netherlands.

Notes
All models are weighted with the log of enterprise size*proportion of non-missing data for education, include year dummies and control for organizational innovation and enterprise size.
* $p<0.05$, ** $p<0.01$, *** $p<0.001$ (2-sided); standard errors in parentheses.

demand for workers who are qualified to work with the new technology (Autor, 2015); middle educated workforce that are less qualified are replaced by those who possess the knowledge and skills to work with and alongside new technologies (Holzer, 2015). Needless to say, such replacement processes require a steady supply of workers trained to work with the new technology. The Dutch labor context is likely to create the prerequisites: the Netherlands has a vocationally-oriented educational system characterized by close links between educational programs and the labor market (Van de Werfhorst, 2004). This system improves the match between the skill demands of employers and the skill supply of employees through, for instance, internships and company placements embedded in vocational training, as well as the higher possibility of information exchange between educational institutions and employers about skill requirements (Holzer, 2015). This explanation raises a more fundamental question: the extent to which the technology–labor composition relationship depends on the institutionalized features of skill creation (e.g., the existence of formal ties between organizations and educational institutions). We leave this interesting avenue for future studies that use a cross-country comparative design.

Our main finding regarding age compositional change is an unexpected increase in the proportion of workers aged 50+ in the workforces. This finding suggests that organizations may value older workers' experience and skills in times of technological investment more than skill-based theories might imply. For instance, organizations may consider older, experienced workers more suitable for tasks such as change management or consultancy, which are highly valued during periods of organizational change. Future research could investigate the relationship between the type of jobs created during periods of technological change and the age of their incumbents, to gain more insight into which types of older workers are attracted to enterprises in times of technological change. Nevertheless, some findings also support the notion that technology favors younger workers (see Bartell & Sicherman, 1993; Beckmann, 2007), as the proportion of older workers leaving enterprises increases, while the proportion of younger workers leaving enterprises decreases following technological change.

Our results regarding institutional variation are puzzling and, in any case, do not lend a simple interpretation of uniformly weaker effects in more unionized contexts. Remarkably, within unionized industries, technology implementation leads to lower percentages of less educated workers entering and leaving. This pattern may actually support, rather than refute, the influence of institutions: in unionized contexts, one way for employers to circumvent protection against layoff is to decrease the hiring of lower educated workers (Fernandez, 2001). Findings regarding age seem to point to institutional influences, albeit through different mechanisms. Within more unionized industries, we find the proportion of 50+ workers leaving enterprises under technological change to be significantly greater. Favorable early retirement schemes agreed by unions and employers are one possible explanation (see Raymo, Warren, Sweeney, Hauser, & Ho, 2011), but one may need to follow the destination of leavers – whether retirement, unemployment or a new job – to corroborate this.

Based on our results, the signs for workforce sustainability are generally positive, although there are also reasons to be concerned about the advance of new technologies. Lower educated workers seem to fare worse during technological change, and the extent to which unionism still provides them with protection, given the declining power of unions and increasing liberalization of labor markets, is questionable (Thelen, 2014). National policy efforts should in any case focus on the employment opportunities of these workers. Another source of concern is the labor market position of middle educated and older groups of workers after leaving jobs, a question we did not touch upon in this study. This topic definitely warrants attention, as the skills these groups bring to the labor market may prove unfitting in an environment where technologies keep advancing (Weber, 2014). On a positive note, the general pattern of our findings does not suggest that experienced, older workers and middle educated workers lose much ground in organizations. A careful consideration of organizational and labor market mechanisms is needed to identify the groups that are at risk during the process of technological change.

Notes

1 The Netherlands is a relevant case for conducting the study as it is among the top-ranking countries regarding innovation (Cornell University, INSEAD, & WIPO, 2015).

2 The results are based on calculations by Utrecht University using non-public micro-data from Statistics Netherlands. Under certain conditions, these micro-data are accessible for statistical and scientific research. Contact microdata@cbs.nl for further information.

14 A sustainable workforce in Europe

Future challenges

Tanja van der Lippe and Éva Fodor

Introduction

The evidence provided in the chapters of this book helps us to understand why achieving a sustainable workforce is a complex challenge in the present age. The aim of this book was threefold. The first goal was to provide insight into the availability of organizational policies for a sustainable workforce and their use by employees in different sectors in European countries. The second goal was to analyze the consequences of the availability and use of employers' investments in productive and satisfied employees and cohesive and profitable workplaces. The third goal was to integrate the meso (organizational) level into research on the micro and macro levels of employment. This final chapter brings together the results and conclusions of the foregoing chapters. As such, it shows which employees use different types of organizational investments and what the consequences are for a range of outcomes. We discuss the strengths and weaknesses of studying the organizational level in addition to the employee and country level. The chapter concludes by identifying future challenges for a sustainable workforce.

Synthesis of results

Investments in employees

A general conclusion that can be drawn from the studies in this book is that organizations want to invest in their employees, whether by means of training, leave, flexibility, or health policies. However, it is also clear that there is no uniform approach in this regard. How employers invest in employees appears to be contingent on the specific policy, the employees concerned, and the organizational conditions. Here, we discuss the findings for each policy separately and link them to employee characteristics, as this book shows that policies cannot be considered separately from the employees involved.

Findings in this book show that it is important to distinguish between *training* provided by a co-worker, by a professional, or through an educational program. Women are less likely than men to receive training from a co-worker or to be enrolled in an educational program. However, there is no gender difference in respect of being trained by a professional (Chapter 4). Training differences are also found between native and immigrant workers. Immigrant workers get less formal training than native workers, but their formal training increases in training intensive firms (Chapter 8). Both findings illustrate the importance of formal rules and regulations for groups that are typically less privileged in the organization, such as women and immigrants. Training by a co-worker might happen on a more casual basis, whereas training by a professional is often more institutionalized. Other research also shows that formal rules and regulations reduce gender and minority differences (see Abendroth, Melzer, Kalev, & Tomaskovic-Devey, 2017). This book also addressed access to training for employees who do not have fixed contracts. Although solo self-employed workers more frequently participate in training that they pay for themselves, both these workers and employees on temporary contracts significantly lag behind those with permanent contracts in their participation in training activities (Chapter 11). Ultimately, this might make it more difficult to achieve a sustainable workforce, since employees on temporary contracts report that they need further training relatively often (Chapter 11).

With respect to *work–family policies*, we studied a specific form, namely, parental leave. We found that organizations play a role in the utilization decisions of men regarding parental leave, but not of women, suggesting that while women are expected to use parental leave, men base the extent of their involvement at home, in part, on pressures within the workplace organizational context (Chapter 5). *Policies for 50+ workers* were also studied extensively in this book. Among 50+ workers, being older still increases the likelihood of participating in phasing-out policies, such as a lighter workload, additional leave, and semi-retirement (Chapter 6). There are also major differences between countries in their *health promotion policies* such as healthy nutrition, participating in sports, ergonomic measures, and health checks. Interestingly enough, employees are less likely to perceive these policies as being available in the organization than the organizations themselves report. We find that when organizations offer a more comprehensive set of health policies, employees are also more likely to perceive these policies as being available (Chapter 7). Offering a package of different arrangements makes it more likely that there will be something to appeal to every employee. Organizations would thus do well to offer several policies rather than just one.

In addition to demographic groups such as men and women, younger and older workers, and native and immigrant workers, several employee characteristics also appear to play a role when considering the utilization of such policies. In general, we conclude that a higher educational level and a higher job status goes hand in hand with making more use of all sorts of policies. For example, older employees in high status jobs are more likely to use flexibility policies such as working from home and flexible working hours. Workers who perform physical labor, however, are more likely to use phasing-out arrangements (Chapter 6).

Organizational conditions influence both the investments made by the employer and whether they are used by the employees, but structural conditions matter less than we had anticipated. Nonetheless, organizational size appears to be relevant: bigger organizations provide more parental leave (Chapter 5) and they are also more likely to train all their employees (Chapter 4). However, we also found that immigrants employed in firms that have downsized are more likely to receive training (Chapter 8). The size of the organization plays no role in the training of men and women. While structural characteristics often did not explain variation in employer investments, other organizational characteristics did, especially the role of co-workers and managers. In the case of health policies, team managers' knowledge is an important link between the organizational decision to invest and daily working practices, and our results show that managers play a crucial role when it comes, for example, to informing employees. Moreover, we found that if other colleagues make use of parental leave and if the manager has used parental leave himself/herself, employees are more likely to use parental leave. Colleagues and managers appear to play a decisive role in the uptake of all sorts of policies (see also Van der Lippe & Lippényi, 2018), which indicates that the organization should be included when studying this area.

Consequences for happy and productive employees

This book examined how different sets of investments in sustainable employability impact employee performance and well-being. Similar to the level of investments, the effects of investments are contingent on the specific policy studied, the target group of workers, and the structure of the organization. Some findings corroborate the mutual gains perspective from human resource management research, which argues that policies targeting employee well-being also benefit the performance of the organization. As an indication of this, our results show that worker well-being and performance are positively correlated (Chapter 9). However, policies can have trade-off effects as well, meaning that investments directed at improving employee performance may not increase or may even harm well-being or, conversely, that investments directed at well-being may be harmful for performance. For example, flexible work arrangements may have a direct negative effect on performance, although they positively influence well-being (Chapter 9). Another example is that although training relates to higher employee commitment, it does not improve performance. These findings support the idea that a multi-dimensional analysis of the consequences of policies is needed to understand how such policies produce mutual gains, more productive and cohesive workplaces and, in the end, a sustainable workforce.

The extent to which investments translate into mutual gains for the employee and the organization also depends on the employee. In particular, outcomes may differ by type of contract and whether workers are employed by a firm or are self-employed. That mutual gains are not always forthcoming is certainly true for temporary employees in an organization. Temporary contracts may bring clear labor cost advantages for the organization, but temporary workers experience higher levels of job insecurity than those on permanent contracts (Chapter 10). At the same time, permanent employees experience more job strain and less work–life balance than those on temporary contracts – which may be due to the heavier workload and responsibilities of permanent employees in organizations with a mix of temporary and permanent workers.

We also see different outcomes in how human capital investments are associated with individuals' work engagement and their self-assessed prospects for career advancement (Chapter 11). Among employees on permanent contracts, training has a positive relationship with work engagement and their perceived career prospects. Among those on temporary contracts and solo self-employed workers, human capital investments seem to have more of a 'transactional' function and appear to contribute mainly to how they assess their prospects in their work.

Organizational conditions and structures also shape the outcomes of investments. The presence of female leaders at different levels is an illustrative case. Gender differences in leadership are thought to create mutual gains, but do female employees really profit more from investments when they have a female manager? Analyses show that women do not perceive greater or fewer opportunities for promotion when they work in an organization with a high proportion of female managers, or when they are supervised by a female manager (Chapter 12). Gender differences in perceived promotion opportunities are driven mainly by the arranging of men and women into different teams, which indicates that female managers are not able to reduce gender segregation within organizations. Another investment relates to technology, and this can potentially create conflicting outcomes: technology may be beneficial for the organization and open up new job opportunities, but it can also make workers redundant and lead to job losses, particularly among lower educated and older workers. How the educational and age composition of the workforce responds to technological investments differs across organizational environments: within industries with stronger unions, for example, technology implementation is associated with significantly sharper decreases in the proportion of lower educated employees entering and leaving organizations. This points towards an institutional influence, namely, that union protection makes it difficult to lay off workers and that lower educated employees therefore do not leave the organization (Chapter 13). Although institutional differences across the nine European countries studied in this book are huge (Chapter 2), this does not imply that the consequences of investing in employees always differ from one country to another (see, for example, the findings in Chapter 11). This might also have to do with the way in which we selected the organizations, as we deliberately studied the same six sectors in these countries.

The merit of integrating the organizational level

The European Sustainable Workforce Survey (ESWS) is one of the first multi-country, multi-level surveys of organizations in Europe and includes data on employees, their managers, and their organization. The ESWS made it possible for us to study all three levels and assess whether the suggested mechanisms play out differently in different countries or are universal. Investments and their consequences differ between organizations and depend on a number of organizational characteristics, such as the role of co-workers and managers and the size of the firm. Studies based solely on the employee level are at risk of overlooking the significance of the organizational context, whereas studies that focus solely on the organizational level are likely to underestimate the importance of differences between employees. The ESWS also made it possible to test the interplay between the behavior of employees, department managers, and human resource (HR) managers, which is a considerable innovation. While the multi-country, multi-level approach is a strength, it also has some limitations. Our employees are a select group, as they only capture the proportion of the workforce that is currently employed by an organization. We acknowledge this, and in Chapter 11 we were also able to include the self-employed, a growing group of workers; indeed, the results show that for this group, different investment principles are relevant. We were not, however, able to include those who are unemployed in this study.

The nine countries we studied represent ample variation in institutional and cultural conditions, and collecting multi-level organizational data in such diverse contexts proved to be an enormous practical challenge. Nonetheless, nine countries are still too few to quantify – and formally test – the influence of country-level characteristics (Snijders & Bosker, 1999). Do we then recommend collecting information in even more countries? It might be better to perform small-scale case studies with specific and restricted questions, and focus on comparisons of countries that are generally similar but differ on a few key institutional features; for example, comparing Sweden and Finland could shed light on subtle forms of variation. Another alternative is to collect longitudinal data to analyze some of the issues we studied, as it is certainly possible to track nine countries over time. Future research addressing these issues is especially relevant in respect of establishing more sustainable work relations.

Future challenges

This book offers insights into the current state of the workforce in nine European countries. However, there may be other challenges ahead that have implications for achieving a sustainable workforce in the future. Let us explore that future a little further.

Future of work

The nature of work is changing. Understanding and dealing with the impact of technological innovation has become a key scientific and societal challenge. Automation, robotization, digitalization, and the emergence of the platform economy have profound socioeconomic effects. Some workers will benefit from new technologies in their jobs, their productivity, their job prospects, and their work–life balance. Others, however, may be excluded from these benefits or even experience negative consequences in terms of employability, well-being, health, or the blurring of boundaries between work and private life.

Recent analyses have shown that the impact of technology on work and individuals is far from straightforward (McAfee & Brynjolfsson, 2014; Eurofound, 2016; Organisation for Economic Co-operation and Development [OECD], 2017a). As yet, we do not have enough information to know how it will impact the number of jobs and what they will consist of (Frey & Osborne, 2013). We also do not know how technology will change the type of investments that can or will need to be made in the workforce. Teleworking is one example: it is clearly a technology-enabled, new form of working. The question is whether and how people use and adapt to these types of technology-enabled investments and whether they pay off in terms of well-being, individual employee performance, and the cohesion and productivity of the organization.

One future challenge, then, is to study the impact that technological innovations have in order to propose relevant managerial and organizational guidelines and policies aimed at a sustainable workforce. We included a chapter in this book on the impact of technology on workforce composition (Chapter 13), but clearly more research is needed. Organizations are already deciding which directions to take, and researchers need to keep close track of these developments so that they are able to address possible consequences. Railroad companies are deciding whether to introduce driverless trains, hospitals are deciding to what extent robots can assist surgeons, sales organizations are deciding whether account managers can be replaced by algorithms, banks are deciding whether local offices should be replaced by call centers and to what extent employees can work from home, etc. (Krzywdzinski, 2018; Sergeeva, Huysman, Soekijad, & Van den Hooff, 2017). In doing so, they will also determine which investments are necessary, what types of training, which flexibility arrangements, how quickly employees working in unhealthy work conditions can be replaced by robots, which workers run the risk of becoming obsolete, and what challenges being permanently online pose for individuals' and families' work–life balance (Wotschack, 2017).

Family and community in addition to organization

This book has focused on organizations where employees have paid jobs, but other domains could be relevant as well. To achieve a sustainable workforce, we might need to go a step further. After all, time never stands still in the present day and people move between many different domains of life. This implies that work-related decisions depend not only on the organization, but also on the employee's family and the community in which he or she lives. Individuals are not just employees; they fulfill different roles over their life course. Negative spillover between work, family, and community increases the pressures they face. A future challenge will be how to align potentially conflicting domains and work towards enrichment. It is precisely because people have different roles that it is important to allow for the needs of differing groups of employees in various phases of their lives, and offer them opportunities to work towards common goals and common identities.

For example, individuals can have stable and mutually satisfying relationships both with their family at home and with their colleagues at work, and yet interference between these two domains may challenge the sustainability of these relationships. The competing demands of work and family place increasing pressure on sustainable cooperation in all family structures, but particularly in dual-earner households with children (Peters & Van der Lippe, 2007) and blended families (Van der Heijden, Poortman, & Van der Lippe, 2016). How can balancing work and private life be facilitated?

A related factor is that employees increasingly belong to different family configurations. They might be divorced, have older parents to take care of, or have grandchildren. Organizations must figure out how to deal with such variations and ensure that employees, of whatever sort or type, are able to do a good job. It is another reason why we need to consider not only the organization but also the other life domains that employees inhabit.

A socioeconomic divide in achieving a sustainable workforce?

As we consider the investments made by organizations discussed in this book, we may question whether all employees in the workplace benefit in the same way and, specifically, whether employees of low and high socioeconomic status (SES) do so. There is a growing SES divide in Europe (OECD, 2017a), but very few researchers have studied this divide in relation to work–life policies. A future challenge is to fill this void and gain insight into organizational work–life policies in relation to the SES of employees.

Previous research on organizational work–life policies has focused on the availability of these policies and not so much on their use or on the consequences for lower and higher SES employees, as we do. Existing findings suggest that workers in the same company vary in 'available' work–life support in ways not fully accounted for by differences in need among employees (Blair-Loy & Wharton, 2002). Formal work–life benefits and programs that have been developed for full-time or higher-level positions are typically not made available to workers in low-income positions (Lambert & Haley-Lock, 2004). However, if we do not study the consequences, we will not know whether the skewed distribution of opportunities among different SES groups is problematic. We recommend studying formal availability provided by the organization, availability as perceived by the employee, utilization, and the consequences thereof for employees.

This is all the more urgent because the ongoing devaluation of low-level and vocational degrees in today's society could imply that low SES groups will end up at the margins of organizations even more than they do now, and not benefit from the investments that more resourceful employees receive (Kalleberg,

2011). Moreover, it is possible that organizations that used to unify low educated and high educated workforces into systems of internal labor markets for the benefit of the former group will diminish in importance (Osterman, 2014). This has significant implications, not only for how much investment workers receive directly, but also for how much workers benefit from being employed in resourceful workplaces with resourceful co-workers.

We therefore need to understand how inequality shapes the choices of employers – even more so when those choices affect employees and their families. In addition, organizations are embedded in societies and thus are affected – either positively or negatively – by the levels of economic inequality in that society. Although previous studies have frequently associated national policies with the intersection of SES and gender (Korpi, Ferrarini, & Englund, 2013; Mandel & Semyonov, 2005, 2006), and there are ongoing public policy debates about how to support low-income workers and reduce poverty and income inequality in the process (Lambert, 2009), research has focused less on the role of the organization.

Inequality between countries in achieving a sustainable workforce

This book revealed major institutional differences between the nine European countries with respect to economic, labor market, and demographic trends, as well as to commonality and variance in employment, work–family policies, and health policies in each participating country. We have not yet addressed another key factor that explains at least some of the variation across countries: the presence or absence of stable democratic institutions. Democratic backsliding is particularly prevalent in Central East European countries; one of these, Hungary, is included in our study. Democratic institutions enable organizational policies by securing the rights of workers to negotiate and protest and ensuring that they can stand up for these rights when they consider them to be violated. Ignoring or openly questioning such rights could enable organizations to reduce the benefits they offer. Such shifts in the balance of power between worker and organization may even lead to the organization formally or informally sabotaging the use of national-level policies such as parental leave regulations. Finally, states play an important role in upholding the principles of redistribution outside of and inside companies, such as meritocracy and the equal treatment of minorities. Principles upheld by the state will likely prompt a similar logic to be applied within organizations, by direct or indirect means.

Creating workforce sustainability

Organizations face new and complex challenges in keeping their workforces sustainable, as this book has shown. The growing diversity of the workforce has made it more difficult to predict what investments will lead to more engaged, healthy, and productive employees. At a time when many people are facing job insecurity and governments have reined in social welfare spending, organizations often face the challenge of an overburdened workforce. It is critical that they have the right tools to assess what their employees need in order to be – and remain – effective at their jobs, i.e., to assess their workforce sustainability. The large-scale survey underlying the studies in this book focused mainly on large organizations. Small and medium-sized enterprises (SMEs) have limited access to expensive and time-consuming HR analytics to help them tackle these HR challenges, giving larger organizations a distinct advantage in pursuing workforce sustainability. It should be noted, however, that there are more than 1.5 million SMEs in the European Union employing approximately 48 million people.

Organizations need to know which groups of employees have certain needs and the extent to which they are aware of the investments available to them. Many organizations lack the tools to research this appropriately; they are therefore unable to assess their HR practices and how they impact workforce sustainability. The European Research Council Sustainable Workforce project has significantly advanced our knowledge of how employees respond to such investments. This knowledge has created a unique opportunity to help organizations understand the effects of their HR practices and advise them on how to address the potential shortcomings of their policies. It therefore represents a unique opportunity to offer organizations – whether small, medium-sized, or large – tailored advice, helping them fine-tune their HR policies and create a more engaged and productive workforce. By delivering evidence-based, contextualized advice, this will help organizations, regardless of their size, to understand the impact of their investments and the policy consequences of their workforce composition.

Appendix 1

Collecting cross-country comparative multilevel data in organizations (Chapter 3)

The tables below provide comprehensive lists of the modules for the employee, manager, and organization questionnaires.

Table A1.1 Modules and instruments in the employee questionnaire

Module name	*Short description and topics*
Your job	Job characteristics (occupation, position, contract type, tenure, working hours, commuting time and travel costs reimbursement)
Background information	Demographic characteristics (age, gender, country of birth, country-specific education)
Work flexibility	Knowledge about and use of flexible working arrangements (time, location, part-time)
Training	Participation in training (internal, external, adult education) and utility for current job
Health arrangements	Knowledge about and use of health arrangements at the workplace (catering, sport, health checks, ergonomic measures); physical activity during work
Leave and childcare arrangements	Knowledge about and use of leave and childcare arrangements (maternity and paternity leave, parental leave, assistance with childcare); use of childcare arrangements of partner; perception of support from organization towards employees with family commitments.
Age-related work arrangements	Knowledge about and use of age-related work arrangements (additional leave, specific training, lighter workload, semi-retirement); promotion and demotion of older workers; retirement intentions; subjective age; perceptions of age discrimination; retirement norms
Work climate	Perceptions of work unit cohesiveness; self-reported OCB-I (horizontal cooperation), organizational commitment; perception of supervisory support
Work evaluation	Self-reported job autonomy; role overload; task performance and contextual performance
Well-being and satisfaction	Job satisfaction; work–life balance; work–family strain; work–family enrichment; work–life segmentation preferences; time pressures; general health
Job outlook	Career uncertainty, employment uncertainty, job uncertainty, turnover intentions
Your household	Partner's education, employment situation, working hours and commuting time; children living at home and their age
Housework and care responsibilities	Own and partner's time spent on childcare; domestic duties; elderly care; grandchildren; gender norm perceptions
Final questions	Monthly wage and household income

Table A1.2 Modules and instruments in the manager questionnaire

Module name	*Short description and topics*
Your department	Work unit size; work unit age, gender, skill and contract-type composition; temporary contract extension; presence of agency workers; part-time work; prevalence of recruitment and performance related problems; characteristics of the work of workers in unit (autonomy, interdependency, team work, project-based work, skill specificity)
Work flexibility	Availability and use of flexible working arrangements (time, location, part-time)
Training	Facilitation of and employee participation in training (internal, external, adult education); evaluation of training needs of employee groups
Health arrangements	Availability and employees' use of health arrangements at the workplace (catering, sport, health checks, ergonomic measures)
Leave and childcare arrangements	Availability and employees' use of leave and childcare arrangements (maternity and paternity leave, parental leave, part-time, assistance with childcare); family-supportiveness of manager and workplace
Age-related work arrangements	Availability and older employees' use of age-related work arrangements (additional leave, specific training, lighter workload, health promoting measures, coaching younger colleagues, semi-retirement, early retirement); promotion and demotion of older workers; use of mixed-age teams; attitudes towards older workers
Productivity and performance	Productivity and work climate of work unit, OCB in work unit (horizontal and vertical cooperation); department culture
Your job	Job characteristics (tenure, managerial tenure, working hours, working from home)
Work evaluation	Task and contextual performance; managerial style
Well-being	Work–family strain; work–family enrichment; work–life balance; time pressures; work–family segmentation preferences; gender role norms
Your household	Demographic characteristics (gender, age, education, partner, partner's employment situation and working hours, children, use of childcare arrangements)
Income	Monthly wage

Table A1.3 Modules and instruments in the organization questionnaire

Module name	*Short description and topics*
Your establishment	Establishment characteristics (type, private/public ownership, domestic/international ownership)
The employees	Employee and management characteristics (number of employees, demographic, skill and contract-type composition, flexible hiring policies, presence of temporary agency workers, part-time work, prevalence of recruitment and performance related problems, hierarchical structure of establishment, size and gender composition of management, men and women in higher management, collective bargaining, protection against lay-off, internal hiring for jobs)
Work flexibility	Availability and use of flexible working arrangements (time, location, part-time)
Training	Facilitation of and employee participation in training (internal, external, adult education); evaluation of training needs of employee groups
Health arrangements	Availability and employees' use of health arrangements at the workplace (catering, sport, health checks, ergonomic measures)
Leave and childcare arrangements	Availability and employees' use of leave and childcare arrangements (maternity and paternity leave, parental leave, part-time, assistance with childcare)
Age-related work arrangements	Availability and older employees' use of age-related work arrangements (additional leave, specific training, lighter workload, health promoting measures, coaching younger colleagues, semi-retirement, early retirement); promotion and demotion of older workers; use of mixed-age teams; implementation of new HR policies aimed at older employees; labor costs and productivity of older employees
Performance and productivity	Performance and productivity indicators (change of organizational size; financial situation; labor productivity), external competition
Organizational culture	Organizational culture
Payment	Individual and team performance–related payment scheme

Appendix 2

The differential influence of employee and organization characteristics on men and women's training participation (Chapter 4)

Table A2.1 shows the full results of the average marginal effects from analyses of training participation.

Table A2.1 Average marginal effects from logistic multi-level analyses of training participation among male and female employees

	Male		*Female*	
	B	*s.e.*	B	*s.e.*
Training by a co-worker				
Years of education	0.01	0.01	0.03**	0.01
Permanent contract	–0.07*	0.03	–0.11***	0.03
Age	–0.06***	0.01	–0.04***	0.01
Public	–0.04	0.05	0.01	0.04
Organization size (ref. = small)				
Medium	0.09*	0.04	0.13***	
Large	0.10*	0.04	0.11**	0.04
Collective labor agreements	0.05	0.04	0.01	0.04
Training by a professional				
Years of education	0.06***	0.01	0.08***	0.01
Permanent contract	0.10**	0.03	0.06*	0.03
Age	–0.04***	0.01	–0.02*	0.01
Public	–0.11*	0.05	–0.03	0.05
Organization size (ref. = small)				
Medium	0.02	0.05	–0.02	0.04
Large	0.07	0.04	0.03	0.04
Collective labor agreements	0.07	0.04	0.06	0.04
Educational program				
Years of education	0.02*	0.01	0.06***	0.01
Permanent contract	–0.01	0.03	–0.01	0.02
Age	–0.05***	0.01	–0.04***	0.01
Public	0.03	0.03	0.02	0.03
Organization size (ref. = small)				
Medium	0.05	0.03	0.02	0.03
Large	0.06*	0.03	0.01	0.03
Collective labor agreements	0.04	0.02	0.03	0.02

Notes
All continuous variables are standardized.
*$p < 0.05$, **$p < 0.01$, ***$p < 0.001$ (2-sided).

Appendix 3

Do female managers improve women's promotional opportunities? – Discussion of country-specific analyses (Chapter 12)

Tables A3.1 and A3.2 illustrate Model 5 for each country separately. Country-specific analyses display the same picture as analyses in which the nine countries are combined: women's and men's perceived promotional opportunities are not differently affected by the proportion of female managers in the organization, nor by themselves having a female manager. For Portugal, country-specific analyses with fixed effects reveals a significant interaction effect between proportion of women in management and female, indicating that with a higher number of women in management women perceive better job opportunities. The same is true for Finland. However, differences in working hours between men and women seem to determine this result in Finland. Since the number of organizations per country is limited, we need to be cautious about the interpretation of the country-specific results.

Table A3.1 Model 5 separately for Finland, Sweden, Germany, the Netherlands (NL) and the United Kingdom (UK)

	Finland	*Sweden*	*Germany*	*NL*	*UK*
Employee variables					
Female	–0.29	0.02	–0.12	–0.11	–0.19
	(0.20)	(0.16)	(0.15)	(0.09)	(0.22)
Age	–0.02***	–0.03***	–0.01**	–0.02***	–0.02***
	(0.01)	(0.01)	(0.01)	(0.00)	(0.00)
Educational level	0.00	0.02	0.03	0.01	0.05
	(0.04)	(0.03)	(0.03)	(0.02)	(0.04)
Partner	–.018†	–0.05	–0.01	–0.03	–0.30**
	(0.10)	(0.09)	(0.10)	(0.05)	(0.11)
Dependent children	0.06	0.19*	0.05	–0.01	0.18†
	(0.09)	(0.08)	(0.08)	(0.05)	(0.09)
Tenure	–0.03***	–0.01*	–0.02**	–0.02***	–0.03***
	(0.01)	(0.01)	(0.01)	(0.00)	(0.01)
Contract hours	0.00	–0.00	0.01	0.01**	0.01†
	(0.01)	(0.01)	(0.01)	(0.00)	(0.01)
Department variables					
Female manager	–0.29	0.18	0.03	0.12	0.14
	(0.20)	(0.17)	(0.17)	(0.12)	(0.20)
Organizational variables					
Proportion female managers	–1.04*	–0.11	0.35	0.34	0.32
	(0.49)	(0.55)	(0.40)	(0.47)	(0.89)
Proportion female employees	0.72	–0.66	0.02	–0.01	–1.44
	(0.60)	(0.44)	(0.54)	(0.35)	(0.95)
Number of employees	0.00	0.00	0.00	0.00	0.00
	(0.00)	(0.00)	(0.00)	(0.00)	(0.00)
Number of employees (natural log)	–0.34	–0.11	–0.04	–0.05	0.05
	(0.27)	(0.11)	(0.13)	(0.06)	(0.11)
Interactions with female					
× proportion female managers	0.04	–0.27	0.10	–0.01	–0.08
	(0.24)	(0.21)	(0.20)	(0.12)	(0.21)
× female manager	0.49	0.15	0.03	0.23	0.48
	(0.42)	(0.49)	(0.28)	(0.32)	(0.65)
Intercept	3.86***	3.52***	2.19**	2.46***	2.71***
	(0.99)	(0.67)	(0.70)	(0.38)	(0.62)
Random variance terms					
Organization (intercept)	0.00	0.27	0.13	0.18	0.00
Female (slope organizations)	0.00	0.01	0.02	0.09	0.00
Department (intercept)	0.00	0.21	0.06	0.20	0.36
Female (slope departments)	0.32	0.01	0.01	0.00	0.24
Employee variance	0.96	0.97	0.99	0.90	0.97
N	574	735	645	1,809	547

Notes

† $p<0.1$, * $p<0.05$, ** $p<0.01$, *** $p<0.001$ (2-sided); standard errors in parentheses.

Occupation (ISCO) indicators are included but not shown in the table.

Table A3.2 Model 5 separately for Portugal, Spain, Hungary and Bulgaria

	Portugal	*Spain*	*Hungary*	*Bulgaria*
Employee variables				
Female	–0.28	–0.32	–0.22	0.27†
	(0.19)	(0.21)	(0.15)	(0.16)
Age	–0.00	–0.01*	–0.01***	–0.00
	(0.01)	(0.01)	(0.00)	(0.00)
Educational level	–0.00	0.09*	0.04	0.03
	(0.04)	(0.04)	(0.02)	(0.03)
Partner	0.05	0.07	0.02	–0.05
	(0.09)	(0.11)	(0.07)	(0.08)
Dependent children	–0.02	–0.04	0.11†	–0.03
	(0.08)	(0.10)	(0.06)	(0.07)
Tenure	–0.02**	–0.01†	–0.01	–0.01**
	(0.01)	(0.01)	(0.00)	(0.01)
Contract hours	0.01*	–0.01	0.00	–0.01
	(0.01)	(0.01)	(0.01)	(0.00)
Department variables				
Female manager	0.14	0.01	0.03	–0.09
	(0.15)	(0.19)	(0.12)	(0.15)
Organizational variables				
Proportion female managers	–0.76	0.18	–0.98	0.29
	(0.59)	(1.06)	(0.82)	(0.39)
Proportion female employees	0.29	–0.12	0.70	–0.17
	(0.38)	(1.01)	(0.98)	(0.44)
Number of employees	0.00	0.00	–0.00†	0.00
	(0.00)	(0.00)	(0.00)	(0.00)
Number of employees (natural log)	–0.02	–0.04	0.11	0.11
	(0.07)	(0.20)	(0.11)	(0.15)
Interactions with female				
× proportion female managers	–0.19	0.07	0.02	–0.02
	(0.18)	(0.20)	(0.15)	(0.17)
× female manager	0.83	0.70	0.10	–0.35
	(0.52)	(0.50)	(0.27)	(0.32)
Intercept	1.53**	2.08*	1.11	1.81*
	(0.56)	(1.03)	(0.74)	(0.83)
Random variance terms				
Organization (intercept)	0.34	0.32	0.38	0.38
Female (slope organizations)	0.28	0.19	0.19	0.15
Department (intercept)	0.00	0.23	0.00	0.38
Female (slope departments)	0.00	0.04	0.00	0.15
Employee variance	1.00	0.98	0.89	0.38
N	776	579	963	1,041

Notes
† $p<0.1$, * $p<0.05$, ** $p<0.01$, *** $p<0.001$ (2-sided); standard errors in parentheses.
Occupation (ISCO) indicators are included but not shown in the table.

References

Abendroth, A. K., & Den Dulk, L. (2011). Support for the work–life balance in Europe: The impact of state, workplace and family support on work–life balance satisfaction. *Work, Employment and Society*, *25*(2), 234–256.

Abendroth, A. K., Melzer, S., Kalev, A., & Tomaskovic-Devey, D. (2017). Women at work: Women's access to power and the gender earnings gap. *Industrial and Labor Relations Review*, *70*(1), 190–222.

Abendroth, A. K., Van der Lippe, T., & Maas, I. (2012). Social support and the working hours of employed mothers in Europe: The relevance of the state, the workplace, and the family. *Social Science Research*, *41*(3), 581–597.

Acemoglu, D., & Autor, D. (2011). Skills, tasks and technologies: Implications for employment and earnings. *Handbook of Labor Economics*, *4*, 1043–1171.

Acker, J. (1990). Hierarchies, jobs, bodies: A theory of gendered organizations. *Gender & Society*, *4*(2), 139–158.

Acker, J. (2006). Inequality regimes: Gender, class, and race in organizations. *Gender & Society*, *20*(4), 441–464.

Adams, L., Winterbotham, M., Oldfield, K., McLeish, J., Large, A., Stuart, A., … Selner, S. (2016). *Pregnancy and maternity-related discrimination and disadvantage: Experience of mothers research findings*. Retrieved from Equality and Human Rights Commission website: www.equalityhumanrights.com/en/managing-pregnancy-and-maternity-workplace/pregnancy-and-maternity-discrimination-research-findings.

Aldana, S. G., Anderson, D. R., Adams, T. B., Whitmer, R. W., Merrill, R. M., George, V., & Noyce, J. (2012). A review of the knowledge base on healthy worksite culture. *Journal of Occupational and Environmental Medicine*, *54*(4), 414–419.

Algan, Y., Dustmann, C., Glitz, A., & Manning, A. (2010). The economic situation of first and second-generation immigrants in France, Germany and the United Kingdom. *The Economic Journal*, *120*, F4–F30.

Allen, N. J., & Meyer, J. P. (1996). Affective, continuance and normative commitment to the organization: An examination of construct validity. *Journal of Vocational Behavior*, *49*(3), 252–276.

Allen, T. D. (2001). Family-supportive work environments: The role of organizational perceptions. *Journal of Vocational Behavior*, *58*, 414–435.

Amuedo-Dorantes, C. (2000). Work transitions into and out of involuntary temporary employment in a segmented market: Evidence from Spain. *Industrial & Labor Relations Review*, *53*(2), 309–325.

Anaya, C., Ayuso, J. L., & Fries-Tersch, E. (2015). *Safer and healthier work at any age*. Bilbao, Spain: Country Inventory.

Anderson, C. D., & Tomaskovic-Devey, D. (1995). Patriarchal pressures: An exploration of organizational processes that exacerbate and erode gender earnings inequality. *Work and Occupations*, *22*(3), 328–356.

Anderson, L. M., Quinn, T. A., Glanz, K., Ramirez, G., Kahwati, L. C., Johnson, D. B., ... Katz, D. L. (2009). The effectiveness of worksite nutrition and physical activity interventions for controlling employee overweight and obesity. A systematic review. *American Journal of Preventive Medicine*, 37(4), 340–357.

Anseel, F., Lievens, F., Schollaert, E., & Choragwicka, B. (2010). Response rates in organizational science, 1995–2008: A meta-analytic review and guidelines for survey researchers. *Journal of Business and Psychology*, *25*(3), 335–349.

Anxo, D., Fagan, C., Letablier, M. T., Perraudin, C., & Smith, M. (2007). *Parental leave in European companies: Establishment survey on working time 2004–2005*. Dublin: European Foundation.

Appelbaum, E., Bailey, T., Berg, P., & Kalleberg, A. L. (2000). *Manufacturing advantage: Why high-performance work systems pay off*. Ithaca, NY: Cornell University Press.

Armstrong-Stassen, M. (2008). Human resource practices for mature workers – And why aren't employers using them? *Asia Pacific Journal of Human Resources*, *46*(3), 334–352.

Armstrong-Stassen, M., & Cattaneo, J. (2010). The effect of downsizing on organizational practices targeting older workers. *Journal of Management Development*, *29*(4), 344–363.

Armstrong-Stassen, M., & Ursel, N. D. (2009). Perceived organizational support, career satisfaction, and the retention of older workers. *Journal of Occupational and Organizational Psychology*, *82*(1), 201–220.

Arts, W. A., & Gelissen, J. P. T. M. (2002). Three worlds of welfare capitalism or more? A state-of-the-art report. *Journal of European Social Policy*, *12*(2), 137–158.

Arulampalam, W., & Booth, A. L. (1998). Who gets over the training hurdle? A study of the training experiences of young men and women in Britain. *Journal of Population Economics*, *10*, 197–217.

Arulampalam, W., Booth, A. L., & Bryan, M. L. (2004). Training in Europe. *Journal of the European Economic Association*, *2*(2–3), 346–360.

Arulampalam, W., Booth, A. L., & Bryan, M. L. (2007). Is there a glass ceiling over Europe? Exploring the gender pay gap across the wage distribution. *Industrial and Labor Relations Review*, *60*(2), 163–186.

Ashford, S. J., George, E., & Blatt, R. (2007). Old assumptions, new work: The opportunities and challenges of research on nonstandard employment. *The Academy of Management Annals*, *1*(1), 65–117.

Atkinson, J. (1984). Manpower strategies for flexible organizations. *Personnel Management*, *16*(8), 28–31.

Autor, D. H. (2015). Why are there still so many jobs? The history and future of workplace automation. *Journal of Economic Perspectives*, *29*(3), 3–30.

Autor, D. H., Katz, L. F., & Krueger, A. B. (1998). Computing inequality: Have computers changed the labor market? *The Quarterly Journal of Economics*, *113*(4), 1169–1213.

Autor, D. H., Levy, F., & Murnane, R. J. (2003). The skill content of recent technological change: An empirical exploration. *The Quarterly Journal of Economics*, *118*(4), 1279–1333.

Avdagic, S. (2015). Does deregulation work? Reassessing the unemployment effects of employment protection. *British Journal of Industrial Relations*, *53*(1), 6–26.

Avent-Holt, D., & Tomaskovic-Devey, D. (2012a). Relational inequality: Gender earnings inequality in US and Japanese manufacturing plants in the early 1980s. *Social Forces*, *91*(1), 157–180.
Avent-Holt, D., & Tomaskovic-Devey, D. (2012b). A relational theory of earnings inequality. *American Behavioral Scientist*, 58(3), 379–399.
Avent-Holt, D., & Tomaskovic-Devey, D. (2014). A relational theory of earnings inequality. *American Behavioral Scientist*, 58(3), 379–399.
Bäck-Wiklund, M., Van der Lippe, T., Den Dulk, L., & Van Doorne-Huiskes, A. (2011). *Quality of life and work in Europe: Theory, practice and policy*. London: Palgrave Macmillan.
Baird, C. L., & Reynolds, J. R. (2004). Employee awareness of family leave benefits: The effects of family, work, and gender. *The Sociological Quarterly*, *45*(2), 325–353.
Bal, M. P., Kooij, D. T. A. M., & De Jong, S. B. (2013). How do developmental and accommodative HRM enhance employee engagement and commitment? The role of psychological contract and SOC strategies. *Journal of Management Studies*, 50(4), 545–572.
Baltes, B. B., Briggs, T. E., Huff, J. W., Wright, J. A., & Neuman, G. A. (1999). Flexible and compressed workweek schedules: A meta-analysis of their effects on work-related criteria. *Journal of Applied Psychology*, *84*(4), 496–513.
Bardasi, E., & Francesconi, M. (2004). The impact of atypical employment on individual wellbeing: Evidence from a panel of British workers. *Social Science & Medicine*, 58(9), 1671–1688.
Barley, S. R., & Kunda, G. (2001). Bringing work back in. *Organization Science*, *12*(1), 76–95.
Barley, S. R., & Kunda, G. (2006). *Gurus, hired guns, and warm bodies: Itinerant experts in a knowledge economy*. Princeton, NJ: Princeton University Press.
Baron, J. N., & Bielby, W. T. (1980). Bringing the firms back in: Stratification, Segmentation, and the organization of work. *American Sociological Review*, 45(5), 737–765.
Barrett, A., McGuinness, S., O'Brien, M., & O'Connell, P. (2013). Immigrants and employer-provided training. *Journal of Labor Research*, *34*, 52–78.
Bartell, A. P. (1995). Training wage growth, and job performance: Evidence from a company database. *Journal of Labor Economics*, *3*, 401–425.
Bartell, A. P., & Sicherman, N. (1993). Technological change and retirement decisions of older workers. Journal of Labor Economics, 11(1), 162–183.
Baruch, Y., & Holtom, B. C. (2008). Survey response rate levels and trends in organizational research. *Human Relations*, *61*(8), 1139–1160.
Bassanini, A., Booth, A., Brunello, G., De Paola, M., & Leuven, E. (2005). *Workplace training in Europe* (IZA Discussion Papers No. 1640). Bonn: Institute for the Study of Labor.
Bauer, T. K., & Bender, S. (2004). Technological change, organizational change, and job turnover. *Labour Economics*, *11*(3), 265–291.
Beaudry, P., Green, D. A., & Sand, B. M. (2016). The great reversal in the demand for skill and cognitive tasks. *Journal of Labor Economics*, *34*(S1), S199–S247.
Beauregard, T. A. (2011). Corporate work–life balance initiatives: Use and effectiveness. In S. Kaiser, M. J. Ringlstetter, D. R. Eikhof, & M. Pina e Cunha (Eds.), *Creating balance? International perspectives on the work–life integration of professionals* (pp. 193–208). Berlin/Heidelberg: Springer.
Beauregard, T. A., & Henry, L. C. (2009). Making the link between work–life balance practices and organizational performance. *Human Resource Management Review*, *19*(1), 9–22.

Becker, G. S. (1962). Investment in human capital: A theoretical analysis. *Journal of Political Economy*, *70*(5), 9–49.

Becker, G. S. (1964). *Human capital: A theoretical and empirical analysis, with special reference to education*. Chicago, IL: University of Chicago Press.

Becker, G. S. (1975). *Human capital* (2nd ed.). New York: Columbia University Press.

Beckmann, M. (2007). *Age-biased technological and organizational change: Firm-level evidence and management implications* (WWZ Discussion Paper No. 05/07). Basel: Center of Business and Economics.

Been, W. M. (2015). *European top-managers' support for work–life arrangements*. Ridderkerk, Netherlands: Ridderprint.

Been, W. M., Den Dulk, L., & Van der Lippe, T. (2017a). A business case or social responsibility? How top managers' support for work–life arrangements relates to the national context. *Community, Work and Family*, *20*(5), 573–599.

Been, W. M., Van der Lippe, T., Den Dulk, L., Das Dores Horta Guerreiro, M., Kanjuo Mrčela, A., & Niemistö, C. (2017b). European top managers' support for work–life arrangements. *Social Science Research*, *65*, 60–74.

Beham, B., Drobnič, S., Präg, P., Baierl, A., & Eckner, J. (2018). Part-time work and gender inequality in Europe: A comparative analysis of satisfaction with work–life balance. *European Societies*. Advance online publication. doi:10.1080/14616696.2018.1473627

Bellmann, L., & Düll, H. (2001). Die zeitliche Lage and Kostenaufteilung von Weiterbildungsmaßnahmen – Empirische Ergebnisse auf der Grundlage des IAB Betriebspanels. In R. Dobischat & H. Seifert (Eds.), *Lernzeiten neu organisieren* (pp. 317–352). Berlin: Edition Sigma.

Benz, M., & Frey, B. S. (2008). Being independent is a great thing: Subjective evaluations of self-employment and hierarchy. *Economica*, *75*(298), 362–383.

Berman, E., Bound, J., & Griliches, Z. (1994). Changes in the demand for skilled labor within US manufacturing: Evidence from the annual survey of manufactures. *The Quarterly Journal of Economics*, *109*(2), 367–397.

Berntson, E., & Marklund, S. (2007). The relationship between perceived employability and subsequent health. *Work & Stress*, *21*(3), 279–292.

Bezrukova, K., Jehn, K. A., & Spell, C. S. (2012). Reviewing diversity training: Where we have been and where we should go. *Academy of Management Learning & Education*, *11*(2), 207–227.

Biebly, W. T., & Baron, J. S. (1986). Men and women at work: Sex segregation and statistical discrimination. *American Journal of Sociology*, *91*(4), 759–799.

Birnholtz, J. P., Horn, D. B., Finholt, T. A., & Bae, S. J. (2004). The effects of cash, electronic, and paper gift certificates as respondent incentives for a web-based survey of technologically sophisticated respondents. *Social Science Computer Review*, *22*(3), 355–362.

Black, D. A., Noel, B. J., & Wang, Z. (1999). On-the-job training, establishment size, and firm size: Evidence for economies of scale in the production of human capital. *Southern Economic Journal*, *66*(1), 82–100.

Blackaby, D. H., Clark, K., Leslie, D. G., & Murphy, P. D. (1994). Black–white male earnings and employment prospects in the 1970s and 1980s. *Economics Letters*, *46*, 273–279.

Blair-Loy, M., & Wharton, A. S. (2002). Employees' use of work–family policies and the workplace social context. *Social Forces*, *80*(3), 813–845.

Blanchflower, D. G. (2000). Self-employment in OECD countries. *Labour Economics*, *7*(5), 471–505.

Blau, F. D., Ferber, M., & Winkler, A. (2006). *The economics of women, men, and work* (5th ed.). New York, NY: Prentice Hall.
Blechinger, D., & Pfeiffer, F. (1996). *Technological change and skill obsolescence: The case of German apprenticeship training* (ZEW Discussion Paper No. 96–15). Mannheim: Zentrum für Europäische Wirtschaftsforschung.
Blossfeld, H. P., & Hofmeister, H. (2006). *Globalization, uncertainty and women's careers: An international comparison*. Cheltenham, UK: Edward Elgar.
Blum, T., Fields, D., & Goodman, J. (1994). Organizational level determinants of women in management. *Academy of Management Journal, 37*(2), 241–268.
Blundell, R., Daerden, L., & Meghir, C. (1996). *The determinants and effects of work-related training in Britain*. London: Institute for Fiscal Studies.
Boon, C., Paauwe, J., Boselie, P., & Den Hartog, D. (2009). Institutional pressures and HRM: Developing institutional fit. *Personnel Review, 38*(5), 492–508.
Booth, A. L., Francesconi, M., & Frank, J. (2003). A sticky floors model of promotion, pay, and gender. *European Economic Review, 47*, 295–322.
Booth, A. L., & Van Ours, J. C. (2009). Hours of work and gender identity: Does part-time work make the family happier? *Economica, 76*(301), 176–196.
Boselie, P. (2010). *Strategic human resource management: A balanced approach*. Maidenhead, UK: McGraw-Hill Education.
Boswell, W. R., Boudreau, J. W., & Tichy, J. (2005). The relationship between employee job change and job satisfaction: The honeymoon-hangover effect. *Journal of Applied Psychology, 90*(5), 882–892.
Boxall, P., Guthrie, J. P., & Paauwe, J. (2016). Editorial introduction: Progressing our understanding of the mediating variables linking HRM, employee well-being and organisational performance. *Human Resource Management Journal, 26*(2), 103–111.
Boxall, P., & Macky, K. (2009). Research and theory on high-performance work systems: Progressing the high-involvement stream. *Human Resource Management Journal, 19*(1), 3–23.
Boxall, P., & Purcell, J. (2015). *Strategy and human resource management*. Basingstoke, UK: Palgrave Macmillan.
Boyce, A. S., Ryan, A. M., Imus, A. L., & Morgeson, F. P. (2007). Temporary worker, permanent loser? A model of the stigmatization of temporary workers. *Journal of Management, 33*(1), 5–29.
Boye, K., & Grönlund, A. (2018). Workplace skill investments – An early career glass ceiling? Job complexity and wages among young professionals in Sweden. *Work, Employment and Society, 32*(2), 368–386.
Boyne, G. A. (2002). Public and private management: What's the difference? *Journal of Management Studies, 39*(1), 97–122.
Bresnahan, T. F., Brynjolfsson, E., & Hitt, L. M. (2002). Information technology, workplace organization, and the demand for skilled labor: Firm-level evidence. *The Quarterly Journal of Economics, 117*(1), 339–376.
Brinton, M. C., & Mun, E. (2016). Between state and family: Managers' implementation and evaluation of parental leave policies in Japan. *Socio-Economic Review, 14*(2), 257–281.
Briscoe, F., & Kellogg, K. C. (2011). The initial assignment effect: Local employer practices and positive career outcomes for work–family program users. *American Sociological Review, 76*(2), 291–319.
Broschak, J. P., Davis-Blake, A., & Block, E. S. (2008). Nonstandard, not substandard: The relationship among work arrangements, work attitudes, and job performance. *Work and Occupations, 35*(1), 3–43.

Brough, P., Timms, C., O'Driscoll, M. P., Kalliath, T., Siu, O. L., Sit, C., & Lo, D. (2014). Work–life balance: A longitudinal evaluation of a new measure across Australia and New Zealand workers. *International Journal of Human Resource Management, 25*(19), 2724–2744.

Broughton, A., Green, M., Rickard, C., Swift, S., Eichhorst, W., Tobsch, V., & Tros, F. (2016). *Precarious employment in Europe: Patterns, trends and policy strategies*. Brussels: European Parliament Directorate General for Internal Policies.

Brown, A., Forde, C., Spencer, D., & Charlwood, A. (2008). Changes in HRM and job satisfaction, 1998–2004: Evidence from the Workplace Employment Relations Survey. *Human Resource Management Journal, 18*(3), 237–256.

Brown, J. N. (1989). Why do wages increase with tenure? On-the-job training and life-cycle wage growth observed within firms. *The American Economic Review, 79*(5), 971–991.

Brunello, G. (2001). *On the complementarity between education and training in Europe* (IZA Discussion Paper Series, No. 309). Bonn: Institute for the Study of Labor.

Bryson, C. (2004). The consequences for women in the academic profession of the widespread use of fixed term contracts. *Gender, Work & Organization, 11*(2), 187–206.

Buchanan, D., Boddy, D., & McCalman, J. (1988). Getting in, getting on, getting out and getting back. In A. Bryman (Ed.), *Doing research in organizations* (pp. 53–67). New York: Routledge.

Buddelmeyer, H., McVicar, D., & Wooden, M. (2015). Non-standard "contingent" employment and job satisfaction: A panel data analysis. *Industrial Relations: A Journal of Economy and Society, 54*(2), 256–275.

Bull, S. S., Gillette, C., Glasgow, R. E., & Estabrooks, P. (2003). Work site health promotion research: To what extent can we generalize the results and what is needed to translate research to practice? *Health Education and Behavior, 30*(5), 537–549.

Burgoon, B., & Dekker, F. (2010). Flexible employment, economic insecurity and social policy preferences in Europe. *Journal of European Social Policy, 20*(2), 126–141.

Büsch, V., Dahl, S. Å., & Dittrich, D. A. V. (2009). An empirical study of age discrimination in Norway and Germany. *Applied Economics, 41*(5), 633–651.

Buskens, V., Raub, W., & Snijders, C. (2003). Theoretical and empirical perspectives on the governance of relations in markets and organizations. In V. Buskens, W. Raub, & C. Snijders (Eds.), *The governance of relations in markets and organizations* (pp. 1–18). Bingley, UK: Emerald Group Publishing.

Butts, M. M., Casper, W. J., & Yang, T. S. (2013). How important are work–family support policies? A meta-analytic investigation of their effects on employee outcomes. *Journal of Applied Psychology*, 98(1), 1–25.

Bygren, M., & Duvander, A. Z. (2006). Parents' workplace situation and fathers' parental leave use. Journal of Marriage and Family, 68(2), 363–372.

Bygren, M., Gahler, M., Elisabeth, B. G., Morris, Z. B. G. D., & Magnus, N. (2012). Family formation and men's and women's attainment of workplace authority. *Social Forces*, 90(3), 795–816.

Cameron, K. S., & Quinn, R. E. (2006). *Diagnosing and changing organizational culture: Based on the competing values framework*. San Francisco, CA: John Wiley & Sons.

Camps, J., Oltra, V., Aldás-Manzano, J., Buenaventura-Vera, G., & Torres-Carballo, F. (2016). Individual performance in turbulent environments: The role of organizational learning capability and employee flexibility. *Human Resource Management, 55*(3), 363–383.

Cappelli, P. (1999). *The new deal at work*. Boston, MA: Harvard Business School Press.

Cappelli, P. (2008). Talent on demand – Managing talent in an age of uncertainty. *Strategic Direction, 25*(3). doi:10.1108/sd.2009.05625cae.001

Card, D., & DiNardo, J. E. (2002). Skill-biased technological change and rising wage inequality: Some problems and puzzles. *Journal of labor economics*, *20*(4), 733–783.

Carmichael, F., & Ercolani, M. G. (2014). Age-training gaps in the European Union. *Ageing and Society*, *34*(1), 129–156.

Carmichael, F., Fenton, S. J., Pinilla Roncancio, M., Sadhra, S., & Sing, M. (2016). *Workplace wellbeing programmes and their impact on employees and their employing organisations: A scoping review of the evidence base*. Birmingham, UK: University of Birmingham.

Castilla, E. J. (2011). Bringing managers back in: Managerial influences on workplace inequality. *American Sociological Review*, *76*(5), 667–694.

Castilla, E. J., & Benard, S. (2010). The paradox of meritocracy in organizations. *Administrative Science Quarterly*, *55*(4), 543–676.

Central Bureau voor de Statistiek. (2017). *Flexibele arbeid en de gevolgen voor relatie- en gezinsvorming*. [Flexible employment and its consequences for relationships and family formation]. The Hague: Author.

Chadi, A., & Hetschko, C. (2013). *Flexibilisation without hesitation? Temporary contracts and workers' satisfaction* (IAAEU Discussion Paper Series in Economics, No. 04/2013). Trier: Institute for Labour Law and Industrial Relations in the European Union.

Chan, C. K., & Anteby, M. (2016). Task segregation as a mechanism for within-job inequality: Women and men of the transportation security administration. *Administrative Science Quarterly*, *61*(2), 184–216.

Chand, M. (2010). The impact of HRM practices on service quality, customer satisfaction and performance in the Indian hotel industry. *International Journal of Resource Management*, *21*(4), 551–566.

Chang, K., & Smithikrai, C. (2010). Counterproductive behaviour at work: An investigation into reduction strategies. *International Journal of Resource Management*, *21*(8), 1272–1288.

Charles, M., & Grusky, D. B. (2004). *Occupational ghettos: The worldwide segregation of women and men*. Stanford, CA: Stanford University Press.

Christofides, L. N., Polycarpou, A., & Vrachimis, K. (2013). Gender wage gaps, "sticky floors" and "glass ceilings" in Europe. *Labour Economics*, *21*, 86–102.

Clark, A. E. (2005). Your money or your life: Changing job quality in OECD countries. *British Journal of Industrial Relations*, *43*(3), 377–400.

Clark, S. C. (2000). Work/family border theory: A new theory of work/family balance. *Human relations*, *53*(6), 747–770.

Clarke, M. (2008). Understanding and managing employability in changing career contexts. *Journal of European Industrial Training*, *32*(4), 258–284.

Cohen, L., & Broschak, J. (1998). And then there were more? The effect of organizational sex composition on the hiring and promotion of managers. *American Sociological Review*, *63*(5), 711–727.

Cohen, P. N., & Huffman, M. L. (2007). Working for the woman? Female managers and the gender wage gap. *American Sociological Review*, *72*(5), 681–704.

Conen, W. S. (2018). *Do we have to worry about the "new"* solo *self-employed? Self-sufficiency and precariousness among workers with different types of contract* (Host Country Discussion Paper – The Netherlands). Brussels: European Commission.

Conen, W. S., Henkens, K., & Schippers, J. (2012). Employers' attitudes and actions towards the extension of working lives in Europe. *International Journal of Manpower*, *33*(6), 648–665.

Conen, W. S., Schippers, J. J., & Schulze Buschoff, K. (2016). *Self-employed without personnel. Between freedom and insecurity*. Düsseldorf: Hans-Böckler-Stiftung.

Conen, W. S., Van Dalen, H. P., & Henkens, K. (2012). Ageing and employers' perceptions of labour costs and productivity: A survey among European employers. *International Journal of Manpower, 33*(6), 629–647.

Conen, W. S., Van Dalen, H. P., Henkens, K., & Schippers, J. (2011). *Activating senior potential in ageing Europe: An employers' perspective* (ASPA Project Report). The Hague: Netherlands Interdisciplinary Demographic Institute.

Conn, V. S., Hafdahl, A. R., Cooper, P. S., Brown, L. M., & Lusk, S. L. (2009). Meta-analysis of workplace physical activity interventions. *American Journal of Preventive Medicine, 37*(4), 330–339.

Connell, P. J. O., & Byrne, D. (2010). The determinants and effects of training at work: Bringing the workplace back in. European Sociological Review, 28(3), 283–300.

Cook, A., & Glass, C. (2015). Diversity begets diversity? The effects of board composition on the appointment and success of women CEOs. *Social Science Research, 53*, 137–147.

Cornell University, INSEAD, & WIPO (2015). *The Global Innovation Index 2015: Effective innovation policies for development*. Fontainebleau, Ithaca, and Geneva: Authors.

Corrigall, E. A., & Konrad, A. M. (2006). The relationship of job attribute preferences to employment, hours of paid work, and family responsibilities: An analysis comparing women and men. *Sex Roles, 54*(1–2), 95–111.

Corrigall, E. A., & Konrad, A. M. (2007). Gender role attitudes and careers: A longitudinal Study. *Sex Roles, 56*(11–12), 847–855.

Cortes, G. M., & Salvatori, A. (2016). *Delving into the demand side: Changes in workplace specialization and job polarization* (IZA Discussion Papers, No. 10120). Bonn: Institute for the Study of Labor (IZA).

Courtenay, W. H., McCreary, D. R., & Merighi, J. R. (2002). Gender and ethnic differences in health beliefs and behaviors. *Journal of Health Psychology, 7*(3), 219–231.

Crook, T. R., Todd, S. Y., Combs, J. G., Woehr, D. J., & Ketchen Jr., D. J. (2011). Does human capital matter? A meta-analysis of the relationship between human capital and firm performance. *Journal of Applied Psychology, 96*(3), 443–456.

Cuddy, A. J. C., Fiske, S. T., & Glick, P. (2004). When professionals become mothers, warmth doesn't cut the ice. *Journal of Social Issues, 60*(4), 701–718.

Cutler, D., & Lleras-Muney, A. (2006). *Education and health: Evaluating theories and evidence* (Working Paper Series, No. 06–19). Ann Arbor, MI: University of Michigan, National Poverty Center.

Cutuli, G., & Guetto, R. (2013). Fixed-term contracts, economic conjuncture, and training opportunities: A comparative analysis across European labour markets. *European Sociological Review, 29*(3), 616–629.

Cycyota, C. S., & Harrison, D. A. (2006). What (not) to expect when surveying executives: A meta-analysis of top manager response rates and techniques over time. *Organizational Research Methods, 9*(2), 133–160.

D'Netto, B., & Sohal, A. S. (1999). Human resource practices and workforce diversity: An empirical assessment. *International Journal of Manpower, 20*(8), 530–547.

Dailey, S. L., & Zhu, Y. (2017). Communicating health at work: Organizational wellness programs as identity bridges. *Health Communication, 32*(3), 261–268.

Damman, M., & Henkens, K. (2018). Gender differences in perceived workplace flexibility among older workers in the Netherlands: A brief report. *Journal of Applied Gerontology*. Advance online publication. Advance online publication. doi:10.1177/0733464818800651

Davis-Blake, A., & Uzzi, B. (1993). Determinants of employment externalization: A study of temporary workers and independent contractors. *Administrative Science Quarterly*, *38*, 195–223.

De Cuyper, N., De Jong, J., De Witte, H., Isaksson, K., Rigotti, T., & Schalk, R. (2008). Literature review of theory and research on the psychological impact of temporary employment: Towards a conceptual model. *International Journal of Management Reviews*, *10*(1), 25–51.

De Cuyper, N., & De Witte, H. (2005). Job insecurity: Mediator or moderator of the relationship between type of contract and various outcomes? *SA Journal of Industrial Psychology*, *31*(4), 79–86.

De Cuyper, N., & De Witte, H. (2011). The management paradox: Self-rated employability and organizational commitment and performance. *Personnel Review*, *40*(2), 152–172.

De Cuyper, N., Sulea, C., Philippaers, K., Fischmann, G., Iliescu, D., & De Witte, H. (2014). Perceived employability and performance: Moderation by felt job insecurity. *Personnel Review*, *43*(4), 536–552.

De Grip, A., Fouarge, D., & Montizaan, R. (2015). *Goede inzetbaarheid oudere medewerkers vereist beter HR-beleid*. Tilburg: Netspar.

De Menezes, L. M., & Kelliher, C. (2011). Flexible working and performance: A systematic review of the evidence for a business case. *International Journal of Management Reviews*, *13*(4), 452–474.

De Sivatte, I., & Guadamillas, F. (2013). Antecedents and outcomes of implementing flexibility policies in organizations. *International Journal of Human Resource Management*, *24*(7), 1327–1345.

De Witte, H., & Näswall, K. (2003). Objective vs subjective job insecurity: Consequences of temporary work for job satisfaction and organizational commitment in four European countries. *Economic and Industrial Democracy*, *24*(2), 149–188.

Dearden, L., Reed, H., & Van Reenen, J. (2006). The impact of training on productivity and wages: Evidence from British panel data. *Oxford Bulletin of Economics and Statistics*, *68*(4), 397–421.

Dearing, H. (2016). Gender equality in the division of work: How to assess European leave policies regarding their compliance with an ideal leave model. *Journal of European Social Policy*, *26*(3), 234–247.

Deepchand, K., Drever, E., Gilby, N., Prestage, Y., Purdon, S., Tipping, S., Wood, W. (2013). *Workplace Employment Relations Study (WERS) 2011/2012*. London: NatCen Social Research.

Dejoy, D. M., Parker, K. M., Padilla, H. M., Wilson, M. G., Roemer, E. C., & Goetzel, R. Z. (2011). Combining environmental and individual weight management interventions in a work setting: Results from the Dow chemical study. *Journal of Occupational and Environmental Medicine*, *53*(3), 245–252.

Den Dulk, L. (2001). *Work–family arrangements in organisations: A cross-national study in the Netherlands, Italy, the United Kingdom and Sweden*. Amsterdam: Rozenberg Publishers.

Den Dulk, L., & De Ruijter, J. (2005). Werk/privé-cultuur en de houding van managers ten aanzien van werk/privé beleid in de financiële sector. *Gedrag & Organisatie*, *18*(5), 260–275.

Den Dulk, L., & De Ruijter, J. (2008). Managing work–life policies: Disruption versus dependency arguments. Explaining managerial attitudes towards employee utilization of work–life policies. *International Journal of Human Resource Management*, *19*(7), 1222–1236.

Den Dulk, L., & Groeneveld, S. (2013). Work–life balance support in the public sector in Europe. *Review of Public Personnel Administration*, *33*(4), 384–405.

Den Dulk, L., Groeneveld, S., Ollier-Malaterre, A., & Valcour, M. (2013). National context in work–life research: A multi-level cross-national analysis of the adoption of workplace work–life arrangements in Europe. *European Management Journal*, *31*(5), 478–494.

Den Dulk, L., & Peper, B. (2007). Working parents' use of work–life policies. *Sociologia, Problemas e Práticas*, *53*, 51–70.

Den Dulk, L., Peper, B., Kanjuo Mrčela, A., & Ignjatović, M. (2016). Supervisory support in Slovenian and Dutch organizations: A contextualizing approach. *Community, Work & Family*, *19*(2), 193–212.

Den Dulk, L., Peters, P., & Poutsma, E. (2012). Variations in adoption of workplace work–family arrangements in Europe: The influence of welfare-state regime and organizational characteristics. *International Journal of Human Resource Management*, *23*(13), 2785–2808.

Den Dulk, L., Peters, P., Poutsma, E., & Ligthart, P. E. (2010). The extended business case for childcare and leave arrangements in Western and Eastern Europe. *Baltic Journal of Management*, *5*, 156–184.

Derks, B., Ellemers, N., Van Laar, C., & De Groot, K. (2011). Do sexist organizational cultures create the queen bee? *British Journal of Social Psychology*, *50*(3), 519–535.

Derks, B., Van Laar, C., & Ellemers, N. (2016). The queen bee phenomenon: Why women leaders distance themselves from junior women. *Leadership Quarterly*, *27*(3), 456–469.

Di Fabio, A. (2017). The psychology of sustainability and sustainable development for well-being in organizations. *Frontiers in Psychology*, *8*, 1534.

Dickens, L. (2000). Collective bargaining and the promotion of gender equality at work: Opportunities and challenges for trade unions. *Transfer: European Review of Labour and Research*, *6*(2), 193–208.

Dieckhoff, M., & Steiber, N. (2011). A re-assessment of common theoretical approaches to explain gender differences in continuing training participation. *British Journal of Industrial Relations*, *49*, s135–s157.

Dikkers, J. S. E., Geurts, S. A. E., Den Dulk, L., Peper, B., Taris, T. W., & Kompier, M. A. J. (2007). Dimensions of work–home culture and their relations with the use of work–home arrangements and work–home interaction. *Work and Stress*, *21*(2), 155–172.

Dillman, D. A. (2011). *Mail and internet surveys: The tailored design method – Update with new internet, visual, and mixed-mode guide*. Hoboken, NJ: John Wiley & Sons.

DiMaggio, P. J., & Powell, W. W. (1983). The iron cage revisited: Institutional isomorphism and collective rationality in organizational fields. *American Sociological Association*, *48*(2), 147–160.

Dobbin, F. (2009). *Inventing equal opportunity*. Princeton, NJ: Princeton University Press.

Dobbin, F., Kim, S., & Kalev, A. (2011). You can't always get what you need. *American Sociological Review*, *76*(3), 386–411.

Duncan, G. J., & Hoffman, S. (1979). On-the-job training and earnings differences by race and sex. *The Review of Economics and Statistics*, *61*(4), 594–603.

Dutta-Bergman, M. J. (2004). Primary sources of health information: Comparisons in the domain of health attitudes, health cognitions, and health behaviors. *Health Communication*, *16*(3), 273–288.

Ehrich, L. C., & Kimber, M. (2015). The purpose and place of mentoring for women managers in organisations: An Australian perspective. In M. L. Connerley & J. Wu (Eds.), *Handbook on well-being of working women* (pp. 225–242). Dordrecht: Springer.

Eikemo, T. A., Bambra, C., Huijts, T., & Fitzgerald, R. (2017). The first pan-European sociological health inequalities survey of the general population: The European social survey rotating module on the social determinants of health. *European Sociological Review*, *33*(1), 137–153.

Ellemers, N., Van den Heuvel, H., de Gilder, D., Maass, A., & Bonvini, A. (2004). The underrepresentation of women in science: Differential commitment or the queen bee syndrome? *British Journal of Social Psychology*, *43*(3), 315–338.

Elliott, J. R., & Smith, R. A. (2004). Race, gender, and workplace power. *American Sociological Review*, *69*(3), 365–386.

Elvira, M. M., & Graham, M. E. (2002). Not just a formality: Pay system formalization and sex-related earnings effects. *Organization Science*, *13*(6), 601–617.

Ely, R. J. (1995). The power in demography: Women's social constructions of gender identity at work. *The Academy of Management Journal*, *38*(3), 589–634.

Engbers, L. H., Van Poppel, M. N. M., Chin, M. J. M., Paw, A., & Van Mechelen, W. (2005). Worksite health promotion programs with environmental changes: A systematic review. *American Journal of Preventive Medicine*, *29*(1), 61–70.

Engellandt, A., & Riphahn, R. T. (2005). Temporary contracts and employee effort. *Labour economics*, *12*(3), 281–299.

England, P. (2005). Gender inequality in labor markets: The role of motherhood and segregation. *Social Politics*, *12*(2), 264–288.

England, P. (2010). The gender revolution: Uneven and stalled. *Gender & Society*, *24*(2), 149–166.

England, P., & Folbre, N. (2005). Gender and economic sociology. In N. J. Smelser & R. Swedberg (Eds.), *The handbook of economic sociology* (pp. 627–649). Princeton NJ: Princeton University Press.

Esping-Andersen, G. (1990). *The three worlds of welfare capitalism*. Oxford: Polity Press.

Esping-Andersen, G. (2009). *The incomplete revolution*. Cambridge: Polity Press.

Eurofound. (2007). *Parental leave in European companies*. Luxembourg: Publications Office of the European Union.

Eurofound. (2015a). *European Working Conditions Survey* (4th ed.) [computer file]. Colchester, UK: UK Data Archive [distributor].

Eurofound. (2015b). *Sixth European Working Conditions Survey: 2015*. Retrieved from: www.eurofound.europa.eu/surveys/european-working-conditions-surveys/sixth-european-working-conditions-survey-2015.

Eurofound. (2016). *Sixth European Working Conditions Survey – Overview report*.

Eurofound. (2017a). *Exploring self-employment in the European Union*. Luxembourg: Publications Office of the European Union.

Eurofound. (2017b). *Non-standard forms of employment: Recent trends and future prospects*. Luxembourg: Publications Office of the European Union.

Eurofound. (2017c). *Developments in working life in Europe 2016: EurWORK annual review*. Luxembourg: Author.

European Agency for Safety and Health at Work. (2015). *Second European Survey of Enterprises on New and Emerging Risks (ESENER-2): Main findings*. Luxembourg: Publications Office of the European Union.

European Commission. (2010a). *Europe 2020*. Brussels: European Commission.

European Commission. (2010b). *Self-employment in Europe 2010*. Luxembourg: Publications Office of the European Union.

European Commission. (2015). *Gender equality*. Retrieved from https://ec.europa.eu/europeaid/sectors/human-rights-and-governance/gender_en.

European Commission. (2016a). *EU employment and social situation – Quarterly review*. Retrieved from: http://ec.europa.eu/social/BlobServlet?docId=15397&langId=en.

European Commission. (2016b). *Smarter, greener, more inclusive? Indicators to support the Europe 2020 strategy*. Luxembourg: Publications Office of the European Union.

European Commission's European Political Strategy Centre (EPCS). (2016). *The future of work. Skills and resilience for a world of change*. Retrieved from: http://ec.europa.eu/epsc/publications/strategic-notes/future-work_en.

European Network for Workplace Health Promotion. (2009). *MOVE Europe – A campaign for the improvement of lifestyle-related workplace health promotion in Europe*. Retrieved from www.enwhp.org/fileadmin/downloads/7th_Initiative_MoveEU/Move_europe_Business_Report.pdf.

European Observatory of Working Life. (2018). *Collective bargaining*. Retrieved from: www.eurofound.europa.eu/observatories/eurwork/collective-wage-bargaining/context.

European Parliament. (2015). *Maternity, paternity and parental leave: Data related to duration and compensation rates in the European Union*. Brussels: European Parliament, Policy Department C – Citizens' Rights and Constitutional Affairs.

Eurostat. (2013). *Statistics in focus* (14/2013). Retrieved from: https://ec.europa.eu/eurostat/statistics-explained/index.php?title=Archive:Labour_force_survey_overview_2012.

Eurostat. (2015). *Quality of life in Europe – facts and views – employment*. Retrieved from: https://ec.europa.eu/eurostat/statistics-explained/index.php/Quality_of_life_in_Europe_-_facts_and_views_-_employment.

Evans, P., & Bartolome, F. (1980). The relationship between professional and private life. In C. B. Derr (Ed.), *Work, family and career* (pp. 281–317). New York: Praeger.

Evertsson, M. (2004). Formal on-the-job training: A gender-typed experience and wage-related advantage? *European Sociological Review*, *20*(1), 79–94.

Evertsson, M., & Duvander, A. Z. (2011). Parental leave – possibility or trap? Does family leave length effect Swedish women's labour market opportunities? *European Sociological Review*, *27*(4), 435–450.

Felstead, A. (2010). Closing the age gap? Age, skills and the experience of work in Great Britain. *Ageing & Society*, *30*, 1293–1314.

Fernandez, R. M. (2001). Skill-biased technological change and wage inequality: Evidence from a plant retooling. *American Journal of Sociology*, *107*(2), 273–320.

Ferrera, M. (1996). The "southern model" of welfare in social Europe. *Journal of European Social Policy*, 6(1), 17–37.

Fielding, J. E., & Piserchia, P. V. (1989). Frequency of worksite health promotion activities. *American Journal of Public Health*, *79*(1), 16–20.

Fleischmann, M., & Koster, F. (2017). Older workers and employer-provided training in the Netherlands: A vignette study. *Ageing and Society*, *38*(10), 1995–2018.

Fleischmann, M., Koster, F., & Schippers, J. (2015). Nothing ventured, nothing gained! How and under which conditions employers provide employability-enhancing practices to their older workers. *International Journal of Human Resource Management*, *26*(22), 2908–2925.

Forrier, A., & Sels, L. (2003). Temporary employment and employability: Training opportunities and efforts of temporary and permanent employees in Belgium. *Work, Employment & Society*, *17*(4), 641–666.

Forrier, A., Verbruggen, M., & De Cuyper, N. (2015). Integrating different notions of employability in a dynamic chain: The relationship between job transitions, movement capital and perceived employability. *Journal of Vocational Behavior*, *89*, 56–64.

Fouarge, D., De Grip, A., Smits, W., & De Vries, R. (2012). Flexible contracts and human capital investments. *De Economist, 160*(2), 177–195.

Fouarge, D., & Schils, T. (2009). The effect of early retirement incentives on the training participation of older workers. *Labour, 23*(Special Issue), 85–109.

Frazis, H., Gittleman, M., & Joyce, M. (2000). Correlates of training: An analysis using both employer and employee characteristics. *ILR Review, 53*(3), 443–462.

Frazis, H., & Loewenstein, M. A. (2005). Reexamining the returns to training: Functional form, magnitude, and interpretation. *Journal of Human Resources, 15*(2), 453–476.

Frey, C. B., & Osborne, M. A. (2013). *The future of employment*. Retrieved from Oxford Martin School, University of Oxford website: www.oxfordmartin.ox.ac.uk/The_Future_of_Employment.pdf.

Frey, C. B., & Osborne, M. A. (2017). The future of employment: How susceptible are jobs to computerisation? *Technological Forecasting and Social Change, 114*, 254–280.

Funk, R. (2013). Making the most of where you are: Geography, networks and innovation in organizations. *Academy of Management Journal, 2*, 1–56.

Gajic, A., Cameron, D., & Hurley, J. (2012). The cost-effectiveness of cash versus lottery incentives for a web-based, stated-preference community survey. *European Journal of Health Economics, 13*(6), 789–799.

Galinsky, E., David, J., & Hughes, D. (1990). Trends in corporate family-supportive policies. *Marriage & Family Review, 15*(3–4), 75–94.

Gallie, D. (2007). Production regimes and the quality of employment in Europe. *Annual Review of Sociology, 33*(1), 85–104.

Gallie, D. (2009). *Employment regimes and the quality of work*. Oxford: Oxford University Press.

Garhammer, M. (2002). Pace of life and enjoyment of life. *Journal of Happiness Studies, 3*(3), 217–256.

Gash, V. (2008). Bridge or trap? Temporary workers' transitions to unemployment and to the standard employment contract. *European Sociological Review, 24*(5), 651–668.

Gathmann, C., & Schönberg, U. (2010). How general is human capital? A task-based approach. *Journal of Labor Economics, 28*(1), 1–49.

Giannikis, S. K., & Mihail, D. M. (2011). Flexible work arrangements in Greece: A study of employee perceptions. *International Journal of Resource Management, 22*(2), 417–432.

Gibson, J. (2002). Decomposing ethnic differences in the incidence of employer-provided training in New Zealand. *Applied Economic Letters*, 9, 121–126.

Giunchi, M., Emanuel, F., Chambel, M. J., & Ghislieri, C. (2016). Job insecurity, workload and job exhaustion in temporary agency workers (TAWs): Gender differences. *Career Development International, 21*(1), 3–18.

Glass, J. L., & Noonan, M. C. (2016). Telecommuting and earnings trajectories among American women and men 1989–2008. *Social Forces, 95*(1), 217–250.

Göbel, C., & Zwick, T. (2013). Are personnel measures effective in increasing productivity of old workers? *Labour Economics, 22*, 80–93.

Goetzel, R. Z., & Ozminkowski, R. J. (2008). The health and cost benefits of work site health-promotion programs. *Annual Review of Public Health, 29*, 303–323.

Golden, T. D., & Veiga, J. F. (2005). The impact of extent of telecommuting on job satisfaction: Resolving inconsistent findings. *Journal of Management, 31*(2), 301–318.

Goodstein, J. D. (1994). Institutional pressures and strategic responsiveness: Employer involvement in work–family issues. *Academy of Management Journal, 37*(2), 350–382.

Goos, M., & Manning, A. (2007). Lousy and lovely jobs: The rising polarization of work in Britain. *Review of Economics and Statistics*, 89(1), 118–133.

Goos, M., Manning, A., & Salomons, A. (2009). Job polarization in Europe. *American Economic Review*, 99(2), 58–63.

Goos, M., Manning, A., & Salomons, A. (2014). Explaining job polarization: Routine-biased technological change and offshoring. *American Economic Review*, *104*(8), 2509–2526.

Grawitch, M. J., Gottschalk, M., & Munz, D. C. (2006). The path to a healthy workplace: A critical review linking healthy workplace practices, employee well-being, and organizational improvements. *Consulting Psychology Journal: Practice and Research*, 58(3), 129–147.

Gray, L., & McGregor, J. (2003). Human resource development and older workers: Stereotypes in New Zealand. *Asia Pacific Journal of Human Resources*, *41*(3), 338–353.

Green, C. P., & Heywood, J. S. (2008). *Are flexible contracts bad for workers? Evidence from job satisfaction data*. Retrieved from SSRN website: https://ssrn.com/abstract=1033436.

Green, F., Machin, S., & Wilkinson, D. (1999). Trade unions and training practices in British workplaces. *ILR Review*, 52(2), 179–195.

Greenhalgh, L., & Rosenblatt, Z. (1984). Job insecurity: Toward conceptual clarity. *Academy of Management Review*, 9(3), 438–448.

Greenhaus, J. H. (1988). The intersection of work and family roles: Individual, interpersonal, and organizational issues. *Journal of Social Behavior and Personality*, 3(4), 23–45.

Greenhaus, J. H., Collins, K. M., & Shaw, J. D. (2003). The relation between work–family balance and quality of life. *Journal of vocational behavior*, 63(3), 510–531.

Groeneveld, S., Steijn, B., & Van der Parre, P. (2009). Joining the Dutch civil service: Influencing motives in a changing economic context. *Public Management Review*, *11*(2), 173–189.

Grönlund, A. (2017). On different tracks? Gender, professional strategies, and early career wage gaps. *Nordic Journal of Working Life Studies*, *7*(2), 9–25.

Grönlund, A., Halldén, K., & Magnusson, C. (2017). A Scandinavian success story? Women's labour market outcomes in Denmark, Finland, Norway and Sweden. *Acta Sociologica*, 60(2), 97–119.

Grossmeier, J., Fabius, R., Flynn, J. P., Noeldner, S. P., Fabius, D., Goetzel, R. Z., & Anderson, D. R. (2016). Linking workplace health promotion best practices and organizational financial performance: Tracking market performance of companies with highest scores on the HERO scorecard. *Journal of Occupational and Environmental Medicine*, 58(1), 16–23.

Grover, S., & Crooker, K. (1995). Who appreciates family-responsive human resource policies: The impact of family-friendly policies on the organizational attachment of parents and non-parents. *Personnel Psychology*, 48, 271–288.

Grund, C., & Martin, J. (2012). Determinants of further training – Evidence for Germany. *International Journal of Human Resource Management*, 23(17), 3536–3558.

Grunow, D., Begall, K., & Buchler, S. (2018). Gender ideologies in Europe: A multidimensional framework. *Journal of Marriage and Family*, 80(1), 42–60.

Grusky, D., & England, P. (2004). *Occupational ghettos: The worldwide segregation of women and men*. Stanford, CA: Stanford University Press.

Guazzi, M., Faggiano, P., Mureddu, G. F., Faden, G., Niebauer, J., & Temporelli, P. L. (2014). Worksite health and wellness in the European Union. *Progress in Cardiovascular Diseases*, 56(5), 508–514.

Guerrazzi, M. (2014). Workforce ageing and the training propensity of Italian firms: Cross-sectional evidence from the INDACO Survey. *European Journal of Training and Development*, *38*(9), 803–821.

Guest, D. E. (2002). Perspectives on the study of work–life balance. *Social Science Information*, *41*(2), 255–279.

Guest, D. E. (2004). Flexible employment contracts, the psychological contract and employee outcomes: An analysis and review of the evidence. *International Journal of Management Reviews*, 5(1), 1–19.

Guest, D. E. (2017). Human resource management and employee well-being: Towards a new analytic framework. *Human Resource Management Journal*, *27*(1), 22–38.

Haar, J. M., Russo, M., Suñe, A., & Ollier-Malaterre, A. (2014). Outcomes of work–life balance on job satisfaction, life satisfaction and mental health: A study across seven cultures. *Journal of Vocational Behavior*, *85*(3), 361–373.

Haas, L., Allard, K., & Hwang, P. (2002). The impact of organizational culture on men's use of parental leave in Sweden. *Community, Work & Family*, 5(3), 319–342.

Haas, L., & Hwang, C. P. (2009). Is fatherhood becoming more visible at work? Trends in corporate support for fathers taking parental leave in Sweden. *Fathering: A Journal of Theory, Research, and Practice about Men as Fathers*, *7*(3), 303–321.

Haas, L., & Hwang, C. P. (2016). "It's about time!": Company support for fathers' entitlement to reduced work hours in Sweden. *Social Politics*, *23*(1), 142–167.

Haelermans, C., & Borghans, L. (2012). Wage effects of on-the-job training: A meta-analysis. *British Journal of Industrial Relations*, *50*(3), 502–528.

Hakim, C. (1990). Core and periphery in employers' workforce strategies: evidence from the 1987 ELUS survey. *Work, employment and society*, 4(2), 157–188.

Halldén, K. (2015). Taking training to task: Sex of the immediate supervisor and men's and women's time in initial on-the-job training. *Work and Occupations*, *42*(1), 73–102.

Halpert, J. A., Wilson, M. L., & Hickman, J. L. (1993). Pregnancy as a source of bias in performance appraisals. *Journal of Organizational Behavior*, *14*(7), 649–663.

Hammer, S. S., Liebherr, M., Kersten, S., & Haas, C. T. (2015). Adherence to worksite health interventions: Practical recommendations based on a theoretical framework. *Journal of Workplace Behavioral Health*, *30*(4), 325–343.

Hank, K., & Jürges, H. (2007). Gender and the division of household labor in older couples. *Journal of Family Issues*, *28*(3), 399–421.

Hansson, B. (2007). Company-based determinants of training and the impact of training on company performance: Results from an international HRM survey. *Personnel Review*, *36*(2), 311–331.

Hashi, I., & Stojcic, N. (2014). The impact of innovation activities on firm performance using a multi-stage model: Evidence from the Community Innovation Survey 4. *Research Policy*, *42*(2), 353–366.

Hedström, P., & Ylikoski, P. (2011). Analytical sociology. In A. Tashakkori & C. Teddlie (Eds), *Sage handbook of mixed methods in social & behavioral research* (pp. 386–398). Thousand Oaks, CA: Sage.

Hegewisch, A., & Gornick, J. C. (2011). The impact of work–family policies on women's employment: A review of research from OECD countries. *Community, Work & Family*, *14*(2), 119–138.

Hellevik, O. (2009). Linear versus logistic regression when the dependent variable is a dichotomy. *Quality and Quantity*, *43*(1), 59–74.

Hermansen, A. (2015). Retaining older workers: The effect of phased retirement on delaying early retirement. *Nordic Journal of Social Research*, 6, 44–67.

Hill, E. J., Hawkins, A. J., Ferris, M., & Weitzman, M. (2001). Finding an extra day a week: The positive influence of perceived job flexibility on work and family life balance. *Family relations*, *50*(1), 49–58.

Hillmert, S., Hartung, A., & Weßling, K. (2017). A decomposition of local labour-market conditions and their relevance for inequalities in transitions to vocational training. *European Sociological Review*, *333*(4), 534–550.

Holman, D. (2013). Job types and job quality in Europe. *Human Relations*, *66*(4), 475–502.

Holtmann, A. G., & Idson, T. L. (1991). Employer size and on-the-job training decisions. *Southern Economic Journal*, *58*(2), 339–355.

Holzer, H. (2015). *Job market polarization and US worker skills: A tale of two middles.* Washington, DC: The Brookings Institution.

Hoobler, J. M., Wayne, S. J., & Lemmon, G. (2009). Bosses' perceptions of family–work conflict and women's promotability: Glass ceiling effects. *Academy of Management Journal*, *52*(5), 939–957.

Hoque, K., & Bacon, N. (2006). The antecedents of training activity in British small and medium-sized enterprises. *Work, Employment and Society*, *20*(3), 531–552.

Houseman, S. N., Kalleberg, A. L., & Erickcek, G. A. (2003). The role of temporary agency employment in tight labor markets. *ILR Review*, *57*, 105–127.

Hox, J. J. (2010). *Multilevel analysis: Techniques and applications*. Hove, UK: Routledge.

Huffman, M. L. (2016). Does the presence of women in management impact gender inequality? In M. L. Connerley & J. Wu (Eds.), *Handbook on well-being of working women* (pp. 175–187). Dordrecht: Springer Netherlands.

Huffman, M. L., Cohen, P. N., & Pearlman, J. (2010). Engendering change: Organizational dynamics and workplace gender desegregation, 1975–2005. *Administrative Science Quarterly*, *55*(2), 255–277.

Huffman, M. L., & Torres, L. (2002). It's not only "who you know" that matters – Gender, personal contacts, and job lead quality. *Gender and Society*, *16*(6), 793–813.

Huijts, T., Stornes, P., Eikemo, T. A., Bambra, C., Beckfield, J., Wendt, C., ... Gkiouleka, A. (2017). The social and behavioural determinants of health in Europe: Findings from the European Social Survey (2014) special module on the social determinants of health. *European Journal of Public Health*, *27*(1), 55–62.

Hum, D., & Simpson, W. (2003). Job-related training activity by immigrants to Canada. *Canadian Public Policy*, *29*(4), 469–490.

Hundley, G. (2001). Why and when are the self-employed more satisfied with their work? *Industrial Relations: A Journal of Economy and Society*, *40*(2), 293–316.

Ingram, P., & Simons, T. (1995). Institutional and resource dependence determinants of responsiveness to work–family issues, *38*(5), 1466–1482.

International Labour Office. (2012). *International Standard Classification of Occupations: ISCO-08*. Geneva: Author.

International Network on Leave Policies and Research. (2016). *12th international review of leave policies and related research 2016*. Retrieved from: www.leavenetwork.org/file admin/user_upload/k_leavenetwork/annual_reviews/2016_Full_draft_20_July.pdf.

Jacobs, J. A. (1992). Women's entry into management: Trends in earnings, authority, and values among salaried managers. *Administrative Science Quarterly*, *37*(2), 282–301.

Jacobs, J. A., Lukens, M., & Useem, M. (1996). Organizational, job, and individual determinants of workplace training: Evidence from the National Organizations Survey. *Social Science Quarterly*, *77*(1), 159–176.

Jiang, K., Lepak, D., Hu, J., & Baer, J. C. (2012). How does human resource management influence organizational outcomes? A meta-analytic investigation of mediating mechanisms. *Academy of Management Journal*, *55*(6), 1264–1294.

Jobber, D., & O'Reilly, D. (1998). Industrial mail surveys: A methodological update. *Industrial Marketing Management*, *27*(2), 95–107.

Jones, F., Burke, R. J., & Westman, M. (Eds.). (2013). *Work–life balance: A psychological perspective*. Hove, UK: Psychology Press.

Jovanovic, B. (1979). Job matching and the theory of turnover. *Journal of Political Economy*, *87*(5, Part 1), 972–990.

Kahn, L. M. (2012). Temporary jobs and job search effort in Europe. *Labour Economics*, *19*(1), 113–128.

Kalleberg, A. L. (2000). Nonstandard employment relations: Part-time, temporary and contract work. *Annual Review of Sociology*, *26*, 341–365.

Kalleberg, A. L. (2009). Precarious work, insecure workers: Employment relations in transition. *American sociological review*, *74*(1), 1–22.

Kalleberg, A. L. (2011). *Good jobs, bad jobs*. New York: Russel Sage Foundation.

Kalleberg, A. L. (2012). Job quality and precarious work: Clarifications, controversies, and challenges. *Work and Occupations*, *39*(4), 427–448.

Kalleberg, A. L., Marsden, P. V., Aldrich, H. E., & Cassell, J. W. (1990). Comparing organizational sampling frames. *Administrative Science Quarterly*, *35*, 658–688.

Kalleberg, A. L., Marsden, P. V., Reynolds, J., & Knoke, D. (2006). Beyond profit? Sectoral differences in high-performance work practices. *Work and Occupations*, *33*(3), 271–302.

Kalleberg, A. L., Wallace, M., & Althauser, R. P. (1981). Economic segmentation, worker power, and income inequality. *American Journal of Sociology*, *87*(3), 651–683.

Kampkötter, P., & Marggraf, K. (2015). Do employees reciprocate to intra-firm trainings? An analysis of absenteeism and turnover rates. *International Journal of Human Resource Management*, *26*(22), 2888–2907.

Kanji, S., & Samuel, R. (2017). Male breadwinning revisited: How specialisation, gender role attitudes and work characteristics affect overwork and underwork in Europe. *Sociology*, *51*(2), 339–356.

Kanter, R. M. (1977). *Men and women of the corporation*. New York: Basic Books.

Karasek, R. A. (1979). Job demands, job decision latitude, and mental strain: Implications for job redesign. *Administrative Science Quarterly*, *24*, 285–308.

Katz, L. F., & Murphy, K. M. (1992). Changes in relative wages, 1963–1987: Supply and demand factors. *Quarterly Journal of Economics*, *107*(1), 35–78.

Kaufman, G. (2017). Barriers to equality: Why British fathers do not use parental leave. *Community, Work and Family*, *21*(3), 310–325.

Kauhanen, M., & Nätti, J. (2014). Involuntary temporary and part-time work, job quality and well-being at work. *Social Indicators Research*, *120*(3), 783–799.

Kautonen, T., Down, S., Welter, F., Vainio, P., Palmroos, J., Althoff, K., & Kolb, S. (2010). "Involuntary self-employment" as a public policy issue: A cross-country European review. *International Journal of Entrepreneurial Behaviour & Research*, *16*(2), 112–129.

Kelly, E. L. (2003). The strange history of employer-sponsored child care: Interested actors, uncertainty, and the transformation of law in organizational fields. *American Journal of Sociology*, *109*(3), 606–649.

Kelly, E. L., Kossek, E. E., Hammer, L. B., Durham, M., Bray, J., Chermack, K., … Kaskubar, D. (2008). Getting there from here: Research on the effects of work–family initiatives on work–family conflict and business outcomes. *Academy of Management Annals*, *2*(1), 305–349.

Kennedy, S., Drago, R., Sloan, J., & Wooden, M. (1994). The effect of trade unions on the provision of training: Australian evidence. *British Journal of Industrial Relations, 32*(4), 565–580.

Kilpatrick, M., Blizzard, L., Sanderson, K., Teale, B., & Venn, A. (2015). Factors associated with availability of, and employee participation in, comprehensive workplace health promotion in a large and diverse Australian public sector setting. *Journal of Occupational and Environmental Medicine, 57*(11), 1197–1206.

King, J., Reichelt, M., & Huffman, M. L. (2017). Computerization and wage inequality between and within German work establishments. *Research in Social Stratification and Mobility, 47*, 67–77.

Kinnunen, U., Mäkikangas, A., Mauno, S., Siponen, K., & Nätti, J. (2011). Perceived employability: Investigating outcomes among involuntary and voluntary temporary employees compared to permanent employees. *Career Development International, 16*(2), 140–160.

Kirves, K., Kinnunen, U., De Cuyper, N., & Mäkikangas, A. (2014). Trajectories of perceived employability and their associations with well-being at work. *Journal of Personnel Psychology, 13*(1), 46–57.

Knies, E., Leisink, P., & Van de Schoot, R. (2017). People management: Developing and testing a measurement scale. *The International Journal of Human Resource Management*. Advance online publication. doi:10.1080/09585192.2017.1375963

Kofodimos, J. R. (1993). *Balancing act*. San Francisco, CA: Jossey-Bass.

Kogan, I. (2004). Last hired, first fired? The unemployment dynamics of male immigrants in Germany. *European Sociological Review, 20*(5), 445–461.

Kogan, I. (2006). Labor markets and economic incorporation among recent immigrants in Europe. *Social Forces, 85*(2), 697–721.

Kolenikov, S., & Angeles, G. (2004). *The use of discrete data in principal component analysis with applications to socio-economic indices* (CPC/MEASURE Working Paper No. WP-04-85). Chapel Hill, NC: MEASURE Evaluation/ Carolina Population Center.

Konings, J., & Vanormelingen, S. (2010). *The impact of training on productivity and wages* (LICOS Discussion Paper Series 244/2009). Leuven: LICOS Centre for Institutions and Economic Performance.

Kooij, D. T., Jansen, P. G., Dikkers, J. S., & de Lange, A. H. (2014). Managing aging workers: A mixed methods study on bundles of HR practices for aging workers. *The International Journal of Human Resource Management, 25*(15), 2192–2212.

Koopmans, L., Bernaards, C. M., Hildebrandt, V. H., De Vet, H. C., & Van der Beek, A. J. (2014). Construct validity of the individual work performance questionnaire. *Journal of Occupational and Environmental Medicine, 56*(3), 331–337.

Kopelman, R. E., Prottas, D. J., Thompson, C. A., Jahn, E. W., Kopelman, R. E., Prottas, D. J., & Jahn, E. W. (2006). A multilevel examination of work–life practices: Is more always better? *Journal of Managerial Issues, 18*(2), 232–253.

Korpi, W., Ferrarini, T., & Englund, S. (2013). Women's opportunities under different family policy constellations: Gender, class, and inequality tradeoffs in Western countries re-examined. *Social Politics: International Studies in Gender, State & Society, 20*(1), 1–40.

Kossek, E. E., & Friede, A. (2006). The business case: Managerial perspectives on work and the family. In M. Pitt-Catsouphes, E. E. Kossek, & S. Sweet (Eds.), *The work and family handbook: Multidisciplinary perspectives, methods and approaches* (pp. 611–628). New York, NY: Routledge.

Kossek, E. E., Lautsch, B. A., & Eaton, S. C. (2006). Telecommuting, control, and boundary management: Correlates of policy use and practice, job control, and work–family effectiveness. *Journal of Vocational Behavior*, 68(2), 347–367.

Kossek, E. E., & Michel, J. (2010). Flexible work scheduling. In S. Zedeck (Ed.), *Handbook of industrial-organizational psychology*. Washington, DC: American Psychological Association.

Kossek, E. E., & Thompson, R. J. (2016). Workplace flexibility: Integrating employer and employee perspectives to close the research–practice implementation gap. In T. D. Allen & L. T. Eby (Eds.), *The Oxford handbook of work and family* (pp. 255–270). Oxford: Oxford University Press.

Kossek, E. E., Valcour, M., & Lirio, P. (2014). The sustainable workforce organizational strategies for promoting work–life balance and wellbeing. In P. Chen & C. Cooper (Eds.), *Wellbeing: A complete reference guide: Vol III – Work and wellbeing* (pp. 295–318). Oxford: Wiley-Blackwell.

Kotiso, A., & Lokhorst, B. (2009). *Van ontzien naar duurzaam ontwikkelen. Alternatieven voor seniorenregelingen in CAO's*. Utrecht: Expertisecentrum LEEFtijd.

Kristal, T. (2013). The capitalist machine: Computerization, workers' power, and the decline in labor's share within US industries. *American Sociological Review*, 78(3), 361–389.

Kristal, T. (2017). Who gets and who gives employer-provided benefits? Evidence from matched employer–employee data. *Social Forces*, 96(1), 31–64.

Kristiansen, C. M. (1990). The role of values in the relation between gender and health behaviour. *Social Behaviour*, 5(2), 127–133.

Krueger, A. B. (1993). How computers have changed the wage structure: Evidence from microdata, 1984–1989. *Quarterly Journal of Economics*, 108(1), 33–60.

Krzywdzinski, M. (2018), Wie gute Arbeit in der Industrie 4.0 geschaffen werden kann. *Böll.Thema – Das Magazin der Heinrich–Böll–Stiftung*, 1, 11–13.

Kurtulus, F. A., & Tomaskovic-Devey, D. (2012). Do female top managers help women to advance? A panel study using EEO-1 records. *The ANNALS of the American Academy of Political and Social Science*, 639(1), 173–197.

Lambert, S. J. (2009). Lessons from the policy world: How the economy, work supports, and education matter for low-income workers. *Work and Occupations*, 36(1), 56–65.

Lambert, S. J., & Haley-Lock, A. (2004). The organizational stratification of opportunities for work–life balance: Addressing issues of equality and social justice in the workplace. *Community, work & family*, 7(2), 179–195.

Lambooij, M., Flache, A., Sanders, K., & Siegers, J. (2007). Encouraging employees to co-operate: The effects of sponsored training and promotion practices on employees' willingness to work overtime. *The International Journal of Human Resource Management*, 18(10), 1748–1767.

Lautsch, B. A. (2002). Uncovering and explaining variance in the features and outcomes of contingent work. *Industrial & Labor Relations Review*, 56, 23–43.

Lautsch, B. A. (2003). The influence of regular work systems on compensation for contingent workers. *Industrial Relations: A Journal of Economy and Society*, 42(4), 565–588.

Lazear, E. P. (2009). Firm-specific human capital: A skill-weights approach. *Journal of Political Economy*, 117(5), 914–940.

Lazear, E. P., & Shaw, K. L. (2007). Personnel economics: The economist's view of human resources. *Journal of Economic Perspectives*, 21(4), 92–114.

Lechthaler, W., & Snower, D. J. (2008). Minimum wages and training. *Labour Economics*, 15, 1223–1237.

Legge, K. (1995). *HRM: Rhetorics and realities*. London: Macmillan Business.

Lepak, D. P., & Snell, S. A. (2002). Examining the human resource architecture: The relationships among human capital, employment, and human resource configurations. *Journal of Management, 28*(4), 517–543.

Leppel, K., Brucker, E., & Cochran, J. (2012). The importance of job training to job satisfaction of older workers. *Journal of Aging and Social Policy, 24*(1), 62–76.

Leslie, L. M., Manchester, C. F., Park, T-Y., & Mehng, S. A. (2012). Flexible work practices: A source of career premiums or penalties? *Academy of Management Journal, 55*(6), 1407–1429.

Leuven, E., & Oosterbeek, H. (1999). The demand and supply of work-related training: Evidence from four countries. *Research in Labor Economics, 18*, 303–330.

Lewis, J. (2009). *Work–family balance, gender and policy*. Cheltenham, UK: Edward Elgar Publishing.

Lewis, S., & Den Dulk, L. (2008). Parents' experiences of flexible work arrangements in changing European workplaces: A multi-layer contextual approach. *Sociological Problems, IL–II*, 5–28.

Lewis, S., & Smithson, J. (2001). Sense of entitlement to support for the reconciliation of employment and family life. *Human Relations, 54*(11), 1455–1481.

Liao, H., Toya, K., Lepak, D. P., & Hong, Y. (2009). Do they see eye to eye? Management and employee perspectives of high-performance work systems and influence processes on service quality. *Journal of Applied Psychology, 94*(2), 371–391.

Liden, R. C., Wayne, S, J., Kraimer, M. L., & Sparrowe, R. T. (2003). The dual commitments of contingent workers: An examination of contingents' commitment to the agency and the organization. *Journal of Organizational Behavior, 24*, 609–625.

Linehan, M., & Walsh, J. S. (2000). Work–family conflict and the senior female international manager. *British Journal of Management, 11*(Special Issue), 49–58.

Linnan, L., Bowling, M., Childress, J., Lindsay, G., Blakey, C., Pronk, S., ... Royall, P. (2008). Results of the 2004 National Worksite Health Promotion Survey. *American Journal of Public Health*, 98(8), 1503–1509.

Linnan, L. A., Sorensen, G., Colditz, G., Klar, N., & Emmons, K. M. (2001). Using theory to understand the multiple determinants of low participation in worksite health promotion programs. *Health Education & Behavior, 28*(5), 591–607.

Linnan, L., Weiner, B., Graham, A., & Emmons, K. (2007). Manager beliefs regarding worksite health promotion: Findings from the working healthy project 2. *American Journal of Health Promotion, 21*(6), 521–528.

Loretto, W., & White, P. (2006). Employers' attitudes, practices and policies towards older workers. *Human Resource Management Journal, 16*(3), 313–330.

Lössbroek, J. (2018). *Personnel policies for older workers in 22 EU countries: An overview* [Research note]. Utrecht: Utrecht University.

Lössbroek, J., Lancee, B., Van der Lippe, T., & Schippers, J. (2017). Understanding old-age adaptation policies in Europe: The influence of profit, principles and pressures. *Ageing and Society*. Advance online publication. doi:10.1017/S0144686X17001295

Lössbroek, J., & Radl, J. (2018). Teaching older workers new tricks. Workplace practices and gender training differences in nine European countries. *Ageing and Society*. Advance online publication. doi:10.1017/S0144686X1800079X

Lozza, E., Libreri, C., & Bosio, A. C. (2013). Temporary employment, job insecurity and their extraorganizational outcomes. *Economic and Industrial Democracy, 34*(1), 89–105.

Lynch, L. M. (1991) The role of off-the-job vs. on-the-job training for the mobility of women workers. *The American Economic Review, 81*(2), 151–156.

Lynch, L. M., & Black, S. E. (1998). Beyond the incidence of employer-provided training. *ILR Review*, *52*(1), 64–81.

Lyness, K. S., & Kropf, M. B. (2005). The relationships of national gender equality and organizational support with work–family balance: A study of European managers. *Human Relations*, 58(1), 33–60.

Lyonette, C. (2015). Part-time work, work–life balance and gender equality. *Journal of Social Welfare and Family Law*, *37*(3), 321–333.

Maas, C. J. M., & Hox, J. J. (2005). Sufficient sample sizes for multilevel modelling. *Methodology: European Journal of Research Methods for the Behavioral and Social Sciences*, *1*(3), 85–91.

Mackenbach, J. P., Bopp, M., Deboosere, P., Kovacs, K., Leinsalu, M., Martikainen, P., … De Gelder, R. (2017). Determinants of the magnitude of socioeconomic inequalities in mortality: A study of 17 European countries. *Health & Place*, *47*, 44–53.

Maes, L., Van Cauwenberghe, E., Van Lippevelde, W., Spittaels, H., De Pauw, E., Oppert, J. M., … De Bourdeaudhuij, I. (2012). Effectiveness of workplace interventions in Europe promoting healthy eating: A systematic review. *European Journal of Public Health*, *22*(5), 677–683.

Magnavita, N., Capitanelli, I., Falvo, R., La Milia, D. I., Borghini, A., Moscato, U., … Ricciardi, W. (2017). Workplace health promotion programs in different areas of Europe. *Epidemiology, Biostatistics and Public Health*, *14*(2), 1–8.

Mandel, H., & Semyonov, M. (2005). Family policies, wage structures, and gender gaps: Sources of earnings inequality in 20 countries. *American Sociological Review*, *70*(6), 949–967.

Mandel, H., & Semyonov, M. (2006). A welfare state paradox: State interventions and women's employment opportunities in 22 countries. *American Journal of Sociology*, *111*(6), 1910–1949.

Manyika, J., Chui, M., Miremadi, M., Bughin, J., George, K., Willmott, P., & Dewhurst, M. (2017). *A future that works: Automation, employment, and productivity*. New York, NY: McKinsey Global Institute.

Marler, J. H., Woodard Barringer, M., & Milkovich, G. T. (2002). Boundaryless and traditional contingent employees: Worlds apart. *Journal of Organizational Behavior*, *23*(4), 425–453.

Martin, G., Dymock, D., Billett, S., & Johnson, G. (2014). In the name of meritocracy: Managers' perceptions of policies and practices for training older workers. *Ageing and Society*, *34*(6), 992–1018.

Masters, J. K., & Miles, G. (2002). Predicting the use of external labor arrangements: A test of the transaction costs perspective. *Academy of Management Journal*, *45*, 431–442.

Mastin, T. (1998). Employees' understanding of employer-sponsored retirement plans, a knowledge gap perspective. *Public Relations Review*, *24*(4), 521–534.

Matos, C. (2013). The shifting welfare state in Hungary and Latvia. *American Journal of Economics and Sociology*, *72*(4), 851–891.

Maume, D. J. (2011). Meet the new boss … same as the old boss? Female supervisors and subordinate career prospects. *Social Science Research*, *40*(1), 287–298.

Maume, D. J., & Ruppanner, L. (2015). State liberalism, female supervisors, and the gender wage gap. *Social Science Research*, *50*, 126–138.

McAfee, A., & Brynjolfsson, E. (2014). *The second machine age*. New York: Norton.

McClean, E. J., Burris, E. R., & Detert, J. R. (2013). When does voice lead to exit? It depends on leadership. *Academy of Management Journal*, *56*(2), 525–548.

McCleary, K., Goetzel, R. Z., Roemer, E. C., Berko, J., Kent, K., & De La Torre, H. (2017). Employer and employee opinions about workplace health promotion (wellness) programs: Results of the 2015 Harris Poll Nielsen Survey. *Journal of Occupational and Environmental Medicine*, 59(3), 256–263.

McDonald, D. J., & Makin, P. J. (2000). The psychological contract, organizational commitment and job satisfaction of temporary staff. *Leadership & Organization Development Journal, 21*(2), 84–91.

McDonald, P. K., Brown, K., & Bradley, L. M. (2005). Explanations for the provision-utilisation gap in work–life policy. *Women in Management Review, 20*(1), 37–55.

McEachan, R. R. C., Lawton, R. J., & Conner, M. (2010). Classifying health-related behaviours: Exploring similarities and differences amongst behaviours. *British Journal of Health Psychology, 15*(2), 347–366.

McGinnity, F., & Whelan, C. T. (2009). Comparing work–life conflict in Europe: Evidence from the European Social Survey. *Social Indicator Research,* 93(3), 433–444.

McGrath, D. M., & Keister, L. A. (2008). The effect of temporary employment on asset accumulation processes. *Work and Occupations, 35*(2), 196–222.

McPherson, M., Smith-Lovin, L., & Cook, J. M. (2001). Birds of a feather: Homophily in social networks. *Annual Review of Sociology, 27*, 415–444.

McVicar, D., Wooden, M., Leung, F., & Li, N. (2016). Work-related training and the probability of transitioning from non-permanent to permanent employment. *British Journal of Industrial Relations*, 54(3), 623–646.

Melzer, S. M. (2018). The influence of firms on immigrant–native wage gaps in Germany: A comparison of economic and sociological organizational approaches. Unpublished manuscript, University of Bielefeld, Germany.

Melzer, S. M., Tomaskovic-Devey, D., Schunck, R., & Jacobebbinghaus, P. (2018). A relational inequality approach to first- and second-generation immigrant earnings in German workplaces. *Social Forces*, 97(1), 91–128.

Méndez, F., & Sepúlveda, F. (2015). A comparative study of training in the private and public sector: Evidence from the United Kingdom and the United States. *Contemporary Economic Policy*, 34(1), 107–118.

Meng, L., Galyardt, A. K., Robinson, K. T., Dejoy, D. M., Padilla, H. M., Zuercher, H., … Smith, M. L. (2017). Factors associated with interest in worksite health-related discussions/events among employed adults with chronic conditions. *Journal of Occupational and Environmental Medicine*, 59(7), e145–e149.

Michaels, G., Natraj, A., & Van Reenen, J. (2014). Has ICT polarized skill demand? Evidence from eleven countries over twenty-five years. *Review of Economics and Statistics*, 96(1), 60–77.

Midtsundstad, T. I., Hermansen, A., & Nielsen, R. A. (2012). Effects of companies' initiatives to reduce early retirement among older workers. *Nordic Journal of Working Life Studies*, 2(3), 89–108.

Millán, J. M., Hessels, J., Thurik, R., & Aguado, R. (2013). Determinants of job satisfaction: A European comparison of self-employed and paid employees. *Small Business Economics*, 40(3), 651–670.

Miller, P. W. (1994). Gender discrimination in training: An Australian perspective. *British Journal of Industrial Relations*, 32(4), 539–564.

Mintz, B., & Krymkowski, D. H. (2010). The ethnic, race, and gender gaps in workplace authority: Changes over time in the United States. *Sociological Quarterly*, *51*(1), 20–45.

Mishel, L., Schmitt, J., & Shierholz, H. (2013). *Assessing the job polarization explanation of growing wage inequality* [Working paper]. Berkeley, CA: University of California, Economic Policy Institute.

Mitchell, O. S. (1988). Worker knowledge of pension provisions. *Journal of Labor Economics*, 6(1), 21–39.

Moen, P., Kelly, E. L., Fan, W., Lee, S., Almeida, D., Kossek, E., & Buxton, O. M. (2016). Does a flexibility/support organizational initiative improve high-tech employees' well-being? Evidence from the Work, Family, and Health Network. *American Sociological Review*, 81(1), 134–164.

Moen, P., Kojola, E., Kelly, E. L., & Karakaya, Y. (2016). Men and women expecting to work longer: Do changing work conditions matter? *Work, Aging and Retirement*, *2*(3), 321–344.

Mood, C. (2010). Logistic regression: Why we cannot do what we think we can do, and what we can do about it. *European Sociological Review*, *26*(1), 67–82.

Morrison, E. W., & Robinson, S. L. (1997). When employees feel betrayed: A model of how psychological contract violation develops. *Academy of Management Review*, *22*(1), 226–256.

Mortensen, P. S., & Bloch, C. W. (2005). *Oslo manual: Guidelines for collecting and interpreting innovation data*. Paris: Organisation for Economic Co-operation and Development (OECD).

Moss, P. (2011). *International review of leave policies and related research 2011*. Retrieved from International Network on Leave Policies & Research website: www.leavenetwork.org/fileadmin/user_upload/k_leavenetwork/annual_reviews/2011_annual_review.pdf.

Moss, P. (2017). *13th international review of leave policies and related research 2017*. Retrieved from International Network on Leave Policies & Research website: www.leavenetwork.org/fileadmin/user_upload/k_leavenetwork/annual_reviews/2017_Leave_Review_2017_final2.pdf.

Mulvaney, M. A. (2014). Leave programs/time off and work-stress family employee benefits programs, organizational commitment, and self-efficacy among municipal employees. *Public Personnel Management*, *43*(4), 459–489.

Munn, S. L., & Greer, T. W. (2015). Beyond the "ideal" worker: Including men in work-family discussions. In M. J. Mills (Ed.), *Gender and the work–family experience: An intersection of two domains* (pp. 1–38). New York, NY: Springer International Publishing.

Mutual Information System on Social Protection (MISSOC) (2018). *Comparative tables on sickness – cash benefits*. Retrieved from: www.missoc.org/missoc-database/comparative-tables/results/.

Nabe-Nielsen, K., Garde, A. H., Clausen, T., & Jørgensen, M. B. (2015). Does workplace health promotion reach shift workers? *Scandinavian Journal of Work, Environment & Health*, *41*(1), 84–93.

Navarro, J. G., Dewhurst, F. W., & Eldridge, S. (2010). Linking chief knowledge officers with customer capital through knowledge management practices in the Spanish construction industry. *The International Journal of Resource Management*, *21*(3), 389–404.

Nedelkoska, L. (2013). Occupations at risk: Job tasks, job security, and wages. *Industrial and Corporate Change*, *22*(6), 1587–1628.

Nenovsky, N., & MIlev, J. (2014). *Bulgarian welfare system (1989–2014) during the transition and the crisis* (MPRA Paper No. 62039). CRIISEA, University of Picardie, Amiens and University of World and National Economy, Sofia.

Ng, T. W. H., & Feldman, D. C. (2012). Evaluating six common stereotypes about older workers with meta-analytical data. *Personnel Psychology*, *65*(4), 821–858.

Nikandrou, I., Aspospori, E., Panayotopoulou, L., Stavrou, E. T., & Papalexancris, N. (2008). Training and firm performance in Europe: The impact of national and organizational characteristics. *International Journal of Human Resource Management, 19*(11), 2057–2078.

Nöhammer, E., Stummer, H., & Schusterschitz, C. (2014). Employee perceived barriers to participation in worksite health promotion. *Journal of Public Health, 22*(1), 23–31.

Nutbeam, D. (2008). The evolving concept of health literacy. *Social Science & Medicine, 67*(12), 2072–2078.

O'Connell, P. J., & Byrne, D. (2012). The determinants and effects of training at work: Bringing the workplace back in. *European Sociological Review, 28*(3), 283–300.

O'Connell, P. J., & Jungblut, J. (2008). What do we know about training at work? In K. U. Mayer & H. Solga (Eds.), *Skill formation: Interdisciplinary and cross-national perspectives* (pp. 109–125). Cambridge: Cambridge University Press.

O'Halloran, P. L. (2008). Gender differences in formal on-the-job training: Incidence, duration, and intensity. *LABOUR: Review of Labour Economics & Industrial Relations, 22*(4), 629–659.

Ogbonnaya, C., & Messersmith, J. (2018). Employee performance, well-being, and differential effects of human resource management subdimensions: Mutual gains or conflicting outcomes? *Human Resource Management Journal*. Advance online publication. doi:10.1111/1748-8583.12203

Olson, A., & Chaney, J. D. (2009). Overcoming barriers to employee participation in WHP programs. *American Journal of Health Studies, 24*(3), 353–357.

Oosterbeek, H. (1998). Unravelling supply and demand factors in work-related training. *Oxford Economic Papers, 50*(2), 266–283.

Organisation for Economic Co-operation and Development (OECD). (2000). The partial renaissance of self-employment. In *Employment outlook 2000*. Paris: Author.

Organisation for Economic Co-operation and Development (OECD). (2005). *Education at a glance*. Paris: Author.

Organisation for Economic Co-operation and Development (OECD). (2012). *PISA 2012 technical report*. Retrieved from: www.oecd.org/pisa/pisaproducts/PISA-2012-technical-report-final.pdf.

Organisation for Economic Co-operation and Development (OECD). (2013). Protecting jobs, enhancing flexibility: A new look at employment protection legislation. In *Employment outlook 2013* (pp. 65–126). Paris: Author.

Organisation for Economic Co-operation and Development (OECD). (2016). *Use of childbirth-related leave by mothers and fathers, 1–3*. Retrieved from www.oecd.org/els/family/PF2-2-Use-childbirth-leave.pdf.

Organisation for Economic Co-operation and Development (OECD). (2017a). *Employment outlook 2017*. Paris: Author.

Organisation for Economic Co-operation and Development (OECD. (2017b). OECD family database. Retrieved from: www.oecd.org/els/family/database.htm.

Organisation for Economic Co-operation and Development (OECD). (2017c). Labour force statistics. Employment by Permanency. Incidence of temporary employment. Retrieved from: www.oecd.org/sdd/labour-stats/.

Organisation for Economic Co-operation and Development (OECD). (2018). OECD stat: Trade union membership and trade union density. Retrieved from: https://stats.oecd.org/Index.aspx?DataSetCode=CBCC.

Organisation for Economic Co-operation and Development/Eurostat/UNESCO Institute for Statistics. (2015). *ISCED 2011 operational manual: Guidelines for classifying national education programmes and related qualifications*. Paris: OECD Publishing.

Origo, F., & Pagani, L. (2008). *Flexicurity and workers well-being in Europe: Is temporary employment always bad?* (Working Paper Series No. 141). Milan: University of Milan-Bicocca.

Orlikowski, W. J., & Barley, S. R. (2001). Technology and institutions: What can research on information technology and research on organizations learn from each other? *MIS Quarterly*, *25*(2), 145–165.

Osnowitz, D. (2010). *Freelancing expertise: Contract professionals in the new economy*. Ithaca, NY: Cornell University Press.

Osterman, P. (2014). *Securing prosperity: The American labor market: How it has changed and what to do about it*. Princeton, NJ: Princeton University Press.

Ostroff, C. (1993). Comparing correlations based on individual-level and aggregated data. *Journal of Applied Psychology*, *78*(4), 569–582.

Oude Mulders, J., Henkens, K., Liu, Y., Schippers, J., & Wang, M. (2018). Managers' interview invitation decisions about older job applicants: Human capital, economic conditions and job demands. *Ageing and Society*, *38*(4), 839–864.

Oude Mulders, J., Henkens, K., & Van Dalen, H. P. (2018). Werkgevers bezorgd over langer doorwerken. *Demos*, *34*(1), 1–4.

Pampel, F. C., Krueger, P. M., & Denney, J. T. (2010). Socioeconomic disparities in health behaviors. *The Annual Review of Sociology*, *36*, 349–370.

Parker, R. E. (1994). *Flesh peddlers and warm bodies: The temporary help industry and its workers*. New Brunswick, NJ: Rutgers University Press.

Parker, S. K., Griffin, M. A., Sprigg, C. A., & Wall, T. D. (2002). Effect of temporary contracts on perceived work characteristics and job strain: A longitudinal study. *Personnel psychology*, *55*(3), 689–719.

Parks, K. M., & Steelman, L. A. (2008). Organizational wellness programs: A meta-analysis. *Journal of Occupational Health Psychology*, *13*(1), 58–68.

Pasamar, S. (2015). Availability and use of work-life benefits: What's in between? *Personnel Review*, *44*(6), 949–969.

Pasamar, S., & Alegre, J. (2015). Adoption and use of work–life initiatives: Looking at the influence of institutional pressures and gender. *European Management Journal*, *33*(3), 214–224.

Passey, D. G., Brown, M. C., Hammerback, K., Harris, J. R., & Hannon, P. A. (2018). Managers' support for employee wellness programs: An integrative review. *American Journal of Health Promotion*, *32*(8), 1789–1799.

Pearce, J. L. (1993). Toward an organizational behavior of contract laborers: Their psychological involvement and effects on employee co-workers. *Academy of Management Journal*, *36*, 1082–1096.

Peccei, R. E., Van de Voorde, F. C., & Van Veldhoven, M. (2013). HRM, well-being and performance: A theoretical and empirical review. In J. Paauwe, D. E. Guest, & P. M. Wright (Eds.), *HRM & performance: Achievements & challenges* (pp. 15–46). Chichester, UK: Wiley.

Pejtersen, J. H., Kristensen, T. S., Borg, V., & Bjorner, J. B. (2010). The second version of the Copenhagen Psychosocial Questionnaire. *Scandinavian Journal of Public Health*, *38*(3), 8–24.

Perek-Białas, J., & Turek, K. (2012). Organisation-level policy towards older workers in Poland. *International Journal of Social Welfare*, *21*(s1), 101–116.

Perlow, L. A. (1995). Putting the work back into work/family. *Group & Organization Management*, *20*(2), 227–239.

Peters, P., Den Dulk, L., & Van der Lippe, T. (2009). The effects of time-spatial flexibility and new working conditions on employees' work–life balance: The Dutch case. *Community, Work and Family*, *12*(3), 279–297.

Peters, P., & Van der Lippe, T. (2007). Home-based telework: A gendered strategy to cope with demanding work and family responsibilities. *International Journal of HRM, 18*, 430–447.

Pettigrew, R. N. (2014). *Parental leave use by male employees: Corporate culture, managerial attitudes & employees' perceptions*. Unpublished manuscript, University of Manitoba, Canada.

Pfeffer, J. (2010). Building sustainable organizations: The human factor. *Academy of Management Perspectives, 24*(1), 34–45.

Picchio, M., & Van Ours, J. C. (2013). Retaining through training even for older workers. *Economics of Education Review, 32*(1), 29–48.

Pitt-Catsouphes, M., & Matz-Costa, C. (2008). The multi-generational workforce: Workplace flexibility and engagement. *Community, Work and Family, 11*(2), 215–229.

Podsakoff, P. M., MacKenzie, S. B., Lee, J.-Y., & Podsakoff, N. P. (2003). Common method biases in behavioral research: A critical review of the literature and recommended remedies. *Journal of Applied Psychology*, 88(5), 879–903.

Polachek, S. W. (1981). Occupational self-selection: A human capital approach to sex differences in occupational structure. *The Review of Economics and Statistics, 63*(1), 60–69.

Polavieja, J. G. (2003). Temporary contracts and labour market segmentation in Spain: An employment-rent approach. *European Sociological Review, 19*, 501–517.

Portegijs, W., & Den Brakel, M. (2016). *Emancipatie monitor 2016*. The Hague, Netherlands: Sociaal en Cultureel Planbureau (SCP)/Centraal Bureau voor de Statistiek (CBS).

Posthuma, R. A., & Campion, M. A. (2009). Age stereotypes in the workplace: Common stereotypes, moderators, and future research directions. *Journal of Management, 35*(1), 158–188.

Principi, A., Fabbietti, P., & Lamura, G. (2015). Perceived qualities of older workers and age management in companies: Does the age of HR managers matter? *Personnel Review, 44*(5), 801–810.

Principi, A., Lamura, G., Sirolla, C., Mestheneos, L., Bie , B., Brown, J., ... Döhner, H. (2014). Work restrictions experienced by midlife family care-givers of older people: Evidence from six European countries. *Ageing and Society, 34*(2), 209–231.

Prottas, D. J., Thompson, C. A., Kopelman, R. E., & Jahn, E. W. (2007). Work–family programs: Factors affecting employee knowledge and accuracy. *Personnel Review, 36*(2), 163–189.

Ramsdal, H., & Skorstad, J. (2016). *Flexible organizations and the new working life: A European perspective*. New York, NY: Routledge.

Raymo, J. M., Warren, J. R., Sweeney, M. M., Hauser, R. M., & Ho, J. H. (2011). Precarious employment, bad jobs, labor unions, and early retirement. *Journals of Gerontology Series B: Psychological Sciences and Social Sciences*, 66(2), 249–259.

Remery, C., Henkens, K., Schippers, J., & Ekamper, P. (2003). Managing an aging workforce and a tight labor market: Views held by Dutch employers. *Population Research and Policy Review, 22*, 21–40.

Renaud, S., Lakhdari, M., & Morin, L. (2004). The determinants of participation in non-mandatory training. *Industrial Relations*, 59(4), 724–743.

Reskin, B. F. (2000). The proximate causes of employment discrimination. *Contemporary Sociology, 29*(2), 319–328.

Reskin, B. F., & Bielby, D. D. (2005). A sociological perspective on gender and career outcomes. *Journal of Economic Perspectives, 19*(1), 71–86.

Richter, A., Näswall, K., & Sverke, M. (2010). Job insecurity and its relation to work–family conflict: Mediation with a longitudinal data set. *Economic and Industrial Democracy, 31*(2), 265–280.

Ridgeway, C. L. (1997). Interaction and the conservation of gender inequality: Considering employment. *American Sociological Review*, 62(2), 218–235.

Ridgeway, C. L. (2001). Gender, status, and leadership. *Journal of Social Issues*, 57(4), 637–655.

Ridgeway, C. L. (2011). *Framed by gender: How gender inequality persists in the modern world*. Oxford: Oxford University Press.

Robroek, S. J. W., Van Lenthe, F. J., Van Empelen, P., & Burdorf, A. (2009). Determinants of participation in worksite health promotion programmes: A systematic review. *International Journal of Behavioral Nutrition and Physical Activity*, 6(1), 26.

Rodriguez, J. K., Johnstone, S., & Procter, S. (2017). Regulation of work and employment: Advances, tensions and future directions in research in international and comparative HRM. *Human Resource Management*, 28(21), 2957–2982.

Roeters, A., & Craig, L. (2014). Part-time work, women's work–life conflict, and job satisfaction: A cross-national comparison of Australia, the Netherlands, Germany, Sweden, and the United Kingdom. *International Journal of Comparative Sociology*, 55(3), 185–203.

Rogers, J. K. (2000). *Temps: The many faces of the changing workplace*. Ithaca, NY: Cornell University Press.

Rongen, A., Robroek, S. J. W., & Burdorf, A. (2014a). The importance of internal health beliefs for employees' participation in health promotion programs. *Preventive Medicine*, 67, 330–334.

Rongen, A., Robroek, S. J. W., Van Ginkel, W., Lindeboom, D., Pet, M., & Burdorf, A. (2014b). How needs and preferences of employees influence participation in health promotion programs: A six-month follow-up study. *BMC Public Health, 14*(1), 1277–1284.

Rongen, A., Robroek, S. J. W., Van Lenthe, F. J., & Burdorf, A. (2013). Workplace health promotion: A meta-analysis of effectiveness. *American Journal of Preventive Medicine*, 44(4), 406–415.

Rose, D., & Harrison, E. (2007). The European socio-economic classification: A new social class schema for comparative European research. *European Societies*, 9(3), 459–490.

Rose, D. S., Sidle, S. D., & Griffith, K. H. (2007). A penny for your thoughts: Monetary incentives improve response rates for company-sponsored employee surveys. *Organizational Research Methods*, 10(2), 225–240.

Rose, M. (2005). Job satisfaction in Britain: Coping with complexity. *British Journal of Industrial Relations*, 43(3), 455–468.

Rosen, S. (1986). The theory of equalizing differences. In O. C. Ashenfelter & R. Layard (Eds.), *Handbook of labor economics* (pp. 641–692). Amsterdam, Elsevier.

Rothbard, N., & Dumas, T. (2006). Research perspectives: Managing the work–home interface. In F. Jones, R. J. Burke, & M. Westman (Eds.), *Work–life balance: A psychological perspective* (pp. 71–89). New York, NY: Psychology Press.

Rothbard, N. P., Phillips, K. W., & Dumas, T. L. (2005). Managing multiple roles: Work-family policies and individuals' desires for segmentation. *Organization Science, 16*(3), 243–258.

Rothwell, A., & Arnold, J. (2007). Self-perceived employability: Development and validation of a scale. *Personnel review*, 36(1), 23–41.

Rousseau, D. M. (2011). The individual–organization relationship: The psychological contract. In S. Zedeck (Ed.), *APA handbook of industrial and organizational psychology: Vol. 3 – Maintaining, expanding, and contracting the organization* (pp. 191–220). Washington, DC: American Psychological Association.

Rousseau, D. M., Ho, V. T., & Greenberg, J. (2006). I-deals: Idiosyncratic terms in employment relationships. *Academy of Management Review, 31*(4), 977–994.

Royalty, A. B. (1996). The effects of job turnover on the training of men and women. *ILR Review, 49*(3), 506–521.

Rubery, J., Bosch, G., & Lehndorff., S. (2008). Surviving the EU? The future for national employment models in Europe. *Industrial Relations Journal, 39*, 488–509.

Rudman, L. A., & Mescher, K. (2013). Penalizing men who request a family leave: Is flexibility stigma a femininity stigma? *Journal of Social Issues, 69*(2), 322–340.

Ryan, A., & Kossek, E. E. (2008). Work–life policy implementation: Breaking down or creating barriers to inclusiveness? *Human Resource Management, 47*, 295–310.

Saloniemi, A., & Zeytinoglu, I. U. (2007). Achieving flexibility through insecurity: A comparison of work environments in fixed-term and permanent jobs in Finland and Canada. *European Journal of Industrial Relations, 13*(1), 109–128.

Sandelowski, M. (2000). Combining qualitative and quantitative sampling, data collection, and analysis techniques in mixed-method studies. *Research in Nursing & Health, 23*(3), 246–255.

Saunders, M. N. (2012). Web versus mail: The influence of survey distribution mode on employees' response. *Field Methods, 24*(1), 56–73.

Saunders, M., Lewis, P., & Thornhill, A. (2006). Negotiating access and research ethics. In M. Saunders, A. Thornhill, & P. Lewis (Eds.), *Research methods for business students* (pp. 168– 209). Harlow, UK: Pearson Education.

Schalk, R., & Van Veldhoven, M. (2010). Moving European research on work and ageing forward: Overview and agenda. *European Journal of Work and Organizational Psychology, 19*, 76–101.

Schaufeli, W. B. (2017). *Work engagement in Europe: Relations with national economy, governance, and culture* [Internal report]. Leuven, Belgium: KU Leuven, Research Unit Occupational & Organizational Psychology and Professional Learning.

Schein, V. E., Mueller, R., Lituchy, T., & Liu, J. (1996). Think manager – Think male: A global phenomenon? *Journal of Organizational Behavior, 17*(1), 33–41.

Scherer, S. (2009). The social consequences of insecure jobs. *Social Indicators Research, 93*(3), 527–547.

Schmidt-Catran, A. W., & Fairbrother, M. (2016). The random effects in multilevel models: Getting them wrong and getting them right. *European Sociological Review, 32*(1), 23–38.

Schneider, S. L., & Kogan, I. (2008). *The International Standard Classification of Education 1997: Challenges in the application to national data and the implementation in cross-national surveys*. The International Standard Classification of Education (ISCED-97). Mannheim: MZES.

Schulze Buschoff, K., & Schmidt, C. (2009). Adapting labour law and social security to the needs of the "new self-employed" – Comparing the UK, Germany and the Netherlands. *Journal of European Social Policy, 19*(2), 147–159.

Scott, W. R. (2014). *Institutions and organizations: Ideas, interests, and identities* (4th ed.). Los Angeles, CA: Sage Publications.

Scott, W. R., & Davis, G. F. (2015). *Organizations and organizing*. London: Routledge.

Sequeda, M. F., De Grip, A., & Van der Velden, R. (2015). *Does informal learning at work differ between temporary and permanent workers? Evidence from 20 OECD countries* (IZA Discussion Paper Series No. 9322). Bonn: IZA.

Sergeeva, A., Huysman, M., Soekijad, M., & Van den Hooff, B. (2017). Through the eyes of others. *MIS Quarterly*, *41*(4), 1153–1178.

Setti, I., Dordoni, P., Piccoli, B., Bellotto, M., & Argentero, P. (2015). Proactive personality and training motivation among older workers. *European Journal of Training and Development*, *39*(8), 681–699.

Sexton, E. A., & Olsen, R. N. (1994). The returns to on-the-job training: Are they the same for blacks and whites? *Southern Economic Association*, *61*(2), 328–342.

Shacklock, K., & Brunetto, Y. (2011). A model of older workers' intentions to continue working. *Personnel Review*, *40*(2), 252–274.

Shanafelt, T. D., Boone, S., Tan, L., Dyrbye, L. N., Sotile, W., Satele, D., ... Oreskovich, M. R. (2012). Burnout and satisfaction with work–life balance among US physicians relative to the general US population. *Archives of Internal Medicine*, *172*(18), 1377–1385.

Shavit, Y., & Muller, W. (1998). *From school to work. A comparative study of educational qualifications and occupational destinations*. Oxford: Oxford University Press.

Shelton, B. A. (1990). The distribution of household tasks. Does wife's employment status make a difference? *Journal of Family Issues*, *11*(2), 115–135.

Sheridan, A. (2004). Chronic presenteeism: The multiple dimensions to men's absence from part-time work. *Gender, Work and Organisation*, *11*(2), 207–225.

Shields, M. A., & Wheatley Price, S. (1999a). Ethnic differences in the incidence and determinants of employer-funded training in Britain. *Scottish Journal of Political Economy*, *46*(5), 523–551.

Shields, M. A., & Wheatley Price, S. (1999b). Ethnic differences in British employer-funded on and off-the-job training. *Applied Economic Letters*, 6(7), 421–429.

Shih, T. H., & Fan, X. (2008). Comparing response rates from web and mail surveys: A meta-analysis. *Field Methods*, *20*, 249–271.

Shore, L. M., & Goldberg, C. B. (2013). Age discrimination in the workplace. In R. L. Dipboye & A. Colella (Eds.), *Discrimination at work: The psychological and organizational bases* (pp. 203–225).New York, NY: Psychology Press.

Siegel, D. S. (1998). The impact of technological change on employment: Evidence from a firm-level survey of Long Island manufacturers. *Economics of Innovation and New Technology*, 5(2–4), 227–246.

Simpson, P. A., & Stroh, L. K. (2002). Revisiting gender variation in training. *Feminist Economics*, 8(3), 21–53.

Skaggs, S., Stainback, K., & Duncan, P. (2012). Shaking things up or business as usual? The influence of female corporate executives and board of directors on women's managerial representation. *Social Science Research*, *41*(4), 936–948.

Sloan, R., & Gruman, J. (1988). Participation in workplace health promotion programs: The contribution of health and organizational factors. *Health Education Quarterly*, *15*(3), 269–288.

Smelser, N. J., & Swedberg, R. (Eds.). (2010). *The handbook of economic sociology*. Princeton, NJ: Princeton University Press.

Smith, J., & Gardner, D. (2007). Factors affecting employee use of work–life balance initiatives. *New Zealand Journal of Psychology*, 36(1), 3–12.

Smith, V. (2002). *Crossing the great divide: Worker risk and opportunity in the new economy*. Ithaca, NY: Cornell University Press.

Smith, V. (2010). Enhancing employability: Human, cultural, and social capital in an era of turbulent unpredictability. *Human Relations*, 63(2), 279–300.

Snijders, T., & Bosker, R. (1999). *Multilevel analysis: An introduction to basic and applied multilevel analysis*. London: Sage publications.

Solberg, E., & Dysvik, A. (2015). Employees' perceptions of HR investment and their efforts to remain internally employable: Testing the exchange-based mechanisms of the "new psychological contract." *International Journal of Human Resource Management*, 27(9), 909–927.

Sora, B., Caballer, A., & Hoege, T. (2012). Job insecurity and its cross-domain effect on family satisfaction: The role of employees' affective well-being and detachment. *International Journal of Psychology*, *47*, 520–531.

Spasova, S., Bouget, D., & Vanhercke, B. (2016). *Sick pay and sickness benefit schemes in the European Union. Background report for the Social Protection Committee's in-depth review on sickness benefits*. Brussels: European Commission, European Social Policy Network (ESPN).

Spence, M. (1973). Job market signaling. *Quarterly Journal of Economics*, 87(3), 355–374.

Spitz-Oener, A. (2006). Technical change, job tasks, and rising educational demands: Looking outside the wage structure. *Journal of Labor Economics*, 24(2), 235–270.

Srivastava, S. B., & Sherman, E. L. (2015). Agents of change or cogs in the machine ? Re-examining the influence of female managers on the gender wage gap. *American Journal of Sociology*, 120(6), 1778–1808.

Stainback, K., Kleiner, S., & Skaggs, S. (2016). Women in power. *Gender & Society*, 30(1), 109–135.

Staines, G., Tavris, C., & Jayaratne, T. E. (1974). The queen bee syndrome. *Psychology Today*, 7(8), 55–60.

Statistics Netherlands. (2012, May 31). *Organisatiegraad van werknemers 1995–2011*. Retrieved from: www.cbs.nl/nl-nl/maatwerk/2012/22/organisatiegraad-van-werknemers-1995-2011.

Stavrou, E. T. (2005). Flexible work bundles and organizational competitiveness: A cross-national study of the European work context. *Journal of Organizational Behavior*, 26(8), 923–947.

Stegmueller, D. (2013). How many countries for multilevel modeling? A comparison of frequentist and Bayesian approaches. *American Journal of Political Science*, 57(3), 748–761.

Stigler, G. J. (1961). The economics of information. *Journal of Political Economy*, 69(3), 213–225.

Stone, K. V. (2006). Legal protections for atypical employees: Employment law for workers without workplaces and employees without employers. *Berkeley Journal of Employment & Labour Law*, 27(2), 251–286.

Sturges, J., & Guest, D. (2004). Working to live or living to work? Work/life balance early in the career. *Human Resource Management Journal*, 14(4), 5–20.

Supiot, A. (2001). *Beyond employment: Changes in work and the future of labour law in Europe*. Oxford: Oxford University Press.

Szücs, S., Drobnič, S., Den Dulk, L., & Verbiede, R. (2011). Quality of life and satisfaction with the work–life balance. In M. Bäck-Wiklund, T. Van der Lippe, L. Den Dulk, & A. Doorne-Huiskes (Eds.), *Quality of life and work in Europe. Theory, practice and policy* (pp. 95–117). Basingstoke, UK: Palgrave Macmillan.

Takeuchi, R., Chen, G., & Lepak, D. P. (2009). Through the looking glass of a social system: Cross-level effects of high-performance work systems on employees' attitudes. *Personnel Psychology*, 62(1), 1–29.

Tam, M. Y. M., & Chiu, S. (2010). Job training provision by employers – An institutional analysis of employees in Hong Kong. *International Journal of Human Resource Management*, *21*(12), 2194–2217.

Taylor, P., Loretto, W., Marshall, V., Earl, C., & Phillipson, C. (2016). The older worker: Identifying a critical research agenda. *Social Policy & Society*, *15*(4), 675–689.

Taylor, P., & Urwin, P. (2001). Age and participation in vocational education and training. *Work, Employment & Society*, *15*(4), 763–779.

Taylor, P., & Walker, A. (1998). Employers and older workers: Attitudes and employment practices. *Ageing and Society*, *18*(6), 641–658.

Ter Hoeven, C. L., Miller, V. D., Peper, B., & Den Dulk, L. (2017). "The work must go on": The role of employee and managerial communication in the use of work–life policies. *Management Communication Quarterly*, *31*(2), 194–229.

The Netherlands Scientific Council for Government Policy (WRR). (2013). *Naar een lerende economie* [Towards a learning economy]. Amsterdam: Amsterdam University Press.

Thelen, K. (2014). *Varieties of liberalization and the new politics of social solidarity*. Cambridge: Cambridge University Press.

Thijssen, J. G., Van der Heijden, B. I., & Rocco, T. S. (2008). Toward the employability-link model: Current employment transition to future employment perspectives. *Human Resource Development Review*, *7*(2), 165–183.

Thompson, C. A., Beauvais, L. L., & Lyness, K. S. (1999). When work–family benefits are not enough: The influence of work–family culture on benefit utilization, organizational attachment, and work–family conflict. *Journal of Vocational Behavior*, *54*, 392–415.

Thunnissen, M., Boselie, P., & Fruytier, B. (2013). Talent management and the relevance of context: Towards a pluralistic approach. *Human Resource Management Review*, *23*(4), 326–336.

Tichenor, P. J., Donohue, G. A., & Olien, C. N. (1970). Mass media flow and differential growth in knowledge. *Public Opinion Quarterly*, *34*(2), 159–170.

Tijdens, K. G. (2012). Measuring work activities and skill requirements of occupations: Experiences from a European pilot study with a web-survey. *European Journal of Training and Development*, *36*(7), 751–763.

Tomaskovic-Devey, D., Hällsten, M., & Avent-Holt, D. (2015). Where do immigrants fare worse? Modeling workplace wage gap variation with longitudinal employer–employee data. *American Journal of Sociology*, *120*(14), 1095–1143.

Tomaskovic-Devey, D., Thomas, M., & Johnson, K. (2005). Race and the accumulation of human capital across the career: A theoretical model and fixed-effects application. *American Journal of Sociology*, *111*(1), 58–89.

Tomlinson, J., Baird, M., Berg, P., & Cooper, R. (2018). Flexible careers across the life course: Advancing theory, research and practice. *Human Relations*, *71*(1), 4–22.

Topel, R. (1991). Specific capital, mobility, and wages: Wages rise with job seniority. *Journal of Political Economy*, 99(1), 145–176.

Torrini, R. (2005). Cross-country differences in self-employment rates: The role of institutions. *Labour Economics*, *12*(5), 661–683.

Tros, F. (2010). Flexibility and security for older workers: HRM-arrangements in four European countries. In *Working and ageing: Emerging theories and empirical perspectives* (pp. 132–165). Luxembourg: European Centre for the Development of Vocational Training (Cedefop),

Tsui, A., & Gutek, B. (1999). *Demographic differences in organizations: Current research and future directions*. Lanham, MD: Lexington Books.

Tsui, A. S., Pearce, J. L., Porter, L. W., & Tripoli, A. M. (1997). Alternative approaches to the employee–organization relationship: Does investment in employees pay off? *Academy of Management Journal*, *40*(5), 1089–1121.

Universities and Colleges Admissions Service (UCAS). (2017). *Progression pathways 2017*. Cheltenham, UK: Author.

Valcour, M. (2007). Work-based resources as moderators of the relationship between work hours and satisfaction with work–family balance. *Journal of Applied Psychology*, *92*(6), 1512–1523.

Van Belle, J. (2016). *Paternity and parental leave policies across the European Union*. Cambridge: Rand.

Van Breeschoten, L., Roeters, A., & Van der Lippe, T. (2018). Reasons to reduce: A vignette-experiment examining men and women's considerations to scale back following childbirth. *Social Politics: International Studies in Gender, State & Society*, *25*(2), 169–200.

Van Buuren, S., & Oudshoorn, K. (1999). *Flexible multivariate imputation by MICE*. Leiden: TNO Prevention Center.

Van Dalen, H. P., Henkens, K., & Schippers, J. (2007). *Oudere werknemers door de lens van de werkgever* (NIDI Report No. 74). The Hague: Netherlands Interdisciplinary Demographic Institute.

Van Dalen, H. P., Henkens, K., & Schippers, J. (2009). Dealing with older workers in Europe: A comparative survey of employers' attitudes and actions. *Journal of European Social Policy*, *19*(1), 47–60.

Van Dalen, H. P., Henkens, K., & Schippers, J. (2010a). How do employers cope with an ageing workforce? *Demographic Research*, *22*(32), 1015–1036.

Van Dalen, H. P., Henkens, K., & Schippers, J. (2010b). Productivity of older workers: Perceptions of employers and employees. *Population and Development Review*, *36*(2), 309–330.

Van Dalen, H. P., Henkens, K., & Wang, M. (2015). Recharging or retiring older workers? Uncovering the age-based strategies of European employers. *The Gerontologist*, *55*(5), 814–824.

Van de Voorde, K., Paauwe, J., & Van Veldhoven, M. (2012). Employee well-being and the HRM-organizational performance relationship: A review of quantitative studies. *International Journal of Management Reviews*, *14*(4), 391–407.

Van de Werfhorst, H. G. (2004). Systems of educational specialization and labor market outcomes in Norway, Australia, and the Netherlands. *International Journal of Comparative Sociology*, *45*(5), 315–335.

Van den Broeck, A., De Cuyper, N., Baillien, E., Vanbelle, E., Vanhercke, D., & De Witte, H. (2014). Perception of organization's value support and perceived employability: Insights from self-determination theory. *International Journal of Human Resource Management*, *25*(13), 1904–1918.

Van den Heuvel, A., & Wooden, M. (1997). Participation of non-English-speaking-background immigrants in work-related training. *Ethnic and Racial Studies*, *20*(4), 830–848.

Van der Heijde, C. M., & Van der Heijden, B. I. (2006). A competence-based and multidimensional operationalization and measurement of employability. *Human Resource Management*, *45*(3), 449–476.

Van der Heijden, F. I., Poortman, A., & Van der Lippe, T. (2016). Children's postdivorce residence arrangements and parental experienced time pressure. *Journal of Marriage and Family*, *78*, 468–481.

Van der Horst, M., Van der Lippe, T., & Kluwer, E. (2014). Aspirations and occupational achievements of Dutch fathers and mothers. *Career Development International*, *19*(4), 447–468.

Van der Lippe, T. (2007). Dutch workers and time pressure. *Work, Employment and Society*, *21*, 693–711.

Van der Lippe, T., De Ruijter, J., De Ruijter, E., & Raub, W. (2010). Persistent inequalities in time use between men and women: A detailed look at the influence of economic circumstances, policies, and culture. *European Sociological Review*, *27*(2), 164–179.

Van der Lippe, T., Den Dulk, L., Van Doorne-Huiskes, A., Schippers, J., Lane, L., & Bäck-Wiklund, M. (2009). *Quality of life in a changing Europe: Final report*. Utrecht: Utrecht University.

Van der Lippe, T., & Glebbeek, A. (2003). *Time Competition Survey*. Interuniversity Center for Social Science Theory and Methodology (ICS), Utrecht University/ University of Groningen.

Van der Lippe, T., Havekes, E., Lippényi, Z., Lössbroek, J., Van Breeschoten, L., & Van Gerwen, N. (2015a). Sustainable Workforce Survey: Employee questionnaire. Deliverable 2.1 of FP7 EU-project Sustainable Workforce (ERC Advanced Grant 340045).

Van der Lippe, T., Havekes, E., Lippényi, Z., Lössbroek, J., Van Breeschoten, L., & Van Gerwen, N. (2015b). Sustainable Workforce Survey: Manager questionnaire. Deliverable 2.2 of FP7 EU-project Sustainable Workforce (ERC Advanced Grant 340045).

Van der Lippe, T., Havekes, E., Lippényi, Z., Lössbroek, J., Van Breeschoten, L., & Van Gerwen, N. (2015c). Sustainable Workforce Survey: Organization questionnaire. Deliverable 2.3 of FP7 EU-project Sustainable Workforce (ERC Advanced Grant 340045).

Van der Lippe, T., & Lippényi, Z. (2018). Beyond formal access: Organizational context, working from home, and work–family conflict of men and women in European workplaces. *Social Indicators Research*. Advance online publication. doi:10.1007/s11205-018-1993-1

Van der Lippe, T., Lippényi, Z., Lössbroek, J., van Breeschoten, L., Van Gerwen, N., & Martens, T. (2016). *European Sustainable Workforce Survey* (ESWS). Utrecht: Utrecht University.

Van der Lippe, T., Van Doorne-Huiskes, A., & Blommaert, L. (2014). De toename van vrouwen in leidinggevende functies. *ESB Vrouw & Economie*, 99(4689 & 4690), 456–458.

Van Dyne, L., & Ang, S. (1998). Organizational citizenship behavior of contingent workers in Singapore. *Academy of Management Journal*, *41*(6), 692–703.

Van Echtelt, P., Croezen, S., Vlasblom, J. D., De Voogd-Hamelink, M., & Mattijssen, L. (2016). *Aanbod van arbeid 2016* [Supply of labour 2016]. The Hague: The Netherlands Institute for Social Research.

Van Emmerik, I. J., Schreurs, B., De Cuyper, N., Jawahar, I. M., & Peeters, M. C. (2012). The route to employability: Examining resources and the mediating role of motivation. *Career Development International*, *17*(2), 104–119.

Van Es, F., & Van Vuuren, D. J. (2011). A decomposition of the growth in self-employment. *Applied Economics Letters*, *18*(17), 1665–1669.

Van Gerwen, N., Buskens, V., & Van der Lippe, T. (2018). Individual training and employees' cooperative behavior: Evidence from a contextualized laboratory experiment. *Rationality and Society*, *30*(4), 432–462.

Van Harten, J., De Cuyper, N., Guest, D., Fugate, M., Knies, E., & Forrier, A. (2017). Special issue of international human resource management journal HRM and employability: An international perspective. *The International Journal of Human Resource Management*, *28*(19), 2831–2835.

Van Harten, J., Knies, E., & Leisink, P. (2015). Employer's investments in hospital workers' employability and employment opportunities. *Personnel Review, 45*(1), 84–102.

Van Solinge, H., & Henkens, K. (2014). Work-related factors as predictors in the retirement decision-making process of older workers in the Netherlands. *Ageing and Society, 34*(9), 1551–1574.

Vandello, J. A., Hettinger, V. E., Bosson, J. K., & Siddiqi, J. (2013). When equal isn't really equal: The masculine dilemma of seeking work flexibility. *Journal of Social Issues, 69*(2), 303–321.

Veld, M., Semeijn, J., & Vuuren, T. V. (2015). Enhancing perceived employability: An interactionist perspective on responsibilities of organizations and employees. *Personnel Review, 44*(6), 866–882.

Verra, S. E., Benzerga, A., Jiao, B., & Ruggeri, K. (2019). Health promotion at work: A comparison of policy and practice across Europe. *Safety and Health at Work, 10*(1), 21–29.

Vidovićová, L. (2014). *Conceptual framework of the active ageing policies in employment in Czech Republic* (CASE Network Studies & Analyses No. 469/2014). Warsaw: CASE.

Virtanen, M., Kivimäki, M., Elovainio, M., Vahtera, J., & Ferrie, J. E. (2003). From insecure to secure employment: Changes in work, health, health related behaviours, and sickness absence. *Occupational and Environmental Medicine, 60*(12), 948–953.

Visser, J. (2002). The first part-time economy in the world: A model to be followed? *Journal of European Social Policy, 12*(1), 23–42.

Visser, J. (2016). ICTWSS Database. Version 5.1. University of Amsterdam, Amsterdam Institute for Advanced Labour Studies (AIAS).

Vogtenhuber, S. (2015). Explaining country variation in employee training: An institutional analysis of education systems and their influence on training and its returns. *European Sociological Review, 31*(1), 77–90.

Von Hippel, C., Mangum, S. L., Greenberger, D. B., Heneman, R. L., & Skoglind, J. D. (1997). Temporary employment: Can organizations and employees both win? *The Academy of Management Executive, 11*(1), 93–104.

Vough, H. C., Broschak, J. P., & Northcraft, G. B. (2005). Here today, gone tomorrow? Effects of nonstandard work status on workgroup processes and outcomes. In M. C. Thomas-Hunt (Ed.), *Research on managing groups and teams:* Volume 7 – *Status and groups* (pp. 229–257). Bingley, UK: Emerald Group Publishing.

Voydanoff, P. (2005). Consequences of boundary-spanning demands and resources for work-to-family conflict and perceived stress. *Journal of Occupational Health Psychology, 10*(4), 491–503.

Vroom, V. (2005). On the origins of expectancy theory. In K. G. Smith & M. A. Hitt (Eds.), *Great minds in management: The process of theory development* (pp. 239–258). Oxford: Oxford University Press.

Waddoups, J. C. (2011). Firm size and work-related training: New evidence on incidence, intensity, and training type from Australia. *Journal of Labor Research, 32*, 390–413.

Waddoups, J. C. (2014). Union coverage and work-related training in the construction industry. *ILR Review, 67*(2), 532–555.

Warr, P., & Inceoglu, I. (2018). Work orientations, well-being and job content of self-employed and employed professionals. *Work, Employment and Society, 32*(2), 292–311.

Way, S. A., Lepak, D. P., Fay, C. H., & Thacker, J. W. (2010). Contingent workers' impact on standard employee withdrawal behaviors: Does what you use them for matter? *Human Resource Management, 49*, 109–138.

Weber, S. (2014). Human capital depreciation and education level. *International Journal of Manpower*, *35*(5), 613–642.

West, C., & Zimmerman, D. H. (1987). Doing gender. *Gender & Society*, *1*(2), 125–151.

Westerveld, M. (2012). The "new" self-employed: An issue for social policy? *European Journal of Social Security*, *14*(3), 156–173.

Wheatley, D. (2017). Employee satisfaction and use of flexible working arrangements. *Work, Employment and Society*, *31*(4), 567–585.

Wilkin, C. L. (2013). I can't get no job satisfaction: Meta-analysis comparing permanent and contingent workers. *Journal of Organizational Behavior*, *34*(1), 47–64.

Williams, S. J., & Snow, D. M. (2012). Promoting health in small and medium-sized enterprises. *Journal of Small Business and Enterprise Development*, *19*(4), 729–744.

Williamson, O. E. (1989). Transaction cost economics. In M. Armstrong & R. H. Porter (Eds.), *Handbook of industrial organization* (pp. 135–182). Amsterdam: Elsevier.

Witte, H. D. (1999). Job insecurity and psychological well-being: Review of the literature and exploration of some unresolved issues. *European Journal of Work and Organizational Psychology*, 8(2), 155–177.

Wolff, E. (2001). Productivity convergence and education: Evidence from OECD countries. *Industrial and Corporate Change*, *10*(3), 735–759.

Wood, S., Van Veldhoven, M., Croon, M., & De Menezes, L. M. (2012). Enriched job design, high involvement management and organizational performance: The mediating roles of job satisfaction and well-being. *Human Relations*, *65*(4), 419–445.

Wooldridge, J. M. (2010). *Econometric analysis of cross section and panel data*. Cambridge, MA: The MIT Press.

World Bank. (2016). *World development report 2016: Digital dividends*. Washington, DC: Author.

World Bank Data. (2018). *Population ages 65 and above (% of total)*. Retrieved from: https://data.worldbank.org/indicator/SP.POP.65UP.TO.ZS.

Wotschack, P. (2017). Leave saving options over the life course – Only for the highly skilled? Evidence from two German best-practice companies. *European Societies*, *19*(4), 396–418.

Wright, P. M., & Nishii, L. H. (2007). *Strategic HRM and organizational behavior: Integrating multiple levels of analysis* (CAHRS Working Paper Series No. 07-03). Ithaca, NY: Cornell University, Center for Advanced Human Resource Studies.

Xu, K., & Lin, Z. (2011). Participation in workplace employer-sponsored training in Canada: Role of firm characteristics and worker attributes. *Contemporary Economic Policy*, *29*(3), 416–430.

Ybema, J. F., Geuskens, G., & Oude Hengel, K. (2009). *Oudere werknemers en langer doorwerken: Secundaire analyses van de NEA, het NEA–cohortonderzoek en de WEA*. Hoofddorp, Netherlands: TNO.

Yoshida, Y., & Smith, M. R. (2005). Training and the earnings of immigrant males: Evidence from the Canadian Workplace and Employee Survey. *Social Science Quarterly*, 86, 1218–1241.

Žnidaršič, J., & Dimovski, V. (2009). Age management: A new paradigm in HRM within Slovenian enterprises. *Journal of Applied Business Research*, *25*(3), 111–124.

Zwick, T. (2006). The impact of training intensity on establishment productivity. *Industrial Relations*, *45*(1), 26–46.

Index

Page numbers in **bold** denote tables, those in *italics* denote figures.

For Product Safety Concerns and Information please contact our EU
representative GPSR@taylorandfrancis.com
Taylor & Francis Verlag GmbH, Kaufingerstraße 24, 80331 München, Germany

www.ingramcontent.com/pod-product-compliance
Ingram Content Group UK Ltd.
Pitfield, Milton Keynes, MK11 3LW, UK
UKHW020016200926
475702UK00014B/1919
9780367727949